Transcending unidimensional and strictly national approaches to understanding inequalities, this extraordinary book draws on multiple disciplines to highlight how multiple forms of inequality—across lines not only of income but also of social identities, life chances and ecological vulnerability—reinforce one another and determine the contours of social conflict in the 21st century.

Eric Hershberg, American University, USA.

The book offers a wealth of new research on inequality. Coming from diverse disciplinarian perspectives, the authors look at social inequality from multiple angles. Together they throw light on how the impact that these multiple aspects exert on the others adds complexity to inequality. Thus, rather than simply an assembly of relevant contributions on a common subject, what the book offers to the reader is a fresh view about the interactional character of the multiple dimensions of inequality. Balancing theoretical reflection and solid empirical knowledge, *Global Entangled Inequalities* is a timely publication that expands our knowledge about inequality in Latin America and beyond.

Elisa Reis, Federal University of Rio de Janeiro, Brazil.

This book uses the concept of global entangled inequalities, developed by the *desiguALdades* research network, to stress ever-evolving patterns of inequalities in Latin America. This genuine volume offers a comprehensive take on the production and transformation of inequalities, using case studies from transnational care to ecology, race to gender, and open theoretical venues that challenge disciplinary canons.

Lena Lavinas, Federal University of Rio de Janeiro, Brazil, and The Institute for Advanced Study, Berlin, Germany.

This is a rich collection of globally pertinent Latin American explorations of multidimensional inequalities.

Göran Therborn, Cambridge University, Emeritus, author of *The Killing Fields of Inequality*.

GLOBAL ENTANGLED INEQUALITIES

This book presents studies from across Latin America to take up the challenge of exploring the plurality of social inequalities from a global perspective. Accordingly, it identifies the structural forces of social inequalities on a world scale as they shape asymmetries observed in a wide array of phenomena, such as racial and gender inequality, urbanization, migration, commodity production, indigenous mobilization, ecological conflicts, and the "new middle class." A rich contribution to the study of the interconnections between the global social structure and multiple local and national hierarchies, *Global Entangled Inequalities* brings together a variety of conceptual approaches, ranging from ethnographies to legal genealogies, and will therefore appeal to scholars across the social sciences with interests in social theory, power analysis, intersectionality studies, urban studies, and global social and environmental justice.

Elizabeth Jelin is Senior Researcher at CONICET (Consejo Nacional de Investigaciones Científicas y Técnicas of Argentina) and IDES (Instituto de Desarrollo Económico y Social) in Buenos Aires, Argentina, and Professor at the Social Sciences Graduate Program UNGS-IDES. Her most recent book, *La lucha por el pasado: Cómo construimos la memoria social*, was published in 2017.

Renata Motta is Adjunct Professor in Sociology at the Institute for Latin American Studies at Freie Universität Berlin. Her research interests include political sociology, rural studies, social inequalities, risk sociology, gender, and the environment. She has authored articles in these areas for *Journal of Agrarian Change*, *Social Movement Studies*, *Sociology Compass*, and *Revista Brasileira de Ciências Sociais*, and for the United Nations Economic Commission for Latin America and the Caribbean (ECLAC). She is the author of *Social Mobilization, Global Capitalism and Struggles over Food: A Comparative Study of Social Movements* (Routledge, 2016).

Sérgio Costa is Professor of Sociology at Freie Universität Berlin, where he is the spokesperson of the Maria Sibylla Merian Centre Conviviality in Unequal Societies. Trained in sociology and economics in Brazil and Germany, he specializes in social inequalities, racism and anti-racism, as well as postcolonial theories.

Entangled Inequalities: Exploring Global Asymmetries

Series Editor:
Sérgio Costa, Freie Universität Berlin, Germany

https://www.routledge.com/Entangled-Inequalities-Exploring-Global-Asymmetries/book-series/ASHSER1413

Departing from classical approaches to the study of social inequalities between individuals and social classes within particular national settings, this series emphasises the production and reproduction of inequalities across borders, as well as the multiplicity of categories—whether 'race', 'sex' or 'nationality' amongst others—according to which contemporary inequalities are shaped.

Entangled Inequalities constitutes a forum and a catalyst for discussing recent advancements in inequality research from a transnational, global and intersectional perspective, highlighting the fact that social inequalities are always the product of both global interpenetrations and of complex intersections between different social categorisations. The series therefore welcomes monographs and edited volumes across the social sciences that deal with inequalities from an 'entangled' perspective—with an intersectional or a transnational focus, or both.

Titles in this series
A Moment of Equality for Latin America?
Barbara Fritz and Lena Lavinas
(Ashgate, 2015)

Social Mobilization, Global Capitalism and Struggles over Food
Renata Motta
(Routledge, 2016)

Reducing Inequality in Latin America
María Fernanda Valdés
(Routledge, 2016)

Global Entangled Inequalities
Elizabeth Jelin, Renata Motta, Sérgio Costa
(Routledge, 2017)

GLOBAL ENTANGLED INEQUALITIES

Conceptual Debates and Evidence from Latin America

Edited by Elizabeth Jelin, Renata Motta and Sérgio Costa

LONDON AND NEW YORK

First published 2018
by Routledge
2 Park Square, Milton Park, Abingdon, Oxon OX14 4RN

and by Routledge
711 Third Avenue, New York, NY 10017

Routledge is an imprint of the Taylor & Francis Group, an informa business

© 2018 selection and editorial matter, Elizabeth Jelin, Renata Motta, Sérgio Costa; individual chapters, the contributors

The right of Elizabeth Jelin, Renata Motta, and Sérgio Costa to be identified as the authors of the editorial material, and of the authors for their individual chapters, has been asserted in accordance with sections 77 and 78 of the Copyright, Designs and Patents Act 1988.

All rights reserved. No part of this book may be reprinted or reproduced or utilized in any form or by any electronic, mechanical, or other means, now known or hereafter invented, including photocopying and recording, or in any information storage or retrieval system, without permission in writing from the publishers.

Trademark notice: Product or corporate names may be trademarks or registered trademarks, and are used only for identification and explanation without intent to infringe.

British Library Cataloguing-in-Publication Data
A catalogue record for this book is available from the British Library

Library of Congress Cataloging-in-Publication Data
A catalog record for this book has been requested

ISBN: 978-1-138-74060-0 (hbk)
ISBN: 978-1-315-18335-0 (pbk)
ISBN: 978-1-138-01926-3 (ebk)

Typeset in Bembo
by Deanta Global Publishing Services, Chennai, India

Printed and bound by CPI Group (UK) Ltd, Croydon, CR0 4YY

CONTENTS

List of figures	*ix*
List of tables	*x*
Contributing authors	*xi*

Introduction   1
Renata Motta, Elizabeth Jelin, and Sérgio Costa

PART I
Structuring inequalities   19

1   Inequality: toward a world-historical perspective   21
    Roberto Patricio Korzeniewicz

2   Transregional articulations of law and race in Latin America:
    a legal genealogy of inequality   42
    Manuel Góngora-Mera

3   The urban space and the (re)production of social inequalities:
    decoupling income distribution and patterns of urbanization
    in Latin American cities   59
    Ramiro Segura

4   Researching inequalities from a socio-ecological perspective   76
    Kristina Dietz

viii Contents

PART II
Categorization: the construction and deconstruction of persistent hierarchies

93

5 The social imaginary of inequalities in Latin America: is another view necessary? 95
Juan Pablo Pérez Sáinz

6 Unequal differences: gender, ethnicity/race and citizenship in class societies (historical realities, analytical approaches) 109
Elizabeth Jelin

7 Competing indigeneities: being a (hyper)real ecowarrior in twenty-first-century Bolivia 128
Andrew Canessa

8 The symbolic construction of inequalities 144
Luis Reygadas

PART III
Dynamics of production and transformation of inequalities

159

9 Multiple layers of inequalities and intersectionality 161
Jairo Baquero-Melo

10 Millionaires, the established, the outsiders, and the poor: social structure and political crisis in Brazil 178
Sérgio Costa

11 Transnational care chains and entangled inequalities 196
Anna Katharina Skornia

12 Socio-environmental inequalities and GM crops: class, gender, and knowledge 214
Renata Motta

Final reflections 231
Sérgio Costa, Renata Motta, and Elizabeth Jelin

Index 237

FIGURES

1.1	Global stratification: 850 country deciles ranked from rich to poor	24
1.2	Migration as global social mobility	32
1.3	Percentual distribution of the world population by income levels	38
3.1	Development of unemployment, poverty, and inequality in the metropolitan area of Buenos Aires	68
7.1	TIPNIS *Avatar cartoon*	129
7.2	'Evotar'	130

TABLES

3.1	Inequality and poverty in Latin American cities (1980–2000)	62
8.1	Processes of classification, categorization, and creation of boundaries	147
8.2	Processes of valuation, devaluation, and re-valuation	149
8.3	Relations between difference and inequality	151
8.4	Production, acquisition, and distribution of symbolic capital	153
8.5	Struggles around the legitimacy of inequalities	155
10.1	Recent changes in Brazilian social structure 2003–2014	188

CONTRIBUTING AUTHORS

Jairo Baquero-Melo holds a D.Phil. in Sociology from Freie Universität Berlin and is currently Associate Professor of Sociology at Universidad del Rosario. Formerly, he was a long-term doctoral researcher of the desiguALdades.net network in Berlin, funded by the BMBF (Germany). His research areas are related to social inequalities, sociology of development, economic sociology, armed conflicts, and peace. His main publications include (2015) "The Intersection of Race, Class, and Ethnicity in Agrarian Inequalities, Identities, and the Social Resistance of Peasants in Colombia," *Current Sociology*, 63 (7), 1017–1036; (2015) "Regional Challenges to Land Restitution and Peace in Colombia: The Case of the Lower Atrato," *Journal of Peacebuilding and Development*, 10 (2), 36–51; and (2014) *Layered Inequalities: Land Grabbing, Collective Land Rights and Afro-Descendant Resistance in Colombia*, Berlin: LIT Verlag.

Andrew Canessa is Professor of Anthropology at the University of Essex in the U.K. He has worked on indigenous peoples in Bolivia since the 1980s, focusing on issues of identity, gender, and racialization. His most recent publications are *Intimate Indigeneities: Exploring Race, Sex and History in the Small Spaces of Life* (Duke) and, with Aida Hernandez Género, *Complementariedades y exclusiones en Mesoamérica y los Andes* (ABYA YALA and IWGIA). His current book project, together with political scientist Manuela Picq, is on indigeneity and citizenship, exploring ways in which indigeneity is at the very center (if often invisibly) in how the nation–state is understood.

Kristina Dietz holds a Ph.D. in Political Science from the Department of Social Sciences of Universität Kassel, Germany. Since 2014 she has been joint head (with Bettina Engels) of a Junior Research Group "Global change—local conflicts? Conflicts over land in Latin America and sub-Saharan Africa" at Freie Universität

xii Contributing Authors

Berlin. Recent book publications include *Contested Extractivism, Society and the State: Struggles over Mining and Land* (ed. with Bettina Engels), London: Palgrave Macmillan, 2017; and *The Political Ecology of Agrofuels* (ed. with Bettina Engels, Oliver Pye, and Achim Brunngengräber), London: Routledge, 2017.

Manuel Góngora-Mera is a postdoctoral lecturer at Lateinamerika Institut (Freie Universität Berlin). He studied law and obtained master's degrees in Economic Law (Universidad Javeriana, Bogotá) and in International Economic and Development Policy (Friedrich-Alexander Universität Erlangen-Nürnberg). He received his doctoral degree in Public Law (*summa cum laude*) from Humboldt-Universität zu Berlin. He was visiting researcher at the Inter-American Court of Human Rights (San José, 2008), UNRISD (Geneva, 2011), FLACSO (Quito, 2013), and Universidad de Salamanca (Salamanca, 2016). His publications deal mainly with constitutional and human rights issues, including international human rights law, social rights, racial discrimination, and social inequalities.

Roberto Patricio Korzeniewicz is Professor and Chair of Sociology at the University of Maryland, College Park, U.S., and was a Fellow at DesiguALdades in Freie Universität Berlin in 2014. He has published extensively on global social inequality and stratification and on social movements in Latin America. He is the co-author, with Timothy P. Moran, of *Unveiling Inequality* (Russell Sage Foundation, 2009). His current research focuses on world historical patterns of income inequality, social stratification, and mobility.

Juan Pablo Pérez Sáinz has been a researcher at the Facultad Latinoamericana de Ciencias Sociales (FLACSO), Costa Rica, since 1981. A sociologist, Pérez Sáinz has done research on labor markets, local economic development, social exclusion, and inequalities. His most recent publication is the book *Mercados y bárbaros. La persistencia de las desigualdades de excedente en América Latina* (San José, FLACSO, 2014).

Luis Reygadas is full Professor in Anthropology at Universidad Autónoma Metropolitana Iztapalapa, México. He is the author of six books and several articles on inequalities, industrial anthropology, and work in contemporary capitalism. His publications include (2008) *La apropiación. Destejiendo las redes de la desigualdad*, Barcelona: Anthropos; Paul Gootenberg and Luis Reygadas (eds.) (2010) *Indelible Inequalities in Latin America: Insights from History, Politics, and Culture*, Durham and London: Duke University Press; and (2005) "Imagined inequalities: representations of discrimination and exclusion in Latin America," *Social Identities. Journal for the Study of Race, Nation and Culture*, 11 (5).

Ramiro Segura holds a Ph.D. in Social Sciences (UNGS-IDES) and a postdoc at Freie Universität (FU) Berlin. He is Researcher at the National Council of Scientific and Technical Researches (CONICET, Argentina) and Professor at the National University of La Plata (UNLP) and National University of San Martin

(IDAES/UNSAM). He is author of the book *Vivir afuera. Antropología de la experiencia urbana* (2015), and he recently published "The Uses of Informality: Urban Development and Social Distinction in Mexico City" (*Latin American Perspectives*, 2016; with Frank Müller) and "Space, Urban Borders and Political Imagination in Buenos Aires" (*Latin American and Caribbean Ethnic Studies*, 2016; with Alejandro Grimson).

Anna Katharina Skornia completed her doctorate in Sociology at Freie Universität Berlin as a member of the Research Network on Interdependent Inequalities in Latin America (desiguALdades.net). Her dissertation, entitled "Entangled Inequalities in Transnational Care Chains. Practices Across the Borders of Peru and Italy," was published in 2014. She is an Associate Researcher of desiguALdades.net, Freie Universität Berlin. Her research interests include migration, care, and social inequality from a transnational perspective.

INTRODUCTION[1]

Renata Motta, Elizabeth Jelin, and Sérgio Costa

As a foundational topic of modern social sciences, research on inequalities has followed a long path of development and change. Some issues, concepts, and topics have been constant, such as those related to social stratification and social mobility, while other conceptualizations and concerns have had ups and downs, with different emphases along time and space. Social science agendas have been shaped by developments within each discipline, but also by policy debates at national and mostly international agencies and by the challenges presented by the "real" world, by trends and experiences in different regions of the world.

This book is part of a renewed attention to these issues, with a double face: inequalities in the plural, as an expression of multiple asymmetries, as well as in the singular, since specific inequalities are inserted in a single global social structure.

The 1980s and 1990s were times when many scholars, governments, and international agencies put their attention on poverty rather than on inequalities. Furthermore, the focus of attention was the national level. At that time, inequalities became the subject of econometric approaches that reduced research to measurements of income distribution. Under the dominance of the perspective of human capital, emphasis was placed on the need to invest in the development of human capacities—rather than on changing structures of opportunities, to refer to Amartya Sen's (1999) approach.

At the same time, far from the international concerns for poverty and hunger, Western European sociologists and political scientists, with few exceptions, appeared to be fascinated by a reflexive or second modernity that supposedly opened new spaces for freedom and human creativity after the debacle of socialism and the global expansion of democracy, and virtually banned inequalities from their research agendas (Beck, Giddens, and Lash 1994; Habermas 1998; Beck 1986). Some scholars (Luhmann 1985; Honneth 1992) even proclaimed the unimportance of redistributive conflicts. Struggles for recognition and for individual and

2 Renata Motta, Elizabeth Jelin, and Sérgio Costa

collective differentiation were supposed to be the new claims for justice in substitution of fights to reduce structural material inequalities.

Meanwhile, in other parts of the world such as Latin America and Eastern Europe, transitions from dictatorships and authoritarian regimes were at center stage, and issues of democratization and enlargement of citizenship rights were at stake. Political and civic claims displaced (or shared space with) issues of poverty. Later on, the language of exclusion-inclusion would come to the fore, reviving the discussions on marginality of the 1960s (Nun 1969, 2001; LARR 2004). Here and there, the study of (new and old) social movements and collective identities was shaping a new agenda for research, one that entailed fresh ways of dealing with stubborn and persistent inequalities in the world as well as with the struggles to overcome them. However, research on social movements and social inequalities developed as parallel fields that only recently converged.

From the late 1990s, frustrations accumulated regarding global capitalism and the effects of neoliberal policies that emphasized the centrality of market forces and placed the state in a subsidiary position in guiding distribution and redistribution of valuable resources. Simultaneously, new struggles for redistribution led to a revival of inequality research. These new studies, partially rediscovering virtues of classical authors, have broadened the analytical perspective in different directions. We identified four main shifts in research on social inequalities.

1. There has been a change from an exclusive interest in socioeconomic disparities to a more comprehensive understanding of inequalities. Accordingly, researchers have included power inequalities (Kreckel 2004) as well as vital and existential asymmetries in their approaches (Therborn 2006). Such expansion implies a critique of the concept of social mobility, insofar as it reduces the study of inequality to a matter of calculating the changing distribution of individuals in socioeconomic strata.

A further important conceptual expansion refers to attempts to take environmental inequalities seriously (Krämer 2007; Göbel, Góngora-Mera, and Ulloa 2014). While the sociology of inequalities has often disregarded the environmental question, environmental studies have also ignored inequalities research. In fact, natural resources also constitute relevant societal goods to which individuals and social groups have differential access and rights of use. There are a number of distributive conflicts regarding control over land, water, forests, seeds, etc., also mediated by asymmetrical power relations. The environmental question, however, highlights the existence of another type of distributive conflict, namely over the asymmetrical distribution of environmental damage. Often, the negative impacts of industrial and extractive activities are unequally experienced along social categories such as black/white, man/woman, indigenous peoples/Creole elites, etc. In other words, powerful actors are able to externalize environmental risks and damages, transferring them to less powerful ones. Ecological inequalities also reflect and feed geopolitical asymmetries inasmuch as the industrialized global North defines what are the environmental issues on the international agenda, whereas the countries from the global South not only lack the power to bring their concerns to the agenda, but are

Introduction **3**

also obliged to participate in managing the solutions to the problems of the rich countries (McMichael 2009).

Finally, attention has also been paid to symbolic and subjective dimensions, whereby inequalities are expressed in the location of the self and of others in symbolic hierarchies that play a significant role in practices of discrimination and segregation (Reygadas 2008).

2. A second shift refers to the unit of analysis and the time period considered when trying to understand current patterns of inequalities. An increasing consensus regarding the limitations of methodological nationalism (Fine 2007; Chernilo 2007; Beck 1996) contributed to the rise of studies that have changed the unit of analysis from a national to a transnational or global lens (Korzeniewicz and Moran 2009; Pieterse 2002; Boatcă 2015; Burawoy 2000). This is a crucial shift since between two-thirds and three-quarters of existing social inequalities have a global character (Kreckel 2004). The new interest in global inequalities is mostly associated with new diachronic approaches concerned with explaining persistent patterns of historical inequalities (Randeria 2007; Boatcă 2015). Among recent efforts in overcoming methodological nationalism in the research on inequality, two perspectives can be singled out: the world-systems approach and the transnational approach.

The recent work of Moran and Korzeniewicz (Korzeniewicz and Moran 2009; Korzeniewicz 2011) represents a paradigmatic example of the developments of inequality studies as part of historical, world-systems research. Their studies have shown that inequality patterns found in different countries go as far back as the colonial period. In contrast to the hitherto hegemonic literature, the authors demonstrate that the persistence of countries belonging to low- or high-income inequality categories cannot be explained by domestic factors alone. Instead, a country's potential to remedy existing inequality within its borders through redistributive policies is inextricably tied to the global economy and world politics. Therefore, a country's position in the world economy and its internal distributive patterns are interdependently connected (see Korzeniewicz in this book).

The position of social actors in transnational structures of inequalities is the central focus of transnational approaches in the research on inequality (Pries 2008; Weiß 2005; Weiß and Berger 2008). Following a transnational perspective, authors research inequality in the context of transnational migration and argue that the traditional unit of reference, namely nation-states, does not suffice alone in order to explain how migrants are embedded in structures of inequality. Therefore, it is worthwhile for inequality research to take pluri-local/transnational spaces seriously:

> Alongside these units of analysis—enmeshed like Russian dolls—(local, national, supranational and global), pluri-local as a unit of analysis for phenomena such as household economy or education strategies is of fundamental importance like in the case of transnational migrants and social space distributed over different national societies.
>
> *(Pries 2008: 62)*

4 Renata Motta, Elizabeth Jelin, and Sérgio Costa

3. Inequality research has broadened its focus by integrating multiple categorizations besides classes in shaping contemporary hierarchies. There are multiple other axes of societal differentiation operating in the world: nationality and citizenship, place of residence and origins, gender, race, ethnicity, age, religion, language. These differences are not intrinsically hierarchical but rather horizontal. Yet in the real world, there is a strong—yet variable—relationship between these horizontal differences and vertical inequalities. In fact, the actual historical development of the functioning of these theoretically horizontal axes of difference led to their turning into dimensions of inequality.

In Charles Tilly's (1998) perspective for understanding "durable inequalities," the categories that define differences within populations are at the basis of persistent inequalities when the main mechanisms of the production of inequalities (exploitation, opportunity hoarding) are linked to the construction and maintenance of hierarchically ordered categorical pairs. The link between societal categories of difference and structures of inequalities is historically structured and contingent.

Going beyond Tilly's influential contribution, more recent studies not only take into account categories such as race, ethnicity, and gender; they also study how categories are constructed (for instance: Anthias 2015). This task involves unveiling the ways in which categorizations blend, engage, and disengage themselves from each other along historical time. This is to be looked at in three ways—its variable historical salience as a structuring dimension for inequalities, the salience and visibility that each type of difference gains, and the struggles in which populations engage to overcome these difference-based inequalities. Including the multiplicity of social categorizations in the analysis of social inequalities requires the development of various important conceptualizations: horizontal and vertical inequalities, intersectionality, and the discussion of inequality and difference.

The term "horizontal inequality" has been coined by development economist Frances Stewart (Stewart 2000; Stewart 2010; Stewart, Brown, and Mancini 2005). According to Stewart, an individual's social position in a given society corresponds to the sum of vertical and horizontal inequalities. The former refers to the differences between individuals on a social scale, and the latter to the differences between groups. By focusing on horizontal inequalities, Stewart aims to broaden the conventional economic view about the causes of social inequality. She distinguishes groups not only using economic factors, but also applying political, religious, ethnic, racial, and gender-specific criteria. However, the question of group definition is still difficult to answer: given that an individual can at the same time feel a sense of belonging to different groups, how does one define a group? Additionally, considering the inequalities that group affiliations engender, a causal relationship between group membership and inequality is by no means obvious. Stewart accordingly argues the following:

> To some extent, then, group boundaries become endogenous to group inequality. If people suffer discrimination (i.e. experience horizontal inequality)

they may then feel cultural identity more strongly, particularly if others categorise them into groups for the express purpose of exercising discrimination (thereby creating or enforcing HIs [horizontal inequalities]).

(Stewart, Brown, and Mancini 2005: 9)

Intersectionality, in turn, is more than a concept. Originated in the 1980s in the realm of U.S.- black and feminist activism, the term characterizes today a broad field of studies disputed by scholars defending different positions and views (Célleri Endara et al. 2013). The common denominator in this field is the search for understanding positions of individuals in social hierarchies as interpenetrations and articulations of different categorizations as described by Roth (2013: 2):

> Rather than examining gender, race, class, nation, etc. as distinct social hierarchies, approaches dedicated to an intersectionality perspective examine how various axes of stratification mutually construct one another and how inequalities are articulated through and connected with differences. An intersectional perspective always takes the multidimensional character, the entanglements, the analogies and simultaneities of various axis of stratification into account.

The multiple axes of societal differentiation are not intrinsically hierarchical but rather horizontal. Yet, as just discussed, they become axes of inequality. At a world level, the most daring inequalities are those between nation-states. Life chances, access to goods and services, even life expectancy widely differ by the "chance" of being born in one place or in another. As Brubaker (2015) points out, this seemingly neutral or "horizontal" difference of citizenship or place of birth is intimately tied into the structure of inequalities. And these birth inequalities are reinforced and rigidified by the policies on migration and refugees, and by limits to the free movement of people in the world. Passports and citizenship become marks of privilege and distinction. These ascribed categorizations are perhaps the most durable, and even growing in the contemporary world. They have been, however, seldom incorporated into social science analysis, which has focused on within-country inequalities (see also Shachar 2009 and Boatcă 2015).

4. These three (new) directions in research perspectives have been accompanied by a change in the methodologies applied to researching social inequalities. Thus, following the incorporation of multiple categories of structuration of inequalities, there has been a shift from studies based on socio-structural data to studies based on qualitative as well as quantitative findings at the political and symbolic dimensions. This required a methodological diversification in which stratification and mobility studies are less dominant, paving the way for the introduction of a critical analysis of the construction of social categorizations themselves (Anthias 2013, 2015). Equally influential became ethnographic methodologies that enable researchers to study the effects of inequality in everyday interactions and multi-sited networks (Skornia 2014).

6 Renata Motta, Elizabeth Jelin, and Sérgio Costa

Searching for a broader perspective on inequalities, one that enables scholars to understand dynamics of inequality production and reproduction beyond national borders, also opens the question regarding the types of data and analysis commonly used. Indeed, Piketty (2014) and his collaborators offered a key methodological innovation in collecting data from the top tax payers and analyzing cross-national data historically. However, a main obstacle for advancing in this research agenda is the lack of available data in many countries as well as a lack of global inter-crossed data for linking, for instance, environmental damage caused by soybean production in Paraguay and welfare improvements derived from soybean consumption in Europe or China.

Studying dynamics of global entangled inequalities

Until now, these advancements have formed specific subfields within inequality research. This means that scholars involved in investigations related to each of the developments cited above mostly ignored progress observed in the next subfield. In fact, however, these advancements are clearly complementary. The challenge of analytically combining them constitutes the core of the research agenda of *desiguALdades.net*, a scientific network established in 2009. The network strives in collecting and systematizing empirical findings of single investigations conducted within different disciplines in order to produce conceptual advancements in research on inequalities. Accordingly, the network makes a twofold contribution to inequality research: it introduces its own input in each of the four subfields outlined above *and* combines these inputs into a coherent analytical framework to study social inequalities.

The present book draws on findings of *desiguALdades.net* and seeks to offer a systematic overview of advancements achieved within the network and to identify shortcomings in these results in order to open new research agendas. We start with a relatively straightforward understanding of "entangled social inequalities" as "the distances between positions, which individuals or groups of individuals assume in the context of a hierarchically organized access to relevant societal goods (income, wealth, etc.) and power resources (rights, political participation, political positions, etc.)" (Braig, Costa, and Göbel 2013: 2).

This book takes this hierarchical organization as its guiding principle. Four considerations have to be introduced at this point. First, the realization that this ordering results from the operation of multiple forces—institutional, structural—that produce the hierarchical ordering (socioeconomic, sociopolitical, socioecological, cultural).

Second, the dynamics of inequalities are to be seen from a multi-scalar and relational perspective, focusing on the interdependencies between phenomena at different levels, from global historical trends to local negotiations. The premise is that even local (community or household) patterns of inequalities are never isolated from national and international forces. This does not imply to adopt global social structures as the preferred units of analysis as in world-system research or to exclusively concentrate on transnational spaces as "methodological transnationalists" (Khagram and Levitt 2007) do. Since the production and reproduction but also the contestation and mitigation of social inequalities always reflect an interplay of global (inter)dependencies, national politics, and everyday negotiations, geographical or political-administrative units of analysis (municipalities, nation-states, or the entire globe) are not adequate for studying dynamic entangled inequalities. Flexible relational units of analysis, constructed during the inquiry process itself, are required in order to encompass all relevant hierarchies associated with concrete social positions occupied by individuals or groups in the different spheres in which inequalities emerge. Dynamic relational units of analysis also enable researchers to follow the construction (implying de-constructions and re-constructions) of social categorizations relevant to shaping inequalities. Accordingly, categorizations that have been, for instance, a source for discrimination and exclusion at the level of everyday life in a certain period can be later reframed as justification for compensations or even reparations at the level of policies or legal framework. Care chains (Skornia in this book) and regimes of inequalities (Góngora-Mera in this book) are examples of relational units of analysis applied to study entangled inequalities.

Third, inequalities are plural, involving multiple socially constructed hierarchical categorizations, following historical developments and social struggles against discrimination and devaluation. Categories come to be socially defined, recognized, and reinforced—and eventually blurred or erased. The dimensions along which hierarchies and categorizations are constructed are not discrete but interrelated.

Fourth, social inequalities are always embedded in dynamics of transformation and change, which can entail both emancipatory change as well as the transformations required in order to, paradoxically, leave structures of inequality unchanged. In the first case, one might inquire into the conditions and forms that resistance to domination might take, including organized social movements or more subtle, individual forms of rejecting the dominant order. In short, the dynamics of transformation include struggles over resources and meanings, considering the reinforcing ways in which symbolic and material domination operate (Brubaker 2015).

The structure of the book

Following these considerations, the book is organized in three sections: structures, categorizations, and dynamics of change. The multi-scalar and relational perspective embedded in the concept of global entangled inequalities has oriented all authors when conducting their research. Therefore, it will be present, to a greater or lesser extent, in all parts of the book.

1. Structures: shaping inequalities. Established scholarship used to place the emphasis on socioeconomic inequalities reflected in income distribution or socioeconomic strata based on levels of schooling or positions in the labor market. Additionally, there are considerations of the role of political institutions—particularly the state—in deepening or mitigating the functioning of markets in producing inequalities. While acknowledging the functioning of these institutions in the structuring of inequalities, the first section of the book looks at other—often neglected—institutions

8 Renata Motta, Elizabeth Jelin, and Sérgio Costa

and arenas that impinge upon inequalities: the realm of law, the role of space and territory, in terms of spatial segregation and appropriation and in terms of environmental concerns, the relationship between society and nature. The main argument shared by the chapters in this section is that the dynamics of these realms are not solely the consequence of socioeconomic and sociopolitical structures of inequalities. Rather, they have an active role on their own in producing and reproducing social inequalities.

The chapter by Roberto Patricio Korzeniewicz focuses attention on the global level, in order to understand the structuration of socioeconomic inequalities. The global unit of analysis brings new light to an old phenomenon, namely income distribution. By adopting a world-historical perspective, the chapter contributes to overcoming the methodological individualism still dominant in research on inequality and, more specifically, in studies on stratification. The chapter shows that positions assumed by individuals within the global social structure are to a great extent determined by birth within a certain nation-state. Contrary to the liberal ideology of meritocracy, individual efforts and achievements have very little impact on social mobility at the global level.

While Korzeniewicz deals with income inequality at the global level, the other chapters in this section deal with different arenas where inequalities are generated. Thus, choosing a transregional unit of analysis to show persistent patterns of inequality, Góngora-Mera describes in his chapter the manifold nexus (in his words, articulations) between law and racial inequalities in Latin America. Since the constitutional recognition of and corresponding legal entitlements for Afro-descendants and indigenous peoples only took place at the end of the 20th century, he poses the question of how could the structural discrimination against these groups, expressed in socioeconomic and political inequalities, remain hidden for so long. In order to address the problem, Góngora-Mera suggests two analytical steps: a shift from domestic to a transregional legal approach; the use of Foucauldian conceptual lenses to understand the role of law and norms in the structuring of social relations. These steps are combined in the concept of inequality regime.

Differing from most nationally bounded studies of race, he starts by critically examining the category of race itself and arguing that race generates transregional inequality. Since the concept has been furnished to rationalize a hierarchical categorization of peoples, race performed a distinctly European way of naturalizing its domination. Race ordered the colonial system that included all world regions: Europe, the Americas, Asia, Oceania, and Africa. By treating race as a discursive and legal construction, Góngora-Mera provides us with a genealogy of law that seeks to deconstruct regimes of truth that normalized social inequalities. Relying on rich historical research from European, Latin American, and international jurisprudence, his genealogy is organized around four inequality regimes, ranging from the colonial period until the multicultural turn in international law. This chapter, based on discourse analysis of legal texts, offers a cogent example of how inequality research can benefit from a broader conceptual and methodological approach, as well as from a wider analytical scope by espousing a transregional and diachronic analysis.

Ramiro Segura's chapter turns the focus to space and, more specifically, to urban space. He argues that urban space, understood as a constitutive dimension of social life, with its own materiality and temporality, not only expresses inequalities in terms of the quality of housing and surroundings. Rather, urban space also conditions the (re)production of inequalities, affecting various aspects of social life such as job opportunities, the quality of education, access and costs related to mobility and transport, and the symbolic status of segregated neighborhoods. When studied at the level of their impact on urban spaces, the pro-poor policies adopted during the last decade in virtually all Latin American countries reveal their ambivalent impacts on social inequalities. Focused on cash transfer rather than on the consolidation of welfare structures (urban infrastructure, public education and health, etc.), these policies have contributed to reducing income inequalities and to stimulating consumption among lower strata. However, the lack of investments in the production of public goods has deteriorated the quality of life, especially of the poor.[2]

Research on Latin America from a global and entangled perspective also calls attention to the environmental inequalities among world regions arising from global capitalism. Socio-environmental inequalities are both material and symbolic because they are sustained by asymmetries of knowledge over nature and disputed by conflicts over social and cultural representations of nature. For instance, commodification and valorization of nature, such as the idea of payment for environmental services, clash with other values and understandings of nature that reject bringing its values under the same denominator of market products. In short, unequally distributed environmental impacts reinforce existing social inequalities.

In her chapter in this section, Kristina Dietz argues that the environment is not socially or politically neutral and that in order to understand the constitutive role of nature in the structuring of social inequalities, it is necessary to overcome the ontological dualism in modern thinking that has constructed nature and society as separate ontological entities. It is precisely the interaction of nature and power structures that is key to studying social inequalities in their ecological dimension. She starts from the premise that the ways in which societies transform and appropriate nature as natural resources or vital conditions, the institutions that regulate its accessibility and distribution, and how it is being conceived and known, make a difference in the way social relations of inequality unfold. Her point is that social inequalities are not only *a consequence of* specific ways of transforming nature, but also *inherent* to them.

Dietz draws on the related fields of political ecology and environmental justice to develop a conceptual proposal regarding the interdependencies between nature and inequalities. While the former calls attention to the structuring forces that co-constitute environmental inequalities, such as the political economy of resource extraction, the gender domination, and the disputes between representations of nature, latter highlights the intersectionality of structures of discrimination (race, gender, class, etc.) in the unequal distribution of environmental damage as well as of access to environmental resources. In reviewing such literature, Dietz develops the argument that it is not that the socioecological dimensions of inequality

10 Renata Motta, Elizabeth Jelin, and Sérgio Costa

reflect other structural forces, but that they are forged together, as racialized, gendered, and classed relations to nature further justifies other dimensions of inequality. Furthermore, relying on critical theory and historical-materialism, Dietz makes the case that both the materiality and meanings of nature are fundamental to a non-dualistic understanding of nature-society relations and, therefore, of the nexus between inequality and nature. Her main contribution consists in developing a conceptual proposal to theorize and research socioecological inequalities in three ways: social inequalities characterize the multiple ecological crises; the social production of nature also explains the social production of other dimensions of inequalities; the materiality of nature has implications for social inequalities.

2. Categorizations: constructing and de-constructing persistent hierarchies. This section looks at the way in which social categories are conceptualized and negotiated by social actors (including academics). Categories are salient in the contemporary world in both senses of visibility—they matter when looking at inequalities; they have been the motor of protest and claims for redress. Symbolic and interactive processes are linked to discrimination, inferiorization, and segregation of those characterized as "different," and, in this way, they have an impact on inequalities, insofar as these processes involve barriers for the underprivileged in entering desirable positions.

The chapters in this section share a concern with the need to critically scrutinize concepts such as difference, and more specifically gender, race, and indigeneity. If it is true that these concepts have "real" impacts on social life, our position as analysts oblige us to insist on their contingent, historical character. For instance, and following this logic, social actors, state agents, and scholars who phrase the issue of land concentration in certain Andean regions as a distributive conflict between peasants and large landowners can, in another context or moment, identify a cultural contest involving indigenous peoples and Creole farmers. Attention to the constructed and dynamic character of social categorizations is found in all chapters of the section. Some of them share also a common concern in understanding the consequences of the neoliberal legacy for the debate and policy on categorizations and inequalities. Under neoliberalism, narrowing inequality to income measures and fighting it with poverty reduction converged with policies involving a celebration of difference and a multicultural turn. Grounded in experiences and debates from Latin America, the chapters show how the region has been dealing with the ever-changing question of "inequality between whom?"

In his chapter, Juan Pablo Pérez Sáinz applies the theoretical framework from *Durable Inequality* (Tilly 1998) to Latin America. His work provides a radical critique of the liberal understanding of inequalities as defined by income for its blindness to previous social processes. Accordingly to Pérez Sáinz, when focusing on household income, one is observing the end result of a process of redistribution. Yet a previous distribution has taken place in markets, and these do not operate in a neutral manner but rather are mediated by power asymmetries and struggles. These distributional issues are seldom taken into consideration; they are accepted and taken for granted. He argues that this liberal understanding has contributed to depoliticizing the social question in the region, and his main claim is to bring the political dimension back into the analysis of social inequalities. Pérez Sáinz pays attention to processes instead of results, in which there are power relations between social subjects that are always characterized by asymmetries. One case in point is to understand that the reduction in the income gap of wage labor has been achieved by leveling down qualified labor at the cost of increasing the power of capital vis-à-vis labor.

Pérez Sáinz poses the need to distinguish between the social spheres of production and reproduction and, concomitantly, between struggles over surpluses in markets (such as between labor and capital), which are distributive conflicts, and social spending targeted at households, which involves redistributive policies. The state plays a key role both in regulating markets and in addressing the social question. At the same time, low budget policies of conditioned cash transfers targeted at the poorest households explain how Latin American governments managed to significantly reduce poverty rates while refraining from implementing structural changes in labor, land, and financial markets, and, with that, avoiding social conflict. With these clarifications, it comes as no surprise that the celebrated reduction in poverty (not inequalities) in the region has often occurred concomitantly with a higher concentration of rents at the higher social strata. In sum, to analyze inequalities one needs a concept of power and social conflict, bringing to the center of analysis not only final redistributive outcomes but also processes of empowerment and destitution.

The chapter by Elizabeth Jelin goes in this direction, guided by the concern with the relationship between inequality and difference, insofar as the multidimensional character of inequalities calls for a systematic analysis of the link between hierarchical inequalities of class relations, on the one hand, and those based on socially defined categorical differences on the other. Recalling that the emerging social science in the mid-20th century in Latin America framed this link as part of the discussion of capitalist development and evolving class relations, she sets the task to recover seminal works that can serve as a counterpoint to more contemporary discussions about inequalities and differences. In her chapter, she reviews how authors discussed gender (Larguía, Saffiotti), ethnicity (Stavenhagen), or race (Fernandes) cleavages within the framework of class relations. She also notes that global entanglements were framed in center-periphery and dependency approaches. The increasing recognition of the hierarchical nature of gender, ethnicity, and race relations led to a "cultural turn," whereby gender, ethnicity, and race were conceived on an equal (or even more salient) footing with economic stratification and class relations, as expressed in the perspective of "intersectionality." Jelin's main argument is to bring back the centrality of class, looking at the multiple dimensions and social categorizations involved in the resulting pattern of social inequalities.

One of the clearest symbolic impacts of the celebration of difference and multiculturalism in Latin America was felt in Bolivia with the election, for the first time in the world's history, of a self-declared indigenous president. In his chapter, Andrew Canessa explores how the category of indigenous, once key to making

12 Renata Motta, Elizabeth Jelin, and Sérgio Costa

demands for recognition of cultural difference and rights of minority groups to the state, loses such a clear role when citizenship is blurred with indigeneity. What happens when all, including the state, become indigenous? With an analysis of a conflict around the national park and indigenous territory TIPNIS, Canessa follows the transformation of Morales' office and its contradictions when its deployment of indigeneity as a tool of statecraft has privileged some indigenous peoples over others. Indeed, Morales' display of an indigenous rhetoric at global fora, claiming a moral weight to Bolivia's indigenous state in the defense of natural resources, is at odds with his domestic promotion of extractive industries (gas, oil, and lithium) in the name of development. His government has therefore sparked typically indigenous social mobilizations against the dispossession of their rights, while favoring small capitalist farmers and the urban poor. Canessa argues that "thinking of indigeneity in terms of discourses of the post-colonial dispossessed is simply unhelpful in navigating through these tensions and contradictions."

With a long ethnographic experience in the country, Canessa suggests not to think of indigeneity as a fixed category but rather as discourses with often competing senses, which also vary according to the scale of use. At the global scale it is straightforwardly understood as a defense of the environment, yet indigeneity can be equally deployed by Morales (the state) and by localized groups. It is at the national and local scales that conflicts arise showing conflicting senses of what indigeneity stands for and for whom. Taking Bolivia as a case study, Canessa engages with broader issues, such as some ambiguous consequences of the global transformation of the term "indigenous" from a category to describe (and dispossess) subject peoples in colonial regimes to it becoming a self-declared identity of liberation and rights. Among these, Canessa warns of the need to analyze the internal differentiation, and against the danger of "assuming that indigenous people are always and everywhere in the right or even that they are the colonized, never the colonizers." He concludes with the suggestion that, in order to address the paradoxes created when indigeneity works both to create new hierarchies and to dismantle them, one has to inquire into the diversity of indigenous voices and demands.

Reygadas' chapter explores social inequalities from the symbolic perspective. Drawing on previous anthropological and sociological scholarship, the author seeks to offer a systematic answer to the question, "How do symbols shape inequalities?" Accordingly, he identifies five main symbolic processes of production, reproduction, and contestation of social inequalities: creation of categories and boundaries; attribution of values to the created categories; conversion of categories (differences) into inequalities; creation and distribution of social capital; struggles over the legitimacy of inequalities. The author describes these symbolic patterns of reproducing inequalities not as a static repetition of existing asymmetries but as dynamic fields of forces in which actors using strategies for maintaining social distances compete with actors interested in mitigating inequalities. Even if some of these symbolic mechanisms have been already researched by previous studies, the effort made by Reygadas to critically reconstruct these processes in detail, and also to demonstrate how they interact, represents an important enlargement of existing studies on inequality. Thus, the chapter integrates symbolic processes that take place at different levels and in different social spheres (economy, politics, institutions, everyday life) into a coherent and encompassing analytical matrix. Seen through the lens of this matrix, one can precisely ascertain the complex nexus between material and symbolic processes that configure existing inequalities.

3. Dynamics of production and transformation of inequalities. The third and last section of the book concerns dynamics that produce inequalities but also processes of transformation and the reactions that the latter may cause. Such dynamics involve conflicts and disputes developed in different arenas using multiple repertoires of action—from public scandalization to lobbying and corruption. The case studies presented in this section follow processes in which inequalities are generated and maintained, also revealing their political and contested character. Although they deal with conflicts observed in concrete localities and nation-states, they share a common concern with interpreting local struggles in the context of their global and historical interdependencies. For this, the chapters re-elaborate concepts that seek to trace the temporal continuity (layered inequalities) and the transnational linkages of processes of production, trade, and consumption (global commodity chain) as well as of social reproduction (global care chain).

From a synchronic perspective, the chapters in this section address recent changes in social structure associated with individual strategies of mobility (migration) as well as with public policies (poverty reduction schemes, "multicultural" policies, and neoextractivist arrangements). This set of transformations has opened up new lines of conflict and also posed new conceptual questions for inequality scholars. It refers to controversies around policies that (re-)create differences such as affirmative action in Brazil or special land rights for Afro-descendent rural communities in Colombia.

In his chapter, Jairo Baquero-Melo deploys the concept of layered inequalities to grasp the overlapping of economic, political, and social processes that have been, historically and currently, producing and reproducing inequalities in the region of Lower Arato in Colombia. He claims that although social categories are fundamental to analyze the overlapping of inequalities, such processes simultaneously affect multiple social groups. More specifically, in his case study, while the expansion of multicultural collective land rights since the nineties has benefited Afro-descendants, other groups that have also been historically dispossessed of their land and labor rights, such as mestizo peasants, are further disregarded by the state. Currently, they share an experience of land conflicts and violence linked to global agribusiness, which continues to re-concentrate land and thus counters the forces promoting equality. Such "legalization" of difference, as he conceptualizes it, has been a contradictory result of multicultural policies. Therefore, he argues, the intersection of social categories of class, race, and ethnicity must be taken into account across the various groups of the dispossessed.

Baquero-Melo follows the historical processes that configured asymmetrical relations among various social groups across categories of class, race, and ethnicity,

14 Renata Motta, Elizabeth Jelin, and Sérgio Costa

from colonial times to contemporary Colombia plagued by armed conflict. His study of the Lower Arato region, where forced evictions are part of the routine experience of mestizo peasants and Afro-descendants, is an example of the relations between inequality and violence, deployed as a mechanism that produces and reproduces inequalities.

Sérgio Costa's chapter takes up the case of Brazil, where the recent cycle of economic growth combined with increasing social expenditures has led to a huge expansion of consumption, especially of durable goods. Combining Marxist and Weberian approaches in the study of inequalities and particularly the contributions of Kreckel (2004) and Therborn (2013), the chapter strives to reconstruct the connections between recent changes in Brazilian social structure and the political conflicts that led to the impeachment of Brazilian president Rousseff in August of 2016. The chapter outlines a multidimensional matrix, according to which five main vectors are relevant for defining classes or strata in Brazil: wealth, position in hierarchical spaces, knowledge, exclusive associations, and existential rights. Even if social distances, measured in terms of income and other assets, have remained untouched, the emergence of a new contingent of consumers has challenged the established middle class, which lost its monopoly to use certain services and commercial spaces (universities, shopping malls, airports, etc.). This explains its resistance against the governments conducted by the Workers' Party, even during the period of rapid economic growth in which the established middle class registered important material gains. Since 2014, economic stagnation has brought heavy material losses for all social classes, aggravating also the symbolic conflicts. This, combined with the investigations on corruption that have obstructed the illegal associations between politicians and business elites, undermined Rousseff's popular and parliamentarian sustentation.

From a world-historical perspective, as suggested by Korzeniewicz in this volume, migration appears as a mechanism to reduce inequalities; yet from a transnational perspective, one that follows the linkages and relations between households that emerge from migration, new patterns of inequalities stand out. Migration produces inequalities within the family and beyond, in gender-specific ways that also interact with social classes. The chapter by Anna Skornia explores some of these multiple meanings and effects of migration on social inequalities.

The incorporation of the link between the spheres of production and reproduction calls for a concern with households and families as sites of production and reproduction of inequalities. Households and families, and men and women within them, however, are also actors in specific markets, national and even global. In her chapter, Skornia looks at the dynamics of global labor migration processes linked to what seemed to be private family-related tasks: care work for the elderly. Care deficits in the global North are increasingly met by female migration from the South. Women's entry into the labor force in Northern countries has not implied a substantial change in the gendered division of labor, but an outsourcing of care labor to migrant workers in the domestic sphere. These new care relationships have important implications for the reproduction of social inequalities across national borders and beyond. With the purchase of care services, provided by migrant workers in the global North, care has become an unfairly distributed resource, which is withdrawn from one country and household and imported to another.

Studying Peruvian migrant workers in Italy, Skornia discusses how the particularities of national social-institutional and policy configurations play an essential role in contributing to the reproduction of inequalities related to care. She calls attention to the role of the state in providing welfare or failing to do so and its effects on inequalities, in this case, based on age, a category often disregarded in research on inequalities. In addition, by looking into the family, Skornia recalls an important topic of the social sciences, namely the role of the family as an intermediate between the individual and the collective, and, in the case at hand, in reducing or reproducing inequalities.

Tracing the local effects of the production of global agrarian commodities in Latin America bears a wider relevance for sociological theory. A renewed attention to inequalities implies questioning the urban and industrial bias in sociology, starting with the acknowledgment that almost half of the world population is rural, of which three-quarters are poor. In this direction, in her chapter in this volume, Renata Motta looks into the mobilization of the rural poor against social-environmental inequalities associated with the expansion of genetically modified (GM) crops in Argentina and Brazil. While often the dynamics that generate new inequalities operate at multiple scales, such as global capitalist markets and national development projects, the effects are locally experienced—at the level of the household, such as in the case of health problems, and at the level of the small farm, as peasants are deprived of their control over seeds. It is also at those levels of the directly affected that resistance is built up.

Engaging with the literature of gender and environment and, in particular, with the conceptual triad of economic, social, and environmental (re)production, Motta draws on two cases of social mobilization to argue that, not coincidentally, the market expansion of agro-biotechnology relied on the erosion of state and corporate responsibilities for both social and environmental reproduction. The connection between these phenomena is to be found in neoliberal agrarian capitalism, characterized by state lax regulation about their health and environmental effects while at the same time pressuring for a strong state presence for enforcing intellectual property rights. In this, Motta claims that social mobilization is the key process to contest the disjuncture between the productive and reproductive spheres on which the defenders of GM crops rely.

Notes

1   We would like to thank the Research Network Interdependent Inequalities in Latin America (*desiguALdades.net*), sponsored by the German Federal Ministry of Education and Research, for supporting our research and this publication. Our sincere thanks to all authors who kindly accepted our invitation to participate in this joint project, and revised their work so many times, responding to our queries and comments. We are

16 Renata Motta, Elizabeth Jelin, and Sérgio Costa

indebted to Neil Jordan as a very collaborative editor, the anonymous reviewers, and Tom Norton, for his copyediting work.

2 The former mayor of São Paulo, Fernando Haddad, a political scientist, properly formulated this contradiction in his successful campaign for the municipal elections in 2012: "Thanks to Lula and Dilma [former Brazilian presidents], the Brazilian poor are consuming more. As a mayor, I want to help you to extend this achievement, not only better consuming but also using public services of good quality, having better education, transportation and housing. Therefore, I state that Lula and Dilma improved your life inside your home; as a mayor, I will give my best to improve your quality of life outside your home door" (Haddad 2012).

References

Anthias, F. (2013): "Social Categories, Embodied Practices, Intersectionality: Towards a Translocational Approach." In *Interdependencies of Social Categorisations*, edited by Célleri, D., Schwarz, T., and Wittger, B., 27–40. *Ethnicity, Citizenship and Belonging in Latin America*. Madrid: Iberoamericana.

Anthias, F. (2016): "Interconnecting Boundaries of Identity and Belonging and Hierarchy-Making within Transnational Mobility Studies: Framing Inequalities." *Current Sociology* 64 (2): 172–190.

Beck, U. (1986): *Risikogesellschaft. Auf Dem Weg in eine andere Moderne*. Frankfurt am Main: Suhrkamp Verlag.

Beck, U. (1996): "World Risk Society as Cosmopolitan Society?: Ecological Questions in a Framework of Manufactured Uncertainties." *Theory, Culture and Society* 13(4): 1–32.

Beck, U., Giddens, A., and Lash, S. (1994): *Reflexive Modernization: Politics, Tradition and Aesthetics in the Modern Social Order*. Stanford, CA: Stanford University Press.

Berger, P. A. (2008): *Transnationalisierung sozialer Ungleichheit*. Wiesbaden: VS Verlag für Sozialwissenschaften.

Boatcă, M. (2015): *Global Inequalities beyond Occidentalism*. Farnham: Ashgate.

Braig, M., Costa, S., and Göbel, B. (2013): "Soziale Ungleichheiten und globale Interdependenzen in Lateinamerika: eine Zwischenbilanz." Berlin: desiguALdades.net, Working Paper No. 4.

Brubaker, R. (2015): *Grounds for Difference*. Cambridge, MA: Harvard University Press.

Burawoy, M. (2000): *Global Ethnography: Forces, Connections, and Imaginations in a Postmodern World*. Berkeley, CA: University of California Press.

Célleri Endara, D., Schwarz, T., Wittiger, B., and Digitalia (2013): *Interdependencies of Social Categorisations*. Madrid; Frankfurt am Main: Vervuet.

Chernilo, D. (2007): *A Social Theory of the Nation-State: The Political Forms of Modernity beyond Methodological Nationalism*. Critical Realism. London: Routledge.

Connell, R. (2007): *Southern Theory: Social Science and the Global Dynamics of Knowledge*. Cambridge and Malden: Polity.

Fine, R. (2007): *Cosmopolitanism. Key Ideas*. London: Routledge.

Göbel, B., Góngora-Mera, M., and Ulloa, A. (eds.) (2014): *Desigualdades Socioambientales en América Latina*. Bogotá: Universidad Nacional de Colómbia.

Gonzales de la Rocha, M., Perlman, J., Safa, H., Jelin, E., Roberts, B. R., and Ward, P. M. (2004): "From the Marginality of the 1960s to the 'New Poverty' of Today: A LARR Research Forum." *Latin American Research Review* 39 (1): 183–203

Habermas, J. (1998): *Die Postnationale Konstellation: Politische Essays*. Frankfurt am Main: Suhrkamp Verlag.

Haddad, F. (2012): Electoral advertisement. Available at: https://www.youtube.com/watch?v=WY95GnE-YnU, last accessed on 27 November, 2016.

Honneth, A. (1992): Kampf um Anerkennung. Zur moralischen Grammatik sozialer Konflikte. Frankfurt am Main: Suhrkamp Verlag .

Khagram, S. and Levitt, P. (2007): "Constructing Transnational Studies." In Khagran, S. and Levitt, P. (eds.): *The Transnational Studies Reader*. London/New York: Routledge, pp. 1–39.

Korzeniewicz, R. P. and Moran, T. P. (2009): *Unveiling Inequality: A World-Historical Perspective*. New York: The Russel Sage Foundation.

Kraemer, K. (2007): "Umwelt und soziale Ungleichheit." *Leviathan* 35(3): 348–372.

Kreckel, R. (2004): *Politische Soziologie der sozialen Ungleichheit*. Frankfurt am Main: Campus.

Luhmann, N. (1985): "Zum Begriff der sozialen Klasse." In Luhmann, Niklas (ed.): *Soziale Differenzierung. Zur Geschichte einer Idee*. Opladen: Westdeutscher Verlag, pp. 119–162.

McMichael, P. (2009): *Contesting Development: Critical Struggles for Social Change*. London: Routledge.

Nun, J. (1969): "Superpoblación relativa, ejército industrial de reserva y masa marginal." *Revista Latinoamericana de Sociología* 2: 178–236.

Nun, J. (2001): *Marginalidad y Exclusión Social*. Buenos Aires: Fondo de Cultura Económica.

Pérez Sáinz, J. P. (2014): *Mercados Y Bárbaros: La Persistencia de las Desigualdades de Excedente en América Latina*. San José: FLACSO.

Pieterse, J. N. (2002): "Global Inequality: Bringing Politics Back In." *Third World Quarterly* 23 (6): 1023–1046.

Piketty, T. (2014): *Capital in the Twenty-First Century*. Cambridge, MA: The Belknap Press of Harvard University Press.

Pries, Ludger (2008): "Transnationalisierung und soziale Ungleichheit. Konzeptuelle Überlegungen und empirische Befunde aus der Migrationsforschung." In Berger, Peter A. and Weiß, A. (eds.): *Transnationalisierung sozialer Ungleichheiten*. Wiesbaden: VS, 41–64.

Randeria, S. (2007): "The State of Globalization: Legal Plurality, Overlapping Sovereignties and Ambiguous Alliances between Civil Society and the Cunning State in India." *Theory, Culture & Society* 24 (1): 1–34.

Reygadas, L. (2008): *La apropiación. Destejiendo las Redes de la Desigualdad*, Barcelona: Anthropos.

Roth, J. (2013): *Entangled Inequalities as Intersectionalities: Towards an Epistemic Sensibilization*. Berlin: desiguALdade.snet, Working Paper No. 43.

Shachar, A. (2009): *The Birthright Lottery: Citizenship and Global Inequality*. Cambridge, MA: Harvard University Press.

Sen, A. (1999): *Development as Freedom*. Oxford University Press.

Skornia, A. K. (2014): *Entangled Inequalities in Transnational Care Chains: Practices across the Borders of Peru and Italy*. Bielefeld: transcript.

Stewart, F., Brown, G., and Mancini, L. (2005): *Why Horizontal Inequalities Matter: Some Implications for Measurement*. Oxford: University of Oxford, CRISE Working Paper No. 19.

Therborn, G. (2006): "Meaning, Mechanisms, Patterns, and Forces: An Introduction," in: Therborn, G. (ed.): *Inequalities of the World*. London: Verso, pp. 1–58.

Tilly, C. (1998): *Durable Inequality*. Berkeley, CA: University. of California Press.

Weiß, A. (2005): "The transnationalization of social inequality. Conceptualizing social positions on a world scale." *Current Sociology* 53 (4): 707–728.

PART I
Structuring inequalities

1

INEQUALITY

Toward a world-historical perspective

Roberto Patricio Korzeniewicz

1 Why a world-historical unit of analysis?

One of the most deeply ingrained assumptions in the social sciences is that inequality and stratification across the world are shaped primarily by forces operating within nations. This assumption is so fundamental and deeply rooted that the choice of nations as the privileged unit of analysis has come to be most often not theoretically informed. Instead, driven by a combination of common sense, academic custom, and the format in which relevant data have come to be most easily available, much of the work on inequality and stratification in the contemporary social sciences naturalizes nations as the spaces that contain within their boundaries the fundamental processes relevant to understanding the subject matter.

For a more productive study of stratification and inequality, we draw on a different tradition, and argue that greater critical thought should be given to what should constitute an appropriate unit of analysis. What is an appropriate unit of analysis? One that contains within its boundaries the social processes that are relevant for understanding the phenomenon under investigation (Weber 1996 [1905]). For the study of stratification and inequality, the appropriate unit of analysis is global and historical.[1]

A foundational text of the modern social sciences, Adam Smith's *The Wealth of Nations*, serves to illustrate the importance of choosing an appropriate unit of analysis. In several passages of *The Wealth of Nations*, Smith discusses wealth disparities within and between town and country, in ways that echo discussions of such disparities within and between wealthy and poor nations today. Rather than following the existing common sense to explain the wealth of towns and the poverty of the country in the late eighteenth century as the outcome of processes occurring independently within each of these bounded territories, *The Wealth of Nations* chooses an alternative unit of analysis, one that encompasses both sets of spaces (town and country).

In Smith's account, the citizens of towns historically used corporate association to regulate production and trade in ways that restricted competition from the country.[2] As a result of such arrangements, in their dealings with the country ("and in these latter dealings consists the whole trade which supports and enriches every town") town dwellers were "great gainers" able to "purchase, with a smaller quantity of their labor, the produce of a greater quantity of the labor of the country" (Smith 1976 [1776]: I, 139–140). In this account, the wealth of towns and the poverty of the country become inextricably related, as it was largely to regulate and shape the flows (e.g., of goods, capital, and people) constituting this very relation that territorial boundaries between town and country were constructed and enforced.

While such arrangements tended to raise the wages that town employers had to pay, "in recompense, they were enabled to sell their own just as much dearer; so that so far it was as broad as long, as they say; and in the dealings of the different classes within the town with one another, none of them were losers by these regulations" (Smith 1976 [1776]: I, 139). What Smith thereby describes is a process of selective exclusion: through institutional arrangements establishing a social compact that restricted entry to markets, town dwellers attained a virtuous combination of growth, political autonomy, and relative equity that simultaneously transferred competitive pressures to the countryside.

Adam Smith provides important insights into the crucial role played by opportunity hoarding in shaping the relative prevalence of wealth and scarcity in town and country. But these insights would have been missed if his unit of analysis in *The Wealth of Nations* had failed to encompass both sets of spaces (towns and country) and their interaction in his narrative. For example, Smith could have attributed the wealth of towns to the individual effort, frugality, and/or values of their citizens—thereby explaining the relative poverty of rural peoples as the consequence of insufficient achievement in each or any of these dimensions. But his account avoided such a naturalization of town/country boundaries, and emphasized instead the relational processes (including the creation and enforcement of the boundaries demarcating "town" and "country") that in his account play a central role in explaining the uneven distribution of wealth across these spaces.

Similarly, Korzeniewicz and Moran (2009) argue that accounts of contemporary inequality and stratification that assume the nation-state to constitute the fundamental unit of analysis—and moreover, as is most often the case, restrict their observations to wealthy nations—are bound to miss key processes that shape these phenomena even within the wealthy populations they study.[3] The key processes shaping social inequality and stratification have unfolded globally and over a long period of time—and the study of these phenomena requires a world-historical perspective.[4] Such a perspective reveals that the institutional arrangements shaping inequality within and between countries have always been simultaneously national and global, that the most significant patterns of social mobility involve challenges to existing patterns of inequality between nations, and that ascribed criteria continue to play a fundamental role in sustaining inequality at a global level. Our understanding of each of these issues changes dramatically once such relationships are taken into account—and this can only be done by broadening the scope of our analysis to the world as a whole.

Efforts to construct such a mapping have been constrained by both the scarcity of adequate comparable data and the theoretical assumptions hitherto guiding research on stratification and mobility. In fact, the empirical constraints we face are linked to prevailing theoretical assumptions. For the most part, social stratification and mobility have been conceived as taking place primarily—if not wholly—within national boundaries, and these assumptions became deeply entrenched in data collection as the latter developed over the last century. Most data on inequality, for example, therefore have been drawn from national surveys of individuals and/or households, collected primarily by national statistical agencies for the purpose of shaping policies at a national level. Moreover, these national data, collected primarily in wealthy countries, have been used throughout the social sciences to identify trends and patterns in (and construct "universal" narratives about) stratification, inequality, and social mobility.

How different are our accounts of inequality and stratification when looking at these processes and outcomes from a global rather than a national perspective? What constitutes social mobility when seen from the world as a whole? Who has the relative ability to access different routes to social mobility, and to what extent, over time?

Shifting the unit of analysis in this manner produces an alternative perspective on inequality and stratification. Rather than being nationally bounded, institutional arrangements constitute relational mechanisms of regulation, operating within countries while simultaneously shaping interactions and flows between them. Depicting such a conclusion empirically is not easy, as the data necessary to construct such a depiction are not readily available. An empirically precise model, extended over time and space in a true world-historical perspective, will require the creation of data on a global (not national) scale, data that heretofore do not exist. In the absence of such data, the following are merely two illustrations of what such mapping might look like.

Korzeniewicz and Moran (2009) took 85 countries having decile-level income distribution data (the percentage, or share, of income accruing to each 1/10 of the population) available circa 2007, and calculated for each decile its average income—for example, the income share accruing to the richest 10% of the United States (USA10) is almost 28%, translating into an average income for the decile of $127,500 based on the GNI per capita for the United States in 2007. These 850 country deciles were ranked from poor to rich to establish world deciles (that is, each with 10% of the sampled population), their boundaries, and their composition. For example, the first box at the top of Figure 1.1 represents the richest 10% of our world sample, country deciles with an average income above $27,894 (in US dollars). Although the population size of a decile is equivalent, each world decile contains different numbers of country deciles because countries have different national populations (the large number of deciles in the richest two world deciles thus reflects the small populations in that part of the world).

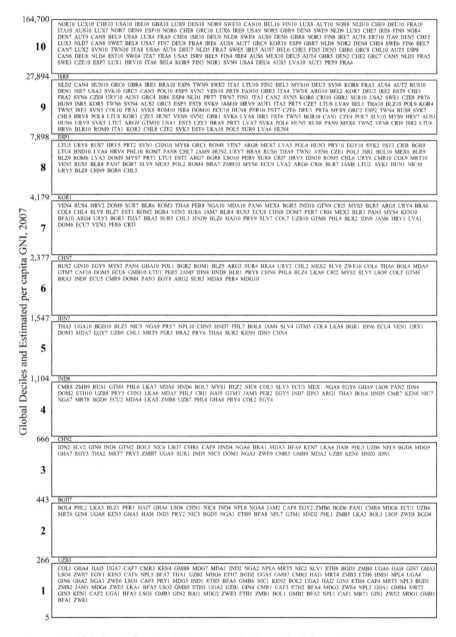

FIGURE 1.1 Global stratification: 850 country deciles ranked from rich to poor.

Source: Korzeniewicz, Robert Patricio, and Moran, Timothy Patrick. 2009. *Unveiling Inequality: A World Historical Perspective*. © Russell Sage Foundation, 112 East 64th Street, New York, NY 10065. Reprinted with permission.

As can be seen in Figure 1.1, virtually all the deciles of high-income nations are contained within the wealthiest two world deciles, illustrating why studies of mobility and stratification that focus solely on such countries are bound to produce a very narrow interpretation of these phenomena. As we will see later, what stands as mobility in these studies, for example moving up the occupational ladder, is recast from a global perspective into movement within what in fact constitutes a world elite (i.e., movement *within* the richest 20% of the world). More significant mobility, as noted below, entails the jumping of borders to secure a more dramatic improvement in income. Producing a better account of global stratification and world inequality to identify such patterns of mobility requires a different (world-historical) approach to the collection and interpretation of social-scientific data.

To arrive at a more precise mapping of how stratification and mobility have changed over recent decades, for example, we would be best served by data that combine information on within-country distributions (say, between rural and urban populations, men and women, the skilled and the unskilled) with measures of how these within-country populations are performing relative to the populations of other countries. Such a mapping would provide a more productive assessment of changes in the relative position of various populations vis-à-vis one another (e.g., different occupations within a country, or similar occupations across nations) and of the changing returns to various strategies of social mobility (e.g., returns to skill and/or education).

Pursuing such an effort, Korzeniewicz and Albrecht (2012) have mapped changes in global occupational stratification between 1982 and 2009 by drawing on the wage data available through the periodical publications of the Union Bank of Switzerland (UBS). Since 1971, the UBS has been publishing, every three years, a survey of prices and salaries that can be used to reconstruct, for over three dozen cities across the world (including cities in high-, middle-, and low-income nations), average wages for over a dozen occupational categories (ranging from construction laborers and unskilled female factory workers, to bus drivers and primary school teachers, to managers and engineers). Such an exercise allows an assessment of how the relative returns to particular occupations have changed over time, the occupations that have been characterized by lesser or greater global convergence in their returns, and the extent to which changes in relative incomes might be traced to various possible processes of upward and/or downward mobility (e.g., returns to education, national economic growth, and/or migration).

Throughout the 1982–2009 period, wages varied more between cities located in high- and low-income nations than they did between occupations. To take one example, throughout the period, the average hourly wage in New York based on 12 surveyed occupations was more than 10 times higher than in Mumbai, and the range of hourly wages within Mumbai (with a $4.04 wage difference between building laborers and department heads) was less than half the gap between the highest wage in Mumbai and the lowest reported wage in New York (a $9.06 difference). In other words, once again, the potential gains a worker in Mumbai can derive through economic growth over time or by increasing their individual human capital (say, by acquiring the education and skills required to become an engineer rather than a construction worker) are small compared to the relative gains a Mumbai worker can acquire by moving to New York.

Mumbai is not the only city to have its wages dwarfed by those in New York. Among the 12 occupations surveyed in 1982, the lowest hourly wage in New York City was for female factory workers, who earned an average of $5.34 in current dollars: in that same year, this was above the highest paid occupation (usually engineers or department heads) in Bogota (Colombia), Cairo (Egypt), Istanbul (Turkey), Jakarta (Indonesia), Manila (Philippines), Mexico City (Mexico), and Mumbai (India). In the 2009 survey, almost 30 years later, the lowest hourly wage in New York City was for car mechanics, who earned an average of $13.46 in current dollars: in that same year (when more lower income cities were sampled than in 1982), this was above the highest paid occupation in Bratislava (Slovakia), Bucharest (Romania), Buenos Aires (Argentina), Caracas (Venezuela), Delhi and Mumbai (India), Jakarta (Indonesia), Kiev (Ukraine), Kuala Lumpur (Malaysia), Manila (Philippines), Mexico City (Mexico), Nairobi (Kenya), Prague (Czech Republic), Riga (Latvia), Santiago de Chile (Chile), Sofia (Bulgaria), Tallinn (Estonia), and Warsaw (Poland).

A second finding that confirms arguments presented in Korzeniewicz and Moran (2009) is that there is considerable stability in the relative ranking of the various occupation and city combinations included in the Korzeniewicz and Albrecht (2012) study. Moreover, throughout the 1982–2009 period, there was considerable stability in the relative wage gap between high-income countries (such as the United States) and middle-income countries (such as most of Latin America).

But, of course, some crucial data are missing from the discussion that this section has advanced so far: the UBS project has begun including mainland cities in China in its survey only since 2006. Add China, with the outstanding rates of growth of the last decades, and the global profile of occupational stratification changes in significant ways. If we had data available on comparable wages for our 12 occupations in 1982 China, the relative distribution and ranking of these wages in all probability would have looked similar to those described earlier for Mumbai. By 2009, wages in Beijing have undergone considerable growth. Wages for the higher-paid occupations in China now surpass those of higher-paid occupations in many Latin American countries.

The absolute increase in wages in Chinese cities—which the UBS data analyzed in Korzeniewicz and Albrecht (2012) only capture for the 2006–2009 interval, but is even more evident when subsequent years are taken into account (e.g., see Albrecht and Korzeniewicz 2014)—is reflective of broader patterns of economic growth in China that are in effect transforming global stratification, as discussed in greater detail below. Before moving to a more specific discussion of the effects of growth in China (and, to a lesser extent, India) on global stratification, however, a brief detour is useful to highlight some implications of these arguments for how to understand some broader implications of adopting a global perspective on social inequality, stratification, and mobility.

2 Global patterns of social mobility

Much of the existing literature on social mobility focuses on how the latter is shaped primarily by (1) changes (up or down) in the relative position of individuals or groups within national income distributions. But, from a global perspective, there have been two main paths to social mobility involving (2) changes in the relative position of nations within the international income distribution, and (3) shifts in the relative location of individuals and/or groups within the global distribution of income attained by "jumping" categorical locations.

Although studies of socioeconomic mobility in wealthy nations generally assume that their conclusions are universally relevant, these conclusions are drawn from the limited range of interactions taking place among and within relatively wealthy strata in the world (mainly, the two top world income deciles in Figure 1.1). Such a narrow focus provides a very partial perspective on mobility patterns. To make a historical parallel, it would be as if we were to assume that a study of individual trajectories in the French or British nobility in the fifteenth century served to represent the overall character of social stratification and mobility at the time. Taking the world as the relevant unit of analysis allows us to reassess the three main paths that in fact have characterized social mobility.

2.1 Path A: Within-country mobility

This is the most apparent path of mobility. Through this path, for example, individuals and/or groups change their relative standing within national income distributions through the upgrading or devaluation of human capital (most importantly, skills and education). Cast more broadly as evidence for the gradual displacement of ascription by achievement as the primary criterion shaping social stratification, the pursuit of this strategy at an individual level has been the principal focus in the study of mobility by much of the social sciences over the twentieth century.

Studies focusing on intergenerational mobility in wealthy countries end up measuring movement at the very top of the global income distribution, the ninth and tenth deciles of Figure 1.1. In 2005, the median earnings for a high school graduate in the United States was over $31,500, while the same figure for someone with a Bachelor's degree or higher was over $56,000 (US Census Bureau 2006). Shifting from one income to the other certainly represents a major attainment for individuals and/or groups making such a transition: within the United States, this educational attainment would imply a move from USA4 to USA8. But even such a major within-country transition represents, in Figure 1.1, a more limited movement in global stratification, as both the $31,500 and $56,000 earnings are contained within global income decile 10.

On the other hand, global mobility through educational attainment is today more significant (1) the higher the level of within-country inequality, and (2) particularly in middle-income nations. After all, restricted access to education is precisely one of the principal mechanisms through which high levels of inequality were reproduced in some nations throughout the twentieth century. In a country such as Brazil, where levels of inequality are extremely high, and less than 10% of the population has a college degree, a shift for an individual or a group similar to the one described for the United States would probably entail a movement from BRA5 or BRA6 to BRA10, translating into a shift from global decile 7 to global decile 9. From the point of view of relative standing in global stratification, the returns to education in such high-inequality, middle-income nations are even more considerable than in wealthy nations.

Complicating this path to mobility, however, are significant obstacles. Most importantly, the relative returns to any given level of human capital and/or educational attainment undergo significant change over time. For example, attaining a primary school education was a standard of high educational achievement in the late nineteenth century, but is not considered as a high marker of human capital attainment today. Computer literacy virtually did not exist 40 years ago, but is certainly a crucial skill today. Particularly in poorer nations, efforts at capturing the returns associated with enhanced human capital and greater educational attainment often involve engaging in a race whose finishing posts are constantly being moved forward.

In much of the prevailing mainstream literature, changes in the differential returns to skilled and unskilled labor and in who has access to such opportunities are fundamental in understanding social stratification and mobility. These changing returns are, indeed, one of the fundamental axes around which inequality has been constituted historically. But what is often missing in the mainstream literature, and what a world-historical perspective leads us to focus on, are the changing ways in which "skill" has been constructed over time as a criterion through which to differentially distribute returns to various populations.

Such a perspective helps understanding of, for example, why certain criteria (e.g., "literacy," "elementary education," "secondary education," "computer skills") serve to claim (or justify) higher returns in one period but not later on in time, why some jobs are perceived as "unskilled" in some countries but "skilled" in others, or why new production processes might be read as "deskilling" in some countries but as "upgrading" in others. A world-historical perspective, in other words, highlights that the "human capital" criteria that underpin inequality are themselves an outcome of institutional arrangements linked to Schumpeterian processes of creative destruction.

Schumpeter suggests that instead of a single transition from one state of equilibrium to another, we should conceive of capitalism as entailing continuous transformation:

> [C]apitalism is by nature a form or method of economic change and not only never is but never can be stationary. The opening up of new markets, foreign or domestic, and the organizational development from the craft shop and factory to such concerns as U.S. Steel illustrate the same process of industrial mutation—if I may use that biological term—that incessantly revolutionizes the economic structure from within, incessantly destroying the old one,

incessantly creating a new one. This process of Creative Destruction is the essential fact about capitalism. It is what capitalism consists in and what every capitalist concern has got to live in.

(Schumpeter 1942: 82–83)

In the Schumpeterian model, the introduction and clustering of innovations disturb existing economic and social arrangements. Over time, this is the fundamental process driving cycles of prosperity (characterized by intense investment in new productive opportunities) and depression (characterized by the broader absorption of innovative practices and the elimination of older activities).

Rather than reflecting an objective capacity to meet certain technical requirements (or anything related to actual tasks performed in production), the assortment of relevant populations across the world into the skilled and unskilled categories is linked to processes of creative destruction. For the most part, the "skilled" within any particular distributional array are constituted by those who are involved in the more "creative" end of the processes of creative destruction described by Schumpeter. Deskilling and the creation of the unskilled is precisely the outcome of constant "destruction," and processes of construction of categorical inequality are linked precisely to the criteria that are used at any given historical moment to assort populations into the "skilled" and "unskilled" categories (for example, "unskilled" today refers for the most part to those activities, once considered "skilled," that are now carried out by populations in or from outside the top two global income deciles of Figure 1.1). Historically, entry into skilled positions has been constrained by the regulation of competition (e.g., as in the towns described by Adam Smith). The use of ascriptive criteria to sort populations and thereby construct what is "skilled" or "unskilled" (e.g., town and country, but also women and men, blacks or whites, poor nations or rich nations) has been constitutive of the very creation and reproduction of inequality.

While the strategies reviewed above focus on mobility at an individual level, within-country mobility has included the various forms of collective action (e.g., social movements, corporate organization) and political mobilization (e.g., from electoral participation to lobbying to revolutions) through which various actors have sought to enhance their command over resources within national boundaries—what Hirschman (1970) described as the exercise of voice.[5] To a significant extent, the very constitution of nation-states over the development of the world economy has been part and parcel of the exercise of "voice" by relevant social actors.

From a world-historical perspective, the impact of these strategies has always been complicated: the success of claims by one actor (e.g., organized labor in wealthy countries) might go hand-in-hand with the exclusion of others (e.g., immigrants from poorer countries). Thus, one and the same process (e.g., the pursuit of a more equitable distribution of resources by welfare states in wealthy countries) can have very different outcomes depending on whether we examine its impact solely within the boundaries of individual nation-states or the world as a whole.

So how should advocates for greater equity assess the outcome of struggles that simultaneously enhance wealth and well-being for some (e.g., male urban workers in post-World War II higher-income countries) while strengthening institutional arrangements leading to the exclusion of others (e.g., immigrants from poorer countries)?

Many answers are possible. Some argue that all countries have their respective disadvantaged populations, who can only be expected to define themselves and their aims primarily in relation to their national surroundings, and that the struggle of poorer populations in wealthy countries is not only meaningful in and of itself, but also helps raise the bar for standards of well-being across the world. Others would focus on the effects of exclusion in increasing relative inequality and facilitating the reproduction of absolute deprivation in poorer countries, and argue that the gains made by disadvantaged populations in wealthy countries are trivial relative to the needs of the majority of the world's population. And of course, most advocates of greater equity would probably reject approaching the question as a dilemma, and instead would seek to recognize as valuable all efforts to advance the interests of the underprivileged relative to wealthier populations—no matter whether these efforts take place within national or global boundaries.

2.2 Path B: Between-country mobility

The second path to mobility in global social stratification has entailed the pursuit of national economic growth. China and India today embody much of the optimism about the potential rewards of such a path. As we noted earlier, if the current rates of growth of these two countries remain as high as they are today, they would eventually change the face of global stratification. Historically, there has always been mobility of individual nations, such as in the cases of Sweden in the late nineteenth century, Japan in the immediate post-World War II era, or South Korea in the 1970s and 1980s. But, in the past, the upward mobility of individual nations took place within a setting in which systemic inequality continued or became even more pronounced. The larger size of China and India makes the story different than before, as their effective mobility, even if limited to these two individual cases, would imply a shift in the logic that has prevailed until now in the world economy.

Over the last two centuries, the development of high inequality between countries was closely linked to the institutional arrangements that came to characterize significantly lower levels of within-country inequality in wealthier nations around the world. In a sense, such institutional arrangements—a particular way of distributing the relative gains and losses arising from more day-to-day processes of creative destruction—have constituted a historical Schumpeterian innovation. But, eventually, the very institutional arrangements created through innovation themselves become characterized by rigidities, creating new competitive opportunities for global mobility—for example, as in Adam Smith's town and country example, the very effectiveness of barriers to entry has generated new niches of opportunity, as in the cheap labor mobilized in China or India during their first decades of sustained high growth.

We should note here that the pursuit of national economic growth is often portrayed in terms of a willingness of people to allow for greater inequality in their own country in exchange for the growth of the overall wealth available for distribution. Leaving aside the fact that not all strategies of economic growth entail rising within-country inequality (as indicated by the "growth with equity" literature), even the existence of such a tradeoff would not be indicative of a lack of concern with inequality. The pursuit of economic growth involves a recognition of the crucial role of between-country inequality in shaping world stratification. When people in South Korea and/or China come to endorse policies designed to generate economic growth, rather than leaving concerns for inequality behind, they are recognizing the potential significance of such a path for engaging in upward social mobility within a global system of stratification.

But such a road of national economic growth has not been easily accessible to vast parts of the world, and success stories have been the exception rather than the rule for most of the world's population. For most of the past two centuries, the path of social mobility through national economic growth has failed to deliver its promise. Even in the case of Mexico, tied as it has been for the past 15 years to a free trade agreement with Canada and the United States, economic growth has not been sufficiently high to allow a single country decile to catch up relative to the United States.

As in the case of educational attainment, this is again a situation in which the goal posts are constantly being moved forward. It is, at bottom, what Schumpeter's notion of creative destruction is all about. Constant processes of innovation historically have ensured the eventual obsolescence of whatever prevailing standards characterized a particular moment in time, for example, standards of education or productive technologies. In a country such as Mexico, this might mean running very fast to simply stand still—if not fall further behind. For the past two centuries, this has been the most prevalent story for most countries in the world. The development and implementation of growth panaceas (Japan in the 1970s, South Korea in the 1980s, or China today) seldom have provided a replicable model for success, and in fact have been part and parcel of the constant creation of obsolescence.

2.3 Path C: Jumping categorical inequality

We thus arrive at the single most immediate and effective means of global social mobility for populations in most countries of the world: migration. Given the crucial role of nationality in shaping global stratification, "jumping" categories by moving from a poorer country to a wealthier one is a highly effective strategy of mobility (see Figure 1.2).

Figure 1.2 returns to our global stratification sample to highlight certain patterns of international migration. The figure used 2007 data to stylistically present the relative global standing of country deciles of six nations from Figure 1.1 that have considerable migration flows among them: Guatemala, Mexico, and the United

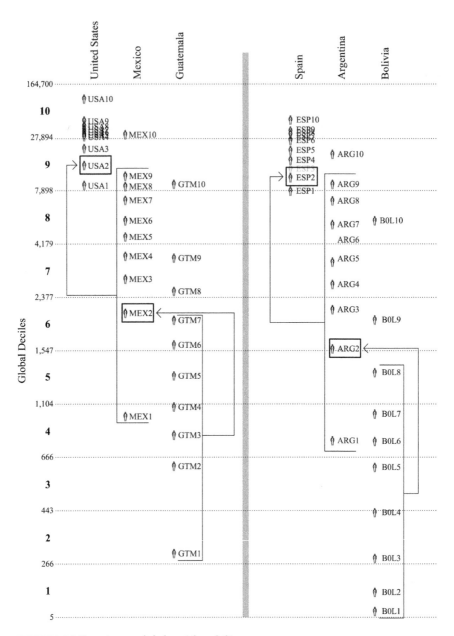

FIGURE 1.2 Migration as global social mobility.

Source: Korzeniewicz, Robert Patricio, and Moran, Timothy Patrick. 2009. *Unveiling Inequality: A World Historical Perspective*. © Russell Sage Foundation, 112 East 64th Street, New York, NY 10065. Reprinted with permission.

States on one side of the figure; Bolivia, Argentina, and Spain on the other. Mexico is a receiving country for migrants from Guatemala, and a sending country to the United States, just as Argentina is a receiving country for migrants from Bolivia, and a sending country of migrants to Spain. The main point of the figure is to illustrate how global stratification produces strong incentives for migration for individuals and/or groups of people in relatively poorer countries. In the case of Guatemala, for example, in 2007, anyone belonging to the poorest seven deciles would be engaging in upward mobility by gaining access to the average income of the second poorest decile in Mexico. In the case of Mexico, the incentives are even more striking, as all but the wealthiest decile would find upward mobility in gaining access to the average income of the second poorest USA decile.

Like the other example, in Bolivia, anyone belonging to the poorest eight deciles would be engaging in upward mobility by gaining access to the average income of the second poorest decile in Argentina. In the case of Argentina, relative to a wealthier country (2007 Spain), the incentives again are even more striking, as all but the wealthiest decile of Argentina, in 2007, would have found upward mobility in gaining access to the average income of the second poorest decile in Spain[6] (and, of course, the reversal of some migration flows between Spain and Argentina over the last ten years, as unemployment in Spain increased, further illustrates the extent to which such flows are contingent on the evolution of income differentials). Such disparities help to explain why economic migrants often are willing to abandon a professional status in their country of origin to work in relatively more menial positions in their country of destination—once again underlining the contingent meaning of "skill" and "human capital."

Of course, migration is not merely the product of differentials in income incentives. Engaging in migration requires access to manifold resources—from those needed to meet the costs of transportation and entry into a foreign country, to those involving social networks that can facilitate access to housing and jobs—and these resources are not equally available to all populations within a given country. And even in the presence (or absence) of strong income incentives, decisions to migrate are also based upon broader considerations regarding security, safety, well-being, and personal attachments. However, Albrecht and Korzeniewicz (2015) and Korzeniewicz and Albrecht (2016) indicate that even when taking into account such broader considerations, income differentials remain the most significant variable accounting for global patterns in migration flows.

The two previous paths of mobility, the upgrading of human capital and the pursuit of national economic growth, both require a long time to generate their intended returns, and are fraught by a high degree of uncertainty whether such returns will be available as expected. By contrast, the third path of mobility in global stratification, migration, while often requiring a high level of courageous determination, tends to offer much more immediate and certain returns (although a different type of uncertainty might be precisely what calls for high doses of courageous determination, particularly for undocumented migrants). Thus, while academics might remain convinced that national borders provide the appropriate boundaries for understanding social mobility, migrants, in their crossing of such borders, reveal the boundaries of stratification to be global.

Mechanisms of institutionalized selective exclusion had a direct impact on trends in inequality, helping to reduce inequality within countries, while restricting migration and thereby increasing inequality between countries. Thus, the decline in inequality experienced in several wealthy countries earlier in the twentieth century was to a large extent the consequence of the introduction of wage-setting institutions across those countries that in effect limited competition in their labor markets.[7] True, much of the literature emphasizes the importance of macroeconomic trends that enhanced the demand for unskilled labor (thereby reducing wage differentials), unionization, or favorable state policies, but the introduction of restrictive international migration policies was the *sine qua non* for the operation of each of these variables (e.g., Williamson 1991).[8]

Such an interpretation, in fact, dovetails with *The Wealth of Nations'* account of the evolution of town/country wealth differentials. For Smith, the effectiveness of the institutional barriers imposed by towns on the mobility of populations from the country was demonstrated by deepening inequalities between town and country. But, over the long run, for Smith, these inequalities—and low prices and wages in the country—would inevitably generate incentives for employers in towns to defect from the existing institutional compact to take advantage of greater profit opportunities outside town boundaries. This would initiate the demise of the corporate association of towns.

As in Smith's town-country scenario, growing income disparities between nations over time themselves have generated strong incentives (e.g., drastically lower wages in poor countries) for "outsourcing" skilled and unskilled jobs to peripheral countries in a "market bypass" that in effect overcomes twentieth-century constraints on labor flows. Rising world inequality becomes a driving force as well for migration, and the latter holds the promise of providing a quick path for overcoming the gap between wealth and poverty. In this sense, migration embodies social mobility. A truly free flow of people across the world, in fact, would provide the fastest means for thoroughly transforming the equilibria that have characterized global stratification for the past two hundred years.

3 The transformation of global inequality

Korzeniewicz and Moran (2009) argue that persistent patterns of high inequality within countries, as in much of Latin America and Africa, appear to be originally linked to the exploitation of coerced labor and the restricted access of large segments of the population to property and/or political rights, and to entail the persistence of what we call selective exclusion. Such exclusion generally is justified by categorical criteria. By comparison, patterns of lower inequality in wealthier countries, where free workers and small property owners have considerable access to property and political rights, appear to involve relatively greater inclusion—through redistributive state policies, the ability of labor to use trade organizations to

Inequality: a world-historical perspective **35**

enhance their bargaining power, and/or the effective use of education to enhance skills and thus wages.

But, in fact, while institutional arrangements centered around selective exclusion and categorical inequality appear to be the most salient distinguishing characteristic of high within-country inequality patterns, selective exclusion and the deployment of categorical inequality have been just as central to the development and persistence of what appear to constitute patterns of low within-country inequality.

In the high within-country inequality pattern, institutional arrangements enhance economic opportunities for some while simultaneously restricting the access of large sectors of the population to various forms of opportunity (e.g., "educational," "political," "economic"). Enhanced opportunities for some and the restricted access of the majority are related: selective exclusion serves to reduce competition among elites through institutional arrangements that simultaneously enhance competitive pressures among excluded populations (in the arenas or markets to which these populations are restricted). In the high within-country inequality pattern, this selective exclusion operates fundamentally within national borders.

The role of selective exclusion is less evident in the low within-country inequality pattern. In fact, the institutional arrangements characteristic of wealthy countries with the low inequality pattern appear to differ from those involving the high within-country inequality pattern precisely by the extent to which they provide for their overall population broader access to educational, political, and/or economic opportunity. Whereas countries characterized by the high inequality patterns are most manifestly characterized by exclusion, ascription, and categorical inequality, countries with the low inequality pattern appear as the very embodiment of universal opportunity and ensuring the possibility of success through individual achievement.

But the institutional arrangements characteristic of countries with the low inequality pattern do restrict access to opportunity for large sectors of the population, except that excluded populations now are located primarily outside national borders. Selective exclusion, in this case, operates fundamentally through the very existence of national borders, reducing competitive pressures within these borders, while simultaneously increasing competitive pressures among the excluded populations outside those very same borders (again, in the arenas or markets to which these populations are restricted). Hence, the establishment of the low inequality pattern and the persistence of high inequalities between countries did not evolve as two separate processes: rather, they are the outcome of fundamental institutional arrangements undergirding world inequality.

Around the late nineteenth and early twentieth centuries, there were relatively high and more open flows of people from poorer areas of the world into richer ones. At this time, as observed by authors such as Williamson (1991), national barriers to entry were relatively less pronounced. By the twentieth century, national barriers to entry became more pronounced, as part of an effort to restrict competitive pressures and/or reduce inequality within wealthier nations.

36 Roberto Patricio Korzeniewicz

Again, such patterns of interaction bear a striking resemblance to how Adam Smith (1976 [1776]) described the relationship between town and country in the brief review we provided in the first section of this chapter. What Smith described is a process of selective exclusion: through institutional arrangements establishing a social compact that restricted entry to markets, town dwellers attained a virtuous combination of growth, political autonomy, and relative equity that simultaneously transferred competitive pressures to the countryside.

Of course, we do not mean to imply that the uneven global distribution of competitive advantages and disadvantages resulted solely from institutional arrangements transferring competitive pressures from one location to another. Surely, the story is much more complicated. Areas that strengthened and protected their own property rights (most generally, restricted to limited sectors of their populations) did provide phenomenal incentives to potential producers that were absent elsewhere. Here, as in Adam Smith's (1976 [1776]: I, 426) towns, "[o]rder and good government, and along with them the liberty and security of individuals, were, in this manner, established […], at a time when the occupiers of land [elsewhere] were exposed to every sort of violence."[9] Moreover, once having gained a certain competitive edge, areas characterized by relatively lower inequality tended to have at their disposal a much greater amount of resources to maintain and extend such an edge (for example, through technological innovation and a more constant upgrading of the labor force).

But when focusing only on wealthy nations, as is the practice of most of the social sciences, these institutional arrangements indeed appear, as those of Adam Smith's towns, to be characterized primarily by inclusion; and, likewise, economic growth and markets seem to constitute virtuous spheres where gain is fundamentally an outcome of effort. From such a perspective, success appears to be the outcome of individual achievement, as measured by universal criteria, in spheres (e.g., education, labor markets) characterized by relatively unrestricted access.

As in Smith's town and country, the interaction of such virtuosity with processes of selective exclusion can only be observed when we shift our unit of analysis to encompass the world as a whole. Such a shift reveals that the prevalence of what appear to be "achieved" characteristics in today's wealthy nations is predicated upon processes operating between nations that hide away how "virtuous" institutional arrangements simultaneously entail privileges based on exclusion and "ascription."[10]

In fact, from the perspective we advance in this chapter, ascriptive criteria centered on national identity even today continue to be the fundamental basis of stratification and inequality in the contemporary world. From such a perspective, the current uneven distribution of income and wealth in the world would unlikely exist in the absence of the institutional arrangements that limit access to markets and political rights on the basis of national borders. In this sense, while it is not the case that the populations of wealthy nations have attained their privileges by making much of the rest of the world poor, we contend that the relative privileges characterizing high-income nations (constituting no more than 14% of the world's population) historically required the existence of institutional arrangements ensuring the exclusion of the vast majority of others from access to opportunity.

As in the past, the persistence of such categorical inequality is justified by appealing to images and forms of constructing identity that appear as natural rather than as the social artifacts they are. In this sense, the idea of nationhood as a "natural" category has become as deeply embedded in common sense (thereby allowing such ideas to often go unchallenged) as the notion of, say, white supremacy was in the nineteenth century.

Unveiling Inequality (Korzeniewicz and Moran 2009) discusses how current challenges to world inequality have taken two forms: increased migration (both documented and undocumented), and the rise of (mainly) China and (more recently) India. Such challenges would not have surprised Adam Smith. For Smith, as indicated above, the political organization of town dwellers allowed them to get, through selective exclusion, significant competitive advantages vis-à-vis rural inhabitants. But, over time, the very success of these arrangements in generating advantages eventually led to their erosion. The accumulation of stock in towns, for example, eventually led to growing competition among stockholders, and, hence, declining profits. Eventually, according to Smith (1976 [1776]: I, 143), these competitive pressures "forces out stock to the country, where, by creating a new demand for country labor, it necessarily raises its wages." By reintroducing competition among those who hitherto had been protected from such pressures, mechanisms of selective exclusion between town and country began to break down.

À la Smith, the very growth of between-country inequality through most of the last two centuries has become a driving force for the migration of labor and capital. Growing income disparities between nations over time have generated strong incentives (e.g., drastically lower wages in poor countries) for both the migration of workers to higher-wage markets and the "outsourcing" of skilled and unskilled jobs to peripheral countries. Both trends exercise a "market bypass" that in effect overcomes the twentieth-century institutional constraints on labor flows that characterized the development of the low inequality pattern through most of the twentieth century. Such are the processes at hand in the recent decline of between-country inequalities (although the extent of this decline is under debate).

Between-country inequality always has been characterized by the mobility of individual nations. But, in the past, as we show, the upward mobility of individual nations took place within a setting whereby systemic inequality continued or became even more pronounced. The large populations of China and India make today's story different than before, as their effective mobility, even if limited to one of those two countries, implies a potentially dramatic shift in patterns of between-country inequality.

The extent of this transformation is illustrated by the changing contours of global social stratification. Figure 1.3 shows the percentual distribution of the world population according to income levels (calculated on the basis of national income data) in 1980 and 2008. In 1980, this distribution had a clear trimodal distribution, with the world population divided into low-, middle-, and high-income clusters

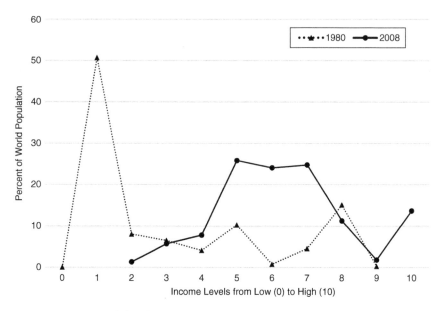

FIGURE 1.3 Percentual distribution of the world population by income levels.

Source: The author's own calculations based on data in World Bank (2013).

(or peripheral, semiperipheral, and core nations), with most of the world population falling into the lower end of the spectrum.

Now compare how the distribution of the world population changed by 2008 as a consequence, primarily, of the rapid growth of China (and to a lesser extent, India). What used to be a trimodal distribution has now become clearly bimodal. The upward movement of wages and incomes in China, discussed earlier, is transforming not only the relative standing of various occupations, but broader patterns of global social stratification as well.

The world-historical interpretation advanced here differs from that which prevails among many contemporary observers, for whom the decline in between-country inequality is normatively interpreted to be either (1) merely a consequence of the gradual diffusion of modernization/industrialization/markets to areas of the world economy that had remained traditional and/or autarchic, and/or (2) an effort by world elites to enhance their privilege through the expansion of markets and exploitative arrangements. From a world-historical perspective, much more is at play. Were the trends of the late twentieth and early twenty-first centuries to continue in a sustained way, between-country inequality could eventually break out of the logic that shaped global stratification for well over a century: the use of institutional arrangements, embedded in national identities, that selectively excluded the vast majority of the world population from access to opportunity.

But such an outcome is not certain, and there are powerful interests resisting such a transformation. How else to understand the current upsurge of nationalist and/or xenophobic political movements in many wealthy nations across the world?

These movements demonstrate the political capital to be gained in wealthy nations by portraying the inclusion of the poorer populations of the world (in their migration flows or their competitive challenges) as a threat. Thus, an effort is evident in wealthy nations to secure and strengthen their borders, to reestablish protected markets, to reconstruct the "golden age" of the mid-twentieth century. Is this not an effort to reassert the privileges of some through "institutional arrangements ensuring the exclusion of the vast majority of others from access to opportunity"?

4 Conclusion

Since the emergence of the social sciences, and in their subsequent development, inequality and stratification have been conceived primarily as processes that occur within national boundaries. Such a focus has produced a number of influential overarching narratives. One such narrative is that the relative well-being of people is shaped most fundamentally by the capacity of home-grown institutions to promote economic growth and/or equity. Another is that people over time have become more stratified by their relative achievement and effort rather than by the characteristics with which they are born. A third one, a corollary of the other two, is that upward social mobility is fundamentally the outcome of the adoption of better domestic institutions by countries, and/or the acquisition of greater human capital by individuals. Looking at the unfolding of social inequality in the world as a whole over a long period of time—in other words, from a world-historical perspective— calls into question these narratives.

Moreover, shifting the relevant unit of analysis from the nation-state to the world-system changes our understanding of what some would call the "relevant positions" from which to assess current tensions associated with "globalization" and inequality.[11] As argued in this chapter, from a global perspective there are indeed tradeoffs: the same institutional mechanisms through which inequality historically has been reduced within some nations often have accentuated the selective exclusion of populations from poorer countries, thereby increasing inequality between nations.

We are thus facing similar dilemmas as those that characterized the expansion of world markets in the late nineteenth century. The latter was another period of uncertainty, in which the growth of markets generated both a constituency for globalization but a protective reaction as well. Current patterns of social stratification, mobility, and inequality might be transformed in the future as a consequence of the very opportunities generated by the growth of between-country inequalities through much of the twentieth century—similar to the way in which Adam Smith discussed how the unequal development of town and country generated the very market forces that would eventually bring such inequality to an end. On the other hand, the interests challenged by such a transformation might engage in the type of protective reaction experienced in the early part of the twentieth century to roll back such challenges (although the size of India and China, together with their linkages to other countries in Asia and elsewhere, might contribute to producing very different outcomes than those of the twentieth century).

40 Roberto Patricio Korzeniewicz

Deciding where to stand when facing these choices will involve difficult decisions for progressive forces across the Western world, but it is important to note that having to make such choices is itself a sign of the relative privilege such forces have hitherto enjoyed.

Notes

1 Many of the arguments in this chapter draw heavily from my collaborative work with Timothy P. Moran and Scott Albrecht.
2 "The inhabitants of a town, being collected into one place, can easily combine together. The most insignificant trades carried on in towns have accordingly, in some place or another, been incorporated; and even where they have never been incorporated, yet the corporation spirit, the jealousy of strangers, the aversion to take apprentices, or to communicate the secret of their trade, generally prevail in them, and often teach them, by voluntary associations and agreements, to prevent that free competition which they cannot prohibit by byelaws" (Smith 1976, 141 [1776]: I).
3 Charles Tilly (1999: 36) notes that focusing on inequality as a relational outcome tends to produce resistance in the social sciences. Korzeniewicz and Moran (2009) argue that such a relational account can only be constructed by embedding it in time and space.
4 This insight has been the methodological heart of what Terence K. Hopkins and Immanuel Wallerstein (1982) eventually came to call a world-systems approach.
5 "To resort to voice, rather than exit, is for the customer or member to make an attempt at changing the practices, policies, and outputs of the firm from which one buys or of the organization to which one belongs. Voice is here defined as any attempt at all to change, rather than to escape from, an objectionable state of affairs, whether through individual or collective petition to the management directly in charge, through appeal to a higher authority with the intention of forcing a change in management, or through various types of actions and protests, including those that are meant to mobilize public opinion" (Hirschman 1970: 30).
6 Using purchasing power parity (PPP) adjusted data alters these findings only slightly. For Mexico, all country deciles below MEX8 (instead of MEX9) are upwardly mobile to USA2. For Guatemala, the results are the same. For Argentina, all country deciles below ARG7 (instead of ARG9) are upwardly mobile into ESP2. For Bolivia, all country deciles below BOL7 (instead of BOL8) are upwardly mobile into ARG2.
7 These institutions also provided opportunities for (some but not other) rural populations to rapidly enhance their incomes by moving to urban areas, thereby contributing further to declines in within-country inequality in wealthier nations.
8 Williamson (1991: 17), for example, argues that declining inequality in industrialized countries after the 1930s was chiefly the outcome of pre-fisc forces altering returns to skilled and unskilled sectors of the labor force in favor of the latter, and indicates that key to these forces was "an erosion in the premium on [...] skills, and [a] relative increase in unskilled labor scarcity."
9 "Whatever stock, therefore, accumulated in the hands of the industrious part of the inhabitants of the country, naturally took refuge in cities, as the only sanctuaries in which it could be secure to the person that acquired it" (Smith 1976, 427 [1776]: I).
10 Of course, not all is exclusion. Institutions of high inequality exclude important sectors of the population of other nations from some markets, but seek to include them in others (for example, such as the one constituted by intellectual property).
11 Rawls (1971: 8) indicates that his theory of justice applies to a national society conceived "as a closed system isolated from other societies." The world-systems perspective adopted in this chapter provides an alternative understanding (particularly insofar as equal citizenship is not forthcoming globally as Rawls assumes it is at a national level).

References

Albrecht, S. and Korzeniewicz, R. P. (2014): "Global Wages and World Inequality: The Impact of the Great Recession," in Suter, C. and Chase-Dunn, C. (eds.) *Structures of the World Political Economy and the Future of Global Conflict and Cooperation*, Berlin: LIT Verlag, pp. 33–52.

Albrecht, S. and Korzeniewicz, R. P. (2015): "Global Migration Flows and Income Differentials," in Pilati, M., Sheick, H., Sperotti, F., and Tilly, C. (eds.) *How Global Migration Changes the Workforce Diversity Equation*, Cambridge, MA: Cambridge Scholars Publishing, pp. 18–54.

Hirschman, A. (1970): *Exit, Voice, and Loyalty: Responses to Decline in Firms, Organizations, and States*, Cambridge, MA: Harvard University Press.

Hopkins, T. and Wallerstein, I. (eds.) (1982): *World-Systems Analysis: Theory and Methodology*, Beverly Hills, CA: Sage Publications.

Korzeniewicz, R. P. and Moran, T. P. (2009): *Unveiling Inequality*, New York, NY: Russell Sage Foundation.

Korzeniewicz, R. P. and Albrecht, S. (2012): "Thinking Globally About Inequality and Stratification: Wages Across the World, 1982–2009," *International Journal of Comparative Sociology*, 53 (5–6): 419–443.

Korzeniewicz, R. P. and Albrecht, S. (2016): "Income Differentials and Global Migration in the Contemporary World-Economy," *Current Sociology* 64 (2): 259–276.

Rawls, J. (1971): *A Theory of Justice*, Cambridge, MA: The Belknap Press of Harvard University.

Schumpeter, J. (1942): *Capitalism, Socialism and Democracy*, New York, NY: Harper and Row.

Smith, A. (1976 [1776]): *An Inquiry into the Nature and Causes of the Wealth of Nations*, Chicago, IL: The University of Chicago Press.

Tilly, C. (1999): *Durable Inequality*, Berkeley, CA: University of California Press.

Union Bank of Switzerland (1971–2009): *Prices and Earnings Around the Globe*, Zurich: Union Bank of Switzerland.

US Census Bureau (2006): *Median Income Levels*, at: www.census.gov (Date of request: 8 October, 2010).

Weber, M. (1996 [1905]): *The Protestant Ethic and the Spirit of Capitalism*, Los Angeles, CA: Roxbury Publishing Company.

Williamson, J. (1991): *Inequality, Poverty, and History: The Kuznets Memorial Lectures of the Economic Growth Center*, New York, NY: Basil Blackwell and Yale University.

World Bank (2010 and 2013): *World Development Indicators*, Washington, DC: World Bank.

2

TRANSREGIONAL ARTICULATIONS OF LAW AND RACE IN LATIN AMERICA

A legal genealogy of inequality

Manuel Góngora-Mera

Introduction

The relationships between law and 'race'[1] throughout world history can be characterized as Janus-faced. On the one hand, law has been used as an instrument to fight racial discrimination (1) by the provision of accessible remedies for individuals who have suffered discrimination or (2) by the provision of preventive measures in order to obtain some tangible reduction in the incidence of racial discrimination, or (3) as a vehicle of social engineering to counteract not only direct discrimination but also the social, cultural, political, and other factors that can underpin indirect discrimination and racial disadvantage (MacEwen 1999: 427). On the other hand, law has been used to naturalize and institutionalize racial discrimination, segregation, and exclusion, for instance, in Apartheid South Africa (e.g., the 1913 Natives Land Act or the 'Pass laws'), Nazi Germany (e.g., the 1933 Law for the Prevention of Hereditarily Diseased Offspring or the 1935 *Reichsbürgergesetz*), Fascist Italy (e.g., the 1938 *leggi razziali*), the United States (e.g., the US anti-miscegenation legislation or the 'Jim Crow Laws'), Indonesia (e.g., the anti-Chinese legislation in force until 1998), or the British colonies (e.g., the British monolingual laws in Hong Kong).

Until quite recently, Latin American countries widely assumed that racial discrimination was a practice that took place elsewhere but not in the region. Dulitzky illustrates this point particularly well, by analyzing the statements of several Latin American countries to the Committee on the Elimination of Racial Discrimination until 2000, where it was argued that racial problems or prejudices "do not exist" or are "practically negligible" and that governments are committed to preserving the region "from the propagation" of racism (Dulitzky 2001: 86, 89–90). In the Declaration of the Conference of the Americas against Racism in Santiago (5–7 December, 2000), all Latin American states admitted for the first time the existence of racism and racial discrimination at both the state and society level. Throughout the twentieth century, most countries embraced the founding myth of being 'racial democracies' by means of a long history of *mestizaje*. Accordingly, racial prejudices were atypical, especially when compared to the United States (Degler 1971; Freyre 2003; Tannenbaum 1946). Additionally, for almost two centuries, a legal veil of formal equality stimulated the intuition that, contrary to the experiences in other world regions, Latin America had escaped the Janus-faced articulations of law and 'race': some countries granted citizenship without racial or ethnic restrictions as early as independence; slavery was legally banned a few decades later; *de jure* segregation systems did not exist; sterilization and anti-miscegenation laws were a rare exception.[2] But this legal idealism masked the arrangements that the Euro-descendant elites made to maintain their privileges and manage social hierarchies. This ultimately resulted in structural discrimination: Afro-descendants and indigenous peoples were de facto not identically situated with 'whites' and were legally ignored and socially excluded from the community of equals. In most Latin American countries, the constitutional recognition of Afro-descendants and indigenous peoples took place only at the end of the twentieth century.[3]

In order to understand how such articulations could remain covered for so long, despite the noticeable inequalities to the disadvantage of Afro-descendants and indigenous peoples in a wide range of socio-economic areas (e.g., education, income, health, housing, patrimony) and in access to political power, this chapter changes the focus on domestic legislation by proposing a legal transregional approach. It is largely inspired by the insights of entangled history (Werner and Zimmermann 2006) and theoretically supported on Foucauldian conceptual lenses (including discipline, discourse, dispositif, dividing practices, genealogy, power/knowledge relations, and regimes of truth). This chapter aims to expose the crucial role that law played in the racialization of society under colonial rule, and the continuities of such a role throughout the twentieth century. For this purpose, I introduce Sérgio Costa's definition of *inequality regime*. This concept serves to depict transregional interconnectedness between legal texts, and to place norms in the center of the analysis of racial inequalities. It is also useful for *longue-durée* studies, as it allows a focusing on regime changes (i.e., major shifts in the racial conceptions and legal standards, and their effects in terms of racial inequalities). The first part of the chapter introduces the legal transregional approach applied here to conceptualize 'race' as transregional inequality and the central role of law in this regard. The second part presents some articulations between law and 'race' in Latin America as conditioning racial discourses, social hierarchies, and inequalities under European rule (*cf.* section 2.1) and some significant continuities of such articulations after independence (*cf.* section 2.2) and in subsequent regime transitions in the twentieth century (*cf.* section 2.3). Particular attention is devoted to transregional and transnational[4] legal influences in times of transition from one regime to another.

This chapter draws on data and reflections derived from a wider research project on interdependent inequalities affecting Afro-descendants in South America conducted over the past five years. It does not include analysis of the situation

44 Manuel Góngora-Mera

after 1989 due to length restrictions, but several topics relating to this period have been discussed in detail elsewhere (see Góngora-Mera 2014, 2015, and 2017). An extended and fully annotated version will be assembled into a forthcoming book.

1 Addressing race as transregional inequality: the central role of law

From its inception, inequality is what 'race' is all about. The concept rationalized the new global political and economic order derived from the transregional interactions of large numbers of populations from Western Europe, sub-Saharan Africa, and America: the operation of a race-based system of transatlantic slavery and the subjugation of Native Americans for the colonization of the 'New World' (Smedley 1998: 690, 693–694). Racial taxonomies progressively emerged as European empires became global and Europeans came into more intimate and permanent contact with peoples of Africa, America, and Asia. 'Race' was an inter-continental category of inequality with a hierarchical vision of humanity, configured as a mechanism that naturalized domination by structuring unequal relations among the newly encountered peoples and establishing a world hierarchy in which white Europeans were deemed innately (or divinely predetermined) superior to all other peoples. 'Race' as a category of inequality is a major feature that distinguishes European colonialism from other previous forms of domination. Accordingly, the global dissemination of the fiction of 'race' and its real consequences in the development of a colonial system based on white supremacy and the enslavement, dispossession, and economic exploitation of the other 'races' represent one of the most prominent cases of a transregionally constructed form of inequality in world history.

Addressing 'race' as a discursive construction that legitimated social and political disparities between conquerors and subjugated peoples allows us to explore the dispositives (e.g., institutions, laws, administrative measures, etc.) employed to impose and normalize this hierarchical ordering in colonial societies. Correspondingly, I speak of a 'legal genealogy of inequality' as a diachronic analysis of the multiscale intercrossing of racial discourses through law. This approach explores the racial representations, discourses, and knowledge that are behind the language of laws and treaties, and their mutually reinforcing connections to social inequalities in post-colonial societies. The analysis focuses on the identification of epistemic continuities and overlappings between changing discourses throughout history, in contrast to a mere chronological/linear narrative focus on events or paradigmatic historic breaks. In this chapter, it is applied to deconstruct the successive regimes of truth that covered legal discrimination and racial inequalities in Latin America until the 1990s.

1.1 The legal lineage of 'race'

The origin of the concept of 'race' and the resulting assumptions and beliefs expressed in racial discourses in Latin America have been transregionally connected through law. Since the early times of Iberian rule in the region, racial identities were constructs produced and reproduced through different regulations. 'Blood purity' statutes (*estatutos de limpieza de sangre*), enacted shortly after the end of the *Reconquista*, were adopted to exclude *conversos* and non-Christians living in the Iberian Peninsula in Europe. This resulted in a discriminatory legal system between Christians, Muslims, and Jews. As Kuznesof (1995: 160) explains, the concept of 'race' in Spain evolved from an issue of religious purity in the fifteenth century into a question of blood relationship to non-Christians. Through the transmission of this way of thinking during the first stages of colonization in America, 'race' became foremost a matter of purity of blood, and lineage a significant social reference (Carrera 2003: 12).

Coexistence between Europeans and indigenous peoples was regulated by the establishment of a 'Republic of Indians' subjected to the servitude of a 'Republic of Spaniards.' But the logic of this binary segregation was broken due to the forced arrival of enslaved Africans and the realities of sexual relationships and procreation between natives, Africans, and Europeans, which has been called 'miscegenation' (*mestizaje*). This resulted in an intricately detailed social stratification ('castes') based on percentages of racial intermixtures between Iberian, Indigenous, and African blood: whites were at the top, followed by mestizos, then descendants of natives, and, at the bottom, slaves and individuals with African blood, who were demeaned with labels that depicted them as animals or human-animal hybrids (e.g., *mulato, coyote, lobo*).

Over the generations, when establishing the lineage and blood mixtures of an individual became more complex, 'race' increasingly became a morphological term (skin color, hair texture, etc.). This led to a wide range of color prejudices and discriminatory regulations (especially against castes with dark skin) in both Spanish and Portuguese laws (Carrera 2003: 13; Degler 1971: 213–220). For instance, defining if an individual must pay taxes or was allowed access to the market or the school depended ultimately on ancestry or color of skin. In other cases, regulations without an explicit racial bias had an adverse impact on mestizos and lower castes. For instance, Iberian civil laws privileged legitimate children for inheritance, which indirectly discriminated against blacks and mestizos (as most of them were born of parents who were not married to one another). This in turn increased the concentration of wealth and the economic distances between the castes, and progressively encouraged the belief in the natural superiority of whites.

In the long term, the *derecho indiano* established an inequality regime that was coherent with the tradition of *iustitia distributiva* (i.e., treating equal persons equally and unequal persons unequally): it granted *privilegia* in canon and civil law and distributed social positions according to racial hierarchies (among other criteria). These positions were internalized through the available disciplinary techniques of the Iberian empires: *encomiendas, mitas, reducciones,* or *resguardos* for indigenous peoples; slaves' markets, barracks, *haciendas,* or large plantations for Africans and their descendants. The strict social stratification in castes served to the *divide et impera* logics of dividing local social structures in order to impede alliances that could

46 Manuel Góngora-Mera

become a menace against the colonial power. In general terms, the colonization of Latin America illustrates the normalizing power of law, as it naturalized the racial discourses surrounding the bodies and defined the social relations and stratifications as common knowledge, as general truth.

1.2 Transregional articulations of inequality regimes

The use of the concept of 'regime' to analyze transregional articulations between law and racial inequality is not unplanned. Contrary to the traditional state-centric approach, which is built on a political unit of analysis, regime analysis defines a focus that is restricted neither to a spatial nor a political unit; it rather adopts a relational, interdependent view on the emergence, maintenance, and transformation of inequalities. It assumes that domestic legal frameworks influence national patterns of social exclusion, but also that they are usually consistent with interrelated legal bodies at different levels beyond the state (regional, transregional, global).

Costa (2011: 16–17) defines 'inequality regime' as a set of logics of stratification/ redistribution classified as static (caste societies), dynamic (class societies), or combined (class with racial/ethnic/gender ascription); political, scientific, and popular discourses according to which individuals or groups interpret and construct their own positions and that of others in society; legal and institutional frameworks (e.g., apartheid, multicultural, or antidiscrimination laws); policies (e.g., racist migration policies, integration or compensatory policies); and models of conviviality (segregating or integrating convivial forms) in everyday life. Relevant here is the fact that none of these components is exclusively restricted to the state borders. Racial hierarchies and other logics of stratification are transregional/transnational; ethnic and racial discourses are globally shared (e.g., the diffusion of scientific racism in the late nineteenth century or the diffusion of race-based affirmative action in the twenty-first century); even domestic legal frameworks and public policies are usually part of (or influenced by) regional/global legal trends; and changes in conviviality are typically marked by processes of international migration. Although the concept of regime includes the multidimensional character of inequalities (legal, political, economic, etc.), in this chapter, I focus on the legal component of racial inequality regimes and particularly on the continuities/discontinuities after regime shifts.

As a core component of racial inequality regimes, law may link to racial inequality in at least four types of articulations: (1) constitutive (law enables or promotes racial discrimination and regulates racial discourses); (2) prohibitive (law proscribes racial discrimination); (3) conservative (law has normalization and legitimation effects over the logics of racial stratification); and (4) corrective (law is used to reduce/counteract racial discrimination and to protect the victims). My interest here is restricted to constitutive and conservative articulations. In turn, the concept of 'articulation' aims to underline the contingent nature of the relations between law and 'race.' It suggests that both can come together with diverse accounts to be part of a temporary unity that is called here 'inequality regime.'

Racial inequality regimes in Latin America

Costa identifies four regimes of inequality that have historically encompassed Afro-descendants in Latin America. Extended to indigenous groups, such regimes can be named as follows: (1) caste regime (from colonial times until the nineteenth century); (2) racist nationalism (from abolition to the 1930s); (3) mestizo nationalism (1930s to 1990s); and (4) compensatory regime (since the 1990s), which he identifies with multiculturalism and post-Durban global anti-racism. These regimes are not conceived as separate containers of national history; they are mutually dependent and may directly influence state behavior and exert a transregional disciplinary power oriented for normalizing differences. Moreover, although they reveal important discontinuities, there are several continuities and their contexts are transregionally interrelated. For instance, social hierarchies in post-colonial Latin America cannot be understood without consideration of the categorizations developed during the Iberian domination or the preservation of slavery in the United States or the British Antilles. Likewise, the legal developments are transnationally articulated: the constitutional adoption of the concept of citizenship and its formal extension to the 'castes' by the 1810s cannot be understood without consideration of the legal discrimination in the Haitian and US Constitutions, the Spanish attempts at legal inclusion in the Constitution of Cadiz, or the English laws that prohibited the transatlantic slave trade. Some of these transregional articulations will be analyzed in this section.

2.1 Transregional articulations of law and 'race' in the caste regime

From the first decades of conquest, the Spanish Crown enacted protective measures to impede annihilation of the Indians (which could jeopardize its imperial economic objectives, based on indigenous labor in mines and plantations). The 1512 Laws of Burgos included quite progressive measures that from a present-day point of view could be named as limited periods of work and rules of rest (Law 13), maternity leave (Law 18), and occupational safety and health (Laws 15, 20, and 24), and fined those *encomenderos* who violated such provisions (in the worst case, they could lose the Indians under their dominion). The 1542 New Laws even called for a gradual end of the *encomienda* system (Article XXIX) and the immediate abolition of Indian slavery (Article XX). On the one hand, the proscription of Indian slavery indirectly fostered the enslavement of Africans, a process that Portugal and other colonizing powers in America accelerated. On the other hand, the New Laws received strong opposition from the *encomenderos*. To avoid (or in some cases, contain) rebellions, several colonial authorities did not enforce this legislation, establishing a custom of formal (almost 'ceremonial') subordination to law while applying it selectively (according to the interests of the local elites), which was epitomized in the saying '*obedezco pero no cumplo*' (I honor but I do not comply with the law). This custom also derived in the unequal application of law in correlation with social status, which in turn created a widespread perception of law as an instrument that impose duties only for the poor while guaranteeing the property rights of the elites. As a matter of fact, the *encomienda* system was effectively abolished only 250 years later.

A similar picture of noncompliance arises from the 'protective' provisions in the legislation for African slaves, but with the aggravating circumstance of its delay. From the times of Louis XIV, France had already a codification to regulate the conditions of African slaves in the French colonies: the 1685 *Code Noir*. Even within its harsh and inhuman regulations, it is possible to find a few provisions that, at least on paper, restricted the power of the masters and operated as legal protection for slaves; for instance, marriages between Catholic slaves would be recognized (Article VIII); slaves must receive determined quantities of food (Article XXII) and clothing (Article XXV) even if they become sick or old (Article XXVII); and slave families (husband, wife, and their young children) were not to be sold separately (Article XLVII). One hundred years later, strongly inspired by these and other provisions of the *Code Noir*, Spain finally developed a comprehensive and codified legislation for African slaves in its colonies: the *Real Cédula* of 1789 ('Instruction for the Education, Treatment and Occupations of the Slaves in all the Possessions of the Indies'). Although African slaves would receive according to this Spanish law a milder treatment in comparison with the French and other European colonial laws, protective measures were widely ignored on the ground. The *Real Cédula* was greeted with firm opposition by slaveholders throughout the Hispanic colonies (in particular, Caracas, La Habana, Louisiana, Santo Domingo, and Tocaima), who used their influence in the local *cabildos* to force a declaration of acknowledgment of the Instruction but with suspension of its legal effects (see in detail, Lucena 1996: 155–178).

Another interesting feature of the relation between law and 'race' in the caste regime should be mentioned: the legal means to purchase a 'higher' racial status. Fifteen years before the beginning of the independent movement, the Crown enacted the Royal Decree of '*Gracias al sacar*,' allowing certain individuals of the castes with mixed African and Spanish ancestry to purchase 'whiteness' to access the social privileges of the white status (Lau 1996: 436–437). This can be seen as a legal strategy for upward mobility in which racial identity was negotiated, and exemplifies that law not only could naturalize racial inequalities and make social hierarchies static, it could also create exemptions and allow vertical movements within an established racial hierarchy. While this reveals that law can create inclusion mechanisms even in contexts of strict hierarchies, it also reinforces racial patterns by excluding those who remain in the lower racial levels.

Thus, four major articulations between law and 'race' in Latin America in the caste regime may be emphasized: (1) a widespread practice of noncompliance with protective provisions while formally honoring strict adherence to the letter of the law, hiding the real situation of Afro-descendants and indigenous peoples under the appearance of legal protection; (2) the consequent tradition of unequal application of law according to the addressees of the norms, with strong correlation to racial hierarchies; (3) the legal normalization of transregional and domestic racial inequalities; and (4) the legal inclusion/exclusion of Afro-descendants and indigenous peoples, in line with the political interests of the elites. While the first and second effects relate to the application of law and have a more stable nature independently of the form of government, the third and fourth effects are more related to the design of law, and consequently should diminish after a regime shift based on republican and democratic procedures. The revolutionary rupture with Iberian rule was founded on egalitarian constitutional ideals, but the mutually reinforcing interconnections between law and 'race' did not significantly change with independence. Rather, remarkable continuities can be observed for most of the post-colonial history.

2.2 From the caste regime to racist nationalism: ruptures and continuities in the articulations of law and race after independence

The Latin American independence movement was closely linked with a transregional chain of events, including the American and French revolutions, the Napoleonic Wars, and the French invasion of Spain, which ultimately made the revolution possible. But all these events did not change the global inequality regime based on white supremacy; with the exception of Haiti, the rebellion was not planned as a rupture with the established racial stratification, it was rather a transition from an externally driven to a nationally driven racist regime. The independence movement was dominated by the white creole elite, whose national project was based on decolonization while maintaining the social status quo.

In the awakening to independent life, one of the first steps in consolidating state power was the creation of a 'national identity' through the proclamation of constitutions and the enactment of legislation. In these efforts of nation-building by law, the new elites were influenced by European thoughts of 'nation' that conceived racial homogeneity of the social body as a prerequisite, and therefore that were incompatible with the inherited caste divisions (Yelvington 2005: 244). In the seventeenth century, European racial discourses associated 'race' with different habits, religions, and languages. Accordingly, Gauls (Celtic peoples) and Franks (Germanic invaders who succeeded in conquering Gaul in the sixth century) in France, or Saxons and Normans (who replaced the Saxons as the ruling elite after the eleventh-century invasion) in England were conceived as different 'races;' such dualism justified revolutions based on the discourse of a 'perpetual race war' between the conquered peoples (in France, the Third Estate, arguing its Gallic ancestry) and the ruling elite (Foucault 2010: 56–83). But for European nationalism at the end of the eighteenth century, 'race' was usually equated with 'nation' and served as a unifying agent amongst the population of a state, and therefore it was possible to speak of an English, French, or Germanic 'race.' This understanding of 'nation' was unable to respond to the challenges of the principle of equality before the law under the conditions of post-colonial slave societies, where the color of skin was already a primordial element of social stratification. The pro-independence elites in Latin

50 Manuel Góngora-Mera

America conceived their societies as 'racially heterogeneous' and concluded that a long-term process of homogenization (in line with European ethnic identity and cultural forms) was required. They based their national liberal project "on their self-perception as a Western, Catholic, racially European people, from which Indians and Negroes were excluded. [...] Indians and blacks [...] were considered a burdensome obstacle to nation building" (Stavenhagen 2002: 25–26). During the independence process, however, the legal inclusion of slaves, indigenous peoples, and *libres de todos los colores* was urgent to impede a 'race war' (Thibaud 2011) and to guarantee their support for independence. For regulations on nationality and citizenship (key concepts for legal inclusion), they looked at the only two colonies that by 1810 had achieved their independence in the Americas: the United States and Haiti.

The original US Constitution did not expressly prohibit racial discrimination; it did neither require the immediate abolition of slavery nor limit its cruelty by providing any kind of rights for slaves. For instance, the US Constitution could have provided that slaves had the right to marry, or that slave families could not be broken up, or that slaves could purchase their freedom (Higginbotham 2010: 101). Furthermore, it left the issue of citizenship unresolved, which granted the Congress major powers to define 'racial composition' via immigration and naturalization laws. Accordingly, from the Naturalization Act of 1790 until 1954, federal naturalization statutes restricted US citizenship to free white persons, and, from the 1880s to 1965, federal laws restricted immigration on the basis of 'race.' Thus, from its origin, the United States excluded non-whites from the community of equals in rights and the privileges of citizenship (Fredrickson 2005). Only after the Fourteenth Amendment in 1868, all blacks born in the United States were considered citizens, and only after the Civil Rights Act of 1964, race-based distinctions in the enjoyment of rights were abolished.

On the other hand, the 1805 Haitian Constitution excluded most whites from the benefits of citizenship and owning land within the *Empire d'Haiti* (Article 12) and declared all citizens 'black' in Article 14, that reads as follows: "All acception of color among the children of one and the same family, of whom the chief magistrate is the father, being necessarily to cease, the Haytians shall hence forward be known only by the generic appellation of Blacks." Slavery was banned during the Haitian revolution, reinstituted in 1802, and finally abolished in 1804. The question of citizenship for blacks was at the core of the slave rebellion, as white plantation owners refused to comply with the decision adopted in 1791 by revolutionary Paris of granting citizenship to free blacks. The brutal exploitation of slaves during the French rule was avenged: white slaveholders and colonial officials were killed or forced into exile (*cf.* Dubois 2005). This new social order implied a striking challenge to racial relations throughout the Americas because both Europeans and *criollos* feared that the successful slave rebellion in Haiti would inspire similar revolts.

The US and Haitian constitutions were foreign laws with indirect influence in Latin America. Two other regulations with transregional effects that directly influenced the subsequent regulation on 'race' and citizenship in the incipient states shall be also mentioned: (1) the Slave Trade Act of 1807, a British law that prohibited British vessels engaging in the slave trade, which was a determinant for the progressive prohibition of slave trade worldwide; and (2) the 1812 Constitution of Cadiz, where the concepts of national sovereignty and citizenship were extensively discussed among *peninsulares* and representatives of overseas Spanish dominions (most of them *criollos*), in particular, the legal inclusion of Indians and blacks (which also implied considerations on the prohibition of slave trade and the abolition of slavery). The adoption of such concepts in the context of independence movements had a strategic significance to gain support for the Spanish Crown among different sectors in the overseas population.

Based on the double influence of the US and Haitian experiences, and internationally restricted by the legal responses of Great Britain and Spain to the shifting patterns of power in Europe and America, during the first decades after independence Latin American countries fell into a certain legal Gatopardism when regulating 'race' and citizenship: everything was changed so that everything stayed the same. Abolition of slavery was not immediate (in spite of British and Haitian pressure), but from the beginning of the independence process, the principle of freedom of wombs (in which children born to slaves were considered free citizens) was adopted progressively in the nascent legal systems;[5] however, in several cases, its effective application was delayed or restricted (following the '*obedezco-pero-no-cumplo*' tradition). Due to the successful opposition of slaveholders and other economic elites, slavery was legally abolished only by the mid-nineteenth century in most independent Latin American countries, but in some of them there were very early steps: for instance, in Mexico, where the abolition was proclaimed by Father Hidalgo on December 6, 1810 (a few months after the *Grito de Dolores*) and echoed in a Decree of January 29, 1813, by José María Morelos; in the 1812 Constitution of Cartagena de Indias, where slave trade was banned (*cf.* Title XIII, Article 2); in the United Provinces in 1813, where it was declared that slaves who by any means enter the nation shall be free by the mere fact of entering the territory of the republic; or in Venezuela, where a 1810 decree of the Supreme Junta of Caracas banned slave trade and the 1811 Constitution established the equality before the law of all citizens, without distinction of origin (Article 154), explicitly including free mulattos (Article 203). Nevertheless, these steps were usually associated with fears of a Haitian-type rebellion and aimed to gain the military support of the 'castes' for independence (or to reduce the royalist slave recruiting). Consequently, legal inclusion through nationality, citizenship, and the promises of freedom was usually conditioned to participation in wars on the side of the *criollos* (*cf.* Blanchard 2008). This early openness to the 'castes' changed rapidly once independence was achieved.

The regional adoption of the principle of citizenship and equal application of law without racial distinctions, parallel to the progressive abolition of slavery, represented a radical rupture with the caste regime. This should allow a generalized upward mobility for all members of the new polities, in contrast to the discriminatory legal paths of the United States or Haiti. But de facto property-owning and income restrictions as well as other legal restrictions (e.g., marriage, literacy, etc.) denied citizen status to most Afro-descendants and indigenous peoples. This indirect

52 Manuel Góngora-Mera

discrimination basically served to give the appearance of inclusion by covering the persistence of race-based social stratifications without any legal or policy intervention to counteract the status quo. As analyzed in the following part, Afro-descendants and indigenous peoples were kept socially excluded through successive legal measures that reinforced race-based hierarchies until the end of the twentieth century.

2.3 From racist nationalism to mestizo nationalism: legal strategies of blanqueamiento

The connection between racial discourses, law, and knowledge adopted a new dimension by the mid-nineteenth century. White supremacy received the recognition of scientific discourse; in Foucaldian terms, this 'truth' was linked in a circular relation with the powers that produced and sustained it. European racial discourses on inherent inequality and natural hierarchies became scientific truths with universal validity (generalizable and transferable). Scientific racism ultimately legitimated the New Imperialism on a global scale: the subjugation of 'non-white' populations was justified in their biological inferiority and their resulting inability to achieve a higher level of civilization and self-government. The 'civilizing mission' is particularly clear in the 1885 General Act of the Berlin Conference (that legitimated the scramble for Africa), but it is also observed in the annihilation of indigenous groups in Latin America by the new republics (e.g., during the 'pacification' of the Araucanía in Chile or the Conquest of the Desert in Argentina; both cases supported by law). Racial thoughts (and their hierarchical order of identities) were globally disseminated to Africa, Asia, and Oceania (Kowner and Demel 2013; Piquet 2006: 129–133), and embraced by the Euro-descendant elites in the independent republics of America, generating local expressions as varied as the Jim Crow laws in the United States or the policies of blanqueamiento in Latin America.

In Latin America, the global diffusion of scientific racism consolidated racist nationalism. Legal attempts to 'ascend' in the global racial hierarchy stimulating white immigration were common throughout the region. Equality and inclusion in the state presupposed homogenization—in the most ideal case, according to Western European racial patterns. Thus, several Latin American states adopted laws promoting the immigration of 'desirable races' (especially white agricultural colonists) and discouraging (or even banning) immigration from certain nations or regions. Here, the transregional influence of the United States is manifest. The US Chinese Exclusion Laws (1882–1943) inaugurated a diffusion process of anti-Chinese legislation throughout the hemisphere, with particular influence in Cuba, Mexico, and Central America. In 1902, the US Chinese Exclusion Laws served as a model for Cuban exclusion of Chinese workers after US occupation of the island (such restrictions were removed only in 1942); Chinese were declared as 'undesirable' or 'pernicious' aliens in El Salvador (1897 and 1944), and the 1933 Migration Law banned immigration from China, Mongolia, and Malaysia; Chinese (plus African, Arabian, and Turk) 'races' were not allowed to enter Costa Rica (Immigration Law of 1887), alleging the risk of 'biological degeneration,' and through Article 5 of

Decree No. 59 of July 1896, the President was empowered "to reject immigration of races that in his opinion are harmful for the country." Similarly, Article 33 of the 1917 Mexican Constitution empowered the President to compel any foreigner whose remaining he may deem undesirable ('*inconveniente*') to abandon the national territory immediately and without previous legal action; this was only one of several legal instruments used for deportations and expulsions of Chinese residents, especially in the 1930s (*cf.* Yankelevich 2004: 726–728). Analyzing immigration norms from 1850 to 2000, Cook-Martín and FitzGerald found that at least nineteen of the twenty-two independent countries of the hemisphere by the late 1930s discriminated against Chinese immigrants; discrimination against people of African origin or black immigrants was slightly less common (observed in thirteen of the twenty-two countries), but peaked at the same time (*cf.* Cook-Martín and FitzGerald 2010: 15).

From the second half of the nineteenth century to World War II, provisions that restricted African and/or Asian immigration and encouraged immigration of 'desirable races' were common in Latin America: for instance, the 1845 Law of Selective Immigration of Chile; the 1890 Immigration Law of Uruguay, which banned immigration of Asians, Africans, and "those individuals usually known as Hungarians or Bohemians;" the 1930 Migration Law of Mexico, which stated that it was of public interest to have the individual or collective immigration of healthy foreigners "belonging to races that for their conditions are easily assimilable to our [social] environment, with benefit for the specie and the economic conditions of the country;" or Article 23 of the 1941 Constitution of Panama, which denied entrance to Panama to immigrants "of the black race whose native language is not Spanish, of the yellow race and the races originating in India, Asia Minor and North Africa." Legal discrimination against non-nationals construed an externally oriented inequality regime in the region, but it indeed reinforced the logics of racial stratification at the domestic level as it was built on the assumptions of white supremacy and the transitory nature of relations with 'undesirable races.' Their numbers would comparatively decline vis-à-vis the white population through immigration or they would become extinct through more direct policies like mass land expropriations (e.g., the Chilean occupation of Araucanía), forced marches (e.g., the massive deportation of the Yaqui to Yucatan), disproportionate army recruitment (e.g., of Afro-Argentineans during the Paraguayan War), and 'ethnic cleansing' (e.g., the extermination of the Selk'nam in Tierra del Fuego). In cases of numeric preponderance of Afro-descendants or indigenous peoples, statutes of indentured or forced labor were enacted (e.g., Decree 126 of 1874 and the 1934 Vagrancy Law of Guatemala[6]). All of this was consistent with the international regime after World War I, which testified the Western reluctance to recognize the unlawfulness of the global racial stratification due to the effects of a binding proscription of racial discrimination in its colonies or even within its own segregation systems.

After the 1929 Wall Street Crash, several governments restricted migration to reserve the labor market for local workers in the face of growing unemployment rates. Additionally, due to meager success in attracting white immigrants or in shifting the general 'racial composition' of the population, some Latin American countries began to reorient their racial discourse: homogenization would be achieved through intermarriage with the Catholic and European-oriented 'white' population. This resulted in a discourse of homogeneity through *mestizaje*,[7] a regional trend that was also associated with certain idealization of the indio (indigenism, which was particularly strong in Mexico, Guatemala, and the Andean region) and the mulatto (e.g., Gilberto Freyre's 1933 book *Casa-Grande & Senzala* in Brazil). Admittedly, it implied criticism of the exploitation of Afro-descendants and indigenous peoples and some vindication of their political institutions and cultural heritage. For instance, indigenous and African dances and musical styles became more widely accepted and appropriated as symbols of national identity. Nevertheless, the discourse was a product of the rise of the middle class to power, self-perceived as *mestiza*, and developed to improve its social status, while concurrently 'modernizing' those subjects that still were considered backward. Therefore, mestizo nationalism did not imply a total rupture with the legacy of prejudices against Afro-descendants and indigenous peoples because it broadly aimed for their assimilation into the European-oriented 'national' culture and a paternalist inclusion in formal citizenship (e.g., by educating them in Spanish or Portuguese) and in civil life (e.g., through guardianship legislation, which implied that they were equated with persons incapable of taking autonomous decisions, like a child or a person with mental illness).

A major change in the global inequality regime occurred when the status quo of European domination was broken with the Second World War. Great powers that followed an imperialist project extensively based on white supremacy were finally willing to acknowledge the unlawfulness of racial discrimination and introduced anti-racism as one of the major purposes of the emergent international human rights system in Article 1(3) of the UN Charter in 1945. However, the veil of *mestizaje* was so successful that even the nascent UN system believed the myth of 'racial democracy,' and the region (particularly Brazil) was highlighted as a positive example for race relations (Maio 2001). This had also transregional effects: for instance, Portuguese politicians co-opted Freyre's thesis of 'lusotropicalism' to support Portugal's continued colonial presence in Africa until 1975 (Bender 1978: 3–9 and 19–22).

The post-1945 anti-racist international agenda was focused on the consequences of the Holocaust in Europe and the Middle East, the persistence of institutionalized discrimination in the United States and South Africa, and the changing power relations derived from the decolonization of Asia and Africa (Füredi 1998; Lauren 1988). In the meantime, Latin America could maintain the assimilation project, although with diverse adaptations during the authoritarian wave of the Cold War. At that time, the available legal protections were restricted, and in several cases indigenous peoples were subjected to persecution (e.g., the extermination of at least two hundred thousand indigenous in Guatemala from 1981 to 1983). The international community tended to be indifferent to these actions because the international anti-racist agenda was conditioned to USSR and US strategic interests in Latin America and in other countries (e.g., Indonesia, Cambodia, Vietnam, Angola, Turkey, and Iraq).

Once the authoritarian regimes were overthrown, some countries established general state obligations to protect Afro-descendants and indigenous peoples in their new constitutions.[8] However, such provisions maintained the paternalist approach (focused on protection rather than autonomy); moreover, the said provisions did not recognize the very multicultural makeup of society as a whole. Thus, prior to the 1990s, Latin American countries espoused a doctrine of racial harmony at the same time that they established a regime that meant to serve as the legal means of implementing a process of racial and cultural assimilation. As a result of this whitening project (enclaves of it can be found even in current constitutions, e.g., Article 25 of the Argentinean Constitution), Afro-descendants and indigenous peoples were made invisible in the national statistics and consequently also in public policies, which reinforced the colonial legacy of structural discrimination.

Conclusion

Looking at the geographical diffusion of transregional, race-structured inequality regimes throughout the centuries elucidates how racialization and colonialism operated as interdependent processes and the key role that law played. For the functioning of a global colonial empire based on the natural supremacy of white Europeans, both parts, the dominant and the subjugated peoples, must believe in its validity and legitimacy. Only after the disastrous experience of World War II, when that hierarchy was questioned on both sides, this global racist regime finally collapsed. Certainly, even if military preponderance seems to be sufficient in the short and middle run for the exploitation of under-defended territories, colonists (who usually had to manage the problem of numeric inferiority) could rule for centuries only because the subjugated peoples internalized racial hierarchies, and deviant behavior was effectively punished. And here is where regulatory and disciplinary technologies of power play a major role. As a technology of power, law was essential to the European colonial project in Latin America by normalizing multiple forms of racial discrimination and legitimating the exploitation of disciplined labor. From Francisco de Vitoria's *De Indis Noviter Inventis* of 1532 (widely considered as the first international law text), law and legal argumentation were instruments to justify colonization and legitimate race-based inequalities (Anghie 2007: 24).

The legal transregional approach proposed here seems crucial for unraveling the historical articulations of law and 'race' and the entanglements of power and racial discourses that have sustained inequality regimes in the region. This approach was built on three elements: (1) the characterization of 'race' as a transregional inequality; (2) the introduction of regime-thinking in order to emphasize the centrality of law for the configuration of racial inequalities and to depict transregional interconnectedness between domestic, foreign, and international norms as factors conditioning social hierarchies over long periods; and (3) the consideration that, through regime shifts, regional inequality regimes may present continuities that depend on transregional and global conditions (global stratifications, transnational and transregional discourses on 'race'/ethnicity, international legal frameworks, etc.).

56 Manuel Góngora-Mera

This approach elucidates the chronological and epistemic coincidence between legal projects of racial stratification (e.g., colonization, slavery, nationalism, imperialism) in different world regions. While racial discourse in law is discontinuous in its metamorphosis from one regime to another (implying different configurations of knowledge producing shifts in racial perceptions, representations, and categorizations), there are several continuities in functional terms, especially regarding constitutive and conservative articulations for normalizing domestic inequalities against Afro-descendants and indigenous peoples.

I identified four major articulations between law and 'race' in Latin America in the caste regime and argued that they have persisted: from general noncompliance with the law and its unequal application according to the addressees of the norms, to the legal naturalization of racial inequalities and the legal exclusion of Afro-descendants and indigenous peoples. The promising egalitarian rules introduced during the independence wars were challenged by conservative forces that gave continuity to the global exclusionary order based on white supremacy; in this way, the region also followed the global trend imposed by scientific racism in the second half of the nineteenth century and established severe restrictions on migration, which in turn reinforced the domestic logics of racial stratification; and it also successfully covered racial discrimination under the legal veil of formal equality and the racial veil of *mestizaje* during most of the twentieth century, while adhering rhetorically to the new rules of international anti-discrimination law.

An uncritical posture vis-à-vis law may obscure the domestic, regional, and global power structures at work and the impact of law in increasing racial inequalities. As current domestic and global inequalities had their origins in colonial racial structures sustained, covered, or tolerated by law, and the post-colonial state continues to be confronted with this legacy, it may be reasonable to make these links explicit and keep them in mind if we do not want to limit our ability to design policies that change these arrangements and to reform regulations that are not coherent with the objective of reducing inequalities. If we really concede enough weight to such an objective, we should move away from simplistic legalist assumptions and bring to light the historical nature of current racial inequalities, the interrelated global inequalities, and the interconnected role that law played and continues playing in the whole process.

Notes

1 The term 'race' is used as a socio-political construct. See in detail, Bangura and Stavenhagen 2005: 3–7.
2 For example, the 1923 Civil Code of the state of Sonora (Mexico) banned marriages between Mexican women and Chinese men.
3 1987 in Nicaragua (Article 8); 1988 in Brazil (Preamble); 1991 in Colombia (Articles 1, 7, and 8); 1992 in Mexico (Article 4) and in Paraguay (Articles 62–67); 1993 in Peru (Article 2, para. 9); 1994 in Argentina (Article 75, para. 17) and in Bolivia (Article 1); 1996 in Ecuador (Article 1); and 1999 in Venezuela.
4 Although the terms 'transnational' and 'transregional' intersect in many contemporary cases, I have attempted to restrict the use of 'transnational' in consideration of the

discussions on an anachronism when it is applied to the Iberian colonial period (strictly speaking, laws enacted in the European metropolis were 'transregional' but not 'transnational') and to the nineteenth century (despite most Latin American countries emerging as 'nation-states' at that time, multinational empires were the dominant world-shaping force until World War I).

5   For example, the Law of Wombs of Chile (1811); Argentina (1813); Colombia (1814 in Antioquia and in 1821 as Law of the Great Colombia, i.e., present-day Ecuador, Colombia, Venezuela, and Panama); Peru (1821); and Uruguay (1825). See Andrews 2004: 55–84.
6   This legislation supposedly applied to all, but in practice only the indigenous population was forced to provide free labor.
7   The political discourse of *mestizaje* must be distinguished from the lived experience of *mestizaje* from below. See Wade 2005.
8   1978 in Ecuador (Article 107); 1979 in Peru (Article 34); 1982 in Honduras (Article 346); and 1985 in Guatemala (Articles 66–70).

References

Andrews, G. (2004): *Afro-Latin America, 1800–2000*, New York (NY): Oxford University Press.

Anghie, A. (2007): *Imperialism, Sovereignty and the Making of International Law*, Cambridge, U.K.: Cambridge University Press.

Bangura, Y. and Stavenhagen, R. (2005): "Introduction: Racism, Citizenship and Social Justice," in: Bangura, Y. and Stavenhagen, R. (eds.) *Racism and Public Policy*, Basingstoke: Palgrave Macmillan, pp. 1–22.

Bender, G. (1978): *Angola under the Portuguese: The Myth and the Reality*, Berkeley (CA): University of California Press.

Blanchard, P. (2008): *Under the Flags of Freedom: Slave Soldiers and the Wars of Independence in Spanish South America*, Pittsburgh (PA): University Pittsburgh Press.

Carrera, M. (2003): *Imagining Identity in New Spain: Race, Lineage, and the Colonial Body in Portraiture and Casta Paintings*, Austin (TX): University of Texas Press.

Cook-Martín, D. and FitzGerald, D. (2010): "Liberalism and the Limits of Inclusion: Race and Immigration Law in the Americas (1850–2000)," in: *Journal of Interdisciplinary History* 41(1): 7–25.

Costa, S. (2011): *Researching Entangled Inequalities in Latin America: The Role of Historical, Social, and Transregional Interdependencies*, Berlin: desigualdades.net, Working Paper 9.

Degler, C. (1971): *Neither Black nor White: Slavery and Race Relations in Brazil and the United States*, New York (NY): Macmillan.

Dubois, L. (2005): *Avengers of the New World: The Story of the Haitian Revolution*, Cambridge (MA): Harvard University Press.

Dulitzky, A. (2001): "A Region in Denial: Racial Discrimination and Racism in Latin America," *Beyond Law* 24: 85–108.

Foucault, M. (2010): *Defender la sociedad*, Buenos Aires: Fondo de Cultura Económica.

Fredrickson, G. (2005): "The Historical Construction of Race and Citizenship in the United States," in: Bangura, Y. and Stavenhagen, R. (eds.) *Racism and Public Policy*, Basingstoke: Palgrave Macmillan, pp. 25–47.

Freyre, G. (2003 [1933]): *Casa-grande & senzala: formação da família brasileira sobre o regime da economia patriarcal*, São Paulo: Global, 50th ed.

Füredi, F. (1998): *The Silent War: Imperialism and the Changing Perception of Race*. New Brunswick (NJ): Rutgers University Press.

Góngora-Mera, M. (2014): "Geopolíticas de la identidad: La difusión de acciones afirmativas en los Andes," *Universitas Humanística* 77: 35–69.

Góngora-Mera, M. (2015): "A judicialização da discriminação estrutural contra povos indigenas e Afrodescendentes na América Latina: Conceptualização e tipologia de um diálogo interamericano," *Quaestio Iuris* 8(2), 826–858.

Góngora-Mera, M. (2017): "El Estado y la reidentificación afrodescendiente en el Pacífico Negro: De la invisibilización al reconocimiento," in: Pérez Herrero, P. (ed.) *Estado, nación, identidades y representaciones en la globalización: el reconocimiento de las diferencias.* Alcalá: Universidad de Alcalá (forthcoming).

Higginbotham, M. (2010): *Race Law—Cases, Commentary, and Questions,* Durham (NC): Carolina Academic Press.

Kowner, R. and Demel, W. (2013): "Modern East Asia and the Rise of Racial Thought: Possible Links, Unique Features and Unsettled Issues," in: Kowner, R. and Demel, W. (eds.) *Race and Racism in Modern East Asia: Western and Eastern Constructions,* Leiden: Brill, pp. 1–40.

Kuznesof, E. (1995): "Ethnic and Gender Influences on 'Spanish' Creole Society in Colonial Spanish America," *Colonial Latin American Review,* 1466–1808, 4(1): 153–176.

Lau, S. (1996): "Can Money Whiten? Exploring Race Practice in Colonial Venezuela and its Implications for Contemporary Race Discourse," *Michigan Journal of Race & Law,* 3: 417–472.

Lauren, P. (1988): *Power and Prejudice: The Politics and Diplomacy of Racial Discrimination,* Boulder (CO): Westview Press.

Lucena Salmoral, M. (1996): "La Instrucción sobre educación, trato y ocupaciones de los esclavos de 1789: una prueba de poder de los amos de esclavos frente a la debilidad de la Corona española," *Estudios de Historia Social y Económica de América,* 13: 155–178.

MacEwen, M. (1999): "Comparative Non-Discrimination Law: An Overview," in: Loenen, T. and Rodrigues, P. (eds.) *Non-Discrimination Law: Comparative Perspectives,* The Hague: Martinus Nijhoff Publishers, pp. 427–436.

Maio, M. (2001): "UNESCO and the Study of Race Relations in Brazil: Regional or National Issue?" *Latin American Research Review,* 36(2): 118–136.

Piquet, M. (2006): "Australian Multicultural Equity and Fair Go," in: Kennedy-Dubourdieu, E. (ed.) *Race and Inequality: World Perspectives on Affirmative Action,* Farnham: Ashgate.

Smedley, A. (1998): "'Race' and the Construction of Human Identity," *American Anthropologist,* New Series 100(3): 690–702.

Stavenhagen, R. (2002): "Indigenous Peoples and the State in Latin America: An Ongoing Debate," in Sieder, R. (ed.) *Multiculturalism in Latin America: Indigenous Rights, Diversity and Democracy,* Basingstoke: Palgrave Macmillan, pp. 24–44.

Tannenbaum, F. (1946): *Slave and Citizen: The Negro in the Americas,* New York (NY): Vintage Books.

Thibaud, C. (2011): "La ley y la sangre. La 'guerra de razas' y la Constitución en la América," *Almanack,* 1: 5–23.

Wade, P. (2005): "Rethinking Mestizaje: Ideology and Lived Experience," *Journal of Latin American Studies,* 37: 239–257.

Werner, M. and Zimmermann, B. (2006): "Beyond Comparison: Histoire Croisée and the Challenge of Reflexivity," *History and Theory,* 45(1): 30–50.

Yankelevich, P. (2004): "Extranjeros indeseables en México (1911–1940): Una aproximación cuantitativa a la aplicación del artículo 33 constitucional," *Historia Mexicana* 53(3): 693–744.

Yelvington, K. (2005): "Patterns of 'Race,' Ethnicity, Class, and Nationalism," in: Hillman, R. S. (ed.) *Understanding Contemporary Latin America,* Boulder (CO): Lynne Rienner, 3rd ed., pp. 237–271.

3

THE URBAN SPACE AND THE (RE)PRODUCTION OF SOCIAL INEQUALITIES

Decoupling income distribution and patterns of urbanization in Latin American cities[1]

Ramiro Segura

Introduction: city and inequality in Latin America

A recent project sponsored by the United Nations Development Program (UNDP) notes that Latin America is the only continent in which income inequality declined during the last decade: "in 12 of the 17 countries on which we have comparable data, at an average rate of 1.1% annually" (López-Calva and Lustig, 2011: 11). This is due both to the narrowing of the gap between the income of skilled and of low-skilled workers and to the increase in cash transfers from the state to the poor.

While some celebrate this positive diagnostic, others question its optimism, pointing out the methodological limitations of indicators such as the Gini coefficient[2] and the reductionism of equating inequality with income distribution (Kessler and Tizziani, 2014; Pérez Sáinz, 2014). Accordingly, even accepting the measurements that indicate a reduction in income inequality, it is necessary to note that this reduction, in a context of economic boom, is modest insofar as "if one takes the Gini coefficient as a point of reference, current inequality has approached the level observed at the beginning of the 1980s" (Burchardt, 2012: 137), so that Latin America maintains its position as the most unequal continent in the world, where the richest decile concentrates up to 50% of the national income (ECLAC, 2010). Furthermore, we must bear in mind that inequality does not only manifest itself in terms of income and assets, but rather "in disparate access to land and essential public goods such as education, health and social security" (Burchardt, 2012: 138).

In this direction, this chapter aims to show that the process of social production and configuration of the urban space captures the complex dynamics by which social inequality is not reduced to income distribution, while at the same time sheds light on the limits of certain redistributive policies and highlights the necessity of problematizing the place of urban space in the (re)production of inequalities.

60 Ramiro Segura

In most studies, the city is treated as a non-problematic locus where independent variables such as 'globalization' or 'neoliberalism' operate and impact dependent variables such as 'the labor market,' and this approach implies losing sight of "possibly the most important of urban processes, the space of the city itself" (Robinson 2011: 18). Therefore, in this chapter, we specifically reflect on the place of the city in the processes of the (re)production of social inequalities. Urban space is a constitutive dimension of social life, with its own materiality and temporality. In fact, the urban space not only expresses social inequalities, but rather it also conditions its (re)production, affecting diverse aspects of social life such as job and education opportunities, access and costs related to mobility and transport, and the symbolic status of the inhabitants of different parts of the city.

As David Harvey cautioned early on, "the individual can earn more (less), he can receive positive (negative) benefits from a change in the value of his property, he can simply have more (less) resources made available to him at a lower (higher) price or he can have any combination of these gains and losses over a particular period," thus placing before us the question about "how changes in the spatial form of a city and changes in the social processes operating within the city bring about changes in an individual's income" (Harvey, 1973: 53–54). In this regard, Harvey formulated incisive hypotheses about the 'hidden mechanisms' of income distribution active in the urban system that, impacting location, accessibility, proximity, and urban resources, usually tend to augment inequalities rather than reduce them. In this way, socially produced space conditions the (re)production of inequalities, influencing not only the quality and the location of housing and urban surroundings, but also opportunities related to education, health, and work, among other dimensions of social life.

This chapter propounds the existence of a paradoxical movement in the relations between the city and inequality in contemporary Latin America: while on the one hand many countries in the region have implemented policies that have achieved a (light) reduction in income inequality in the last decade, on the other hand the expansion of fragmented metropolitan areas, initiated in the 1970s and deepened since the 1990s, continues. This pattern of exclusive urbanization augments not only inequality in the access to the city and its goods, services, and opportunities, but also consolidates—articulated with the segmentation of the educational system and the labor market—socially segregated networks and circuits that reduce possibilities of upward social mobility. We arrive at a complex articulation between a process of falling income inequality and the continuity of a pattern of exclusive urbanization. We are dealing with a decoupling, we hypothesize, that impinges precisely on distributive policies implemented in the region, and limits them.

Neoliberalism, globalization, and inequality in Latin American cities

During the 1970s, in the context of the debate on modernization, development, and dependency in Latin America, a model of 'the Latin American city' was constructed, one that exhibited among its predominant characteristics urban primacy, labor and housing informality, and the social polarization of urban space between consolidated centers and poor peripheries (Gilbert, 1998; Borsdorf, 2003). From this perspective, 'the Latin American city'[3] was the result of different interrelated processes in the framework of the dominant model of import substitution industrialization in the region between 1930 and 1970: a political economy oriented to the internal market, with massive internal migration; a rapid process of urbanization concentrated in one or two cities; growth of an 'informal' working class outside of the modern sector—this being the product of an imbalance between industrialization and internal migration; and an expansion of popular housing in slums and 'irregular' settlements in the peripheries (Portes and Roberts, 2005).

In the wake of the impacts of globalization and neoliberalism, however, the position of major Latin American cities in global spaces, as well as their relationship with their respective national spaces and their socio-spatial configuration, suffered profound transformations. In terms of demography and urban predominance, we observe a modification of the place of major cities in national spaces. While the urban population on the continent continues to grow, a gradual decrease or stabilization of the relative size of the first city is observed, visible in the percentage of the urban population concentrated in these cities, the index of urban predominance, and the evolution of urban and metropolitan growth (Portes and Roberts, 2005; Montoya, 2009). The reasons for this trend include the loss of their economic magnetism for internal migration, related to the end of the model of import substitution industrialization; the fall in the fertility rate in metropolitan areas; and the channeling of migratory flows into other urban centers linked to export and tourism: *maquilas* on the Mexican border, secondary cities in Chile, and the development of other metropolitan areas at the expense of Río de Janeiro and São Paulo in Brazil.

On the other hand, simultaneous with this restructuring of the urban system in the last decades of the 20th century, in the context of the passage from the model of import substitution industrialization to the neoliberal model of the open economy—and contemporary to the rise of the notions of 'globalization' and the 'global city'—inequality was aggravated in the principal Latin American cities. In an investigation comparing the cities of Buenos Aires, Lima, Mexico City, São Paulo, Santiago de Chile, Río de Janeiro, and Montevideo (Portes, Roberts, and Grimson, 2005), it was observed that between 1980 and 2000, in all of these cities, there was an increase in informal labor, inequality (save for Lima), and poverty (with the exception of Santiago), as well as crime rates and the sensation of insecurity (see Table 3.1).

In view of this evidence, a significant question emerges: how are globalization and inequality related (Mills, 2009)? And more specifically, to what extent is the increase in inequality seen in Latin American cities between 1980 and 2000 the product of the processes described in theories on globalization (Perlman, 2010a, 2010b) and/or on the global city (Roberts, 2005)?

We know that whether we are talking about the 'world city' (Friedmann, 1986) or the 'global city' (Sassen, 1991), theory predicts a strong correlation between

62 Ramiro Segura

TABLE 3.1 Inequality and poverty in Latin American cities (1980–2000)

		1980	1990	1995	2000	2002/3
Buenos Aires						
	Inequality (Gini)	0.411	0.437	0.446	0.500	0.540
	Poverty (%)	5	33.7	24.8	28.9	51.7
Río de Janeiro						
	Inequality	----	0.570	0.540	0.600	----
	Poverty	----	----	----	----	----
São Paulo						
	Inequality	----	0.510	0.540	0.550	----
	Poverty	----	37.1	56.6	55.8	----
Santiago						
	Inequality	----	0.560	0.560	0.580	----
	Poverty	33.8	28.5	17.8	12.7	----
Mexico City						
	Inequality	----	0.480	0.500	0.500	----
	Poverty	----	----	----	----	----
Lima						
	Inequality	0.429	0.414	0.386	0.403	----
	Poverty	----	47.8	35.5	45.2	----
Montevideo						
	Inequality	----	0.400	0.400	0.430	----
	Poverty	----	28.6	21.3	23.9	----

Source: The author's own elaboration based on data from Portes and Roberts (2005).

globalization and inequality. On the one hand, growth in inequality is estimated with regard to the unequal concentration of resources and strategic activities between world/global cities and the other cities in each country, with the first cities tending to partially disconnect themselves from their regions. On the other hand, theory postulates the thesis of the 'dualization' of the social structure of world/global cities, where two worlds linked to advanced services coexist: the entrepreneurial elite and low-skilled workers (Sassen, 2007). Lastly, certainly with less emphasis,[4] a relation between globalization and urban structures is postulated, specifically the reconfiguration of metropolitan areas linked to globalization in terms of urban 'fragmentation.'

However, these assertions have been nuanced and/or questioned in recent years in the case of major Latin American cities: the supposed novelty of global networks and interdependencies has been relativized by highlighting their temporal depth (Davis, 2005); researchers have been sought to characterize the specific way in which Latin American cities were inserted into global processes (Duhau and Giglia, 2008); and the question has been posed as to which of the observed transformations in Latin American cities could be attributed to globalization and which were the product of the internal dynamic of each city (Mattos, 2010).

In this direction, Bryan Roberts (2005) notes that, while one can predict some urban changes with the models of the global city (such as the growing functional interdependence and specialization of Latin American cities, observable in the growth of services vis-à-vis production—financial, legal, as well as advertising, among others—in major cities and in cities that specialize in manufacturing for export in Mexico and the Caribbean), the more relevant issues for urban social organization were the reduction of communication costs, economic opening to free trade, the free movement of capital, and the reduction of the intervention of the state in the economy, "including when functional specialization and interdependency do not increase" (Roberts, 2005: 111). In this way, it is the effects of neoliberalism "implemented under the influence and strict direction of global institutions, such as the World Bank and the International Monetary Fund" (Portes and Roberts, 2005: 21) that allow us to comprehend the evolution of inequality in contemporary Latin American cities, rather than the causal relations proposed by the theory on global cities.

Following this line of reasoning, specifically with regard to the processes of management, production, and urban regulation, rather than thinking about inequality as a direct and mechanical effect of globalization, it is more plausible to think that in a context of liberalization and deregulation of the economy and the use of space (Roy, 2010), new conditions, actors, and urban practices that had—and have—a significant impact on urban space and the evolution of inequality are consolidated. In effect, in the context of neoliberal opening and the ensuing liberalization of land use, not only private agents (both local and global ones) had an unparalleled scope of action in the city, being consolidated as the principal actors of the urban transformation (Gorelik, 2004; Mattos, 2010; Ciccolella, 2011); also the state is important, since besides abandoning its central role in the production and regulation of land use, it subsidized the action of private agents (both local and global) in the pursuit of attracting investments and 'being global.' Ultimately, we find ourselves facing a new configuration of relations between society, economy, and territory, in which the city appears as a privileged space for the valorization of capital, commodifying urban development and impacting the urban morphology and dynamic as well as the (re)production of social inequality.

Urban fragmentation and inequality in Latin American cities

In the context of these processes of economic opening, deregulation of land use, and the centrality of urban space in capitalist valorization strategies, major Latin American cities were reconfigured in structural, functional, and territorial terms. Based on the work of Pablo Ciccolella (2011) and of Carlos De Mattos (2010), one can sketch the general outlines of these transformations:

- decline in productive functions and restructuring in relation to the logic of consumerism and advanced services;
- passage from a compact metropolitan space, that progressed like an 'oil blot,' with defined borders and limits, toward a metropolitan growth of diffuse borders and polycentric structure;

64 Ramiro Segura

- processes of large-scale private suburbanization by the elites and growth of the precarious habitat, in the center as well as in the urban periphery;
- proliferation of 'new urban objects,' the product of private investments (local and foreign), basically linked to consumption, such as shopping malls, hypermarkets, show centers, the international hotel industry, restaurants, theme parks, and private urbanization.

These transformations are the result of a process fundamentally controlled by entrepreneurial strategies, and they lean tendentially toward privatization. Correspondingly, their effects on a historically unequal socio-economic-territorial structure have aggravated its inequalities.

This process sparked a debate as to "whether these transformations are leading to the fragmentation of Latin American cities" (Bayón and Saraví, 2012: 36), understanding fragmentation as a mode of spatial organization that, in contrast to segregation, not only consists of an unequal distribution of groups in space, but rather of fenced residential spaces and physical barriers to interaction between groups (Kozak, 2005), thus representing an accentuated segregation that is inscribed into space by means of physical barriers (Thuillier, 2005).

On the one hand, authors like Michael Janoschka (2002) and Axel Borsdorf (2003), inter alia, underline the consolidation of a 'new model of Latin American city' (Janoschka, 2002; Borsdorf, 2003). According to Borsdorf (2003), the principle of spatial structuration of Latin American cities shifted from the characteristic polarization of the Fordist city toward urban fragmentation, toward a new form that separates functions and socio-spatial elements, no longer on a wide scale (center-periphery, rich city-poor city, residential area-industrial area), but rather on a reduced scale. New urban-spatial developments like the free distribution of industrial areas; the localization of commercial centers all over the city, oriented toward freeways and airports; and the presence of gated communities all around the urban perimeter, frequently contiguous to residential spaces of the lower classes, changed the geographic scale of socio-territorial segregation. While at the macro level one can emphasize a greater process of social mixing in the present pattern as compared with the traditional center-periphery model, at the micro level the pattern of segregation is reinforced (Janoschka, 2002), made possible by walls and fences, barriers with which one can separate and insure the isles of prosperity and exclusivity against the poor. In this sense, Prévot-Schapira and Cattaneo Pineda (2008) additionally stress that it is precisely in intermediate spaces between the large concentrations of poverty and gated communities where the process of privatizing atomization, characteristic of socio-spatial fragmentation, was launched.

On the other hand, authors like Duhau and Giglia (2008) "emphasize the continuity in the structure of the social division of urban space and of patterns of segregation, rooting the current tendency toward fragmentation in the previous model" (Bayón and Saraví, 2012: 36). In this direction, they contend that "it is not possible to understand the current relations of the metropolis with globalization without taking into account certain far-reaching socio-economic and socio-spatial processes which, in the case of the principal Latin American metropoles, were developed in the course of the last century in the context of the Fordist economic model" (Duhau and Giglia, 2008: 73). To introduce *longue durée* and history in lieu of the opposition between the new and the old implies that both social-spatial polarization and the coexistence of markets of formal and informal labor (dualization) precede neoliberalism and globalization and, rather than being novel, are rooted in the preexisting relations of production. The authors even point out that Janoschka (2002), one of the creators of the idea of the new model of the Latin American city, explicitly states that the processes of urban development possess great inertia and that the radial and sectoral axes of development and urban expansion corresponding to the Latin American developmental metropolis (centers and peripheries, rich areas and poor areas) still subsist and even continue constituting the source of fundamental spatial organization. Of course, for these authors, the indication of lines of continuity and persistency does not negate the effects of globalization and neoliberalism on the city, but rather alerts to the differential temporalities of economic, social, cultural, and territorial processes that form the cities, and acknowledges the specificity of each city.[5]

Lastly, an intermediate position is perhaps found in the investigation carried out by Teresa Caldeira (2000) on São Paulo, which identified three patterns of spatial segregation: (1) the concentrated and heterogeneous city at the start of industrialization (1890–1940), characterized by the absence of the spatial separation of urban functions and the proximity of social sectors; (2) the dispersed city of the industrial and developmental period (1940–1970), where social sectors lived separated by large distances in a typical disposition of rich center and poor periphery; and, finally, (3) a series of processes developed during the 1980s and 1990s that were superimposed on the configuration type center and periphery, such as the abandonment of the center by some fractions of the upper and middle classes, which translated into greater spatial proximity between classes, who are nevertheless separated by physical barriers and systems of control.

In any case, independent of the positions in the debate, with the progressive blurring of the center-periphery configuration, product of the expansion of new urban forms such as freeways, guarded residential complexes for the middle and upper classes in the periphery, the distribution of hypermarkets and malls and centers of entertainment in the entirety of the urban space, suburbanization of industrial production, and growing isolation of the lower class neighborhoods, "a [tendentially] expanded, diffuse, discontinuous, polycentric agglomeration of regional dimensions" is being consolidated, one that implies fundamental changes in the organization and the very sense of urban life (Mattos, 2010: 96) and that has significant impacts in terms of social and spatial inequalities.

This panorama brings us to the question of the relations between urban space and inequality, more specifically the question of the location of space in the process of (re)production of social inequalities. We are not only referring to the undoubtable objectification of social inequalities in the (unequal) access to the city: place of residence, housing, infrastructure and urban services, access to public space, among

66 Ramiro Segura

other facets of urban life. Urban space, understood as a constitutive dimension of social life, with its own materiality and temporality, not only expresses inequalities in terms of the quality of housing and surroundings, but rather it also conditions its (re)production, affecting diverse aspects of social life, such as job opportunities (Prévot-Schapira, 2001; Groisman, 2008), the quality of education (Katzman, 2001; Peters, 2015), access and costs related to mobility and transport (Jirón, Lange, and Bertrand, 2010; Aguiar, 2011; Lizarraga, 2012), and the symbolic status of the inhabitants of segregated neighborhoods (Kessler, 2012).

In a nutshell, although the evidence remains fragmentary, the available research on urban segregation and fragmentation in recent decades in Latin American cities (Sabatini, Cáceres, and Cerdá, 2001; Prévot-Schapira, 2001; Katzman, 2001; Schteingart, 2001; Rodríguez and Arriagada, 2004; Saraví, 2008; Bayón and Saraví, 2012) has shown that these socio-spatial processes, articulated with a progressive segmentation of the labor market and the educational system, are key to the (re)production of social inequalities. These socio-spatial processes augment the isolation and restrict the social networks of the urban poor as well as reduce the geography of opportunities of low-income residential spaces.

Decoupling income distribution and patterns of urbanization in the Metropolitan Region of Buenos Aires

The relations between inequality and urban space are, as we have been suggesting, complex. Currently, due to the conjunction of the persistence of neoliberal politics that make possible the deregulated use of urban land and the efforts of the governments of the region to implement policies geared toward the redistribution of wealth, we face a paradoxical scenario in Latin America. On the one hand, we have fragmented metropolitan structures, with segregated urban, educational, and social circuits, that impact the reproduction of social and urban inequalities; on the other, public policies of redistribution that have reduced income inequality in the majority of Latin American countries during the last decade. In short, simultaneous with the process of reduction of income inequality, there has been no modification of the dominant patterns of urbanization—its proclivity toward privatization and social and urban fragmentation persisting—nor any policies that exhibit a political will to fight inequality in the management of urban land. Thus, in its very configuration, the metropolis materializes social inequalities structured in space in the medium or long term, which impact the labor and educational opportunities of its inhabitants and which can scarcely be influenced by conjuncture changes in income distribution (Peters, 2015).

Let us take the case of the Metropolitan Region of Buenos Aires (RMBA)[6] to illustrate the paradox and the effects of the decoupling of income distribution and patterns of urbanization. The available data for the decade of 2000 on the evolution of income distribution, patterns of urban development, and residential segregation show a complex and contradictory articulation that warns against linear, reductionist, and unidimensional readings of inequality, questioning the 'mirror's thesis'

The urban space and social inequalities **67**

(Sabatini and Brain, 2008) in the way of relating society and space, and even inviting us to formulate hypotheses that go beyond the necessary recognition of the different temporalities involved in the evolution of different dimensions of social life.

First, in line with the continental tendency, we observe a moderate reduction in income inequality in the urban areas of Argentina. Leonardo Gasparini and Guillermo Cruces (2011) showed that between 1974 and 2006, income inequalities measured using the Gini index rose from 0.344 to 0.487[7], although not in a uniform manner during the period. On the contrary, the indicator undulated between intervals of stability and the reduction of inequality and intervals of the rapid increase in inequality. After having reached its highest level in history, the end of the crisis of 2001–2002 initiated a period of rapid recuperation. Nevertheless, "although inequality decreased considerably vis-à-vis the crisis [2001–2002], inequality in 2006 was not significantly different from that which existed between the middle and the end of the 1990s, despite the fact that the GNP *per capita* and employment were high, labor institutions were stronger and a massive cash transfer program was implemented" (Gasparini and Cruces, 2011: 185–186). Accordingly, bearing in mind both the undulating pattern of the development of inequality in the country and its rapid but moderate reduction in a context of continual economic growth, a question arises as to the possibilities (and the challenge) of maintaining and consolidating the downward tendency of income inequality.

Second, regarding the pattern of urbanization, Pablo Ciccolella and Luis Baer (2011) recently showed that following the end of the 2001 crisis, a dynamic of self-segregation of the upper classes similar to that established in the 1990s was reinstated, and there was the expansion of precarious settlements. In this way, beyond the significant differences in the general economic orientation between the two periods (1990–2002 and 2003–2007) that are observable in the development of the indicators of unemployment, poverty, and inequality in the last two decades (see Figure 3.1),[8] the authors verify a continued pattern of urbanization, visible in the expansion of the real estate market for the middle and upper classes and the persistence of investments in freeways, shopping centers, and gated communities, although at a reduced rate.

The expansion of this pattern of urbanization was breathtaking. While gated communities were a marginal phenomenon in the RMBA at the beginning of the 1990s, occupying only 34 km^2, in the year 2000 there existed around 400 gated communities, covering an area of 305 km^2. In this way, made possible by the new network of urban freeways and without the least public debate and without a plan on a metropolitan scale, in ten years the degree of private urbanization reached 1.7 times more space than the city of Buenos Aires (180 km^2), and was consolidated for no more than 100,000 permanent residents at that time (Thuillier, 2005). The change in economic orientation following the crisis of 2001–2002 did not involve, however, the halting or reversion of this process. The continuity of this pattern in the RMBA is shown in the fact that by 2008 the number of gated communities grew to 540, occupying 400 km^2 (double that of the Autonomous City of Buenos

68 Ramiro Segura

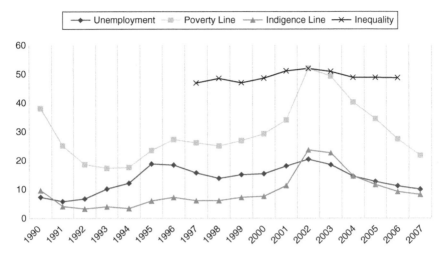

FIGURE 3.1 Development of unemployment, poverty, and inequality in the metropolitan area of Buenos Aires.

Source: The author's own calculations based on Ciccolella and Baer (2011) for unemployment, indigence and poverty, and Alvaredo and Piketty (2011) and Gasparini and Cruces (2011) for inequality.

Aires), which means that 25% of the total developed surface area in the RMBA was occupied only by around 400,000 inhabitants (Fernández Wagner, 2008).

Ultimately, we are facing, as Ciccolella and Baer say:

> a socio-economic situation notably different from that of the 1970s, though this substantial progress does not necessarily imply a pattern of change in urban development, but rather the phantasmagoric or inertial continuity of the 1990s, the exclusive city, even more and more exclusive, only with different rates, both on temporal and territorial scales.
>
> *(Ciccolella and Baer, 2011: 219)*

Indeed, in the context of these processes, with the real estate boom that went hand in hand with the high annual economic growth during the last decade, "the price of land grew at an unparalleled rate" (Ciccolella and Baer, 2011: 233) and, for this reason, "in spite of the favorable evolution of the socio-economic indicators, the worsening of the preexisting territorial segmentation continues" (Ciccolella and Baer, 2011: 235) as "the conditions for obtaining a decent abode on urban land with good services, infrastructure and location were seen to deteriorate" (Ciccolella and Baer, 2011: 239).

Lastly, this decoupling (which reminds us of the fact that correspondence between space and society is neither necessary nor mechanical) of the fragile progress made in the socio-economic indicators and the deepening between the preexisting urban pattern is seen in the evolution of the forms of residential segregation. In a recent report by the United Nations Development Program (UNDP) on residential segregation in urban areas of Argentina, it is pointed out that, simultaneous with the

The urban space and social inequalities **69**

recuperation of the economy and the continuity of the pattern of urbanization based on the suburbanization of the elites, there was, for the period 2001–2006, growth in both the number and the proportion of the urban population living in the slums and informal settlements of the city of Buenos Aires and its conurbation (UNDP, 2009). While in the city of Buenos Aires the population residing in these places grew from 3.9% of the population in 2001 to 4.3% in 2006, in the conurbation this figure increased from 3.9% of the population in 2001 to 10.1% of the population in 2006, which, in absolute numbers for the Metropolitan Area of Buenos Aires (the city of Buenos Aires and its conurbation), represents an increase from 700,000 inhabitants to more than 1,000,000 living in slums and settlements (Cravino, Duarte, and del Río, 2008).

In the same direction, in a recent assessment of inequality in Argentina, Gabriel Kessler (2014) notes that, in general, during the intercensal period of 2001–2010, there was an improvement in the majority of the indicators related to habitat and housing at the national level. However, this general progress has not been able to reverse inequalities between the 'formal' city and the most marginalized areas, like slums and settlements. On the contrary, the social indicators in slums and urban settlements have improved less than the average and, in some cases, the gaps have augmented, putting before us a scenario of general progress with the perpetuation (and, sometimes, the increase) of inequality. The contrasting tendencies in the evolution of inequality that, for this author, characterize the period are manifested in the urban question, giving rise to a scenario in which the economic reactivation itself aggravates the problem of housing and segregation; simultaneously, we observe improvements in family income going hand in hand with growing problems to obtain housing, so that the population residing in slums and settlements continued to grow during the period.

In this context, even the housing programs that were implemented after 2003—and more forcefully toward the end of the last decade and the beginning of the present one—in order to respond to the urgent demand for housing "were designed for the purpose of mobilizing the economy based on public works, generating genuine employment and buoying up the construction market" (UNDP, 2009: 34). Given the absence of reflection in planning and land usage in these housing policies, it is worth asking what their impact has been on residential segregation, to the extent that they are usually limited to the construction of homes in the metropolitan periphery, which contains cheap and available ground, lacks infrastructure, is located far away from services, and costs its residents a great deal of time, money, and energy for commuting.

Without minimizing what it means to obtain housing, we cannot lose sight of the roles that these palliative state policies play in deepening the dynamics of segregation and fragmentation of the urban space, which in the medium term could play a key role in the reproduction of urban inequality with regard to social isolation, disconnection from the formal labor market, access to education, and social stigmas. In this direction, in his analysis of the distributive effects of the expansive phase of Argentina's economy between 2002 and 2007, Fernando Groisman (2008) demonstrated that, although the labor and distributive situation improved in aggregated terms, the social isolation and homogeneity of low-income neighborhoods

70 Ramiro Segura

help us to understand the disparate possibilities in accessing the benefits of growth. Concretely, the author identified a "significant association between residing in a segregated neighborhood and facing certain disadvantage in gaining access to better jobs," due both to the composition of homogeneous social networks as well as to the existence of discriminated neighborhoods with insufficiencies in transport, security, and childcare (Groisman, 2008: 216).

The equation surrounding inequality and urban space thus is not simple. The (moderate) reduction of income inequality, (decelerated) continuity in the pattern of fragmented urbanization, and the (significant) aggravation of the housing problem as well as segregation leave us facing a complex and paradoxical scenario, where income inequality can be reduced and, at the same time, other inequalities can persist and even increase. Further, in this case, it is not a matter (at least not exclusively) of differential temporalities between the (rapid) change in the distribution of income and the (necessarily slower) change in the configuration of urban space. On the contrary, what we are dealing with is the persistence and even worsening of an urban pattern in the context of progress on income distribution. The problem consists precisely in that the urbanization pattern threatens the policy of reduction of inequalities in a wider sense in the medium and long term. As the quoted UNDP report reminds us in its conclusions:

> "if this tendency [toward urban fragmentation] does not reverse the urban story, it could have an ever greater impact on the consolidation of social circuits that reproduce inequality." For this reason, "it is indispensable to virtuously articulate the policies relating to housing, social development and plans for urban development and land-use regulation [...]. This planning may include an intervention in the market, with the aim of restraining real estate speculation and favoring better and more sustainable land usage."
>
> *(UNDP, 2009: 38)*

Epilogue: inequalities, urban space, and public policies

In this chapter, we demonstrate that, in order to reflect on inequality in Latin American cities, we must take into account urban space both as material and as relational reality. It is not merely a matter of recognizing the material and temporal specificity of constructed space, which might not correspond in a mechanical sense to social dynamics, but rather bearing in mind their influence on the (re)production of inequality.

The persistence of a pattern of exclusive urbanization in the context of progress on income distribution leaves us with the challenge of considering urban space when dealing with political processes in the region in pursuit of a reduction of social inequalities: the regulation of the uses of land, the equitable distribution of goods and services, the meanings attributed to the various residential spaces (and their inhabitants), and the accessibility to—and mobility around—the city. We face, undoubtedly, a major challenge, considering further that in the central metropolitan regions of Latin American countries, diverse jurisdictions (national, provincial,

The urban space and social inequalities **71**

and local) converge—and come into tension—frequently with divergent political orientations and constituencies.

Urban structure is not only a product of social processes, but also, as socially produced space, a key factor in the (re)production, expansion, or reduction of inequalities. If social inequality and spatial segregation are not connected in a mechanical or reflexive way, we cannot conceptualize urban structure and hierarchy as a natural and inevitable product of social processes; on the contrary, for its consolidation, a set of social and political vehicles are key, principally the real estate market and urban planning (Duhau, 2013). It is, therefore, imperative to regulate land use (Sabatini and Brain, 2008) and design policies that bring about a more equitable distribution of urban goods and services (Arretche, 2010).

On that point, López-Calva and Lustig (2011) assert that the future of inequality and the possibilities of maintaining and consolidating the downward tendency depend on both improving the quality of education of the labor force, once the goal of accessibility to basic education has been reached (an important achievement, though accomplished through a segmented and unequal educational system), and "breaking the seizure of the state by the affluent and powerful elites," visible in "the difficulty of raising taxes—in particular taxes on income and assets—that prevails in the majority of the countries in Latin America" (p. 34).

Yet the city constitutes an especially relevant field for the implementation of public policies aimed at reducing social inequalities as it is a key factor in the (re) production of educational inequalities and it is a privileged space in the valorization of capital. The task is by no means simple, particularly bearing in mind the place that real estate investment and speculation occupy in the expansion of urban space and the reactivation of the economy and employment in Latin American societies. But it is urban public policy—regulating land use, taxing real estate profit, and investing in access to the city—that is the key to curtailing the deep inequalities of the most urbanized continent in the world.

Notes

1   Translation from Spanish into English by Clay Johnson.
2   The Gini coefficient is an index frequently used to measure income inequality. Among the criticism that it has received is the under-reporting of the sectors with the highest incomes (the richest 10% and 1%) (Alvaredo and Piketty, 2011). In this article, we assert that, beyond the mentioned problems and emphasizing the impossibility of equating social inequalities with income distribution, the evolution of the indicator still shows some general tendencies related to income distribution in the region.
3   We are aware of the dangers that this procedure of categorization involves. As Jennifer Robinson pointed out (2011), the geography of the dominant theory in urban studies (restricted to the experiences and histories of Western cities) has led to the conclusion that cities in other latitudes belonged to a different category of city. The resulting picture of this operation, which contrasted—and continues to contrast—Western cities (associated with the global and modern) with dependent cities (associated with underdevelopment and social and urban problems), not only defines 'the Latin American' city by its distance with respect to Western parameters. It is also unaware of the urban heterogeneity of the continent and the convergences with urban developments in other latitudes.

72 Ramiro Segura

For this reason, without foregoing the significant supports from this research tradition, here we will speak of Latin American cities 'in plural,' pointing out when necessary the convergences and divergences among the metropolitan areas of the region.

4   Although the link between globalization and urban fragmentation has been a topic for a long time, it does not form part of the principal nucleus of the works of John Friedmann and Saskia Sassen. In fact, critics have pointed out a certain insensitivity of these theories to places and the materiality of urban issues, "as they do not consider those factors that have a direct relation with territory or with life experience in a particular city," which allows that, for example, in the ranking of global cities from 2008, Mexico City is located between Amsterdam and Zurich, despite important urban differences between these cities (Moreno Carranco, 2010: 353).

5   Following a similar reasoning, Pablo Ciccolella (2011) distinguishes between different types of urban development in recent decades in Latin America: while in cities like Montevideo, Lima, Río de Janeiro, Buenos Aires, or Bogota, "recent changes seem to simply be an acceleration of present tendencies in the developmental cycle," cities such as Santiago de Chile, San Pablo, and Mexico experienced "territorial metropolitan transformations profound and structural enough to think in terms of a radical rupture with the characteristics of the Latin American developmental city" (p. 82).

6   There are different categories to refer to the Autonomous City of Buenos Aires (CABA) and its conurbation, including Metropolitan Area of Buenos Aires (AMBA), Agglomerated Greater Buenos Aires (AGBA), Metropolitan Zone of Buenos Aires (ZMBA), among others. Each of these is based on different criteria of aggregation and, consequently, delineates different geographic units. For the purposes of this chapter we prefer to take as a unit the Metropolitan Region of Buenos Aires (RMBA), a geographical area that encompasses the totality of the urban settlements and their respective areas of influence, functionally integrated with the principal urban area. The RMBA includes the following jurisdictions: (1) the Autonomous City of Buenos Aires, with a population of 3,100,000 inhabitants; (2) Greater Buenos Aires (1st and 2nd rings or *crowns* of the conurbation), comprising the 25 *partidos* and a population that hovers around 9,000,000 inhabitants; and (3) the rest of the RMBA or '3rd *crown*,' comprising an additional 15 *partidos* and a population of about 1,800,000 inhabitants, giving the RMBA as a whole a population of around 14,000,000 inhabitants (Ciccolella 2011: 130). The RMBA does not constitute a political-administrative unit; on the contrary, there coexist and overlap various government authorities: the national (the CABA is the seat of the national government), the provincial (the 1st, 2nd, and 3rd *crown* form part of the province of Buenos Aires, yet the CABA has an autonomous government equivalent to that of a province), and the municipal (in total, 40 municipalities comprise the RMBA).

7   The calculations from the Gini index are based on the Permanent Household Survey (EPH), which began to be applied in the 1970s in the Buenos Aires conurbation (one-third of the Argentine population) and expanded to encompass all of the urban zones with more than 100,000 inhabitants (two-thirds of the Argentine population). It is this sample that Gasparini and Cruces (2011) used to analyze the evolution of income inequality. By means of fiscal declarations, Alvaredo and Piketty (2011) calculate that, instead of the 0.49 that follows from the survey, the Gini for 2004 could have oscillated between 0.52 and 0.57, depending on the supposition that 0.1% or 1% of individuals with higher incomes, respectively, have not been included in the survey. Both series illustrate, however, a falling tendency in the decade of 2000.

8   Note that the contrast in the values of poverty and unemployment in the decades of 1990 and 2000 is much greater than the variation in the Gini coefficient (income inequality) whose reduction in the last decade was moderate.

References

Aguiar, S. (2011): "Dinámicas de la segregación urbana. Movilidad cotidiana en Montevideo," *Revista de Ciencias Sociales*, 24(28), 55–76.

Alvaredo, F. and Piketty, T. (2011): "La dinámica de la concentración del ingreso en países desarrollados y en desarrollo. Una perspectiva desde los altos ingresos," in López-Calva, L. and Lustig, N. (eds.), *La disminución de la desigualdad en la América Latina ¿Un decenio de progreso?*, Mexico City: Fondo de Cultura Económico, pp. 109–145.

Arretche, M. (2010): *Territorial Justice and Governance: Inequality in Brazilian Metropolitan Regions*, São Paulo: Centro de Estudos da Metrópole, Texto para Discussão 4.

Bayón, M. C. and Saraví, G. (2012): "The Cultural Dimensions of Urban Fragmentation: Segregation, Sociability, and Inequality in Mexico City," *Latin American Perspectives*, 40(189): 35–52.

Borsdorf, A. (2003): "Cómo modelar el desarrollo y la dinámica de la ciudad latinoamericana," *Revista EURE*, 29(86): 37–49.

Burchardt, H. J. (2012): "¿Por qué América Latina es tan desigual? Tentativas de explicación desde una perspectiva inusual," *Nueva Sociedad*, 239: 137–150.

Caldeira, T. (2000): *City of Walls: Crime, Segregation, and Citizenship in São Paulo*, Los Angeles, CA: University of California Press.

Ciccolella, P. (2011): *Metrópolis latinoamericanas. Más allá de la globalización*, Quito: OLACCHI.

Ciccolella, P. and Baer, L. (2011): "Buenos Aires tras la crisis ¿Hacia una metrópoli más integradora o más excluyente?" in Ciccolella, P. (ed.) *Metrópolis latinoamericanas: más allá de la globalización*, Quito: OLACCHI, pp. 213–245.

Cravino, M. C., Duarte, J. and Río, J. (2008): "Un acercamiento a la dimensión cuantitativa de los asentamientos y villas del Área Metropolitana de Buenos Aires," in Cravino, M. C. (ed.): *Los mil barrios informales del Área Metropolitana de Buenos Aires. Aportes para la construcción de un observatorio del hábitat popular*, Buenos Aires: Universidad Nacional de General Sarmiento, pp. 87–152.

Davis, D. (2005): "Cities in Global Context: A Brief Intellectual History," *International Journal of Urban and Regional Research*, 29(1): 92–109.

Duhau, E. (2013): "La división social del espacio metropolitano. Una propuesta de análisis," *Nueva Sociedad*, 243: 79–91.

Duhau, E. and Giglia, A. (2008): *Las reglas del desorden. Habitar la metrópoli*, Mexico: Siglo XXI.

Economic Commission for Latin America and the Caribbean (2007): *Panorama social de América Latina* 2007, Santiago de Chile: ECLAC.

Economic Commission for Latin America and the Caribbean (2010): *Panorama social de América Latina* 2010, Santiago de Chile: ECLAC.

Fernández Wagner, R. (2008): *Democracia y ciudad. Procesos y políticas urbanas en las ciudades argentinas (1983–2008)*, Los Polvorines: Universidad Nacional de General Sarmiento and Buenos Aires: Biblioteca Nacional.

Friedmann, J. (1986): "The World City Hypothesis," *Development and Change*, 17, 69–84.

Gasparini, L. and Cruces, G. (2011): "Una distribución en movimiento. El caso de Argentina," in López-Calva, L. and Lustig, N. (eds.): *La disminución de la desigualdad en la América Latina ¿Un decenio de progreso?*, Mexico City: Fondo de Cultura Económico, pp. 147–191.

Gilbert, A. (1998): *The Latin American City*, New York, NY: The Latin American Bureau.

Gorelik, A. (2004): *Miradas sobre Buenos Aires*, Buenos Aires: Siglo XXI.

Groisman, F. (2008): "Efectos distributivos durante la fase expansiva de Argentina (2002–2007)," *Revista de la CEPAL*, 96: 201–220.

Harvey, D. (1973): *Social Justice and the City*, Oxford: Blackwell Publishers.

Janoschka, M. (2002): "El nuevo modelo de la ciudad latinoamericana. Fragmentación y privatización," *Revista EURE*, 28(85): 11–20.

Jirón, P., Lange, C., and Bertrand, M. (2010): "Exclusión y desigualdad espacial: Retrato desde la movilidad cotidiana," *Revista INVI*, 25(68): 15–57.

Katzman, R. (2001): "Seducidos y abandonados. El aislamiento social de los pobres urbanos," *Revista de la CEPAL*, 75: 171–185.

Kessler, G. (2012): "Las consecuencias de la estigmatización territorial. Reflexiones a partir de un caso particular," *Espacios en Blanco*, 22: 165–197.

Kessler, G. (2014): *Controversias sobre la desigualdad. Argentina, 2003–2013*, Buenos Aires: FCE.

Kessler, G. and Tizziani, A. (2014): "Repensando las desigualdades sociales en América Latina," *Revista Ensambles*, 1: 6–10.

Kozak, D. (2005): "Fragmentación urbana en la ciudad post-industrial," *Revista Café de las ciudades*, 118: 2–10.

Lizarraga, C. (2012): "Expansión metropolitana y movilidad: el caso de Caracas," *Revista EURE*, 38(113): 99–125.

López-Calva, L. and Lustig, N. (2011): "La disminución de la desigualdad en la América Latina. Cambio tecnológico, educación y democracia," in López-Calva, L. and Lustig, N. (eds.): *La disminución de la desigualdad en la América Latina ¿Un decenio de progreso?*, Mexico City: Fondo de Cultura Económico, pp. 11–42.

Mattos, C. de (2010): "Globalización y metamorfosis metropolitana en América Latina. De la ciudad a lo urbano generalizado," *Revista de Geografía Norte Grande*, 47: 81–104.

Mills, M. (2009): "Globalization and Inequality," *European Sociological Review*, 25(1): 1–8.

Montoya, J.W. (2009): "Globalización, dependencia y urbanización. La transformación reciente de la red de ciudades de América Latina," *Revista de Geografía Norte Grande*, 44: 5–27.

Moreno Carranco, M. (2010): "La ciudad de clase mundial. Del discurso académico al discurso urbano," in Mercado Celis, A. (ed.): *Reflexiones sobre el espacio en las ciencias sociales. Enfoques, problemas y líneas de investigación*, Mexico City: Universidad Autónoma Metropolitana, pp. 345–383

Pérez Sáinz, J. P. (2014): *Mercados y bárbaros. La persistencia de desigualdades de excedentes en América Latina*, San José: FLACSO.

Perlman, J. (2010a): "Globalization and the Urban Poor," in Nissanke, M. and Thorbecke, E. (eds.): *The Poor under Globalization in Asia, Latin America, and Africa*, Oxford: Oxford University Press, pp. 255–283.

Perlman, J. (2010b): *Favela: Four Decades of Living on the Edge in Rio de Janeiro*, New York, NY: Oxford University Press.

Peters, S. (2015): "Segregación socioespacial y políticas sociales en América Latina. Vivienda, transporte y educación," *Papeles de Coyuntura*, 40: 6–18.

Portes, A. and Roberts, B. (2005): "Introducción. La ciudad bajo el libre mercado. La urbanización en América Latina durante los años del experimento neoliberal," in Portes, A., Roberts, B., and Grimson, A. (eds.): *Ciudades latinoamericanas. Un análisis comparativo en el umbral del nuevo siglo*, Buenos Aires: Prometeo, pp. 19–74.

Portes, A., Roberts, B., and Grimson, A. (2005): *Ciudades latinoamericanas. Un análisis comparativo en el umbral del nuevo siglo*, Buenos Aires: Prometeo.

Prévot-Schapira, M. F. (2001): "Fragmentación espacial y social. Conceptos y realidades," *Perfiles Latinoamericanos*, 19: 33–56.

Prévot-Schapira, M. F. and Cattaneo, R. (2008): "Buenos Aires. La fragmentación en los intersticios de una sociedad polarizada," *Revista EURE*, 34(103): 73–92.

Roberts, B. (2005): "Globalization and Latin American Cities," *International Journal of Urban and Regional Research*, 29(1): 110–123.

Robinson, J. (2011): "Cities in a World of Cities: The Comparative Gesture," *International Journal of Urban and Regional Research*, 35(1): 1–23.

Rodríguez, J. and Arriagada, C. (2004): "La segregación residencial en la ciudad latinoamericana," *Revista EURE*, 29(89): 5–24.

Roy, A. (2010): "Informality and the Politics of Planning," in Hellier, J. and Healey, P. (eds.): *The Ashgate Research Companion to Planning Theory: Conceptual Challenges for Spatial Planning*, Farnham: Ashgate Publishing, pp. 87–107.

Sabatini, F. and Brain, I. (2008): "La segregación, los guetos y la integración social urbana. Mitos y claves," *Revista EURE*, 34(103): 5–26.

Sabatini, F., Cáceres, G., and Cerdá, J. (2001): "La segregación residencial en las principales ciudades chilenas," *Revista EURE*, 27(82): 21–42.

Saraví, G. (2008): "Mundos aislados. Segregación urbana y desigualdad en la ciudad de México," *Revista EURE*, 34(103): 93–110.

Sassen, S. (1991): *The Global City: New York, London, Tokyo*, Princeton, NJ: Princeton University Press.

Sassen, S. (2007): *Una sociología de la globalización*, Buenos Aires: Katz.

Schteingart, M. (2001): "La división social del espacio en las ciudades," *Perfiles Latinoamericanos*, 19: 13–31.

Thuillier, G. (2005): "El impacto socio-espacial de las urbanizaciones cerradas. El caso de la Región Metropolitana de Buenos Aires," *Revista EURE*, 31(93): 5–20.

4

RESEARCHING INEQUALITIES FROM A SOCIO-ECOLOGICAL PERSPECTIVE

Kristina Dietz

Introduction

The implications of the exploitation of the natural environment, utilitarian representations of nature, and processes of (global) environmental change on inequality are significant. In Latin America, social inequalities are historically rooted in highly unequal systems of allocation of land rights and mining rents, which, in the colonial period, emerged in close relationship with racial hierarchies and slave or indentured labor. Currently, growing capital investments in resources such as land, minerals, metals, fossil fuels, or forests contribute to an increase in multiple patterns of inequality. This is the case since property and labor relations, mechanisms of inclusion and exclusion, cultural representations and meanings of nature, and mechanisms of access to and control over nature tend to change (Borras et al. 2012; Baquero-Melo 2014). Finally, adverse effects of global environmental change or environmentally hazardous industrial production often have an uneven effect on societies, thus either reinforcing existing or generating new inequalities along the lines of class, gender, ethnicity, and 'race' (Auyero and Swiston 2008; Carruthers 2008).

Despite such evidence, studies that make a link between the analysis of social inequalities and (global) environmental change and politics, or dominant social practices of nature appropriation, are still incipient in social science research. Most research has focused on socio-economic and political factors, having the nation-state as a unit of analysis, and considering processes of production and reproduction of social inequality synchronically (for a critique, see Boatcă 2011). A number of recent publications have tried to correct this lacuna. Transnational and world-historical approaches underline the importance of overcoming the methodological nationalism in mainstream social theory and also show how inequalities correspond to historical entanglements between the global, national, and local or between different world regions. Articulations of these entanglements are flows of people, goods, capital, or ideas (Korzeniewicz and Moran 2009; Lillemets 2013). An inter-sectionality approach highlights the multidimensionality of social inequalities and examines how various axes of stratification, for example, gender, class, 'race,' nation, and ethnicity, are mutually constructed and reinforce one another (Roth 2013).

Independent of these promising relational approaches, relations between forms of social domination and representation of nature and social inequalities remain blind spots in most endeavors of understanding persistent social inequalities. Society-nature relations have been traditionally taken up by other research fields and disci-plines such as political geography, political ecology, and environmental justice.

This chapter explores the analytical potentials of conceptual approaches from these fields of research for understanding 'entangled social inequalities,' that is, inequalities that emerge at the intersections "between different regions as well as between diverse social categorisations" (Costa 2011, 16). The aim is threefold: firstly, to identify conceptual approaches from relevant fields that deepen our theoretical understanding of the interdependencies between nature and inequalities; secondly, to develop a conceptual proposal based on these findings; and thirdly, to outline the analytical potential of core categories that prevail in current debates: time, space, and physical materiality. To illustrate how these categories can be applied, I present examples from my own research on struggles over land related to the expansion of palm oil plantations and gold mining in Colombia. I conducted three months of field research on land struggles in 2011 and 2012,[1] and another two months of field research on gold mining in March and September 2015.[2]

I start out from the assumption that 'nature' (its materiality), or how societies transform and appropriate it as a natural resource or institutions that regulate its accessibility and distribution, affects how social relations of inequality unfold.

The chapter is structured as follows: I start with general reflections on the theo-retical foundations and the assumption that only by overcoming the nature-society dualism is it possible to understand how nature interacts with the (re-)production and/or a reduction of unequal power relations. I then proceed to sketch those fields of research that provide crucial insights for a comprehensive understanding of how social nature mediates the production and reproduction of inequalities. The third section represents the core of the chapter, which is grounded in critical theory. I develop a proposal of how to conceptualise the interrelationality of nature and social relations of inequality and discuss core categories of analysis. The chapter concludes with a summary of the conceptual and analytical insights for studying inequalities from a socio-ecological perspective.

Conceptualizing socio-ecological dimensions of inequalities: research fields and theoretical perspectives

A common definition of socio-ecological dimensions of inequalities does not exist, and neither does a consensus on how the relationship between nature and social ine-qualities can be conceptualized and traced. A cursory review of the existing literature on this topic reveals, first of all, what Fitzsimmons called a "peculiar silence on the

78 Kristina Dietz

question of (...) nature" (1989, 106)[3] in the sociological research on inequalities. One indicator of this lacuna is that nature, ecology, the environment, and its related politics are not identified as important fields, theoretical and methodological challenges of sociological research on inequalities in the era of globalization. This 'nature/environment forgottenness' in sociology can be traced back to what Latour (1995) called "epistemic de-hybridization": a categorical separation in modern thinking since the Enlightenment of fundamentally different ontological spheres: human/non-human, society/nature, culture/nature. This "ontological rupture" (Fitzsimmons 1989, 108) historically marked the division of modern academic disciplines into the natural sciences, responsible for the rationalization of nature through a focus on natural principles and laws, and the social sciences, which focus on the explanation of the social via social categories and concepts. The division of natural and social has led to a modern understanding of society based on a differentiation of nature and a denial of society's material dependencies. Social progress and modernity were thus equated with social emancipation from nature via domination, simplification, subordination, mastery, and control (cf. Parsons 1975; for a critique, Plumwood 1993). This dominant dualistic reasoning in Western thought has hindered in particular the social sciences from addressing theoretically and methodologically the socio-ecological phenomena of inequality. I argue that only by overcoming this society/nature and culture/nature dualism, we will be able to further understand how nature interacts with the (re-)production of inequalities, without assuming that nature predetermines culture and social relations and processes.

Since the 1970s, the idea of a non-dualistic view on society and nature has received attention by scholars from different disciplines and fields of research. Depending on epistemological interests and ontological understandings of the relations between nature and society—dialectical, hybrid, monist, or holistic—scholars have addressed these relations in different ways. Two fields of research that have provided insights in this respect are political ecology and environmental justice.

Political ecology

The idea of a co-constitution of society and nature is most prominently encapsulated in the field of political ecology. Political ecology is not a theory. It can best be understood as a cross-disciplinary "'frame of research' consisting of a more or less diverse set of questions, modes of explanation and methods for analysis" (Martín 2013, 4), which has been nourished by various critical theories, disciplines, and strands of research (cf. Watts and Peet 2004; Robbins 2004; Leff 2006; Perreault et al. 2015). Political ecologists ask how social power relations (such as class, gender, 'race,' ethnicity) mediate knowledge about, access to, and control over natural resources.

Over the years, the field has evolved in productive ways. The most prominent examples since the 1970s are neo-Marxian, feminist, and post-structuralist approaches to political ecology.

A neo-Marxian approach in political ecology conceptualizes nature and social inequality in political economic terms, as grounded in the social relations of capitalist production, distribution, and the international division of labor (cf. Blaikie and Brookfield 1987). In the 1980s, this class-based approach succeeded in moving beyond a solely local analysis of socio-ecological changes by way of linking those changes, for example, land degradation and deforestation, to larger transformations in the global political economy. Drawing on critical theories from development studies (dependency theory, world-system theory), scholars from this line of research started to explain environmental degradation in the Global South as a function of the increased integration of peripheral regions into the global capitalist system. Concepts such as the 'development of underdevelopment' (Frank 1969) were applied to problems of resource degradation and complemented by unequal access to and distribution of land or forests (Bunker 1985). Such a view offered a way of making sense "of the power of 'non-place-based' forces" (practices of transnational corporations, instruments and functions of the global (financial) market) "over 'place-based' activities" (e.g., small-scale agricultural production) (Bryant 2001). Many of the current studies on land grabbing, and commodification of nature, stem from this line of research. Here, David Harvey's analytical lexicon on the concept of 'accumulation by dispossession' (Harvey 2003) is often used to locate place-based struggles around the commodification of nature within the wider scope of recent transformations of global capitalism (Fairhead et al. 2012).

In the 1990s, a feminist political ecology gained currency and aimed both to bridge the initial gender gap in political economy narratives and to counter the gendered binary codifications that link nature and emotions to femininity, and culture and reason to masculinity (Plumwood 1993). A key question asked is: is there a gender dimension to the struggles over "knowledge, power and practice, (...) politics, justice and governance" (Watts 2000, 257) that are related to environmental issues. Agarwal (1998, 212) emphasizes thereby the need to consider gendered socio-nature relations through the lens of class. She argues that poor women in rural areas in the Global South are more often exposed to environmental change and hazards and that this fact is a direct outcome of (international) gendered divisions of labor and gendered environmental roles (cf. Rocheleau et al. 1996). Recently, poststructuralist and performative approaches to feminist theory have inspired new directions in feminist political ecology. These studies have explored how gender and gendered subjectivities are constituted alongside other identities and markers of difference (class, 'race,' ethnicity) through the material interaction with and symbolic understandings of nature and changes in the environment. Scholars have examined how symbolic ideas of difference are reproduced and expressed through everyday embodied (materialized) practices (e.g., agro-forestry, food consumption patterns) (cf. Nightingale 2011; Elmhirst 2015).

Parallel with the emergence of a feminist political ecology, a poststructuralist political ecology had gained momentum, mainly promoted by social and cultural anthropologists from different parts of the world. Analyses focused on the micro-dynamics of socio-nature transformation, as well as everyday resistance, subject constructions, and different cultural and discursive articulations, practices, and meanings. The main assumption is that an appreciation of everyday processes that

80 Kristina Dietz

shape people's lives in relation to nature needs a discursive analysis, since questions of nature and lived reality are inseparable from the ways in which nature and reality are represented (Escobar 1996). A pivotal analytical entry point from an anthropological perspective is the recognition of different notions, cultural visions, and situated forms of knowledge about the material world. There is clearly no singular, unique, or universal concept of nature; there are in fact multiple natures. Concepts, visions, and notions of nature are not static but are themselves the results of particular historical situations and cultural experiences. They coexist, overlap, and are constantly contested, especially in times of ecological crises. Drawing on Foucault's (1978) concept of discourse, these knowledge-power relations have gained particular importance in poststructuralist accounts in political ecology. These scholars thus ask how nature is socially constructed via discourse—and how certain ideas and knowledge about nature, ecology, society, and political economy shape and have shaped the way people/societies perceive and use nature as well as how this perception shapes and has shaped subject and power positions as well as forms of eco-governmentality (Escobar 1996, 2008). Thereby, spatial entanglements (global-local) of knowledge constructions and practices are emphasized. Arturo Escobar (ibid.), for example, has shown how specific notions of the environment, such as sustainable development or biodiversity, have been powerfully globalized and in turn have led to the occultation of other notions and forms of knowledge located at the margins of global knowledge production.

Examining the process of normalization of certain forms of knowledge about nature and the environmental crisis is useful for two reasons: firstly, it helps us to understand how new subjectivities are constituted; secondly, it reveals how powerful notions of nature become politically effective across national borders in the way local knowledge and practices are reinterpreted or transformed in the context of the global environmental crisis. In this sense, scholars have critically analysed how local subjectivities have been reconstructed in the context of global conservation and forest policies. Astrid Ulloa (2010) shows, for example, how indigenous people in Colombia were constructed as ecosystem managers or guardians of the forest in the course of a new phase of conservation policies in the 1990s. This, in turn, has contributed to essentialist imaginations of indigeneity based on closeness to nature (cf. Agrawal 2005; Latorre 2012).

Environmental justice

Environmental justice as a political claim and research concept emerged at the beginning of the 1980s in the United States as a response to urban social protests by minority communities of color against unequal exposure to environmental hazards and pollution (Szasz and Meuser 1997). Since then, the concept has been adopted in other countries and applied in varying contexts (e.g., Latin America, rural areas) (cf. Martínez-Alier 1997; Carruthers 2008; special issue of the journal *Society & Natural Resources*, 21(7), 2008). The underlying assumption of the environmental justice concept is that environmental problems "are never socially neutral any more than socio-political arguments [and decisions] are ecologically neutral" (Harvey 1993, 25). With this argument, Harvey emphasizes the fact that an unequal socio-spatial distribution of environmental impact is not an apolitical or arbitrary phenomenon. Because of the close links between local movements and research activities, initially researchers in the U.S. looked mostly at 'race' as the primary explanatory variable for unequal exposure to environmental risks. The issue was even posed as either 'race' or 'class,' as if these and other axes of social stratification were mutually exclusive and "compartmentalizable as discrete things" (Szasz and Meuser 1997, 113). This one-dimensional explanation and reification of social categories was later criticized and revised, especially by scholars who took as their point of departure the conviction that social relations like class, gender, and 'race' interact in complex ways and it is this very interaction that needs to be understood in order to explain the unequal distribution of environmental hazards and risks (cf. Pulido 1996).

Overall, the literature on environmental justice provides all-encompassing evidence that the distribution of environmental risks and impacts is mediated by underlying socially constructed power asymmetries and inequalities. As repercussions of environmental change fall unevenly along the divisions of wealth/poverty, white/non-white, men/women, power/powerlessness, existing social inequalities are reproduced or exacerbated. The question that remains is: in what ways does this happen?

Recent studies focus more on underlying structural and historically rooted processes that lead to uneven outcomes and the reproduction of inequalities via the transformation of nature. A case in point is the work of Sundberg (2008) who explores the ways in which "race works to organize and rationalize environmental inequality" in Latin America (ibid., 26). Based on examples from the colonial era to the present, she illustrates how systems of racial classification come into being in relation to dominant environmental formations and vice versa. Throughout history, (Western) conceptions of 'appropriate' (rational) and 'inappropriate' (irrational, barbarian) land use served colonists and elites in Latin America to claim and grab lands for multiple uses they considered 'legitimate.' Through such practices, forms of difference (racial identities, class interests, etc.) have been linked to environmental politics and resource management, as much as nature is infused with forms of social difference (Kosek 2006; Moore et al. 2003). These findings are important for furthering our understanding of socio-ecological dimensions of inequality as they show that the 'environment' itself is not neutral, but instead racialized, classed, gendered, etc.

Interdependencies of nature and social inequalities—a conceptual proposal grounded in critical theory

The research fields and disciplinary approaches described above share a common ontological vision: a non-dualistic conceptualization of societal nature relations. Rooted in various social theories, they differ in levels and categories of analysis, either highlighting the importance of social structures and social materiality, or the

82 Kristina Dietz

meanings and representations of identity constructions. These levels and categories interrelate when we want to make sense of societal nature relations; though, the focus primarily depends on the research question. In abstract terms, I nevertheless argue that in order to capture the interdependencies between nature and social inequalities, we need to recognize both materiality and meaning. Therefore, I propose a conceptualization of the nature-inequality nexus grounded in a dialectical understanding of the interaction between the material world (nature) and the social world. Building on historical materialism and on critical theory in the tradition of the Frankfurt School, proponents of a dialectic perspective emphasize that society and nature are 'constitutively interrelated' (*vermittelt*) (Görg 2011, 49). Historical materialism is founded on Marx's ontological principle that humans need to transform (metabolize) nature in order to meet existential needs (Marx 2007 [1867]). As Swyngedouw (2004, 130) puts it,

> in order to live, humans transform the world they live in, and this takes place in interaction with others; that is under specific 'social relations of production'. (...) Both nature and humans, materially and culturally, are profoundly social and historical from the very beginning.

Through the transformation of nature, "both humans and 'nature' are changed" (ibid., original emphasis). From this perspective, society, societal development, and subject positions are deeply interwoven by the way in which nature is and has been appropriated, managed, and represented; hence, human history is not independent, but rather is mediated by nature. At the same time, nature is socially constructed in two different but interrelated ways: it is materially produced by economic, technical, and everyday practices and is symbolically and discursively constructed through cultural interpretations, meanings, and ideas (Görg 2011). Nature thus "becomes a socio-physical process infused with political power and cultural meaning" (Swyngedouw 2004, 130; cf. Haraway 1991). Nature becomes social nature. But to take social nature as a point of departure does not mean that nature is social all the way down. Following critical theorists of the 'older' Frankfurt School (Horkheimer and Adorno 1988 [1969]), I start from the premise that the materiality of nature as such is a socially produced materiality. Nature is, at the same time, socially produced and productive, meaning that it may indeed structure social action in some way because of its discrete materiality. But only in social practices, particularly in the appropriation of nature, does this materiality become socially and culturally meaningful and productive. Nevertheless, biophysical materials and processes are not infinitely malleable, as nature cannot be appropriated by society arbitrarily. The more society ignores the specific properties of nature's materiality through endeavors of domination and overexploitation, the more it will be reminded of it through ecological crises. As Castree (2000, 29) states,

> created ecosystems, while intentionally and unintentionally produced by capitalism, possess causal powers of their own and take on agency in relation to

the capitalist processes of which they are a medium and outcome. (...) nature may indeed be 'produced' but produced nature, in turn, cannot be exploited indefinitely: it has a materiality which cannot be ignored.

Scholars following the idea of a 'constitutive interrelationality' assume that social relations of power and domination are constitutive for environmental problems; and, in turn, that the way in which nature is appropriated, transformed, and represented is constitutive for the (re)production of social relations of power, domination, and inequality. However, I do not claim that all forms of nature appropriation, representation, and transformation lead to an increase of social inequality. As previously mentioned, humans, in order to satisfy existential needs (alimentation, housing, clothes), need to transform nature. This transformation is always embedded in a variety of social, political, cultural, and economic conditions, procedures and constellations that operate dynamically at and between geographical scales and places. What matters concerning the inequality implications of society-nature interactions are these conditions and constellations, that is, under what premises is nature appropriated, by whom, and for what? Depending on these modalities, practices of nature transformation and cultural representation of nature might both exacerbate *and* reduce effects for social inequalities.

From this ontological foundation the interdependencies between nature and social inequalities can be conceptualized in at least three different but interrelated ways.

First, social inequalities, understood as distances between positions that individuals or groups occupy in contexts of hierarchically structured access to socially relevant goods (income, wealth, and other assets) and power resources (political rights, participation, voice, etc.) (Kreckel 2004, 17), are part and parcel of the multiple phenomena of the ecological crises. This becomes obvious in relation to climate change in at least two ways: inequalities in the creation of the crises, and inequalities in the distribution of its adverse effects. On a global scale, OECD countries still account for more than 40 percent of the total amount of global CO_2 emissions, deriving from a historically rooted interdependency of fossil fuel consumption and capitalist development. On a societal level, the adverse effects of climate change are distributed highly unevenly. However, this unevenness is not an outcome of climate change itself but a function of the complex interrelationship between society and nature. Vulnerability to climate change is decisively shaped by ethnicity, race, class, and gender as well as political decisions regarding access, control, and the different forms of appropriation of nature (cf. Dietz 2011). All this became very obvious when Hurricane Katrina hit New Orleans in 2005. The overlap of class, gender, and race-specific inequalities, in combination with disastrous urban planning, in which the known risks were deliberately accepted, caused an unequal distribution of vulnerability in New Orleans (Katz 2008). Another example that illustrates the vital importance of social inequalities for understanding current ecological crises is knowledge-power asymmetries: those with the power to voice their own interests and whose knowledge is deemed legitimate make decisions over how societies regulate their relations with nature (Ulloa 2012).

84 Kristina Dietz

Second, nature, and how it is socially produced, known, appropriated, represented, and transformed, constitutes an explanatory variable for the production and reproduction of social inequalities in all dimensions as defined by Therborn (2011, 17f): vital inequalities (socially constructed unequal life chances), existential inequalities (unequal allocations of autonomy and recognition, denial of existential equality), and resource inequalities (unequal distribution of resources to act). Mechanisms through which inequalities are produced and reproduced in the context of nature transformation and environmental change are similar to other contexts: exclusion, hierarchization, concentration, dispossession, privatization, distanciation, or exploitation (ibid.19f).

Third, the adverse effects of socially produced environmental changes reinforce existing structures of inequality. Those who are already marginalized in multiple ways (spatially, economically, socially, and politically) are relatively more vulnerable to climate change impacts, to air or water pollution, to health problems, or to land degradation. Beyond this, the material properties of nature (e.g., water, soil composition, nutritive value) may already become operative in processes of appropriation, control, and representation, which in turn may alter social inequalities in its multiple dimensions. From this point of view, negating the materiality of nature through overexploitation and nature domination may not only result in an exacerbation of the ecological crises, but also serve to deepen social inequalities.

Core categories of analysis: time, space, and materiality

From a dialectical perspective, social practices related to nature are to be considered as contingent, historic, and spatio-temporal-specific processes. Thus, in order to understand how global environmental change or new forms of nature valorization influence the way entangled relations of inequality unfold, we need to incorporate a historical analysis. We may examine the historically specific social, political, and economic power constellations across scales that led to the emergence of certain forms of regimes such as labor, land rights, property, and 'inequality regimes' (Costa 2011). We may also examine the temporal and spatial entanglements of different imaginaries, notions, and meanings, and forms of knowledge and how these changed over time, why, and with what effects on social inequalities.

We may also explore how globalization and current transformations of the global political economic order lead to a transformation of the spatio-temporal coordinates of nature and society and what this means vis-à-vis 'entangled inequalities' (ibid.). The mobility of different forms of capital (financial capital, productive capital, and labor) in the era of globalization is often described as a compression of space and time (Harvey 2001). To illustrate the latter, the increase of capital investments in mining in Latin America since the 1990s (cf. Bebbington and Bury 2013) could be understood and analysed as a 'spatial fix' or 'resource fix' of crisis tendencies of capitalism. Through the term 'spatial fix,' David Harvey (ibid.) describes a crisis-related spatio-temporal relocation of capital (and labor), which leads to a transformation and/or perpetuation of existing socio-spatial orders and configurations, for example, in terms of (global) labor relations and access to land, water, and resources, and in terms of the distribution of adverse environmental effects and economic benefits that derive from mining.

Space: why and how it matters

How space becomes meaningful in the regulation of the relationship between nature and society can be traced by referring to scholarly debates that point to space as socially produced and contested. Core categories in these analyses are: *place* (socially constructed locations, "filled up" with meanings) (Massey 2005); *scale* (the vertical dimension of space, socially produced and politically contested) (Swyngedouw 2004); *territory, territorialization* (border demarcations, spatialization of political power) (Vandergeest and Peluso 1995); and *network* (forms of interspatial interconnections between places, things, actors, and institutions) (Castells 1996). To give an example, I will briefly turn to the notion of territory and territorialization. Territorialization can be understood as processes of spatial-administrative re-organisation (Vandergeest and Peluso 1995). Government agents, private companies, landowners, peasants, or indigenous people aim to establish control over natural resources and human beings, within or beyond a state's territorial borders, thus changing socio-spatial relations of power. Territoriality, Peter Vandergeest and Nancy Peluso argue, is a central element in understanding state-society relations (ibid.). Robert David Sack defines territoriality as "the attempt by an individual or group to affect, influence, or control people, phenomena, and relationships, by delimiting and asserting control over a geographic area" (Sack 1986, 19). Territoriality thus refers to the inclusion and exclusion of people within certain geographic borders. Political rulers territorialize power in order to achieve different goals. Enforcement of taxes and access to valuable natural resources are pivotal. State authority and domination are secured through territorial control, whereby local actors might accept or ignore state practices of territorial control or fight against them.

Current struggles over land in Latin America are not only struggles about access to and control of a material resource, but are most often conflicts over territorial control and processes of territorialization. A case in point is the struggle related to the expansion of oil palm plantations in Colombia (cf. Dietz et al. 2015). The number of oil palm plantations increased greatly after the government of Alvaro Uribe (2002–2010) adopted norms and policies to foster the national production of agrofuels. While in 2001, oil palms were cultivated on around 160,000ha, this area had almost tripled by the year 2011 to 430,000ha (Fedepalma 2012, 23). These developments must be considered against the backdrop of historically rooted conflicts over land in Colombia and ongoing clashes that are primarily "expressed and conducted as territorial struggles" (Ballvé 2013, 239). As a result of oil palm expansion, in many of these regions the contestation of territorial control emerged via either the violent appropriation of fertile land or the introduction of new private property and labor regimes. The latter, thereby, aims to 'include' peasants in the agro-industrial

86 Kristina Dietz

production pattern of palm oil via 'strategic alliances.' Peasant, 'black,' or indigenous subjects are thus made into rural entrepreneurs (Cárdenas 2012, 329).

A salient example is the municipality of María la Baja in the Montes de María region in northwestern Colombia (Coronado Delgado and Dietz 2013). Between 2001 and 2010, the area cultivated with palm crops tripled. Previous to this growth of oil palms, María la Baja had suffered from paramilitary violence and mass displacements (cf. Ojeda et al. 2015). When oil palm cultivation was introduced in 2001, a new era of capitalized rural development began that had adverse socio-spatial effects. Peasants possessing small plots of land became strategic, crop-producing allies of the palm oil companies. Those who could not prove legal land titles, were landless, had been formally displaced, or refused to cooperate with the palm oil industry were territorially excluded. In many communities, communal roads became impassable for local residents because of palm cultivation, cattle that had crossed palm cultivation areas disappeared or had been found dead, and trees and bushes from neighboring areas that hindered the undisturbed development of palm trees had been cut (ibid.). The examples show how the expansion of palm oil plantations in María la Baja was accompanied by strategies of territorialization (claiming buffer zones, introduction of private property rights, fencing of plantations, employment of armed guards to secure property boundaries, etc.) to prevent 'others' from trespassing or from producing other types of crops, thus securing control over land use, economic gains, and political power.

Materiality: why and how the matter matters

Leal and Van Ausdal (2013, 22), in their publication on the environmental histories of the Pacific and Caribbean coasts of Colombia, conclude that "while environmental conditions did not determine the divergent histories, they did shape what was feasible in each place." But how does this happen? How does nature, or the non-human world, become productive in social history and in the (re-)production of social inequalities? Some answers to this question have already been provided: inequality of access, power-knowledge asymmetries related to nature, etc. But others remain open. Does the specific materiality of nature make a difference in the deployment of how humans control, appropriate, or access it? Does nature's materiality make a difference in relation to how social configurations unfold? In other words, can agency be attributed to nature independent of its social context? Those questions are at the center of current debates within the disciplines of geography, political economy, and anthropology (cf. Richardson and Weszkalnys 2014; Bridge 2008; Moore 2015). Against the backdrop of these debates, the following paragraph aims at providing some preliminary theoretical and conceptual reflections on the physical materiality of nature in relation to social inequalities.

Materiality as a concept is nothing new to social theory, especially not in the Marxist tradition. Here, the notion of materiality refers to *social forms* like the state form, that is, social relations to a certain degree have become independent of the multiple actions of individuals and groups and, in turn, orient these actions in a way that enables the reproduction of capitalist societies despite their inherent contradictoriness (Wissen 2015). But following the critical theoretical argument of a 'constitutive interrelationality' between nature and society, I argue that an engagement with materiality can provide a productive way of interrogating persistent questions about the relationship between physical nature (both animate 'nature' and inanimate 'things' or resources) and social relations of inequality. However, this is not an easy or an unproblematic task since it "raises spectres of worn out dualisms, (...) object fetishism and environmental determinism" (Bakker and Bridge 2006, 8). So the question is: how to express the causal role of a material nature without stepping into the naturalism trap? To provide a possible answer, I suggest a non-essentialist concept of materiality, arguing both against the deterministic idea of nature as an external 'thing' that determines social processes and against purely constructivist approaches that reflexively deny any autonomous materiality of nature.

What does this all mean for studying the nature-social inequality nexus in Latin America from a transregional perspective? First of all, it means that "things other than humans make a difference in the way social relations unfold" (ibid., 17f). Starting from this assumption, the analysis must focus on the productive capacities of different materialities. This can happen in the following ways: by structuring global production networks to a certain extent (Bridge 2008), by filling them with meaning, by connecting materialities to production and consumption in specific ways across time and space in processes of valuation (Boyer 2015), or by restructuring access to and control over nature. Take, for example, the materiality of the oil palm fruit. The fact that the fatty acid of the oil palm fruit starts dissolving between 12 and 24 hours after the fruit is harvested leads to the creation of specific agro-industrial palm oil landscapes in order to ensure processing shortly after harvest, with mills that run 24 hours a day and that are surrounded by large plantations. Dietz et al. (2015) demonstrate how the oil palm's materiality matters in valuation processes in the way landscapes are being transformed, including patterns of land use and rural infrastructures. These transformations have challenged and reconfigured patterns of access to and control over land in the recent past, leading to new forms of inclusion and exclusion.

Another case of how the materiality of a resource can influence the (re-)production of social inequalities is gold mining. I will briefly turn to the gold mining boom that has been taking place since the late 1990s in Colombia. This boom is due to several factors: a neoliberal reform of the mining sector, technological innovations, high commodity prices, and an increased global demand for gold for industrial production, for jewelry, and as value reserve. Manifestations of the 21st-century gold boom are manifold: an increase of assigned mining titles and concessions, the expansion of mining sites into areas hitherto sparsely opened up for mining, an increase in foreign capital investments in gold mining, and an increase in ore production. According to national statistics, annual gold production grew between 2009 and 2013 from 48 tonnes (t) to 55.7t, with a peak in 2012 of 66t (UPME 2014, 45), rendering Colombia the 15th most important gold producer in the world (Acquatella et al. 2013, 88).

88 Kristina Dietz

Peter Dicken (2015) has formulated a general material-spatial characteristic of metals and minerals and notes that "they are *locationally specific*. They are where they are (ibid., 244, original emphasis). This means that minerals and metals, as well as mining itself, are "far from footloose" (Bebbington and Bury 2013, 11), but socio-culturally embedded. The question of how patterns of unequal social relations change in relation to valuation processes of metals is therefore a place-based question. Context-specific political and economic structures, gender relations, social group relations, and cultural identities and practices as well as actor-constellations all influence processes of reconfiguring social relations that are related to mining. The fixed spatial location becomes meaningful in its interaction with social-cultural, historical, and political conditions. This means that asymmetries can increase when context-specific livelihoods are being transformed or destroyed through the displacement of former land uses and users, such as farming, peasants, or artisanal miners; when mining concessions and titles are granted to national or transnational companies, thus leading to exclusive rights to exploit gold in the subsoil and the exclusion of other actors.

Patterns of control and access as well as technical requirements and labor processes of extraction vary depending not only on the horizontal spatial dimension of the materiality of gold, but also its vertical dimension (depth) (cf. Bridge 2013). Socio-spatial reconfigurations related to industrial open-pit gold mining are different from those of small-scale or artisanal alluvial gold mining. They comprise different labor relations, different changes in land ownership, territorial access and control, as well as unequal distributions of adverse ecological effects of cyanidation, all of which have multiple repercussions in creating (unequal) social relations. Referencing 'the material' is thus a way of "acknowledging the embeddedness of social action" (Bakker and Bridge 2006, 18), but also its relationality. Nevertheless, acknowledging that materiality makes a difference in the way social relations of inequality unfold means to acknowledge that 'things,' whether they are minerals, metals, or plants, "are not pregiven substrates that variably enable [or] constrain social action, but are themselves historical products of material, representational and symbolic practices" specific in time and space (ibid.).

Conclusion

The aim of this chapter was to identify analytical entry points for the study of social inequalities from a socio-ecological perspective. The main goal was to deepen our theoretical understanding of the interdependencies between nature and social inequalities. From a dialectical perspective on societal relations to nature, I identified three interrelated ways of interdependencies between nature and inequalities:

a   social inequalities are inherent elements of current ecological crises;
b   social nature, its domination, transformation, and representation, constitutes an explanatory variable for the production and reproduction of social inequalities in all its dimensions;
c   the materiality of nature can have implications for how social inequalities unfold.

Further, the chapter aimed to develop an improved theoretical and methodological understanding of the relationship between nature and social inequalities by drawing on different fields of research. In environmental justice debates, socio-ecological dimensions of inequality have been conceptualized as facets or moments of social inequality (Szasz and Meuser 1997, 116), meaning that inequality in the distribution of environmental risks "reinforces and, at the same time reflects, other forms of hierarchy and exploitation along lines of class, race and gender" (Newell 2005, 70). Beyond this understanding, the dialectic perspective on society-nature relations suggests that social inequalities are not only considered as a consequence of specific forms of nature transformation, but also as inherent to them. This implies that we need not only to view the nature-inequality nexus from the point of view of unequal distribution of adverse ecological effects, but also that environmental problems and historically specific forms of nature appropriation and/or conservation themselves need to be viewed as articulations of social inequalities. Class, gender, and race are not only reproduced or perpetuated through new forms of nature transformation, but these social categories of differences are already inscribed in the forms and practices through which nature is appropriated, known, conceived, and imagined.

Based on these observations, I conclude that social inequalities emerge not only at the intersections of different regions and diverse social categorizations, but also in societal nature relations. Transnational processes and entanglements have, at least since the era of colonialism, always played a decisive role in shaping societal nature relations in their material and symbolical dimensions (cf. Mintz 2007), both in European and Latin American societies. Finally, what became clear, both from theoretical reflections but also from empirical studies, is that the categories of time, space, and materiality hold analytical promise for studying inequalities from a socio-ecological perspective in greater depth and beyond the confines of the nation-state.

Notes

1   The research was supported by the German Federal Ministry of Education and Research (BMBF) as part of the project "Fair Fuels?"
2   The research was supported by the German Federal Ministry of Education and Research (BMBF) as part of the project "Global Change—Local Conflicts?"
3   In her statement, Fitzsimmons referred to the discipline of human geography.

References

Acquatella, J., Altomone, H., Arroyo, A. and Larde, J. (2013): "Rentas de recursos naturales no renovables en América Latina y el Caribe: evolución y participación estatal, 1990-2010," *Serie Seminarios y Conferencias* 72, Santiago de Chile: CEPAL.
Agarwal, B. (1998): "The gender and environment debate," in: Keil, R. et al. (ed.): *Political Ecology. Global and Local*, London: Routledge: 193–219.
Agrawal, A. (2005): *Environmentality. Technologies of Government and Making of Subjects*, Durham, NC: Duke University Press.
Auyero, J., and Swiston, D. (2008): "The social production of toxic uncertainty," *American Sociological Review* 73: 357–379.

90 Kristina Dietz

Ballvé, T. (2013): "Territories of life and death on a Colombian frontier," *Antipode* 45 (1): 238–241.

Bakker, K. and Bridge, G. (2006): "Material worlds? Resource geographies and the 'matter of nature,'" *Progress in Human Geography* 30 (1): 5–27.

Baquero-Melo, J. (2014): *Layered Inequalities. Land Grabbing, Collective Land Rights and Afro-descendant Resistance in Colombia*, Münster: LIT Verlag.

Bebbington, A. and Bury, J. (eds.) (2013): *Subterranean Struggles. New Dynamics of Mining, Oil, and Gas in Latin America*, Austin, TX: University of Texas Press.

Blaikie, P. and Brookfield, H. (1987): *Land Degradation and Society*, London: Methuen.

Boatcă, M. (2011): *Global Inequalities*. Berlin: desiguALdades.net, Working Paper 11.

Borras, S. M., Franco, J. C., Gómez, S., Kay, C. and Spoor, M. (2012): "Land grabbing in Latin America and the Caribbean," *The Journal of Peasant Studies* 39 (3–4): 845–872.

Boyer, M. (2015): *Nature Materialities and Economic Valuation. Conceptual Perspectives and their Relevance for the Study of Social Inequalities*, Berlin: desiguALdades.net, Working Paper 85.

Bridge, G. (2008): "Global production networks and the extractive sector: governing resource based development," *Journal of Economic Geography* 8 (3): 389–419.

Bridge, G. (2013): "Territory, now in 3D!" *Political Geography* 34: 55–57.

Bryant, R. L. (2001): "Political ecology: a critical agenda for change?" in: Castree, N. and Braun, B. (ed.): *Social Nature. Theory, Practice, and Politics*, Malden, Oxford: Blackwell: 151–169.

Bunker, S. (1985): *Underdeveloping the Amazon: Extraction, Unequal Exchange, and the Failure of the Modern State*, Urbana, IL: University of Illinois Press.

Cárdenas, R. (2012): "Green multiculturalism: articulations of ethnic and environmental politics in a Colombian 'black community,'" *The Journal of Peasant Studies* 39 (2): 309–333.

Carruthers, D. V. (ed.) (2008): *Environmental Justice in Latin America. Problems, Promise, and Practice*, Cambridge, MA; London: MIT Press.

Castells, M. (1996): *The Rise of the Network Society*, Oxford: Blackwell.

Castree, N. (2000): "Marxism and the Production of Nature," *Capital and Class* 24 (3): 5–36.

Coronado Delgado, S. and Dietz, K. (2013): "Controlando territorios, reestructurando relaciones socio-ecológicas: la globalización de agrocombustibles y sus efectos locales, el caso de Montes de María en Colombia," *Iberoamericana* 49: 93–116.

Costa, S. (2011): *Researching Entangled Inequalities in Latin America. The Role of Historical, Social, and Transregional Interdependencies*, Berlin: desigualdades.net, Working Paper 9.

Dicken, P. (2015): *Global Shift: Mapping the Changing Contours of the World Economy*, London: Sage.

Dietz, K. (2011): *Der Klimawandel als Demokratiefrage. Sozial-ökologische und politische Dimensionen von Vulnerabilität in Nicaragua und Tansania*, Münster: Westfälisches Dampfboot.

Dietz, K., Engels, B. and Pye, O. (2015): Territoriality, scale and networks: the spatial dynamics of agrofuels, in: Dietz, K. et al. (eds.): *The Political Ecology of Agrofuels*. London: Routledge: 34–52.

Elmhirst, R. (2015): "Feminist political ecology," in: Perreault, T. et al. (eds.): *The Routledge Handbook of Political Ecology*, London: Routledge: 519–530.

Escobar, A. (1996): "Construction Nature. Elements for a post-structuralist political ecology," *Futures* 28 (4): 325–343.

Escobar, A. (2008): *Territories of Difference. Place, Movements, Life, Redes*, Durham, NC: Duke University Press.

Fairhead, J., Leach, M. and Scoones, I. (2012): "Green grabbing: a new appropriation of nature?" *Journal of Peasant Studies* 39 (2): 237–261.

Fedepalma (2012): *Anuario Estadístico. La agroindustria de la palma de aceite en Colombia y en el mundo, 2007–2011*, Bogotá: Fedepalma.

Fitzsimmons, M. (1989): "The Matter of Nature," *Antipode* 21 (2): 106–120.

Foucault, M. (1978): *Dispositive der Macht. Über Sexualität, Wissen und Wahrheit,* Berlin: Merve.

Frank, A. G. (1969): "Die Entwicklung der Unterentwicklung," in: Echeverria, B. and Kurnitzky, H. (eds.): *Kritik des Bürgerlichen Anti-Imperialismus.* Berlin: Wagenbach: 30–45.

Görg, C. (2011): "Societal relationship with nature: a dialectical approach to environmental politics," in: Biro, Andrew (ed.): *Critical Ecologies. The Frankfurt School and Contemporary Environmental Crises,* Toronto: University of Toronto Press: 43–72.

Haraway, D. (1991): *Simians, Cyborgs and Women: The Reinvention of Nature,* London: Free Association Books.

Harvey, D. (1993): "The Nature of Environment: The Dialectics of Social and Environmental Change," *Socialist Register,* 29: 1–51.

Harvey, D. (2001): "Globalization and the 'Spatial Fix,'" *Geographische Revue* 3 (2): 23–30.

Harvey, D. (2003): *The New Imperialism,* Oxford: Oxford University Press.

Horkheimer, M. and Adorno, T. W. (1988 [1969]): *Dialektik der Aufklärung. Philosophische Fragmente,* Frankfurt am Main: Fischer.

Katz, C. (2008): "Bad elements: Katrina and the sourced landscape of social reproduction," *Gender, Place & Culture. A Journal of Feminist Geography* 15 (1): 15–29.

Korzeniewicz, R. P., Moran, T. P. (2009): *Unveiling Inequality: A World-Historical Perspective,* New York, NY: The Russel Sage Foundation.

Kosek, J. (2006): *Understories: The Political Life of Forests in Northern New Mexico,* Durham, NC: Duke University Press.

Kreckel, R. (2004): *Politische Soziologie der sozialen Ungleichheit,* Frankfurt am Main: Campus.

Latorre, S. (2012): *Territorialities of Power in the Ecuadorian Coast. The Politics of an Environmentally Dispossessed Group,* Berlin: desiguALdades.net, Working Paper 23.

Latour, B. (1995): *Wir sind nie modern gewesen. Versuch einer symmetrischen Anthropologie,* Berlin: Akademie.

Leal, C. and Van Ausdal, S. (2013): *Landscapes of Freedom and Inequality: Environmental Histories of the Pacific and Caribbean Coasts of Colombia.* Berlin: desiguALdades.net, Working Paper 58.

Leff, E. (2006): "La ecología política en América Latina. Un campo en construcción," in: Alimonda, H. (ed.): *Los Tormentos de la Materia. Aportes para una ecología política latinoamericana,* Buenos Aires: CLACSO: pp. 21–39.

Lillemets, K. (2013): *Global Social Inequalities. Review Essay,* Berlin: desiguALdades.net, Working Paper 45.

Martín, F. (2013): *Latin American Political Ecology and the World Ecological Crisis. Recent developments, contributions and dialogues with the Global Field,* paper presented at the 8th Pan-European Conference on International Relations, 18–21 September, 2013, Warsaw.

Martínez-Alier, J. (1997): "Conflictos de distribución ecológica," *Revista Andina* 15 (1): 41–66.

Marx, K. (2007 [1867]): *Das Kapital. Kritik der politischen Ökonomie,* Berlin: Karl Dietz Verlag, Vol. 1.

Massey, D. (2005): *For Space,* London: Sage.

Mintz, S. W. (2007): *Die süße Macht. Kulturgeschichte des Zuckers,* Frankfurt am Main: Campus.

Moore, D. S., Kosek, J. and Pandian, A. (2003): *Race, Nature, and the Politics of Difference.* Durham, NC: Duke University Press.

Moore, J. W. (2015): "Nature in the limits to capital (and vice versa)," *Radical Philosophy* 193 (Sept/Oct, 2015): 9–19.

Newell, P. (2005): "Race, class and the global politics of environmental inequality," *Global Environmental Politics* 5 (3): 70–94.

Nightingale, A. (2011): "Bounding difference: Intersectionality and the material production of gender, caste, class and environment in Nepal," *Geoforum* 42: 153–162.

Ojeda, D., Petzl, J., Quiroga, C., Rodríquez, A. C. and Guillermo Rojas, J. (2015): "Paisajes del despojo cotidiano: acaparamiento de tierra y agua en Montes de María," *Revista de Estudios Sociales*, 54: 107–119.

Parsons, T. (1975): *Gesellschaften. Evolutionäre und komparative Perspektiven*, Frankfurt am Main: Suhrkamp Verlag.

Perreault, T., Bridge, G. and McCarthy, J. (eds.) (2015): *The Routledge Handbook of Political Ecology*, London: Routledge.

Plumwood, V. (1993): "Nature, self, and gender: feminism, environmental philosophy and the critique of rationalism," In: Zimmermann, M. (ed.) *Environmental Philosophy: From Animal Rights to Radical Ecology*, Englewood Cliffs, NJ: Prentice-Hall: 284–309.

Pulido, L. (1996): "A critical review of the methodology of environmental racism research," *Antipode* 28 (2): 142–159.

Richardson, T. and Weszkalnys, G. (2014): "Resource materialities," *Anthropological Quarterly*, 87 (1): 5–30.

Robbins, P. (2004): *Political Ecology*, Oxford: Blackwell.

Rocheleau, D., Thomas-Slayter, B. and Wangari, E. (eds.) (1996): *Feminist Political Ecology: Global Issues and Local Experiences*, London: Routledge.

Roth, J. (2013): *Entangled Inequalities as Intersectionalities. Towards an Epistemic Sensibilization*, Berlin: desiguALdades.net, Working Paper 43.

Sack, R. (1986): *Human Territoriality. Its Theory and History*, Cambridge, U.K.: Cambridge University Press.

Sundberg, J. (2008): "Tracing race: mapping environmental formations in environmental justice research in Latin America," in: Carruthers, D. V. (ed.): *Environmental Justice in Latin America. Problems, Promise, and Practice*, Cambridge, MA: MIT Press, pp. 25–47.

Swyngedouw, E. (2004): "Scaled geographies: nature, place, and the politics of scale," in: Sheppard, E. and McMaster, R. B. (eds.): *Scale and Geographic Inquiry. Nature, Society, and Method*, Oxford: Wiley, pp. 129–153.

Szasz, A. and Meuser, M. (1997): "Environmental inequalities: literature review and proposals for new directions in research and theory," *Current Sociology* 45 (3): 99–120.

Therborn, G. (2011): *Inequalities and Latin America. From the Enlightenment to the 21st Century*, Berlin: desiguALdades.net, Working Paper 1.

Ulloa, A. (2010): *The Ecological Native: Indigenous Movements and Eco-governmentality in Colombia*, London: Routledge.

Ulloa, A. (2012): *Producción de conocimientos en torno al clima. Procesos históricos de exclusión/ apropiación de saberes y territorios de mujeres y pueblos indígenas*, Berlin: desigualdades.net, Working Paper 21.

Vandergeest, P. and Peluso, N. L. (1995): "Territorialization and state power in Thailand," *Theory and Society* 24: 385–426.

Watts, M. (2000): "Political ecology," in: Sheppard, E. and Barnes, T. J. (ed.): *A Companion to Economic Geography*, Malden, MA: Blackwell Publishers: pp. 257–274.

Watts, M. and Peet, R. (2004): "Liberating political ecology," In: Peet, R. and Watts, M. (eds.): *Liberation Ecologies, Second Edition. Environment, Development, Social Movements*. London: Routledge: pp. 3–47.

Wissen, M. (2015): "The political ecology of agrofuels: conceptual remarks," in: Dietz, K. et al. (eds.): *The Political Ecology of Agrofuels*, London: Routledge: pp. 16–33.

PART II

Categorization

The construction and deconstruction
of persistent hierarchies

5

THE SOCIAL IMAGINARY OF INEQUALITIES IN LATIN AMERICA

Is another view necessary?[1]

Juan Pablo Pérez Sáinz

A key element in the construction of hegemony in a society is the imposition of social imaginaries that, when shared by the majority, end up configuring common sense. Accordingly, one of the greatest achievements of the (neo)liberal order in Latin America has been to depoliticize the social question. This has been achieved via a successful double operation. On the one hand, the *locus* of the social was shifted from the world of production and labor toward reproduction and the household. On the other hand, the problem of basic needs ceased to be approached in terms of social relations and was examined by experts based on fixed standards. In this way, an aseptic discourse was raised in terms of "poverty," where all reference to power and conflict disappeared and, consequently, the social question ended up being configured as an apolitical issue (Pérez Sáinz, 2012).[2]

A second moment where the social issue became central was when the question of inequalities was inscribed in the agenda by international organizations, starting at the end of the last century.[3] Although this formulation could not avoid the concern with power relations—insofar as one can hardly argue that power is not present at the base of inequality—the repoliticization of the social question has been very moderate. Underlying this concern is the imaginary based on the fact that Latin America is the most unequal region on the planet in terms of the distribution of personal income (BID, 1999; De Ferranti et al., 2004; López-Calva and Lustig, 2010). The centrality given to this type of inequality presupposes that when one thinks of inequality, the image that comes to mind is the inequality of income between individuals, estimated by the Gini coefficient based on the data provided by household surveys. This social imaginary has been reinforced in recent years with the idea—which has reached a significant consensus—that this type of inequality decreased in the first deade of the current century (López-Calva and Lustig, 2010, 2012; Gasparini and Lustig, 2011; Lustig and López-Calva, 2012; Lustig et al., 2013).

96 Juan Pablo Pérez Sáinz

The first part of this chapter aims at interrogating this social imaginary by showing its limitations in understanding the phenomenon that it represents. The second section proposes an alternative view, supported by the radical/critical traditions that the important text by Charles Tilly (1999), *Durable Inequality*, revitalized. We conclude by stating the necessity of interrogating the imaginary imposed by the (neo)liberal order and of recuperating the politicization of the social in Latin America.

The predominant social imaginary of inequalities and its limitations

As we just mentioned in the introduction, the imaginary of inequalities that the (neo)liberal order has imposed in the region is expressed in income inequalities between individuals, measured using the Gini coefficient and based on information supplied by household surveys. This way of seeing inequalities has various limitations.

Firstly, when focusing on the household, one is observing redistribution. That is, a previous distribution has taken place that is accepted and that occurs in certain markets whose nature will be seen later when we deal with the radical/critical focus. The argument that the "forces of the market" have acted virtuously is implicit and, in this way, the primary distribution is left undiscussed and is accepted as natural.[4] This perspective responds to the redefinition of the *locus* of the social question that has operated in the (neo)liberal order, as we mentioned in the introduction.

A second disadvantage of this imaginary is that income is a result and, for this reason, we do not focus on the causes of inequalities; we thus risk having a superficial comprehension of the phenomenon. One must not forget that the monetary form of this inequality tends to mystify these processes via abstraction. But the problem is more complex, as family income is no more than the sum of a set of incomes: labor incomes (salary and non-salary) and non-labor incomes (different kinds of earnings, private and public transfers).

In effect, if we follow the proposal put forth by Bobbio (1993) that in any study of inequality two basic questions (inequality "of what" and inequality "between whom") should be formulated, what we have is an amalgamation of different inequalities, or multiple inequalities "of what." Accordingly, for certain types of income, inequality has decreased but, for others, it is possible that it has increased. Thus, it is pertinent to ask inequality "of what," intending to specify to the greatest extent possible which phenomenon we are talking about.[5] Amalgamation, via family income, generates more confusion than clarification.

Nevertheless, from the analytical perspective that has generated this predominant imaginary, there have been attempts to overcome this disadvantage by breaking down family income and identifying its discrete sources. In this regard, an interesting exercise was carried out by López-Calva and Lustig (2010), which lays out the explanation that these authors give for the decrease in income inequality between households in the countries of the region during the first decade of the current century. They assert that there may be two fundamental causes for this decrease.

On the one hand, there have been important non-labor transfers to households, among which the so-called "conditional transfers" stand out because they are the backbone of current policies aimed at reducing "poverty." On the other hand, a decline in the gap in hourly wage between skilled and unskilled workers has taken place. Although these authors note the relevance of institutional factors in certain cases, the principal factor in this phenomenon seems to be the decrease in remuneration for education.[6] In this way, the analysis distances itself from the household and looks into the processes that generate it. The issue ceases to be methodological and becomes interpretative, because it depends on how the evidence is analyzed, as will be seen below.

When breaking down family income in this way, one also breaks down the question "of what," so that it now refers to two inequalities. The first, clearly located in the redistributive sphere, is related to social expenditures and the redistributive role of the state, in this case via conditional transfer programs. The second "of what" refers to inequalities of labor income. In both cases, answers to the basic question (inequalities "between whom") are already implied. This brings us to consider a third limitation in this predominant imaginary because, from a (neo)liberal point of view, the answer to inequality "between whom" is between households, but as these are understood as mere aggregates of persons, the "between whom" becomes between individuals. This has a double consequence.

On the one hand, when prioritizing individuals, the notion of power that is being used is a "soft" one. To our knowledge, the most explicit formulation is that which the United Nations Development Program (PNUD, 2010) has used—a proposal that, furthermore, represents the most successful formulation of Amartya Sen's focus on capabilities, an author of unavoidable reference here. In this view, agency, which presupposes the capabilities of individuals to control their lives, has a projection toward politics in terms of power. This is understood as capability, in this case, because it influences the allotment of resources and wards off arbitrary actions.[7] That is to say, it is a conception that does not demonstrate articulation, at least explicitly, between power and conflict; thus, we characterize it as "soft" and argue that it involves a very moderate repoliticization of the social question.

On the other hand, the incidence of other social subjects is caricaturized or ignored altogether. This occurs with categorical pairs of distinct nature (those of gender, ethnicity, race, territory, etc.) resulting from how differences in the given society are processed. This is a key issue that is absent in this focus and that we will take up again in the next section. Social classes, for their part, tend to be caricaturized. Correspondingly, within this focus of (neo)liberal inspiration, the excessive remuneration of certain types of workers who are identified as privileged as a result of different processes (qualification, formalization, unionization, etc.) has constantly been considered to be one of the principal causes of the high level of inequalities in Latin America (BID, 1999; De Ferranti et al., 2004). This kind of caricaturizing is evident in López-Calva and Lustig's argument (2010) on closing the gap in salary per hour between skilled workers and unskilled ones as the principal explanation for the fall in income inequality between households in countries of the region during the first decade of the current century. If one limits the analysis, as these authors do, to individuals (although they do group them according to their level of qualification), it is of little relevance how the gap is closed, whether "from above" or "from below." Any closing of the gap is synonymous with equity. However, if capital as a social relation is incorporated, even if one distinguishes between workers internally, the "how" is key. If the gap is closed "upwards" because the remuneration of lesser qualified workers tends to approximate that of qualified workers (and these have not suffered deterioration), the result is the empowerment of workers, demonstrating a labor market less asymmetric and thus more equal. Yet, if the gap is closed "downwards," asymmetry is deepened because that which is being strengthened is the power of capital (Pérez Sáinz, 2013).[8]

Correspondingly, in this predominant imaginary and as a consequence of the protagonism conferred on individuals, the conception of power that is being utilized is "soft" and tends to obscure capital, which would seem to have nothing to do with the generation of inequalities.

However, this protagonism points to a fourth limitation in the (neo)liberal imaginary. The source of information utilized, household surveys, does not capture members of the elites, that is, those who wield the power. Their small weight has the effect that the probability of their being incorporated in the sample is minuscule; further, they tend to be refractory toward being interviewed, and if they do permit it, it is reasonable to believe that income not originating from labor will not be reported in its true magnitude. That is to say, we face the problem of truncated information in the right-hand tail end of the income distribution, that is, of higher incomes (Székely and Hilgert, 1999; Cortés, 2001). In other words, the elites and their power do not enter into the analysis.

On that point, it should be mentioned that the Inter-American Development Bank (BID, 1999) attempted to trivialize this problem by proposing a characterization of the "rich Latin Americans" based on the upper decile, estimated in the household surveys. To analyze this group's profile, this organization emphasized that it was dealing with individuals with senior occupations, who inhabit cities, have fewer children, and, in particular, possess a higher level of education. This profile presupposes that the large entrepreneurs are not the only "rich" in the region; in fact, they constitute a minority as they represent just between 10% and 20% of this decile and, consequently, they cannot be made responsible for the acute inequality in the region (BID, 1999: 20–22). With this assertion, there exists the possibility of raising a rhetorical discourse charged with a great deal of cynicism. That is, "rich Latin Americans" are people who have obtained higher education (they probably had access to it by birth but took advantage of the opportunity). They have learned how to recognize their "human capital" on the labor market, and for this reason they have well-paying jobs. Moreover, in "rich" households, women have a higher likelihood of obtaining jobs, for which reason one could say that there is less gender inequality in these households. And, furthermore, they exhibit "rational," not to say "responsible" demographic behavior. In light of this profile, it is worth asking, does this type of person not deserve to be "rich"? The answer could not be more affirmative. In this way, any critical discussion about inequalities is stopped in its tracks seeing as these inequalities are legitimate (Pérez Sáinz, 2014).

Obviously, in order to be able to capture the elites, it is necessary to disaggregate the information at the level of percentiles or even smaller percentages. The household surveys do not permit this, and to achieve it one would have to work with a different type of data, such as fiscal data, in particular those related to taxes. In fact, this is Piketty's proposal (2014), and constitutes his principal contribution—in the way of methodology—to understanding inequalities in our region.[9] In his famed text, there are references made to two previous studies on Latin America that were carried out using *The World Top Incomes Database*.[10] In Argentina, participation of the upper percentile income (1%) in gross income went from 12.4% in 1997 to 16.8% in 2004; and in Colombia, between 1993 and 2010, this same percentile maintained a participation of 20.5% (Gómez Sabaíni and Rossignolo, 2015: 90 and 96). A similar methodology was applied to Uruguay, and between 2009 and 2011, this 1% captured around 12% of the national income (Burdín et al., 2015: Table III.11). A study of similar characteristics was carried out in Chile. The richest 1% appropriated, on average, 30.5% of the total income of this country during the period 2005–2010 (López et al., 2013: Table 13).

This evidence suggests that the fall in income inequalities in the region during the first decade of the current century was of less quantity (Gómez Sabaíni and Rossignolo, 2015) and thus questions the optimistic consensus with regard to it. And the most important, in our opinion: it does not seem that the power of those "above" has been cut back, on the contrary.

Therefore, the imaginary that the (neo)liberal order has imposed on our view of inequalities suffers from a quadruple limitation: it centers on the sphere of redistribution, it shows inequality as a result, it is limited to individuals, and, further, it does not capture the most powerful. Thus, another vision needs to be developed. This is the task that we are going to attempt in the following section.

An alternative view of inequalities based on the radical/critical tradition

One can summarize this alternative view by responding to the two basic questions stated earlier: inequality "of what" and "between whom." In terms of the first question, the response is: power on basic markets to configure conditions that make possible the generation and appropriation of economic surplus. The response to the second question is: apart from between individuals, also between categorical pairs (gender, ethnicity, race, territoriality, etc.) and, of course, between social classes (Pérez Sáinz, 2014). That is to say, we are dealing with a view that shifts to distribution, prioritizes the issue of surplus, and pluralizes the subjects that struggle for this surplus by means of the dynamics of (dis)empowerment. Let us specify each of these premises analytically.

We will begin with the topic of power departing from the supposition that every kind of inequality is sustained in power. Thus, it is a matter of understanding processes of (dis)empowerment and, to do so, it is necessary to assume a "hard" conception of power that implies, fundamentally, relating it to conflict.

The most pertinent author here is Lukes (2004) because, in his proposal, this nexus is clear in that he postulates distinct expressions of power and conflict. Firstly, open conflict is a perfectly observable dimension. In addition, power refers to a second dimension, that of veiled conflicts, because processes of (dis)empowerment, as with any social process, are not consummated; that is to say, there is no total (dis) empowerment, it is always relative.[11] Accordingly, resistance is present although it is not always manifested in an open way as "forms of declared public resistance," but rather exists in disguised modalities as well, hidden as "infrapolitics" (Scott, 2007). There are also latent conflicts, which represent a third dimension of power, when people's desires conflict with their interests. This third dimension of power refers to the problem of legitimacy and will be tackled later on in relation to the processes of individualization that have as a mainstay social citizenship.

The second premise proposes shifting the focus from redistribution to distribution, focusing on the so-called basic markets.[12] In other words, it is in these markets that the conditions of material production in society are defined. We are referring to markets such as the labor, capital, and security markets without forgetting the commodification of land and the subsoil (and, in more general terms, the commodification of nature) and that of one of the key resources in the current process of globalization, the knowledge market. One should remember that the labor force, capital, and land, and perhaps one could incorporate knowledge, are the commodities that Polanyi (1992) deemed "fictitious."[13] This adjective responds to the fact that if the respective market acts in a self-regulating manner it transforms, according to the Hungarian economist's expression, into a "satanic mill" that ends by destroying the corresponding commodity.

As we are speaking of societies that have surpassed the stage of simple reproduction, what is really at stake are the conditions of the production of surplus. That is to say, basic markets are more than spheres where the conditions of material production are defined: they are spaces where the conditions of the generation and appropriation of surplus are configured. This brings us to the third analytical premise of this alternative view.

To deal with this dimension of surplus, we must refer to the proposition concerning inequalities put forth by Tilly (1999), undoubtedly the author who has contributed most to the revitalization and recuperation of the radical focus recently, and who, in our opinion, has propounded the most evocative analytical framework of inequalities in recent decades. Tilly's reflection is complex, and one can borrow various elements from it: those of exploitation, opportunity hoarding, and categorical pairs and matching. Yet, they will be reworked and adapted to the analytical necessities of this proposal.

The first of these elements poses the problem of how social subjects can acquire guarantees in the access to valuable resources and in the appropriation of the fruits of the use of such resources. The solution to this problem is found in the development of two mechanisms: exploitation and opportunity hoarding. For this author, exploitation occurs when powerful and related individuals have at their disposal resources from which significantly incremented returns are extracted via the coordinated effort of unconnected persons who remain excluded from this aggregated value. Opportunity hoarding, on the other hand, occurs when members of a categorically circumscribed network gain access to a valuable and renewable resource that is subject to monopoly because of the activities of this network and that, in turn, is fortified by this network's *modus operandi* (Tilly, 1999: 10). That is to say, this author recuperates the concept of exploitation from the Marxist tradition and that of hoarding from the Weberian tradition's concept of closure.

Contrary to Tilly, we want to localize these processes not in the interior of organizations, but in basic markets, which has a double consequence. On the one hand, one speaks of conditions of exploitation and of hoarding. And, on the other, one distinguishes between two fields of inequalities of surplus: the first refers to the conditions of the exploitation of wage-labor, and the second to the hoarding of the opportunities of accumulation.

The first of these fields, the field concerned with the conditions of exploitation, materializes in the labor market. This supposes that the primordial pulse between capital and labor does not occur in production, but rather previously on the market. Only if capital manages to relativize equality (and liberty), inherent in the exchange, can it generate surplus. On the labor market, he who buys is the owner of the means of production and only he who sells possesses the capacity for work. The exchange, in spite of appearances, neither occurs between equals (their properties are radically different) nor between free individuals (the sellers see themselves compelled to offer their labor capacity to survive).[14]

The second field, on the other hand, that of hoarding the opportunities of accumulation, materializes in a set of markets, that of capital and insurance, without leaving out the commodification of other key resources such as land (including subsoil) and knowledge. Such hoarding is possible because certain types of proprietors have the capacity to erect barriers that generate situations of monopoly/oligopoly. This capacity has multiple origins (innovative Schumpeterian entrepreneurs, political connections, social networks, etc.) and marks the configuration of this field.

At this point in the argument, it is obvious that basic markets are the areas of power. The conception of power that is being assumed here is the Weberian classic of the imposition of one party's will within a social relation, that is, of one social subject over another. However, as Weber (1984) himself pointed out, this is a concept that is sociologically amorphous. In other words, the forms that it can adopt in basic markets must be specified.

In the case of the area of the conditions of exploitation, the struggle settles around the dichotomy, labor *versus* employment, understanding the latter as labor with the statute of non-mercantile guarantees, invoking Castel's (1997) well-known distinction. This supposes that when the conditions of exploitation are configured based on the preeminence of labor, one stands before a field marked by great asymmetry in favor of capital; on the contrary, when employment predominates, asymmetry has been relativized. On the other hand, the field of the hoarding of the opportunities of accumulation should be dealt with in terms of the opposition, inclusion versus exclusion. The first term is synonymous with a context where the asymmetries of this field have been relativized because an opening thereof has taken place, whereas the second refers to the contrary, that is, an area where monopolization or oligopolization of a resource has taken place and—consequently—there exists a situation of closure that bars certain social subjects from the true opportunities of accumulation.

This type of struggle can be specified further, but this already brings us to the question of social subjects who dispute surplus in basic markets and, consequently, to identify the concepts that sustain the response concerning inequality "between whom:" social classes, individuals, and categorical pairs. This plurality of subjects constitutes the fourth analytical premise of this alternative proposal.

As the conditions of the generation and appropriation of surplus on basic markets are disputed, the initial subject to be taken into account—in an analytical sense—is social classes. This does not imply that they are the only one. Bringing back to the analysis the issue of social classes is an urgent necessity, but it should not involve a return to the sociological reductionism of the past in which social classes explained everything. Nor does this premise presuppose that it is necessarily the predominant subject.

Social class is a complex and problematic concept, but it is necessary to make explicit the implicit criteria of this focus. Accordingly, it is postulated that social classes are defined in their struggle for surplus and that they do not exist beyond it. This has various consequences. Firstly, the definition is necessarily relational because if there is struggle, there is more than one class involved. Secondly, as a corollary to the first, power is a key element in this definition; thus, struggle presupposes conflict between two or more classes. In other words, it is not solely a matter of exploitation or opportunity hoarding, but also of the power that permits it; and, in this regard, we must not forget about the differing manifestations of power (observable conflicts, disguised resistances, and latent conflicts). Thirdly, in the case of capitalism, the space of definition of social classes is double: production, certainly, but also exchange. In the latter, social classes struggle to impose their conditions on the basic markets, yet the generation of surplus takes place in the productive process. The struggle lingers in this sphere, which is also defining for the social classes.

We have noted with social subjects that impact areas of inequality of surplus are not exhausted by employing the concept of social classes. It is fairly evident that one cannot obviate individuals because personal biographies are unique and unrepeatable. Yet, to consider individuals as social subjects implies adopting a historical conception of the individual and distancing oneself from understanding it in essentialist terms and, thus, as naturalized and ahistorical.

Accordingly, a historicized approach to individuals is offered to us by Castel (2010) when he argues that individuals are unequally supported because they have varying types of support. Historically, this author has identified two fundamental types of support: private property, and social citizenship, which expresses a sort of social property for those individuals deprived of private property, in terms of the means of production, in other words, laborers. The first reproduces inequalities of surplus while the second, on the contrary, may relativize the dynamics of class in basic markets.[15] In this way, inequalities of surplus can be legitimized because they are postulated as the result of the dynamics of social mobility that reflect compensation for the efforts made by individuals; that is, individual achievement is imposed on belonging to class and on ascriptions.[16] This idea dates back to the famous argument made by Marshall (1998: 21–22) for whom social citizenship, to the extent that it seeks the constitution of a minimum social floor, represents the attempt to recuperate and make effective the principle of equality, and can be constituted in the "architect" of the legitimation of social inequalities.

The last subject to consider is so-called categorical pairs.[17] This subject brings up the issue of processing difference, which is crucial for the understanding of inequalities, but is absent in the (neo)liberal focus. There exist three logics around processing difference that are pertinent for the analytical aims of this radical/critical focus.

The first is what one could call "inferiorization," because the dominant category subordinates the subaltern one in an extreme way and invokes the naturalization of difference (Bastos, 2005).[18] Thus, differences between the sexes transform into gender inequalities, cultural differences become ethnic ones, phenotypical differences becomes racial ones, differences relating to place become territorial ones, etc. The opposite logic would be that of the recognition of difference and presupposes a social construction based on the symmetry of groups involved, normally as a result of the struggle of the subordinated groups for recognition that ends with such imposition. And then there is an intermediate logic where a certain hybridization exists between the groups. Normally, it is not the product of a consensual mix, but rather of an "offer" of the dominant group that achieves—to a certain degree—the assimilation of the other groups (Bastos, 2005).Yet it is important to highlight that the "offer" has different degrees of generosity that count in this intermediate logic of assimilation.

These logics imply different strategies of power (to "inferiorize" the other, to impose upon him or her, assimilation; to attain recognition) that include different configurations of categorical pairs. On that point, it is necessary to make two specifications. The first is that each categorical pair can assume multiple forms and that its contents vary historically. The second is that the asymmetry that defines the pair is inevitably relative because there is always going to exist resistance on the part of the subaltern category; this is the veiled conflict that was referred to at the outset of this section. Therefore, although we speak of a *pair*, we are not dealing with a consummate dichotomization but rather that which reality expresses as grades of asymmetry. Having made these specifications, two basic situations can be identified in terms of the configuration of categorical pairs.

The first corresponds to the processing of differences based on recognition or on an offer of generous assimilation. In this case, the opposition between categories of the pair tends to blur and the configuration of a robust citizenry is made possible, especially in terms of social citizenry, which favors processes of individualization that can impact basic markets by relativizing the asymmetries of class and being able to legitimize inequalities of surplus.

104 Juan Pablo Pérez Sáinz

On the contrary, when processing differences relies on inferiorization or on a non-generous offer of assimilation (which represents an implicit inferiorization) there tend to form contrasting categorical pairs with profound asymmetries. This supposes that subaltern categories accede to basic markets in disadvantage that are reflected by a pair of basic mechanisms in their asymmetric functioning: segregation and discrimination. The former has two moments. The first has to do with the mere access to these markets where belonging to a certain category of a determined pair conditions this access. The second moment operates when access is achieved but segregation is redefined in terms of the segmentation of the market according to the distinction that defines the pair. In other words, within basic markets, there also operate dynamics of segregation that are manifested in the formation of niches. And the second mechanism, that of discrimination, expresses that, although the barriers of segregation have been overcome, the categories of one pair are not found in equivalent situations. Segregation, in any of its two modalities, and discrimination are expressed by the matching of categorical pairs with dynamics of class in basic markets that fortify the latter, causing inequalities of surplus to persist (Pérez Sáinz, 2014).

Consequently, the protagonism that is conferred on individuals as subjects of inequalities in the imaginary imposed by the (neo)liberal order supposes that only the first of these situations is taken into account, ignoring the fact that categorical pairs can be formed that are matched and can reinforce inequalities between classes on basic markets.

Conclusions

We are trapped in an imaginary of inequalities that the (neo)liberal order has imposed on us. The view of the redistributive sphere ensnares us, making us believe that the primary distribution is natural and, therefore, untouchable. It limits us to observing an inequality of result without explaining to us the causes that generate it. It causes us to prioritize individuals as the subjects of inequalities, ignoring other subjects, in particular categorical pairs, or else caricaturizing them, in the case of social classes. Furthermore, with this prioritization, we are incapable of incorporating the truly powerful individuals.

Based on this type of view, the perspective that one can develop is very limited. The proposals of change that seek to attain a less unequal world fall prey to this limitation. The only viable proposals here are those that transform the minimum, leaving the established order almost untouchable, and indeed reproducing it. For this reason, we are facing an imaginary that results from the hegemony imposed by the current (neo)liberal order.

If we want to question this order and achieve proposals that have a truly transformative reach and substantively reduce inequalities, we must begin to develop another type of interpretation that is located in the antipodes of the predominant imaginary. This supposes that the view of inequalities must shift to the sphere of distribution, prioritize the problem of surplus, and pluralize the subjects who struggle for this surplus via the dynamics of (dis)empowerment. Only in this way will we be able to initiate the repoliticization of the social question that is required in Latin America.

Notes

1 Translation from Spanish into English by Clay Johnson.
2 The success of this achievement is such that even "postneoliberal" governments continue to invoke the discourse of "poverty" and to formulate social policies in the same direction, especially those referring to conditional cash transfers. However, the reality shows itself to be more complex and, in practice, these governments have not merely reproduced (neo)liberal social policies.
3 On that point, the contribution made by Vusković Bravo (1993) is to be recognized. His text can be considered the pioneer in the current reflection on inequalities in Latin America, yet went unnoticed beyond the Mexican academic milieu.
4 The functional distribution of income refers to this primary sphere, yet it is a suspiciously marginal methodology in Latin America, as Lindenboim (2008) has pointed out. However, this methodological proposal confronts the difficulty of the labor heterogeneity that characterizes Latin America. An important proportion of labor income does not originate from salary income but rather from self-employment, and this itself is characterized by a great diversity of situations, from subsistence self-employment to highly remunerated professionals.
5 This is exactly the argument that Sen (1995) makes, in his well-known text on inequality, regarding the need to pose the question "of what." Yet this author does not ask the second question ("between whom") since, from his liberal perspective, individuals are the privileged subjects. This implies an important limitation in the understanding of inequalities, as we will argue below.
6 The causes for such decrease are varied (increment in the offer of workers with higher qualifications, fall in the demand for this type of worker, deterioration of the quality of secondary and higher education) and, on the point, there is no consensus (Lustig et al., 2013).
7 The World Bank, in its text about inequalities in Latin America, presents the scheme of a triangle as a proposal for a stylized theoretical framework. In it, the term power would seem to occupy the key vertex in this triangle; indeed, the proposal makes reference to authors such as Bourdieu and Tilly (De Ferranti et al., 2004: Figure 1.1). However, the explicative itinerary of the triangle, as it does not begin with the issue of power, ends up minimizing this vertex; furthermore, the mentioned authors are simple allusions that adorn the text but do not have any explanatory incidence whatsoever (Pérez Sáinz, 2014).
8 On that point, it is illustrative to compare the evolution of the index of the real minimum wage between Brazil and Mexico. Having the value 100 in the year 2000, 13 years later it was lifted—in the first case—to 202.7 while in the Mexican case it remained at 101.8 (OIT, 2014: Statistical Annex, Table 10). According to these authors, in both cases the salary gap was closed, but we think that we face two very different situations in terms of inequality in labor markets.
9 One would have to see in how many countries in the region this type of information is available for processing and analysis.
10 The analysis of Argentina was done by Alvaredo and the analysis of Colombia by this same author and Londoño.
11 This observation is key because when we speak of asymmetries in the area of inequalities, these are never absolute, but relative.
12 We take this qualifier from Figueroa (2000) for whom, from his proposal of a Sigma economy that would correspond to heterogeneous societies such as the Latin American ones, it is in these basic markets that exclusion can be generated.

13 For this author, it is not a matter of real goods that are produced for the sole purpose of sale, as the self-regulating market demands. Labor is intrinsically tied to human life and activity; land is related to nature; and money is a symbol of purchasing power generated by means of banking and state institutions.

14 Marx (1975: 214), just when he concludes his analysis of the purchase and sale of labor at the beginning of his magnum opus, as a prelude to this treatment of the processes of labor and valorization, describes metaphorically and with his habitual sarcasm the triumphal passage to the factory where it is demonstrated, unequivocally, who is the winner (the buyer who now appears as the capitalist) and who is the loser (the seller transformed into the worker). From the outcome of this primordial pulse it is announced what will happen in the productive process.

15 The recent rise of a new type of support for individuals, consumerism, should be mentioned here, which tends to displace inequalities of surplus to a secondary plane.

16 Here, the favorite topic of the liberal focus emerges: equality of opportunities. This myth has been debunked by Dubet (2011: 54) who argues that it is based on the idea that, for each generation, individuals are proportionally distributed on all levels of the social structure independent of their origins and their initial conditions. It is a type of iterative "wiping the slate clean and clearing the accounts."

17 The term *categorical pair* comes from the proposal put forth by Tilly (1999), but we restrict our use of the term here to socio-cultural categories; thus, it does not extend to social classes as the North American sociologist proposes.

18 This logic is inscribed in one of the monocultural rationalities, that of the logic of social classification that De Sousa Santos (2010) identified within what he called the "sociology of absences." Its result is the generation of an inferior party. The other rationalities include the monoculture of knowledge and the rigor of knowledge, the monoculture of linear time, the logic of the dominant scale, and productivist logic. And each one of them, according to the Portuguese author, generates its respective mode of absence or non-existence: the ignorant, the backward, the local or particular, and the unproductive or sterile.

References

Bastos, S. (2005): "Análisis conceptual de la diversidad étnico-cultural en Guatemala. (Reflexiones en torno a lo aparentemente evidente)," in UNDP, *Human Development Report of the UNDP*, Guatemala: UNDP.

BID (1999): *América Latina frente a la desigualdad. Informe 1998–1999*, Washington, DC: Inter-American Development Bank.

Bobbio, N. (1993): *Igualdad y libertad*, Barcelona: Paidós/I.C.E. de la Universidad Autónoma de Barcelona.

Burdín, G., Esponda, F., and Vigorito, A. (2015): "Desigualdad y altas rentas en el Uruguay: un análisis basado en los registros tributarios y las encuestas de hogares del período 2009–2011," in Jiménez, J. P. (ed.): *Desigualdad, concentración del ingreso y tributación sobre las altas rentas en América Latina*, Santiago de Chile: CEPAL/CEF.

Castel, R. (1997): *La metamorfosis de la cuestión social: una crónica del salariado*, Buenos Aires: Paidós.

Castel, R. (2010): *El ascenso de las incertidumbres. Trabajo, protecciones, estatuto del individuo*, Mexico: Fondo de Cultura Económica.

Cortés, F. (2001): "El cálculo de la pobreza en Mexico a partir de las encuestas de ingreso y gasto," *Comercio Exterior*, 19/2001: 879–994.

De Ferranti, D., Perry, G. E., Ferreira, F. H. G., and Walton, M. (2004): *Inequality in Latin America. Breaking with History?*, Washington, DC: World Bank.

De Sousa Santos, B. (2010): *Refundación del Estado en América Latina. Perspectivas desde una epistemología del Sur*, Quito: Abya Yala.

Dubet, F. (2011): *Repensar la justicia social. Contra el mito de la igualdad de oportunidades*, Buenos Aires: Siglo XXI.

Figueroa, A. (2000): "La exclusión social como una teoría de la distribución," in Gacitúa, E., Sojo, C., and Davis, S. H. (eds.): *Exclusión social y reducción de la pobreza en América Latina y El Caribe*, San José: FLACSO/Banco Mundial.

Gasparini, L. and Lustig, N. (2011): *The Rise and Fall of Income Inequality in Latin America*, Verona: ECINEQ Working Paper, 2011, 213.

Gómez Sabaíni, J. C. and Rossignolo, D. (2015): "La tributación sobre las altas rentas en América Latina," in Jiménez, J. P. (ed.): *Desigualdad, concentración del ingreso y tributación sobre las altas rentas en América Latina*, Santiago de Chile: CEPAL/CEF.

Lindenboim, J. (2008): "Distribución funcional del ingreso, un tema olvidado que reclama atención," *Problemas del Desarrollo* 9 (153): 83–117.

López, R., Figueroa B. E., and Gutiérrez C. P. (2013): *La 'parte del león': nuevas estimaciones de la participación de los súper ricos en el ingreso de Chile*, Santiago de Chile: Facultad de Economía y Negocios/Universidad de Chile, Documentos de Trabajo 379.

López-Calva, L. F. and Lustig, N. (2010): "Explaining the Decline in Inequality in Latin America: Technological Change, Educational Upgrading, and Democracy," in López-Calva, L. F. and Lustig, N. (eds.): *Declining Income Inequality in Latin America: A Decade of Progress?* Baltimore, MD: Brookings Institution Press.

López-Calva, L. F. and Lustig, N. (2012): "The Decline in Inequality in Latin America: The Role of Markets and the State," *LASA Forum*, XLIII(3): 4–6.

Lukes, S. (2004): *Power: A Radical View*, London: Palgrave Macmillan.

Lustig, N. and López-Calva, L. F. (2012): "El mercado laboral, el Estado y la dinámica de la desigualdad en América Latina: Brasil, Mexico y Uruguay," *Pensamiento Iberoamericano*, 10: 3–28.

Lustig, N., López-Calva, L. F., and Ortiz-Juarez, E. (2013): *Deconstructing the Decline in Inequality in Latin America*, Washington, DC: Policy Research Working Paper 6552.

Marshall, T. H. (1998): "Ciudadanía y clase social," in Marshall, T. H. and Bottomore, T.(eds.): *Ciudadanía y clase social*, Madrid: Alianza Editorial, pp. 297–344,

Marx, K. (1975): *El Capital. Crítica de la economía política*, Madrid: Siglo XXI, Vol. I.

OIT (2014): *Panorama laboral. América Latina y el Caribe 2014*, Lima: International Labor Organization.

Pérez Sáinz, J. P. (2012): "Exclusión social. Una propuesta crítica para abordar las carencias materiales en América Latina," in Pérez Sáinz, J. P. (ed.): *Sociedades fracturadas. La exclusión social en Centroamérica*, San José: FLACSO.

Pérez Sáinz, J. P. (2013): "¿Disminuyeron las desigualdades sociales en América Latina durante la primera década del siglo XXI? Evidencia e interpretaciones," *Desarrollo Económico*, 53 (209–210): 57–73.

Pérez Sáinz, J. P. (2014): *Mercados y bárbaros. La persistencia de las desigualdades de excedente en América Latina*, San José, FLACSO.

Piketty, T. (2014): *El capital en el siglo XXI*, Mexico City: Fondo de Cultura Económica.

PNUD (2010): "Actuar sobre el futuro: romper la transmisión intergeneracional de la desigualdad," *Informe Regional sobre Desarrollo Humano para América Latina y el Caribe 2010*, New York, NY: UNDP.

Polanyi, K. (1992): *La gran transformación. Los orígenes políticos y económicos de nuestro tiempo*, Mexico City: Fondo de Cultura Económica.

Scott, J. C. (2007): *Los dominados y el arte de la resistencia. discursos ocultos*, Mexico City: Ediciones Era.

Sen, A. (1995): *Inequality Reexamined*, Cambridge, MA: Harvard University Press.

Székely, M. and Hilgert, M. (1999): *What's Behind the Inequality We Measure: An Investigation Using Latin American Data*, Washington, DC: Inter-American Development Bank, Working Paper 409.

Tilly, C. (1999): *Durable Inequality*, Berkeley, CA: University of California Press.

Vusković Bravo, P. (1993): *Pobreza y desigualdad social América Latina*, Mexico City: UNAM.

Weber, M. (1984): *Economía y sociedad. Esbozo de sociología comprensiva*, Mexico City: Fondo de Cultura económica.

6

UNEQUAL DIFFERENCES

Gender, ethnicity/race, and citizenship in class societies (historical realities, analytical approaches)

Elizabeth Jelin[1]

Equality is a concern that, implicitly or explicitly, has been and continues to be at the heart of social struggles. Academic and political debates on the subject have ranged from questions as to whether it is a matter of equality of opportunities or of results and generalized well-being, if it refers to the expansion of the rights of citizenship or to compensatory and redistributive mechanisms in view of the processes of concentration and polarization produced by the functioning of the capitalist market economy, whether it has to do with human capital or with social structures, whether it is a matter of capabilities or of opportunities, to whether a social revolution is required to achieve social equality or there can be processes of gradual reform. These debates are more than theoretical; they have direct consequences for social struggles and social demands at different levels and in different places around the world.

During the last decades, the hegemonic neoliberal and individualistic economic paradigm, casting aside social structures and the central role of institutions, has placed emphasis on individual capabilities, effort, and personal achievement as the motors of well-being—alluding only tangentially to socially structured inequalities. This perspective took for granted the self-regulating functioning of the market, an assumption that had already been criticized and laid to rest decades ago by Karl Polanyi. This dominant ideology did not consider social structures and power relations, be they global or local. Thus, it involved more talk about poverty than about inequalities, and social policies, where they were implemented, were geared toward reducing poverty rather than toward redistributing wealth. Additionally, the language of class and social struggles and the role of the state as a regulator, beyond the implementation of compensatory policies, particularly focalized social policies, were blurred, if not lost altogether.

This neoliberal dominance coincided with an increase in social demands for the recognition of diversity, and these demands generated changes in interpretative frameworks and policies of recognition, focused on the celebration of diversity, multiculturalism, and difference. Undoubtedly, it is more than a matter of coincidences. The affinities between neoliberal individualism and the exaltation of diversity—understood as difference and not as inequality—are noteworthy. Analytical approaches followed these shifts, paying more attention to cultural difference and claims for recognition than to structural inequalities and claims for resources.

This chapter tackles the links between structural inequalities and social differences. As Brubaker states, differences anchored in various ascribed categories, particularly gender, ethnicity, and race; also citizenship:

> are not *intrinsically* linked to inequality; *different* does not necessarily imply *unequal*. The relation between difference and inequality is contingent, not necessary; it is empirical, not conceptual. And the degree to which and manner in which inequality is structured along categorical lines vary widely over time and context.
>
> *(Brubaker 2015: 11)*

Yet the links are not simple: social categories of difference are constructed historically and culturally and their salience may vary along time and place; once in place, they matter in the production and reproduction of inequalities.

It is not my intention to enter into conversations about the various perspectives and approaches that have been developed to tackle these issues. My objective is more limited and concrete: to address how to understand linkages between diverse dimensions of social inequalities, and more specifically, to discuss the contribution of some Latin American thinkers to the analysis of these linkages. In the historical development of Latin American societies and in the history of intellectual debates, the production and reproduction of multiple inequalities have been at the center of attention, rooted in academic traditions and in theoretical-conceptual discussions. They were generated in interaction, dialogue, and active participation in the dynamics of social and political action, insofar as the Latin American intellectuals who formulate theories, models, and interpretations are also active protagonists in the scenarios of public action and of struggle rather than researchers locked up in "ivory towers."

After an initial discussion of multiple inequalities framed around the pair "inequalities-differences," the chapter goes back several decades, to the reality and the analyses developed in Latin America in the middle of the 20th century. At that time, the central concern of analysts and rulers was focused on the issue of capitalist development. After recovering this historical context, the chapter presents the manner in which the analysts of the era discussed and interpreted the relationship between (that which they considered to be) the central dimension of social inequalities—social class—and other dimensions and social cleavages, above all, gender, race, and ethnicity. The concluding section of the chapter takes up these grounded discussions as a point of departure for the discussion of contemporary conceptualizations of the links between inequalities and differences.

An additional note: I read works written in the 1960s and 1970s from the perspective of the 21st century, looking back with current questions and interpretive frameworks. The danger of anachronism is unquestionable. It is unjust to ask the analysts of that era to respond to questions that we pose today. The alternative danger is, perhaps, more serious: to think that everything that we do now is completely novel and original, that the manners of conceptualizing and analyzing social inequalities in the past are obsolete and have been surpassed. It would thus seem that it is not necessary to look toward thinking and elaborations made in the past. I count myself among those who assert that reinventing the wheel is suicidal for the development of knowledge.

Multiple inequalities

The existence of "multiple inequalities," that is, multiple dimensions of stratification and social categorization, is nowadays part of the common sense of social sciences. Yet the multiplicity does not mean that all dimensions are interchangeable, or can be treated in an analogous way. First, it becomes necessary to signal an important differentiation between analytically defined dimensions and the criteria and categories that social actors construct and use in their everyday practices, in their interpersonal relations, and in their struggles for power. From the perspective of the actors in societal scenarios, the categories used to differentiate themselves or identify themselves with others are constructed through their experiences, in the concrete situations in which they find themselves. These categorizations are contingent and empirical; there cannot be a predetermined list of dimensions. That one dimension is problematized and becomes visible, that another is not used explicitly in the frameworks of interpretations of action, that there are diverse regularities and combinations of categories and issues—all this is part of the research questions to be asked and has to be revealed in the process of investigation. From an analytical or *etic* perspective, on the other hand, dimensions and categories are instruments that serve to order and explain what brings the actors to act as they do, even when this is not visible or explicit for these actors.

At a structural level, the concern for inequalities brings social classes to the center of attention. Be it in the analysis of the structure of productive activities and labor markets, or in the analysis of their outcomes in the form of income distribution, this has been, and continues being, the core of social thinking in relation to the dynamics of inequality and the mechanisms of its production and reproduction—be they exploitation or hoarding of opportunities. The issue here is to uncover how class structure is linked to social categorizations and differentiations based on diverse, mostly ascribed cultural and social dimensions, such as ethnicity, "race," gender, age, nationality, religion, language, and so on. Categories and categorizations operate from the outside—"others" (groups, institutions) defining boundaries, rights, and entitlements accruing from belonging, and devaluation and discrimination of the excluded. They also operate from the inside, through subjective feelings, self-identification, and enactment of cultural practices

112 Elizabeth Jelin

(Brubaker 2015). In the midst of political struggles, moreover, actors can develop social categorizations as strategic identifications that help them in defining themselves and their opponents.

The links between these structural positions and relations in social systems on the one hand, and ascribed and culturally bound categorizations on the other, are contingent and change over time. Furthermore, the way these categorizations operate in relation to class and inequalities is not ubiquitous; there are specificities to each dimension. While ethnicity may imply relatively closed communities, segregated and often discriminated against by others, gender cuts across social classes and culturally defined communities.

In contemporary social analysis, the multidimensional aspect of social categorizations and inequalities is being approached through the notion of "intersectionality." Stemming from feminist perspectives concerned with locating gender inequalities in a broader frame, this notion alludes to the fact that gender, ethnicity, and class operate simultaneously in generating and in displaying inequalities (Kerner 2012, Roth 2013.) The corollary of this statement is a methodological warning: any analysis of inequalities will be incomplete if it does not take into account these multiple dimensions of the phenomenon. As a methodological warning, it cannot be contested. At an analytical or theoretical level, however, it does not tell us much about the nature of the links between gender inequalities and other dimensions. Can some generalization and theorization be advanced regarding their interactive patterns? The conceptualization followed here takes as a point of departure the centrality of structural class-related inequalities, and looks at their links to diverse social categorizations and socially constructed differences, considering that each of these categorizations (Tilly's durable categorical paired distinctions [1998]) has dynamics of its own.

The context: Latin America post-Second World War

In the mid-20th century, Latin America experienced a rapid process of urbanization and rural-urban migration, the expansion of education, processes of industrialization, population growth, etc.—all of them signs of "modernization," having important effects on the redistribution and restructuring of social inequalities (Pérez Sáinz 2014). There were multiple specific processes; yet, for our purpose, it is sufficient to sum up their consequences for inequalities. As Thorp concludes,

> Whereas the figures of growth were impressive, and institutional history shows radical changes in many areas, industrialization and import substitution inserted themselves in, and reinforced, the preexisting exceedingly unequal social and economic system. Even the efforts of agrarian reform did not modify the essential panorama of poverty and exclusion. Women and indigenous groups remained relatively deprived and the tendencies of the urban labor market created new inequalities.
>
> *(Thorp 1998: 199)*

In this period, the central issues in the social sciences in the region concerned the type of capitalist development that was materializing. The consideration of inequalities was anchored in this topic: marginality, rural–urban discrepancies, peasantry, salaried work/other forms of work, national bourgeoisies and oligarchies, the formation or absence of middle classes, etc., were considered and analyzed. The formation of a class society, with heavy emphasis on the passage toward merit and stratification anchored more in acquired characteristics than ascribed ones, was on the horizon.

The dynamics of the creation of inequalities combined simultaneously various processes that, according to the thinking of the times, corresponded to different "moments" of theoretically delineated processes: on the one hand, hoarding of resources by means of primitive accumulation—in reference both to the origin of the labor force demanded by capitalist development and to the privatization of land for the expansion of mercantile agriculture, with the displacement of indigenous peoples and peasants, the prevalence of semiservile work in mines and haciendas; on the other hand, exploitation within the capitalist system itself and the hoarding of other resources, especially opportunities to accumulate knowledge and know-how by means of the educational expansion oriented toward the middle classes.

The explanatory axis was centered on the labor market as the force behind the structure and distribution of inequalities. Positions in the labor market were linked to other dimensions: ethnicity interwoven with economic sectors (for example, a peasantry with strong indigenous components in the rural sector), a nascent salaried working class based on European immigration, or the predominance of women of rural origin in urban domestic service. Class structure was the center; other dimensions of inequality were articulated with class dynamics, yet they did not determine them. Other criteria of social categorization, especially ethnicity and race, were mostly seen as "legacies" or vestiges from the past. These ascribed categories would dissolve to the extent that merit and achievement would displace origin as the most important anchor for the definition of social opportunities.

Which were these other categories of inequalities that, besides social class, deserved attention? On the one hand, there was the ethnic and racial composition of the population and the insertion of non-white groups into the lowest positions of the social structure, and immigrant European origin (especially Mediterranean) into the working class. Issues of race and ethnicity had been considered by earlier social thinkers in the region such as José Carlos Mariategui in Peru and Gilberto Freyre in Brazil. The subordinate position of women in the patriarchal structure, however, was a more novel topic, with little or no tradition in Latin American social thinking—even when women thinkers and activists had been problematizing this throughout the 20th century. Spatial differences and inequalities were also significant, always seen in a dynamic manner as part of the process of urbanization.

Inequalities at the international level were interpreted in terms of relations between center and periphery. Capitalist development in Latin America was "peripheral," and the basic goal was to understand its challenges, first in the thinking of Raúl Prebisch and ECLAC. They would come to be interpreted in terms of "dependence" (Cardoso and Faletto 1969, among others who, like Mauro Marini and André Gunder Frank, were more skeptical regarding the potentialities of dependent development). The understanding of inequalities in a world-system perspective (as in Korzeniewicz and Moran 2009, and Korzeniewicz in this volume) was still far into the future. This line is continued in our multiscalar entangled approach, where, as stated in the introduction of this book, the patterns of inequality combine processes at different levels, from the local to the global. Within this framework, when looking at the international scene, belonging to a political community, as conveyed by formal, state-granted citizenship, has to be introduced as a categorical dimension that shapes and determines the strongest inequalities in life chances in the world today (Brubaker 2015).

Florestan Fernandes: capitalism and race

Florestan Fernandes' analysis of capitalist development in Latin America and of the integration of the "Negro" into capitalist development in Brazil is, no doubt, a classic. Fernandes conceptualizes the situation of the region in comparison with the English/European model of capitalist development. Thus, Latin American capitalism is messy, with temporal discrepancies and asynchronies between processes that were simultaneous in other places.[2] It is not only a matter of the region arriving "late"; rather, that capitalist development in the region implies a specific combination of history and structure, and this requires explanation and interpretation.

Fernandes tracks inequalities from the formation—incomplete, specific—of social classes in dependent capitalist development. The double appropriation—of local bourgeoisie and of global capitalism—leaves the "lower" classes in an especially disadvantageous situation. Neither those who are integrated into capitalist production nor those who are marginal have the capacity to struggle, either within the system (because they are not fully integrated) or by means of a revolutionary transformation.

Within this framework of class formation, Fernandes tackles the analysis of the social position of the Negro[3] in Brazil (Fernandes 1965a, 1965b, and 1972; Bastide and Fernandes 1959).[4] The general question is posed in terms of the development of a "competitive social order" as an ineluctable development. The author asks himself about the predispositions and abilities that different human groups have to enter into relations of production required for the "competitive social order." What are the expectations—with regard to that which is expected of the workers—on the part of the system in expansion? Who are the potential workers prepared to insert themselves into this system? In this regard, the Negro is handicapped vis-à-vis the European worker, due to the history of slavery. Fernandes sees the origin of the situation of the Negro in the mid-20th century in the history of slavery and in the challenges faced by ex-slaves after the abolition of slavery in 1888.

The structural conditions are complemented by psychosocial factors—something that decades later would enter into what is currently conceptualized as "subjectivity" and "capacity of action (or of agency)" of subaltern subjects. Social action is not driven only by obscure forces beyond human action (i.e., "structural").

Rather, Fernandes casts his eyes on the (limited) options open to Negroes, and how their ways of acting, learned in the slave past—that which Bauman (2011) calls "class memory"— influence their process of integration into class society.

The Negro is looked at as a person who acts in social settings and scenarios. Facing the conditions set by free labor and the presence of European immigrants, the Negro ex-slave confronts difficulties of various sorts. Even when Fernandes' attention is focused on the structural situation of the ex-slaves, he considers them as human subjects, and he searches into the "moral condition of the person." These are people with rationality, confronting opportunity structures and creating strategies to face them. They also have moral principles. When facing new labor market conditions, "[…] for the Negro or the mulatto all of this was secondary. The essential thing was the moral condition of the person and his liberty to decide how, when and where to work" (Fernandes 1965a: 13). Thus, Negroes and mulattos are understood as subjects that have to face their freedom in an economic and social context for which their previous experience has not prepared them.

In his model of analysis, Fernandes does not incorporate an analysis of gender relations (or relations of the sexes, according to the terminology of his time). Yet when describing and interpreting the situation in São Paulo and entering into a microsocial and interpersonal analysis, men and women gain specificity. In the urban world of São Paulo, he concludes, life appears to be easier for black women. Their insertion into urban domestic work does not imply a deep break in their experience. There are more continuities with their previous experience than in the case of men. Therefore, the black woman is characterized as "a privileged labor agent because she is the only one who can have lasting jobs and a continual source of livelihood" (Fernandes 1965a: 43). It is due to this continuity in their tasks in the urban world that black women run the risk of becoming the sole means of subsistence for the men, yet without the complementary protection of a stable and integrated family. The results of these conditions are social anomy and disorganization in the personal and social life of Negroes. Thus, at this point of his analysis, Fernandes incorporates an explicit consideration of gender relations and how these interact with class and "race" in a specific context.

One of Fernandes' central questions is: Did the city fend off the Negro? His response is that it was not actually an issue of race: "The economic, social, and cultural isolation of the Negro was a product of his relative incapacity to feel, think and act socially as a free man" (Fernandes 1965a: 67). The entrance into the urban world and the competitive social order implied a strong demand: to divest oneself from the previously acquired way of life, and to adopt the psychosocial and moral attributes of a head of the family, salaried worker, citizen, entrepreneur, etc. "Exclusion would have had a specifically racial character if the Negro held these qualities and was nevertheless repelled" (Fernandes 1965a: 68).

The economic, social, and cultural dynamics were and are, undoubtedly, complex. Fernandes goes over the "levels of social disorganization," highlighting conditions of employment and their opportunities, and marking the mediating role of the family as a socializing institution and the different gender roles in the process of

116 Elizabeth Jelin

socialization. Disorganization is not seen as the origin but rather as the consequence of the mismatch and the gap between the slave condition and the requisites of urban life, that is, settings that cannot be controlled; "misplaced" rationalities. As a preview of a subject that would come into the center of attention decades later, Fernandes looks at the centrality of sexuality and the body. Also, interestingly, he deals with the street and the neighborhood as spaces of sociability, as well as with the relationship between this type of sociability and the integration into class society, in the style that would become canonical through the writings of E. P. Thompson (Thompson 1980).

In sum, what Florestan Fernandes does in this type of analysis is, basically, to discard essences and to historicize processes. There is nothing essential in race; there are historical processes that could have been different. For example, he notes that "the aptitude for change does not have to do so much with the contents and the organization of people's cultural horizons or the categories of people, but rather with their localization in the economic structure and power in the city" (Fernandes 1965a: 192). Urban capitalist development, salaried work, and the competitive social order are the structuring axes of social reality. Some trajectories and experiences adapt more easily to them—such as those of immigrant workers—while others hinder processes of integration. Women, used to day-to-day domestic labor, experience more continuity and fewer ruptures in their ways of life. Thus, they can "benefit" from their experience, grounded in their double subordination to their employers and to their partners in the family. This continued survival of patterns of behavior inherited from the slave period is not only present among Negroes and mulattos. "The 'white man' also continued to adhere to a system of social values and of racial domination ... analogous to the one in force in caste society" (Fernandes 1965: 194).

Given the maladjustments in the process of creation of this "competitive social order," with strong lines of racial inequalities and the absence of a racial democracy—despite the myth, where can one seek the seeds of the transformation of social practices and racial hierarchies? Fernandes dedicates a full volume (Fernandes 1965b) to the analysis of collective social movements, on the one hand, and to the "egalitarian impulses" (oriented toward assimilation and integration), on the other. The question is, once again, posed in a relational manner: one needs to study how racial tensions are perceived and socially controlled by various actors, and at the same time to characterize the situation as the "Brazilian racial dilemma."

Rodolfo Stavenhagen: agrarian capitalist development and ethnicity

The issue of interethnic relations within capitalist development, especially in the agrarian sphere, was the focus of attention of Rodolfo Stavenhagen in his book *Las clases sociales en las sociedades agrarias* (*Social Classes in Agrarian Societies*), published in 1969 (Stavenhagen 1969). Stavenhagen is a Mexican anthropologist and sociologist with a long career in the analysis of the relations between development, ethnic inequalities, and the rights of indigenous peoples.[5]

The framework of analysis is capitalist development in the course of history, not as a lineal process that repeats itself in a similar way in different places but as a situated process anchored in the interconnections between the global scale and national and subnational scales. The basic frame of reference is historical: very diverse forms of precapitalist exploitation and domination existed in different places in the world, but "none of these class structures has been able to resist the impact of European expansion without suffering radical modifications" (Stavenhagen 1969: 62). Everywhere, colonialism and the processes of surplus extraction were linked to the way in which commercial capitalism penetrated into preexisting communities. Processes of transformation of class and stratification structures differ from place to place, yet they have significant effects in all cases, stemming from the monetary economy, private property of land, commercial monoculture, work-related migration and rural exodus, urbanization, industrialization, and the national integration of underdeveloped countries. These processes have acted in different ways, according to the preexisting social structures and rhythms of their introduction.

In his analysis of these processes in the Mayan region of Mexico and Guatemala, Stavenhagen takes as his point of departure the passage from the stage of military conquest to the implantation of the colonial system, a product of mercantilist expansion. In this period, the mechanisms of domination were linked to the interests of the powerful social classes of the colonizing country. The indigenous communities became a labor reserve for the colonial economy. In order to maintain this labor reserve, restrictive laws accrued and a centralized system of control was established, maintaining the natives in their position of inferiority vis-à-vis all of the other social strata. This resulted in the loss of the economic base of the old hierarchies within the indigenous communities. In fact, the indigenous communities ended up being only "folk" societies, relatively closed corporate units, under the impact of the Spanish indigenous policy. However, to the extent that they participated in the economic life of the society, they were integrated in a class society.

Both the colonial system and class relations underlay interethnic relations, although in different ways. In colonial terms, indigenous society as a whole confronted the colonial society. Relations were defined in terms of ethnic discrimination, segregation, social inferiority, and economic subjection. Class relations, on the other hand, were defined in terms of labor relations and property; thus, it was not a matter of labor relations between two societies but rather between specific sectors of the same society. Colonial relations responded to mercantilism, class relations to capitalism.

The colonial system functioned on two levels: between the metropolis and the colony, as well as within the colony itself: "What Spain represented for the colony, the colonial metropolis represented for the indigenous communities" (Stavenhagen 1969: 245). For this reason, the post-independence period did not transform the essence of the relations between the *Indios* and the global society. Despite legal equality, various factors maintained colonial relations:

> The *Indios* from the traditional communities once again found themselves in the role of a colonized people: they lost their lands, were compelled to

118 Elizabeth Jelin

> work for the 'foreigners', they were integrated against their will into a new monetary economy, they were subjugated to new forms of political domination. This time, the colonial society was the national society itself, which progressively extended its control over their territory.
>
> *(Stavenhagen 1969: 248)*

The key concept developed by Stavenhagen is that of "internal colonialism."

Stavenhagen sees the dynamic relationship between ethnic relations and class as a duality. On one hand, class relations are embodied in capitalist labor relations that frame subjects as workers and not as ethnicities. On the other hand, ethnicities are anchored in community structures and, to the extent that the community structure is broken, interethnic stratification loses its objective base. Nonetheless, class relations can take on cultural forms, for example, when the struggle for land is carried out in the name of the restitution of communal lands.

The interplay between the two criteria is not simple. Interethnic stratification does not correspond to the emerging class relations—"we are not saying the *Indios* and *Ladinos* are simply two social classes"—since it is deeply rooted in the values of the members of the society. In fact, it functions as a conservative force, halting the development of class relations. To the extent that the process of class formation advances, new bases of stratification, hinging on socioeconomic criteria, develop, even when "ethnic consciousness can, however, weigh more than class consciousness" (Stavenhagen 1969: 250–251).

The reactions of the indigenous can be diverse: acculturation, which may imply the adoption of the symbols of status of the *Ladinos* (consumer goods, for example), even though maintaining the *Indio* cultural identity. Alternatively, it may imply the general economic ascent of indigenous groups, representing a challenge to *Ladino* superiority. Assimilation and individualized adoption of *Ladino* identity may also occur, implying abandoning the community and integrating oneself into the national society, through a process of proletarianization.

In Mexico in the 1960s, Stavenhagen argues, the rapid development of class relations to the detriment of colonial relations produces the development of *indigenismo* as an ideology and a principle for action. This is a "nationalist" position, one that asks for strengthening indigenous government and demanding national political representation of the indigenous people. The paradox is that this can be encouraged by the nation-state itself, as a means of achieving "a goal that represents its absolute negation, namely, the incorporation of the *Indio* into the Mexican nationality, that is to say, the disappearance of the *Indio* as such" (Stavenhagen 1969: 258).

Stavenhagen's complex analysis crosses various axes, in an approach that takes as its central fact the dominant place of the nation-state and the dilemmas involved in constructing nationality, topics that loomed large in the period when the author was writing. Seen from the perspective of the present, the issue is the relationship between two frameworks of interpretation of these dynamics. On the one hand, there is the relationship between development and categorical inequality, which can be read from the perspective of various paradigms: anti-colonialism, Marxism, neoliberalism, or neo-developmentalism. The other is the formation of a national unit—the "integration" that Fernandes was speaking of, Mexican nationality in Stavenhagen's thinking—vis-à-vis the logic of difference, which, historically, spans from scientific racism to multiculturalism.

In the latter, one is faced, once again, with the paradox between equality and difference, posed decades later by Nancy Fraser and Joan Scott (Fraser 1997, Scott 1996). According to this logic, for Stavenhagen, "national integration can only be attained if the contradictions inherent in colonial relations are resolved and overcome. This can be achieved either by suppressing one of the terms of the contradiction or by changing the content of the relationship" (Stavenhagen 1969: 259). For Stavenhagen, the way out of this disjunctive is to achieve national integration not by suppressing the *Indio* but by suppressing him as a colonized being.

Class and gender: Heleieth Saffioti, Isabel Larguía, and John Dumoulin

Differently from race or ethnicity, where inter-category relationships imply inclusions and exclusions, as well as the existence of category-based communities, when dealing with gender one cannot think of the formation of separate communities. Gender is present everywhere—in all classes, in all nationalities, in all ethnic and racial groups. Its universal presence makes it less visible, more "natural," and less subject to analysis and interpretation. Thus, it is not surprising that, in the context of concerns over development and inequalities seen especially through the lens of social marginality and urban development, there was in Latin America a profound blindness concerning inequalities in the relationship between the sexes and the social place of women (the term "gender" was not yet used at that time).

Up to the 1970s, if women were relevant, the matter of concern was the asynchrony between processes of rapid urbanization that the region was experiencing and the persistence of high levels of fertility. The dominant interpretation was the "traditionalism" of women, and the hope was that the modernity that accompanied the processes of urbanization—especially the increase in educational levels—would soon change women's attitudes and behavior. Temporal lags in the process of change could then explain the persistence of this traditionalism. What was taken for granted was that reproductive behavior and attitudes were the patrimony of women. Men had nothing to do with the matter, and their knowledge, attitudes, and practices were irrelevant for such a feminine topic as birth and children.

Toward the end of the 1960s, a new wave of feminism emerged in the central countries, a wave that soon reached women in other parts of the world. This feminist wave had to confront a double challenge: first, to understand and explain the forms of subordination of women, and second, to propose road maps for the struggle to transform this condition. What was the nature of subordination? How to explain it? The debate was intense, the heterogeneity and the theoretical and tactical conflicts permanent. The relationship between research and action was, without doubt, a central concern of feminist academics.

120 Elizabeth Jelin

In this climate of ideas, in 1969 Heleieth Saffioti published her book *A mulher na sociedade de classes. Mito e realidade* (*The Woman in the Class Society. Myth and Reality*) (Saffioti 1969). The product of her doctoral thesis supervised by Florestan Fernandes, the book is framed in Fernandes' research tradition, namely the development of capitalism in general, and particularly in Brazil. Within it, Saffioti looks at the place women occupy in capitalist development. Her analysis is oriented toward showing that "relations between the sexes and, consequently, the position of the woman in the family and in society at large are part of a wider system of domination" (Saffioti 1969: 169).

In this, and in other texts of that time, the reference is to "THE woman" in the singular. Fernandes also speaks of "the Negro" in the singular, and the heterogeneities and differentiations within the category woman or Negro show up only in the specific historically grounded descriptions and analyses. With the passage of time, the plural would become predominant, so as to make clear that hierarchies, relations of dominations and inequalities exist not only among categories of race and gender, but within them as well.

Saffioti traces the origin of the myths and preconceptions that justify the exclusion of women from certain tasks and their segregation in traditional roles and occupations in the way power was organized and distributed in Brazilian slave society. She analyzes the position of male and female slaves and the inconsistencies in racial slave relations—black women slaves had their function in the productive system; they also had a sexual role, and the product—the mulatto—became the focus of social and cultural tensions.

The effects of capitalist development were not uniform. According to Saffioti, it implies a decline in some productive functions that were until then carried out by women, turning them into a source of cheap labor to be used only when capitalism requires it. At the same time, the limited capacity of women to protest and demand produces greater exploitation, while masking the reality of exploitation by appealing to "natural factors" such as sex and race. In this perspective, women represent "anticapitalism," both in reference to their economic activity and to the distance between them and the cultural goals of class societies.

The process is not as lineal as it seems, however. The author analyzes the processes of urbanization and the abolition of slavery in Brazil, processes that jointly with European immigration produced significant changes in the organization of the family, in particular the destabilization of the patriarchal family. Urbanization produces transformations in the social position of urban women: the expansion of cultural horizons, the limitation of childbearing, divorce. Additionally, there is a growing adoption of the Western legal family framework (especially among exslaves) that paradoxically implies the reinforcement of sexual taboos. Cultural factors are at play: the cult of feminine virginity in a world of double standards and the exaltation of the "macho" as the ideal of masculinity. As a result, "certain areas of feminine personality are, as it were, experiencing a modernization linked to novel conceptions of the world and the human being, while other areas remain prisoners of the traditional climate in which the wider process of socialization occurs" (Saffioti 1969: 197).

Family structures and symbolic and cultural practices are also transformed. Yet the articulation between the sexual division of labor in the domestic sphere and the family on the one hand, and the capitalist productive organization on the other, remains unresolved in Saffioti's analysis. This is the topic that Larguía and Dumoulin will tackle.

Their point of departure is the differentiation between "home" and "work," that is, the separation between processes of social production integrated into capitalist markets through the division of labor and processes linked to consumption and reproduction in the domestic sphere, in the private world and in the privacy of the family. In Marxist theory, the focus on modes of production implied looking at the relations between the production of commodities and the means of subsistence. The other side of the equation, the production of human beings who go on to participate in processes of production, was much less developed theoretically. Much was said about the "means of production"; almost nothing about the means of "reproduction." The Marxist feminist debate and specifically the work of Larguía and Dumoulin contributed to this topic. How are human beings, who then sell their labor power, produced? How does reproduction take place in the capitalist economy?

Reproductive activities are carried out in households. In capitalism, the family does not have an economic function. It is not a social class. It stays on as an ethical, ideological, and legal form, and as the locus where the production and reproduction of the workforce takes place. Work used for the production of this "good" is mainly women's labor. It is unpaid and the actual women-producers cannot commercialize it.

In this perspective, patriarchy, as a system of subordination of women, gains analytical importance. If the household-family is the social institution in charge of the organization of everyday life and reproduction, attention has to be paid to its internal organization and to the differentiation of roles of men and women. While the male worker, with his salary, provides the monetary resources required for the maintenance of the working class family, the counterpart of domestic work carried out by the housewife-mother, who transforms this monetary income into the goods and services—including love and affection—for maintenance and social reproduction, remains implicit and invisible.

Larguía and Dumoulin's contribution is grounded in this scenario of theoretical and political discussion. The patriarchal family implies a separation of social life in two sharply differentiated spheres: the public sphere and the domestic sphere (Larguía and Dumoulin 1976). These spheres evolved in a very unequal manner:

> Whereas male and female workers reproduce the labor force by creating commodities for exchange, and in this way for indirect consumption, housewives *replenish the labor force of the entire working class on a daily basis*. Only the existence of an alienating archaic ideology related to sex roles blocks the possibility of perceiving clearly the economic importance of this form of direct private reproduction of the labor force [...] The worker and his family

122 Elizabeth Jelin

do not maintain themselves merely with what they buy with their salary; the housewife and other relatives must invest many hours in domestic work and in other subsistence tasks [...] Women's work remained hidden behind the façade of the monogamous family, remaining *invisible* until our days. It seemed to disappear magically into thin air, as it did not generate an economically visible product like that of men.

(Larguía and Dumoulin 1976: 15–18)

Domestic work ensures social reproduction in its three meanings: the strictly biological reproduction, which at the level of the family means conceiving and having children (and at the societal level refers to the socio-demographic aspects of fertility); the domestic tasks that allow the maintenance and subsistence of the members of the family who, as salaried workers, replenish their vigor and their capacity to continue offering their labor power on a daily basis; and social reproduction, namely the tasks linked to the maintenance of the social system, especially those linked to care and early socialization of children—also caring for the sick and the elderly—including both the physical care and the transmission of norms and patterns of behavior accepted and expected (Larguía and Dumoulin 1976). In this way, biological reproduction is confused with the private reproduction of the workforce.

In sum, the tradition embodied by Larguía and Dumoulin is anchored in the analysis of the social organization and development of capitalism, here linking family and domesticity to the labor market and productive organization. Their aim was to reveal the "social invisibility of women" in unpaid and socially unrecognized domestic work, hidden from public view, and "behind" great men in historical struggles.

In the 1970s, these were among the key topics in the emerging feminist analyses and became a banner in the struggles of the women's movement. Recognition and naming grant social existence, and this visible existence becomes a requirement for the ability to make claims. Thus, feminist researchers turned their attention to day-to-day life, the anti-heroic, the social fabric that it sustains and reproduces. The theoretical debate was intense: What do these women produce when they dedicate themselves to their families and their homes? Who appropriates their labor? The recognition of the housewife as a worker also generated a political debate: Should she be recognized as a worker with labor rights? Should she be granted a salary and a pension? Or, rather, should gender relations in the domestic sphere be transformed? This knowledge, in turn, opened diverse pathways for action to reverse this situation.[6]

Given the reality of the sexual division of labor and the domestic responsibilities of women, it appeared that, as their subordination was anchored in the distinction between the public world and private life, women had to leave the domestic sphere and participate in the public world of employment—until then, predominately masculine. To a certain extent, this was already happening: there was an increase in women's levels of education and in their participation in the workforce. Beginning in the 1970s, the increase of female participation in the workforce in Latin America was very significant (Valdés and Gomariz 1995).

Yet, what happens when women enter the labor market? Saffioti posed the issues involved: there are few opportunities to access "good" jobs, women have to suffer salary discrimination and follow social beliefs about "typically feminine" tasks, namely those that extend and reproduce traditional domestic roles (domestic service, and personal services: secretaries, teachers, and nurses). In short, segregation and discrimination are the rule. Thus, class relations combine with gender subordination in a specific manner, both in the labor market (the organization of social production) and in the domestic domain (the organization of social reproduction). This combination—understood as a "double burden" of women—remained during the following decades as a source of tension, and was the object of diverse kinds of state interventions.[7]

Concluding remarks

It is not the aim of this chapter to draw clear and neat conclusions. Rather, the objective is to inquire into the ways of understanding the relations between the multiple dimensions of inequalities, as well as to understand the logics of these relationships, both in social reality and in the interpretive models developed by the intellectuals of the region. This is important because they require the development of situated knowledge that combines strong theoretical visions with lived social realities and with intentions of contributing to change. The three—concepts, reality, utopia—are interlinked in the writings dealt with here.

What can be learned from this overview in light of some of the debates and dilemmas from the 21st century? First, a comment about time, process, and change. The complex processes of change tied to capitalist development in the region imply different rhythms of transformation in different dimensions. These asynchronies or mismatches, however, are not random. The motor of change was and still is the development of new forms of economic organization, then looked at in each country or nation, nowadays recognizing and considering in a much more visible way the importance of the global level and the interdependencies and entanglements involved. At the level of actors and their scenarios, the questions opened up are about what happens with populations that are in the process of changing their forms of labor and life. Who is prepared for this change? Fernandes shows the strong legacies of slave labor among the black population in Brazil, and the mismatch between their modes of life and values and the demands of the new system. Stavenhagen demonstrates the continuities and new challenges that development poses for agrarian indigenous communities. Saffioti inquired into the changes in the situation of women. In all cases, learned and lived forms do not match the demands of capitalist development.

These disjunctions are central in the experiences of class formation. This relates to Bauman's analysis of "class memory." Bauman refers to "historical memory" or "remembered history" as the "propensity of a group toward certain responsive behaviors rather than others" (Bauman 2011: 10). This remembered history explains the reactions of a group to the change in the circumstances of life. The results may be diverse: disorganization reflected in prophecies of imminent catastrophe; the proliferation of revolutionary utopias; political, social, and cultural realignments. Insofar as the process of articulation of class society is slow, at any historical moment, Bauman says, it is the memorized class strategies that provide the cognitive and normative patterns to deal with what is experienced as critical. Yet something has to be added to Bauman's analysis: the other social categorizations—ethnic, racial, national, gender—are interwoven at the level of the experience of class, and thus enter in an inextricable way in the formation of the memories—or, to use Bourdieu's term, habitus—that will guide the practices of actors.

Second, the issues involved here can be set in the perspective of analyses that look at the tension between demands for equality and redistribution on the one hand, and demands for recognition of specificities, differences, and identities on the other. As an analytical model, this paradigm was developed later (especially by Fraser 1997). In the 1970s, it was felt in the action of historical subjects more than in paradigms or models. It is clear, however, that the analysis centered on capitalist development and class societies cannot be completed without considering gender and ethnicity in an explicit way. Then and now, the feeling of living in a world of inequalities and injustices, and the intent to actively contribute to the struggles for the transformation of the historical situation of discriminated and marginalized groups, act as a strong motivation for probing and carrying out analyses and studies.

Third, to come back once more to the link between inequalities and differences, one can connect the type of analysis presented here with the current discussions on intersectionality. Can relations between the various dimensions involved be established that go beyond the exhortation not to forget something? The authors reviewed here share a theoretical perspective in which capitalist development, and therefore class inequalities, are the key to change at the macrosocial level. Starting from that premise, they consider and analyze, in concrete historical situations, how gender and ethnicity/race play out. Contemporary proposals (Roth 2013) are more open and undefined. An important step in tackling the complex articulation is to follow the path marked by the analytical distinction between class inequalities and the diverse ascribed and cultural differences, looking at the specific ways in which they are entangled in specific historical situations (Brubaker 2015). The interaction of these different dimensions crystalizes historically in structures of inequalities; therefore, the struggle for greater equality requires action at their interdependencies and linkages. No gradual strategy of "one at a time" can act to redress a crystalized complex structure (Fraser 1997, Hirschman 1971 and 1998).

Lastly, a word about the motivation for having carried out this exercise. José Mauricio Domingues (2009) urges Latin American sociology to confront a theoretical task, going beyond regionally based descriptions and not well defined "critical" positions. In order to do so, he calls upon us to go back to the rich tradition embodied in analysts such as Florestan Fernandes, Pablo González Casanova (2009), and Gino Germani (1962). I read this article while I was rereading various texts written by this generation of authors, searching for the way in which they had conceptualized and investigated the diverse dimensions of social inequalities. My search was to a certain extent genealogical, oriented toward the origin or the roots of current ideas and concepts. I was also guided by the belief/intuition/memory that this generation of thinkers combined public-political worries with scientific rigor in their empirical investigations in a very special and fruitful way. And that it is this tradition that we must reinstate. I therefore find an attractive convergence with Domingues' call. The task was to revisit those who conceived the Latin American region from a historical and structural perspective, recognizing that Latin America is part of Western modernity while at the same time occupying a liminal space, a decentered space, marked by a particular insertion in the global world. Regaining this tradition may be a way to contribute to the processes of emancipation, both present and future, on the subcontinent and on a global scale.

Notes

1   I would like to express my gratitude for the comments received on preliminary versions of this text, presented at the Second Colloquium of Political Sociology, Mar del Plata, March 2012, and at the Colloquium of *desiguALdades.net*, November 2013. I am grateful for Sérgio Costa's and Renata Motta's careful reading and suggestions.
2   During the period, the modernization paradigm was dominant, permeating the thinking of Fernandes and other analysts in the region. In that perspective, the "integration" of blacks was, in the long run, inescapable.
3   Although in English there is a more extended use of the word "black," I choose to use Fernandes' terminology in Portuguese, "Negro," when referring to his work.
4   This chapter concentrates on one of Fernandes' texts: *A integração do negro na sociedade de classes: Volume I: O legado da "raça branca"* (Fernandes 1965a).
5   Up until his death in November 2016, Stavenhagen was very active in the field of indigenous rights, as a United Nations Rapporteur and in human rights institutions in Mexico and elsewhere. While his work covers diverse topics, in this chapter I only analyze the relation between social classes and ethnicity developed in the mentioned book.
6   This debate, however, so central in the formation of a gender perspective, did not penetrate into the "establishment" of the social sciences in the region. It was a theoretical and empirical development that remained in a segregated space, built by women academics and militants who defined themselves as feminists and struggled for women's rights. In the 21st century, and driven by "the care deficit" produced by the changes in the position of women, issues of domesticity and family-based maternal tasks are gaining salience in analytical terms and in the discussion of public policies (Esping-Andersen 1990 and 2009, for social policies in Europe; Razavi 2011, and Razavi and Staab 2007, for international comparative analyses; also Esquivel, Faur, and Jelin 2012).
7   In the 21st century, the topic is presented as the politics of the "conciliation of family and work." What is interesting is that, as Faur (2006) pointed out, policies in that direction are still geared only to women, as if the family-work link is an issue only for women.

References

Bastide, R. and Fernandes, F. (1959): *Brancos e negros em Sao Paulo*. São Paulo: Companhia Editora Nacional.

Bauman, Z. (2011): *Memories of Class. The Pre-History and After-Life of Class*, London: Routledge.

Brubaker, R. (2015): *Grounds for Difference*, Cambridge, MA: Harvard University Press.

126 Elizabeth Jelin

Cardoso, F. H. and Faletto, E. (1969): *Dependencia y desarrollo en América Latina*, Mexico City: Siglo XXI.

Domingues, J. M. (2009): "Global Modernization, Coloniality, and Critical Sociology for Contemporary Latin America," *Theory, Culture and Society*, 26(1): 112–133.

Esquivel, V., Faur, E., and Jelin, E. (2012): *Las lógicas del cuidado infantil. Entre las familias, el Estado y el mercado*, Buenos Aires: IDES-UNFPA-Unicef.

Esping-Andersen, G. (1990): *The Three Worlds of Welfare Capitalism,* Princeton, NJ: Princeton University Press.

Esping-Andersen, G. (2009): *The Incomplete Revolution: Adapting to Women's New Roles*, Cambridge, U.K.: Polity Press.

Faur, E. (2006): "Género y reconciliación familia-trabajo. Legislación laboral y subjetividades masculinas en América Latina," in: Mora, L. and Moreno, M. J. (eds.): *Cohesión social, políticas conciliatorias y presupuesto público. Una mirada desde el género*, Mexico City: UNFPA-GTZ, pp. 129–153.

Fernandes, F. (1965a): *A integração do negro na sociedade de classes: Volume I: O legado da "raça branca,"* São Paulo: Dominus and Edusp.

Fernandes, F. (1965b): *A integração do negro na sociedade de classes. Volume II: No limiar de uma nova era*, São Paulo: Dominus Edusp.

Fernandes, F. (1972): *O negro no mundo dos brancos*, São Paulo: Difel.

Fraser, N. (1997): *Iustitia interrupta. Reflexiones críticas desde la posición 'postsocialista,'* Bogota: Universidad de los Andes and Siglo del Hombre.

Germani, G. (1962): *Política y sociedad en una época de transición. De la sociedad tradicional a la sociedad de masas*, Buenos Aires: Paidós.

González Casanova, P. (2009): "El colonialismo interno (1969)," in: González Casanova, P.: *De la sociología del poder a la sociología de la explotación. Pensar América Latina en el siglo XXI*, Bogota. CLACSO and Siglo XXI, pp. 129–156.

Hirschman, A. O. (1971): *Bias for Hope: Essays on Development and Latin America*, New Haven, CT: Yale University Press.

Hirschman, A. O. (1998): *Crossing Boundaries: Selected Writings*, New York, NY: Zone Books.

Kerner, I. (2012): "Questions of Intersectionality: Reflections on the Current Debate in German Gender Studies," *European Journal of Women's Studies*, 19(2): 203–218.

Korzeniewicz, R. P. and Moran, T. P. (2009): *Unveiling Inequality: A World-Historical Perspective*, New York, NY: The Russell Sage Foundation.

Larguía, I. and Dumoulin, J. (1976): *Hacia una ciencia de la liberación de la Mujer*, Barcelona: Anagrama.

Pérez Sáinz, J. P. (2014): *Mercados y bárbaros. La persistencia de las desigualdades de excedente en América Latina*, San José: Flacso.

Razavi, Shahra (ed.) (2011): "Seen, Heard and Counted: Rethinking Care in a Development Context," *Development and Change (Special Issue)*, 42(4): 1–30, Oxford: Wiley-Blackwell.

Razavi, S. and Staab, S. (2007): *The Political and Social Economy of Care in a Development Context: Conceptual Issues, Research Questions* and *Policy Options.* Geneva: United Nations Research Institute for Social Development, Gender and Development Programme Paper 3.

Roth, J. (2013): *Entangled Inequalities as Intersectionalities: Towards an Epistemic Sensibilization*, Berlin: desiguALdades.net, Working Paper 43.

Saffioti, H. (1969): *A mulher na sociedade de classes: Mito e realidade*, São Paulo: Quatro Artes Universitária.

Scott, J. W. (1996): *Only Paradoxes to Offer: French Feminists and the Rights of Man*, Cambridge, MA: Harvard University Press.

Stavenhagen, R. (1969): *Las clases sociales en las sociedades agrarias*, Mexico City: Siglo XXI.

Thompson, E. P. (1980 [1963]): *The Making of the English Working Class*, Harmondsworth: Penguin.

Thorp, R. (1998): *Progreso, pobreza y exclusión. Una historia económica de América Latina en el siglo XX*, Washington, D.C.: BID/EU.

Tilly, C. (1998): *Durable Inequality*, Berkeley, CA: University of California Press.

Valdés, T. and Gomariz, E. (1995): *Mujeres latinoamericanas en cifras. Tomo comparativo*, Santiago: FLACSO/ Instituto de la Mujer.

7

COMPETING INDIGENEITIES

Being a (hyper)real ecowarrior in twenty-first-century Bolivia

Andrew Canessa

Introduction

When John Cameron's 2009 film, *Avatar*, came out in Bolivia, the president, Evo Morales, immediately declared it one of his favorite films. Even though the film was set on a distant planet, the Na'vi, despite their blue skin colour, pointed ears, and long tails, could immediately be identified by global audiences as indigenous: they had a holistic view of nature and culture, they used bows and arrows, they led simple but happy lives, and they were opposed to a ruthless corporation attempting to plunder their natural resources. It is difficult not to sympathize with the Na'vi in this tale as, indeed, it is difficult not to sympathize with the many groups around the world who are being dispossessed of their lands because they stand in the way of 'development.' Although the issue of who is indigenous is a thorny one, if one were to transpose the Na'vi to the Amazon, few people would have any doubt the people attacking tractors with bows and arrows to save their lands could be anything other than indigenous. It is easy, too, to see why an indigenous president would champion a film that empowers indigenous people in the face of big, foreign corporations.

Indeed, his comments, and the fact that he attended the showing in La Paz with his 15-year-old daughter, were widely reported in the press across Latin America as well as Bolivia, and his face appeared blue and Na'vi-like in cartoons and photo montages in numerous publications (see, for example, *La Nación* of Buenos Aires, 12 January 2010). Scholars, too, picked up the theme and the Bebbingtons (2011) entitled one of their articles "An Andean Avatar."

For example, in an image published by the Spanish newspaper, *El Mundo*, in 2010 there is a mock of a film poster by 'MASfilms' referencing Evo Morales' party, MAS (Movimiento al Socialismo), and the tag states, "If you don't turn

Competing indigeneities **129**

FIGURE 7.1 TIPNIS *Avatar cartoon*.
Source: *La Prensa*, 4 August, 2011.

blue, you won't survive the next five years." Morales had indeed made considerable effort to present his indigenous credentials around the world and had been very successful in using the language of indigeneity to campaign against global warming and the autonomy of Bolivia's energy resources. Identifying with *Avatar* and the Na'vi certainly suited him well. By the end of 2011, however, Evo Morales appears as the hostile power in a conflict with indigenous people in lowland Bolivia. As the cartoon (Figure 7.1) from *La Prensa* suggests, the Na'vi are identified with the residents of TIPNIS, the *Territorio Indígena Parque Nacional Isidoro Securé*. It was Evo Morales' government who was proposing a road through the TIPNIS reserve and what is more striking still is that he was imagined by many protestors as being on the *other* side of the Avatar divide (Laing 2015).

The image presented in Figure 7.2, taken on a TIPNIS march by Anna Laing, has Evo in a tractor bulldozing through the jungle, crushing trees, and about to confront a Na'vi with a bow and arrow. Just behind the cab of the tractor is a flag, a multicoloured *wiphala,* the symbol of the indigenous movement in Bolivia. How can 'the world's first indigenous president' be characterized as being on the wrong side of such an eminently clear indigenous struggle surely worthy of a Hollywood film? How was it that, in the space of just a few months, his depiction moved from being a blue-faced Na'vi to being on the side of multinational corporations and their bulldozers? What, moreover, does this say about the discourses of indigeneity in Bolivia that one's symbolic position can be transformed so completely?

FIGURE 7.2 'Evotar'.

Copyright Anna Laing. Published with permission.

The TIPNIS affair to which the cartoons refer was a moment when some of the contradictions of Bolivia's indigenous imagination suddenly broke open, although the signs had been there for quite some time as Morales' government pursued an economic policy favoring extractivist policies (gas, oil, and lithium) (Bebbington and Bebbington 2011; Farthing 2009) even as it pushed for an ever increasing prominence for indigeneity in national life. TIPNIS is The Isidoro Sécure Indigenous Territory and National Park. In its very title it equates indigenous people literally and figuratively with the preservation and protection of wildlife. The issue at hand, which has been widely discussed, revolved around constructing a road through the park to create a better infrastructure between Bolivia and Brazil (e.g., Canessa 2014; Fabricant and Postero 2015; Laing 2015; Lopez Sanchez 2015; McNeish 2013). The protest against the road pitted TIPNIS residents against indigenous coca growers who wanted the road to open up new areas for cultivation. The broader issue, however, was what the Morales government saw as the interest of the nation and economic development that could help pursue the redistribution policies of his government.[1]

There are, at the very least, two competing senses of what 'indigeneity' is in Bolivia and how the image of the indigenous as protector of the environment can be deployed. Long before the issue of TIPNIS arose, Morales placed indigeneity at the very center of how he expressed the legitimacy of his rule and has, moreover, explicitly created a series of very public rituals to match his rhetoric of having created an indigenous state. His administration introduced a new national constitution giving rights to recognised indigenous communities to manage their own resources and the right to be consulted in areas of development. The coca growers' union frequently argues against coca eradication through a discourse centered on the indigenous nature of the coca leaf. At play here are not only competing notions of what Ramos (1994) termed the 'hyperreal Indian,' a simulacrum of the indigenous that operates politically but bears little reference to real people, but, rather, differing perspectives on what indigeneity means in relation to the state. Also at issue here is the scale on which images of indigeneity are deployed. Indigeneity functions on a global scale whose imagery is easily understood across the globe. Many localized groups engage dynamically with these discourses, often mediated by NGOs, to put pressure on national governments in struggles for territories and rights. In Bolivia, however, it is also the national government that presents itself as indigenous as it lobbies for climate change and resource management. The two scales of deployment of images of indigeneity are sometimes in direct conflict in Bolivia and thus explain why the president can, at the same time, be a blue Na'vi fighting global capitalism and a ruthless bulldozing driver of ruthless 'development.'

It is not, however, simply in the person of the president that these contradictions are played out but in conflicts between different constituencies and different indigenous people. After more than two decades of fieldwork among Aymara-speakers in the highlands, and more recently in the lowlands, I am impressed by the diversity of experience even within this linguistic group where discourses of indigeneity can be certainly empowering but also marginalize those less able to articulate official discourses; and in the case of migrants to the lowlands, indigenous discourses can be used to dispossess other indigenous peoples. Thinking of indigeneity in terms of discourses of the post-colonial dispossessed is simply unhelpful in navigating these tensions and contradictions.

In what follows I will explore the example of Bolivia where discourses of indigeneity have been deployed as central elements of statecraft and governance and examine the apparent paradox of the strong opposition by some indigenous communities to what would appear to be the most pro-indigenous government in the nation's, and quite possibly the continent's, post-Conquest history. First, I will outline how indigeneity has become a tool of statecraft and governance in Bolivia.

Evo Morales and the indigenous state

There can be little doubt that Bolivia is an exemplary case of what has been described as indigenous awakening in Latin America and that Evo Morales' winning of the 2005 presidential election is both a product of this 'indigenous awakening' and a contributory factor in setting social and political conditions for an indigenous identity to be increasingly acceptable (Bengoa 2000; Brysk 2000; Stavenhagen 2002). It is important to note, however, that even though mobilization by indigenous people increased following neoliberal reforms in the 1990s, many of these people mobilizing were not doing so as indigenous people *per se* but, rather, as Bolivian citizens who happened to be indigenous (Postero 2007: 221).

This is an important point because it marks a significant shift in indigenous people being on the margins of the nation-state and, at best, represented by mestizos and creoles to a growing position where they were considered best able to defend the national patrimony. This is another scalar shift important in understanding contemporary indigeneity. This shift was shrewdly manipulated by Evo Morales who, in about 2002, started to adopt an indigenous rhetoric positioning indigenous people as the moral guardians of the nation-state, best able to defend its natural resources. Before 2002 he did not publicly self-identify as indigenous but, rather, as the leader of the coca growers' union.

Within a few years he was the world's most famous indigenous leader and a regular speaker at the United Nations. In 2009 he successfully lobbied the UN to declare 22 April 'International Mother Earth Day,' explicitly arguing that the world should show the same respect for the Earth as Andean peoples do for the Pachamama, an earth deity. In September of the same year he was awarded a medal and scroll naming him 'Global Defender of Mother Earth.' In October of 2015 it was Morales himself who, at the World People's Conference on Climate Change and Defense of Life, presented an award to renowned US indigenous activist Leonard Peltier as 'Defender of Indigenous Peoples and Mother Earth,' maintaining his position as global indigenous leader (Native News Online 2015). In September 2015 he successfully lobbied the UN to adopt the Inca precepts of "do not lie; do not steal; and do not be lazy" as a guiding ethos for its bureaucracy. In fact, this slogan is now also enshrined in the Bolivian Constitution and translated into several indigenous languages. Here, as elsewhere, indigeneity becomes decontextualized from its cultural roots and becomes explicitly global. This is also nothing challenging about this Inca moral code; in fact, it is difficult to imagine *any* culture whose moral framework condones people lying, stealing, or being lazy. Indigeneity thus becomes a global commodity accessible to all. This is Evo Morales as Na'vi warrior *par excellence*.

Morales has certainly been a master at deploying indigenous rhetoric on the global stage but in what ways is it meaningful to think of his having transformed Bolivia into an indigenous state? It is constitutionally a multicultural and plurinational state, but the new constitution privileges certain indigenous citizens over others, in particular the kind of citizen described in the constitution as "originary peasant indigenous." Even more importantly, over the course of his tenure, Morales has been developing a rather more homogenous vision of what indigeneity in Bolivia means and indigeneity has been at the center of his statecraft from the day he took office.

Evo Morales immediately marked the indigenous credentials of his administration when he downplayed the constitutional inauguration ceremony for an indigenous ceremony in the country's premier archaeological site, Tiwanaku. Morales made explicit that his legitimacy derived from the authority of the indigenous people and cultures he represented. In his speech he condemned the "colonial State which permitted the permanent sacking of natural resources from this noble earth, a colonial disciplining State, a colonial State which has always seen us, the indigenous people of the world, as savages, as animals." And so, among his first moves he abolished the Department of Indigenous Affairs because from now on *all* national affairs were indigenous. But in Tiwanaku he also directed his rhetoric against a world capitalist system and raised the banner of struggle in defence of the earth and humanity against capitalism and outlined his ideas of 'living well' or 'vivir bien' in which communitarian, indigenous values were raised above the capitalist imperative of extraction and growth. In Tiwanaku he outlined the values of 'vivir bien' as follows:

> To live well means to live in harmony with everyone and everything, between humans and our Mother Earth; and it consequently implies working for the dignity of all. And nowadays it is more important than ever to know how to share, to know how to distribute wealth equitably. What belongs to the people is for the people. To democratise the economy. That is why we nationalise natural resources: in order that these resources return to the Bolivian people.

In fact, the promotion of 'vivir bien' is presented as a state responsibility in Article 8 of the constitution.

Evo has returned to Tiwanaku many times to renew his mandate and to celebrate the 'Aymara New Year,' the winter solstice on 21 June. This celebration, which dates from the late 1980s, has now spread to many communities. Most recently, as the work of Anne Ebert (2015) has shown, the Morales administration dispatches ministers of state to all department capitals in order to celebrate the solstice—the *indigenous* New Year—and so this Andean invented tradition is nationalized and celebrated as part of statecraft in departments and provinces far from the mountains where it originated. This is not simply an andeanization of the state or indigenous culture but surely an attempt to create a new national culture based on indigenous principles. It is somewhat reminiscent of the nation-building movement of many Latin American states, starting with Mexico after the Revolution, which attempted to create a new national culture based on mestizo people, culture, and values. In this case the nation is imagined as indigenous.

If much of the politics of indigeneity is about difference and recognizing the cultural and other rights of minority groups, Evo Morales' government is asserting a very different vision of indigeneity: a homogeneous national culture for the majority. The politics of the 1990s seemed to be about a celebration of diversity and the multiplicity of indigenous cultures, to wit: the formation of a plurinational and multicultural state. Evo Morales seems to be returning to a much older pattern of ethnic relations in which indigenous people are believed to occupy a structurally distinct position, be it as the defeated in conquest, a fiscal category, a racial group, or a social class. Seen from this historical perspective, Morales appears to be trying to create a new kind of relationship between indigenous people and the state. A state where the indigenous is privileged rather than disadvantaged (cf. Blackburn 2009), to be sure, but nevertheless he inherits a long tradition of seeing indigenous people as essentially a homogeneous category; one where they share a political positioning but, it seems, also a set of traditions and beliefs.

Indigenous citizenship

In my own ethnographic research in highland Bolivia in the province of Larecaja I recall Aymara-speaking merchants, children of rural peasants, comment that the rural indigenous people "did not have citizenship" and, in turn, the rural indigenous people agreed: they felt discriminated against by police and judges for being 'Indians' and did not even participate in the national Independence Day celebrations, deeming these of interest only to whites and mestizos. As one Aymara-speaking friend told me, "That time of the 6th of August was when the whites and mestizos made the government of Bolivia appear. Since then the 6th of August has existed." There is no question that across Bolivia people have been empowered by Morales' election night cry "Now we are *all* Presidents!" and what this implied for indigenous Bolivians (cf. Grisaffi 2013).

In Bolivia, moreover, the language of political indigeneity has been clearly used by various groups as an explicit critique of neoliberal globalization (Canessa 2007; Sieder 2002; Van Cott 2002; Postero and Zamosc 2004; Yashar 1998), but it has also been used to argue for a new relationship with the nation-state as well (Postero 2007: 17); that is, a new sense of citizenship and entitlement. This citizenship, however, is clearly not evenly distributed in Bolivia given that some groups are able to mobilize more effectively than others (Escobar 2010; Gustafson 2009). Most celebrated are the coca growers (Grisaffi 2010) who were able to articulate a 'lite' (2010: 433) version of indigeneity that focused on relations with the state rooted in the coca leaf as a metonym for a broader set of colonial and postcolonial injustices. Nicole Fabricant's work with landless peasants in the eastern lowlands (2012) offers a comparable analysis of mobilized groups who use land as an indigenous trope of political engagement. In these two latter cases, these social movements have not only forged new relationships with the state but have become close allies of the state. Not all groups have such privileged access, however.

Current tensions in Bolivia are often seen in simple terms between highlanders and lowlanders but, in fact, the real tension is between what we might call territorialized indigenous groups—be they in the highlands or the lowlands—and deterritorialized groups, some of whom are colonists but many others live in cities. For the former, indigeneity is a discourse relating more closely to autonomy over land, whereas for the latter it is much more about a national identity that includes them at the center and, moreover, where the nation's resources are to be exploited for their benefit in particular and who "maintained a claim to indigeneity despite their reterritorialisation in new geohistorical spaces" (Garcés 2011: 51–52). This is yet another scalar issue that determines indigenous consciousness: a distinction between those who claim indigeneity as Bolivian citizens descended from pre-Columbian peoples, and those who claim indigeneity in terms of a particular *subnational* territory for which they are seeking a certain autonomy from the state. The distinction is crucial because the former claim indigeneity wherever they move in the national territory whereas the latter claim indigeneity in terms of a much smaller territory.

Differentiated indigenous citizens

The contemporary Bolivian state explicitly celebrates diversity by recognizing the pluricultural nature of the state and in, for example, translating 'vivir bien' in various indigenous languages for the constitution. In practice, however, the state is much more keen on celebrating highland values than lowland ones. On a more concrete level, the state supports or even actively encourages the colonization of lowland areas by highlanders.

The collapse of mining in the 1980s generated a massive population movement from the highlands to the lowlands. Some of this movement was to the traditional coca-growing areas of the *yungas*, but a very large number of migrants went from the highlands to areas such as the Chapare region and began cultivating coca leaf. It is in the Chapare that Evo Morales has his political base, and it is here that his political vision was forged. The communities of the Chapare are not the kinds of historically territorialized communities one sees in the highlands as well as the lowlands with a long history of settlement and complex rituals that bind people together but, rather, a set of new communities focusing on an economic activity, which, for decades, has been subject to military, including US military, intervention. Unlike other Aymara and Quechua peasants the coca growers from this and other regions are engaged in cash crop monoculture; they make money, and these areas continue to attract temporary or permanent migrants in search of a better living.

Coca growers are thus one of several groups of people—landless peasants, urban people, highland colonists to the lowlands—who come from 'traditional' indigenous communities and have an historical consciousness of racism and injustice but who nevertheless do not identify closely with the ways of life and cultural values of their communities of origin. In earlier times such economically dynamic people would have been on their way to becoming mestizos and accepting the values of dominant mestizo-creole society. That model of assimilation, however, is largely defunct and what we find are large numbers of people who see themselves neither as mestizos nor as *jaqi* or *runa*, the Aymara and Quechua words for people who follow a particular traditional lifestyle. In urban areas the new rising middle classes are increasingly less likely to identify as mestizo, but will choose to identify as indigenous or *chola* even if their lifestyles would seem to be more consonant with urban middle classes. In Miriam Shakow's recent (2014) book she shows quite clearly that people rising from the rural indigenous peasantry into the professional middle classes are deeply ambivalent about their indigenous identity but what is clear is that they do not identify with the white dominant classes. A situation in which upwardly mobile Bolivians do identify as indigenous is when they are drawing on their backgrounds to legitimize their political aspirations, especially if they are involved with the MAS party. Alessandra Pelligrini's (2016) work with coca growers states this position even more clearly: Aymara-speaking, coca-growing peasants see indigeneity explicitly as a MAS discourse and will look down at their highland cousins who are more traditionally indigenous in their eyes. What is notable here is that Pelligrini's coca growers often earn more than doctors in La Paz but

136 Andrew Canessa

nevertheless eschew any identification with the white or mestizo middle class. For them indigeneity is principally about securing economic and political rights and not at all a matter of cultural identity.

Urban people, coca growers, and highland colonists to the lowlands form a *majority* of those people identified as indigenous in the 2001 census. In fact, it is quite possible that such people constitute an absolute majority of the Bolivian population. It should not be surprising then that the dominant mode of indigeneity in Bolivia today is one that speaks to a dynamic population engaged in market activities seeking economic growth, rather than one that seeks to sacrifice economic growth in favor of 'vivir bien.'[2]

This leads us to a fundamental contradiction in Bolivia's politics of indigeneity wherein the government argues for the rights of indigenous people and the protection of the environment, whereby 'living well' is prioritized over economic growth and Morales is declared 'World Hero of Mother Earth,' even as it pursues an aggressive policy of favoring resource extraction (Bebbington and Humphreys Bebbington 2011; Farthing 2009; Gudynas 2011; Ströbele-Gregor 2012) and monocrop agriculture in the form of coca.

The first point addresses the concerns of small indigenous groups who need protection from agribusinesses and extractive industries. The second is for a development of these industries in favor of the small capitalist farmers and the urban poor. The issue is not so much whether or even what kind of economic development there should be but, rather, who should control it and how the resources will be distributed.

The constitutional insistence that indigenous people have control over their recognized territories and may choose to refuse exploitation on their lands conflicts with the perceived need for economic growth based on extractive industries and intensive agriculture.

Indigenous colonists

The globalized concept explicitly presents indigenous people as being subjects of colonization, and many scholars have argued for a productive engagement with concepts of indigeneity precisely because it is a means through which relatively powerless people can make justice claims. Justice and powerlessness are, however, relative concepts, and there is a danger in assuming that indigenous people are always and everywhere in the right or even that they are the colonized, never the colonizers.

The history of Bolivia can easily be described as the history of the oppression of the descendants of pre-European populations in the service of white-dominated agribusiness and mining. There can be surely no issue in celebrating the removal of power from the white elite by a government that represents the indigenous majority. This is, however, a grossly oversimplified reading of history. There is a serious problem when the concept of indigeneity obscures internal differentiation and, to take a specific Bolivian point, when highland peasants arrive as indigenous citizens to occupy land that is unused or underused in the relatively sparsely populated eastern lowlands—unused, that is, from the perspective of the colonists, but not exactly unused from the perspective of the equally indigenous people who live there. There is a serious problem in always assuming "the shared burden and the equality of indigenous groups" (Pelican 2009: 61; cf. Kenrick and Lewis 2004), that is, the view of indigenous people as always being in the position of the Na'vi in Cameron's film.

On a visit to the lowland town of Rurrenabaque, I spoke to many Aymara and Quechua migrants who had arrived mostly since the opening of the road to the capital in the 1980s that opened the area up for settlement. Today Rurrenabaque is dominated by Aymara and Quechua shopkeepers, and Aymara shopkeeper Rubén told me what it was like:

> I have been here for twenty years. When I first came there was nothing, nothing: just one road and no electricity. It was quiet then, simple, you know. Now it is busy; I liked it more then … These people, you know, didn't know how to do anything. We [the migrants] have made Rurrenabaque what it is today. The people here don't know how to work, we have civilized this place.

The idea that Aymara and Quechua migrants civilized the lowlands is a fairly consistent theme across the region.

Another trader, Marcelino, gave me another, fairly typical account but adds an important gender element:

> Oh yes, I have a wife. She is in Santa Cruz but I also have a wife here, a young girl. She is 22 [Marcelino is 45]. I have a child with her. The people here are very simple. Before I came twenty years ago there was nothing here. We have brought civilization. They don't understand. In those days they would just give you a woman for twenty pesos. [Laughter]. It is very easy to take a woman here.

The juxtaposition of colonization and the 'taking' of indigenous women is not coincidental; it is and has been, in fact, both an image and a practice of conquest since the arrival of the Spanish (Canessa 2012b). The difference here is that it is an Aymara who is invoking this kind of relationship, inserting himself into a colonial relationship as colonizer rather than colonized. As we will see below, the president himself is by no means immune from this kind of language. It is not, however, simply a matter of language since marrying into an indigenous community will give access to land rights as well.[3]

The argument of being indigenous, and thus having a right to settle in whatever indigenous territory one chooses, highlights the necessity for a legal or even conceptual distinction between indigenous groups. This example also demonstrates how certain indigenous groups are perceived—whether from the inside or the outside—to have more legitimacy and power than other groups. Thus, in overlooking

138 Andrew Canessa

fundamental differences between indigenous groups, the state is not only failing to recognize the *hierarchy* of power between indigenous cultures but, in fact, is actually exacerbating it: "recognition by power can, and increasingly does, involve as many problems as the neglect and marginalisation that comes from an absence of state interest" (Dombrowski 2002: 1,071).

It also points, once again, to a scalar issue when considering indigenous issues and identity. Clearly, in some contexts, highlanders adopt the view that they are indigenous wherever they may be in the country and they, as indigenous people, have the right to occupy and cultivate land when they consider it unoccupied. The idea that lowland indigenous people are sitting on vast tracts of unproductive land is shared by president and *colonos* alike, and both show little patience for the views of lowlanders.

The TIPNIS case

The continuing TIPNIS case, with which I opened this chapter, has exposed tensions within the government and it has positively impaled itself on its own contradictions. The remarkable thing, perhaps, is that it took so long for these tensions to emerge.

The road is part of a continental-wide infrastructural investment by Brazil, with the latter providing almost all of the funding for the road. From a more local perspective, the road is important because it connects the Chapare, the coca-growing area, with Brazil without having to go through Santa Cruz, which is the prime locus of opposition to Evo Morales. The road through TIPNIS will also open the area for further colonization by coca growers from the Chapare and, despite the protests, at the time of writing (May 2016), the Morales government is insisting that the road will be built (although no timetable has been set). This colonization is illegal but the state is already unable or unwilling to stop it. There is no question that local people understand that intensive colonization will be the first major consequence of the road. It is not surprising then that the coca growers are fully in support.

As a way of evading the bad publicity in 2011, Morales suggested a wider consultation, including people from outside TIPNIS such as the Chapare. Morales appeared to think he *had* consulted with indigenous people, just not those living in TIPNIS. His government, in any case, represented the majority of indigenous people in the country, and it appears that his political miscalculation rests on his confusion of the place indigenous citizens have in the state he leads and the constitutional right of small groups to resist the state even though legitimized by the support of an indigenous majority.

What is interesting, too, is that in August of that year he echoed the vision of colonization expressed by Marcelino in Rurrenabaque when he was reported as asking (*La Razón*, 1 August 2011) the residents of the Chapare to convince the indigenous people of TIPNIS to give the green light to the construction: "You, compañeras and compañeros, need to explain, to guide the indigenous compañeros.

Their own mayor is moving to convince them not to oppose [the road]." Later he added: "If I had time I would go and seduce (conquistar) the Yuracaré compañeras and convince them not to oppose. That is, young men, you have instructions from the president to seduce the Yuracaré women so that they won't oppose the building of the road." He immediately consulted the residents: "Approved?" and applause was heard from the assembled. The comment is particularly pointed because women were so prominent in the marches from TIPNIS. Often carrying their children, women from TIPNIS frequently were at the head of the march in an effort to defuse violence from the police (Actenberg 2012).

Conclusions: who is blue?

Since the first years of this century and before the election of Morales in 2005 indigeneity offered a new political language in Bolivia. It is not surprising that the *Avatar* film was immediately seized on by a range of groups as well as the president himself. After all, this international blockbuster articulated very well the idea of a globalized notion of indigeneity that pitted 'traditional' people against ruthless multinationals. Indigeneity has become a political discourse at least as much as, in many cases perhaps more than, a personal identity. The result of its wide currency is that people on opposite sides of a conflict may equally claim its mantle.

Much of the recent debate in Bolivia has divided the country into highlands dominated by Aymara and Quechua peasants, the 'natural' supporters of Evo Morales, and lowlands dominated by a white landowning class and including a large number of small, diverse, and marginalized indigenous peoples (but see Perreault and Green 2013). National political divisions often do run along these lines but such a schema obscures important differences. Many highland groups are also excluded from national indigeneity in similar ways to lowland peasants.

Highland communities, such as that of Wila Kjarka where I have conducted fieldwork since 1989, also exhibit ambivalence toward the new indigenous state. Although enthusiastic supporters of the Morales government, they are bemused by some elements of its statecraft. It is other people, many of them mestizos, who are best positioned to invoke the abstract symbolization of earth deities and indigeneity in the broad ecumenical sense and are most able to extract resources from the state. I was very surprised recently to hear a mestizo peasant from a community well known for its historical antipathy toward indigenous people describe himself to me as an Aymara, as I was to witness the enthusiasm of creoles and mestizos for celebrating the Aymara New Year. The Aymara peasants surrounding the town of Sorata in the province of Larecaja do not celebrate the Aymara New Year, and are puzzled by some of the descriptions of the Pachamama as the national symbol of struggle for natural resources and are perplexed when a national politician such as the radical indigenous leader, Felipe Quispe, described natural gas as her fart (interview with author). It cannot be assumed that even in the highlands those who are most rooted in traditional rural ways of life will be the most comfortable with national indigeneity much less the globalized hyperreal image

140 Andrew Canessa

of the indigenous ecowarrior. In fact, it speaks most clearly to a very different constituency; although the rural indigenous people I know have a very intimate relationship with the animate landscape, they are not 'ecological' in the Western sense and are quite happy throwing alkaline batteries and other rubbish into for, example, maize fields.

Discourses of indigeneity have as much potential to create hierarchy as to dismantle it and the empowerment of some indigenous people may entail the disempowerment of others. The paradox of why lowland and other indigenous people are often opposed to the government of the first indigenous president and why he appears to have such little patience for them can be immediately resolved by exploring the diversity of indigenous voices and the different claims they are making. The *Avatar* images of indigeneity and the essentializing characterizations behind them are too easily deployed by a range of actors to offer any clues to what is really going on. Distracting, too, are the common attempts to reduce interethnic conflict in Bolivia to one between highlanders and lowlanders as if these issues could be reduced to the realms of 'culture' and identity. To understand conflict in places such as Bolivia today we need to put aside globalized discourses and the 'hyperreal Indian' and look at the demands people are making on each other and, most importantly, on the state.

In Bolivia today there are, broadly speaking, two indigenous discourses, or two claims on indigenous positionality. One sees indigenous people and values as the foundation of the nation-state and seeks to create an ecumenical indigeneity for a majority of Bolivia's citizens (and perhaps even the world's). The people who most easily embrace this form of indigeneity are deterritorialized citizens who may very well have pre-Columbian ancestors but do not live in indigenous communities *per se*. The other seeks to respect cultural difference in its multiple forms and protection of marginal peoples *from* the state. The people who most clearly embrace this model of indigeneity have territorialized identities and are members of communities with a distinct culture that is reproduced on a daily basis. The two discourses are fundamentally opposed, and sometimes in direct conflict, even as they all claim to be indigenous.

Notes

1   Morales' regime is widely credited with sharply reducing poverty in Bolivia, especially rural poverty, principally through cash payments, *bonos*, to elderly people and children, but also through infrastructure projects that, among other things, have improved rural people's access to electricity and roads.

2   In the 2012 census the number of people identifying as indigenous dropped considerably to 40.3%. The reasons for this dramatic drop are almost certainly to do with the way the questions were formulated and the debate about the lack of inclusion of any *mestizo* category, but it may also have to do with the waning hold of Evo Morales on the imagination of Bolivians and fallout of the TIPNIS case, which was raging in the very year the census was taken.

3   Whereas in the past having a non-indigenous father gave certain advantages now the opposite is often the case since it is through the indigenous mother that one can gain

access to territorial rights. In many cases the same people remain in power (López 2014) but instead of legitimizing their positions through their fathers or grandfathers they do so through their mothers.

Bibliography

Achtenberg, E. (2012): "Women in the frontlines of TIPNIS conflict," *NACLA*, 17 August. Accessed from https://nacla.org/blog/2012/8/17/women-forefront-bolivia's-tipnis-conflict. Accessed on 3 March 2016.

Bebbington, A. and Humphreys Bebbington, D. (2011): "An Andean avatar: post-neoliberal and neoliberal strategies for securing the unobtainable," *New Political Economy*, 15(4): 131–145.

Bengoa, J. (2000): *La emergencia indígena en América Latina*, Mexico City: Fondo de Cultura Económica.

Blackburn, C. (2009): "Differentiating indigenous citizenship: seeking multiplicity in rights, identity, and sovereignty in Canada," *American Ethnologist*, 36(1): 66–78.

Brysk, A. (2000): *From Tribal Village to Global Village: Indian Rights and International Relations in Latin America*, Stanford, CA: Stanford University Press.

Canessa, A. (2007): "Who is indigenous? Self-identification, indigeneity, and claims to justice in contemporary Bolivia," *Urban Anthropology*, 36(3): 14–48.

Canessa, A. (2012a): "New indigenous citizenship in 21st century Bolivia: challenging the liberal model of the state and its subjects," *Latin America and the Caribbean Ethnic Studies*, 7(2): 201–221.

Canessa, A. (2012b): *Intimate Indigeneities: Exploring Race, Sex and History in the Small Places of Andean Life*, Durham, NC: Duke University Press.

Canessa, A. (2014) "Conflict, claim and contradiction in the new 'indigenous' state of Bolivia," *Critique of Anthropology*, 34(2): 151–171.

Dombrowski, K. (2002): "The praxis of indigenism and Alaska native timber policies," *American Anthropologist*, 104(4):1,062–1,073

Ebert, A. (2015): "Reconfiguraciones de 'lo indígena' en Bolivia en el ejemplo de la celebración del Año Nuevo Aymara en Tiwanaku (1980 a 2010)," in: Köhler, R. and Ebert, A. (eds.): *La agencia de lo indígena en la larga era de globalización: Microperspectivas de su constitución y representación desde la época colonial temprana hasta el presente*, Berlin: Gebrüder Mann Verlag, pp. 121–145.

El Mundo (2010): "Evo Morales, el fan de Avatar," 28 January. Accessed from http://www.elmundo.es/america/blogs/nuestra-america-2/2010/01/28/evo-morales-el-fan-de-avatar.html. Accessed on 3 March 2016.

Escobar, A. (2010): "Latin America at a crossroads: alternative modernizations, post-liberalism, or post-development?" *Cultural Studies*, 24(1): 1–65

Fabricant, N. (2012): *Mobilizing Bolivia's Displaced: Indigenous Politics and the Struggle over Land*, Chapel Hill, NC: University of North Carolina Press.

Fabricant, N. and Postero, N. (2015): "Sacrificing indigenous bodies and lands: the political-economic history of lowland Bolivia in light of the recent TIPNIS debate," *Journal of Latin American and Caribbean Anthropology*, 20(3): 452–274.

Farthing, L. (2009): "Bolivia's dilemma: development confronts the legacy of extraction," *NACLA Report on the Americas*, 42(5): 25–29.

Garcés, F. (2011): "The domestication of indigenous autonomies in Bolivia," in: Fabricant, N. and Gustafson, B. (eds.): *Remapping Bolivia: Resources, Territory, and Indigeneity in a Plurinational State*, Santa Fe: SAR Press, pp. 46–67.

Grisaffi, T. (2010): "'We are Originarios ...we just aren't from here': Coca leaf and identity politics in the Chapare, Bolivia," *Bulletin of Latin American Research*, 29(4): 425–439.

Grisati, T. (2013): "'All of us are Presidents': radical democracy and citizenship in the Chapare Province, Bolivia," *Critique of Anthropology*, 33(1): 47–65.

Gudynas, E. (2011): "Sentidos oposiciones y ámbitos de las transciciones al postextractivismo," in: Lang, M. and Mokrani, D. (eds.): *Más allá del desarrollo*, La Paz: Grupo Permanente de Trabajo sobre Alternativas al Desarrollo, Fund. Rosa Luxemburg/Abya Ayala.

Gustafson, B. (2009): "Manipulating cartographies: plurinationalism, autonomy, and indigenous resurgence in Bolivia," *Anthropological Quarterly*, 82: 985–1016.

Instituto Nacional de Estadísticas de Bolívia/UMPA (2003): *Bolivia: características sociodemográficas de la población*, La Paz: INE.

Kenrick, J. and Lewis, J. (2004): "'Indigenous peoples' rights and the politics of the term 'indigenous,'" *Anthropology Today*, 20(2): 4–9.

La Nación (2010): "Evo Morales afirmó que se identifica con la película Avatar," 12 January. Accessed from http://www.lanacion.com.ar/1221148-evo-morales-afirmo-que-se-identifica-con-la-pelicula-avatar. Accessed on 3 March 2016.

Laing, A. (2015): "Resource sovereignties in Bolivia: re-conceptualising the relationship between indigenous identities and the environment during the TIPNIS conflict," *Bulletin of Latin American Research*, 34(2): 149–166.

López Pila, E. (2014): "Constructions of Tacana indigeneity: regionalism, race, and indigenous politics in Amazonian Bolivia," Unpublished Ph.D. thesis, University of Sussex.

McNeish, A. (2013): "Extraction, protest and indigeneity in Bolivia: the TIPNIS effect," *Latin American and Caribbean Ethnic Studies*, 8(2): 221–242.

Native News Online (2015): "Bolivian President Evo Morales acknowledges Leonard Peltier as 'defender of his people and mother earth' calls for his freedom," 13 October. Accessed from http://nativenewsonline.net/currents/bolivian-president-evo-morales-acknowledges-leonard-peltier-as-defender-of-his-people-mother-earth-calls-for-his-freedom/. Accessed on 1 June 2016.

Pelican, M. (2009): "Complexities of autochthony and indigeneity: an African example," *American Ethnologist*, 36(1): 52–65.

Pelligrini, A. (2016): *Beyond Indigeneity: Coca Growing and the Emergence of a New Middle Class in Bolivia*, Tucson, AZ: University of Arizona Press.

Perreault, T. and Green, B. (2013) "Reworking the spaces of indigeneity: the Bolivian ayllu and lowland autonomy movements compared," *Environment and Planning D: Society and Space*, 31: 43–60.

Postero, N. (2007): *Now We Are Citizens: Indigenous Politics in Postmulticultural Bolivia*, Stanford, CA: Stanford University Press.

Postero, N. and Zamosc, L. (2004): *The Struggle for Indigenous Rights in Latin America*, Brighton: Sussex Academic Press.

Ramos, A. (1994): "The hyperreal Indian," *Critique of Anthropology*, 14: 153–171.

Sanchez Lopez, D. (2015): "Reshaping notions of citizenship: the TIPNIS indigenous movement in Bolivia," *Development Studies Research*, 2(1): 20–32.

Sieder, R. (2002): "Introduction," in: Sieder, R. (ed.): *Multiculturalism in Latin America: Indigenous Rights, Diversity and Democracy*, Basingstoke: Palgrave MacMillan.

Shakow, M. (2014): *Along the Bolivian Highway: Social Mobility and Political Culture in a New Middle Class*, Philadelphia, PA: University of Pennsylvania Press.

Stavenhagen, R. (2002): "Indigenous peoples and the state in Latin America: an ongoing debate," in Sieder, R. (ed.): *Multiculturalism in Latin America: Indigenous Rights, Diversity and Democracy*, Basingstoke: Palgrave MacMillan, pp. 24–44.

Ströbele-Gregor, J. (2012): *Litio en Bolivia. El plan gubernamental de producción e industrialización del litio, escenarios de conflictos sociales y ecológicos, y dimensiones de desigualdad social*, Berlin: desiguALdades.net, Working Paper 14.

Van Cott, D. L. (2002): "Constitutional reform in the Andes: redefining indigenous-state relations," in: Sieder. R. (ed.): *Multiculturalism in Latin America: Indigenous Rights, Diversity and Democracy*, Basingstoke: Pallgrave MacMillan, pp. 45–73.

Yashar, D. (1998): "Contesting citizenship: indigenous movements and democracy in Latin America," *Comparative Politics*, 31(1): 23–42.

8

THE SYMBOLIC CONSTRUCTION OF INEQUALITIES[1]

Luis Reygadas

Thomas Piketty says that one of the major results of his book about capital in the twenty-first century is that "the history of inequality is shaped by the way economic, social, and political actors view what is just and what is not, as well as by the relative power of those actors and the collective choices that result" (Piketty 2014: 21). The distribution of goods and services never follows a culturally neutral, "rational" logic, nor does it adjust itself to the functioning of a perfect market, but rather passes through cultural filters that affect the amount of wealth received by each individual and each group. As anthropologist Marshall Sahlins stated, the material appropriation of nature is accompanied by its symbolic appropriation (Sahlins 1988). In Pierre Bourdieu's words:

> The struggles for the appropriation of economic and cultural resources are invariably symbolic struggles for the appropriation of those distinctive signs that are classed or classing resources, *or for the conservation or the subversion of principles of classing of those distinctive properties.*
>
> *(Bourdieu 1988: 247, emphasis in the original)*

Social inequality is not only the outcome of the asymmetrical distribution of advantages and disadvantages in a society; it also expresses the state of culturally mediated power relations.

How do symbols shape inequalities? This chapter explores how inequalities are produced, re-produced, and contested through symbolic processes. I identify five symbolic processes that are key for the generation of inequalities and therefore could also be fundamental in efforts to reduce social asymmetries. These processes are: (1) classification, categorization, and creation of boundaries; (2) valuation, de-valuation, and re-valuation; (3) relations between differences and inequalities; (4) production, acquisition, and distribution of symbolic capital; and (5) struggles

The symbolic construction of inequalities **145**

over the legitimacy of inequalities. In each process, it is possible to find strategies oriented to increase disparities and strategies aimed to contest inequalities as well.

1 Classification, categorization, and creation of boundaries

Among the most important symbolic devices that shape social inequalities, we should foreground the processes of classification, categorization, and creation of boundaries between categories. They are crucial in defining groups, and they are the basis on which many symbolic processes work.

By way of symbols, societies establish limits that define groups. The act of ordering, grouping, and separating objects, animals, plants, people, and institutions marks out differences, limits, and boundaries between them; defines hierarchies; and includes or excludes. Therefore, by classifying things in the world, relationships of inferiority/superiority and exclusion/inclusion are established between them in direct connection with the social order (Durkheim and Mauss 1996: 30 [1903]). Who is in and who is out? Where are the boundaries placed?

On the side of the construction of inequalities, a fundamental strategy is classification of people in categories or groups, ordered in a hierarchic way. Charles Tilly's work about durable inequalities (1998) clearly shows this strategy. What he names categorical inequality comes from the distinction of different socially defined categories of people. These categories are produced culturally, around certain biological or social characteristics. The institutionalization of categories and of the systems of social closure, exclusion, and control that are created according to those categories are what make inequality last. The creation of paired categories establishes boundaries between groups, creates stigmas, and attributes qualities to the actors on each side of the boundaries (Tilly 1998: 66–71).

Boundaries can separate an organization's internal categories (such as those that divide management from workers or doctors from nurses), or they can distinguish external categories, common to an entire society (male/female, black/white). When the internal and external categories coincide, inequality is reinforced (Tilly 1998: 77–79). The use of delimited categories causes persistent inequality by connecting itself with the mechanisms of exploitation and opportunity hoarding. Categorical inequality has cumulative effects. In the long run, it affects individual capacities. Lasting structures of asymmetric resource distribution are created along category lines.

The separation between the groups must also be conserved, which is why the devices that establish limits and maintain social distances also come into play. Thus, the work of re-producing symbolic and emotional barriers produces situations of inclusion-exclusion and maintains material, economic, and political limits that separate groups (Elias 2006; Lamont and Fournier 1992). On the basis of that separation, social closures, glass ceilings, and many other ways of inclusion and exclusion can be created.

Through symbols, human beings not only establish differences and boundaries in a continuous reality, they also do the opposite. They confirm continuities and affinities in realities that would otherwise be discontinuous, fragmented, and

146 Luis Reygadas

unequal. So, we can distinguish a strategy that heads toward equality, by means of re-classification and border transgression. There are symbolic actions that dissolve, relativize, or suspend the differences between social actors, creating among them feelings and notions of equality, solidarity, friendship, and belonging in a community. Leveling and egalitarian myths and narratives work in this way, whether they are religious, political, social, or philosophical in nature. The groups that are at a disadvantage can criticize hegemonic categories, propose alternative classifications, create more inclusive categories, or trespass and ridicule the categories and borders that separate them. The categories should not be seen as something static, but as historical classification and re-classification processes where different agents clash and where the boundaries among groups are continuously redefined.

Just as many symbolic tools generate, reproduce, and reinforce inequalities, there are many others that limit or question them and that are fundamental in the construction of equity. On one hand, there are discourses (and practices) about gifts and reciprocity, which reveal the existence of social mechanisms of equalization, compensation, and redistribution. On the other hand, there are symbolic elements of everyday resistance to inequality and utopias in which social asymmetries are questioned or inverted. Many human interactions are evaluated in terms of a code of reciprocity; the agents involved in them believe that they should be reciprocal. Many inequalities are able to legitimate themselves when they are seen as the result of a pact in which there is mutuality, in contrast to those that are considered illegitimate and the fruit of some imposition. The persistency of reciprocity in social interaction and in the discourses about it (everyday and academic) is related to the strength of the egalitarian narrative, a narrative that stands on a symbolic fabric as dense as the one that sustains the mechanisms of distinction.

There are innumerable lower-class expressions in which the use of irony serves to criticize inequality and to question the symbolic classifications that sustain it. Popular cultures are full of utopian dreaming, mockery and satire of the rich and powerful, rebellious dramatizations, allegorical protests, imaginary figures that reject or invert domination, fantasies, and legends that, taken together, play an important role in breaking down the boundaries of inequality (Comaroff 1985; Gledhill 2000; Keesing 1992; Taussig 1980).

Faced with the boundary work that puts up barriers of inclusion for a few and exclusion for many, there is opposing work that undermines those walls, challenges established classifications, transgresses limits, and criticizes hierarchies and privileges: "Traces of rebellion against authority everywhere creep into the ritual that envelopes the mighty" (Kertzer 1988: 55). Georges Balandier (1994) has described popular mythical figures that utilize symbolic resources to alter, confound, or invert the established order. Through mockery, parody, ridicule, rule-breaking, limit-transgression, and symbolic inversion, disorder flourishes and the fissures, ambiguities, and contradictions of social stratification come to light (Balandier 1994).

Equality and difference are two sides of the same coin, but they are two opposing sides that express tendencies and countertendencies that pervade human groups. Victor Turner presented this confrontation in a suggestive way by referring to the

The symbolic construction of inequalities **147**

TABLE 8.1 Processes of classification, categorization, and creation of boundaries

Symbolic strategies in the construction of inequalities	Symbolic strategies in the deconstruction of inequalities
Classification, categorization, and boundary work	**Reclassification and boundary trespassing**
Classification, ordering, and grouping	Deconstruction of hegemonic categories
Paired categories	Alternative classifications
Creation of boundaries and limits between categories	Inclusive categories, bridging categories
Borders (material, legal, symbolic, visible, invisible, emotional)	Egalitarian utopias and communitarian narratives
Social closures	Ceremonial exchanges, gifts as total social facts
Glass ceilings	Liminality and ritual creation of *communitas*
	Temporal dissolution of boundaries
	Transgression, ridicule, and parody (of categories and boundaries)

Source: The author's own elaboration.

potential that rituals have to create a *communitas*. For him, in the liminal phase of ritual, the differences between the participants temporarily dissolve, while direct and egalitarian bonds are created between them. Those direct bonds ignore, revert, cross, or occur outside the differences of rank and position that characterize everyday social structures. According to Turner, ritual, by creating *communitas*, constructs an "us," launching the message that we are all equal, even though it is a transitory message, so that society may later function in an orderly way within its structural logic of distance, inequality, and exploitation (Turner 1987: 232).

2 Valuation, devaluation, and re-valuation

The second symbolic process related to inequalities has to do with the relative value assigned to the categories. In other words, it implies the mechanisms of valuation, devaluation, and re-valuation. Here, it is possible to identify a dominant strategy of overestimating one's own characteristics. Each agent tries to confer positive characteristics on the social group to which she belongs. The over-valuing of the self, self-qualifications of purity, and those operations that present the privileges held as the result of divine providence or of the possession of special traits operate in this line. The mystique of excellence and distinction would also constitute variants of these mechanisms, in that they present gains in status as the result of effort, intelligence, elegance, good taste, culture, education, beauty, or any other characteristic possessed by the group. As a complement are the symbolic tools that attribute negative characteristics to other groups, such as stigmatization, demonizing, labeling as impure, belittling, or under-valuing the external or the foreign. All of them legitimate the inferior status of the others by identifying physical, social, or cultural traits of lesser value or adequacy.

148 Luis Reygadas

Similarly, the function of social closures, as Weber talked about them, is directly linked to symbolic operations that establish which characteristics are needed to belong to a status group to which a certain positive or negative social value has been assigned (Weber 1996: [1922]: 684–686). Weber goes even further to postulate the existence of ritual marks that accompany the makeup of many status groups (Weber 1996 [1922]: 689).

Mary Douglas employed the analysis of the pure and the impure, of the clean and the contaminated, to understand the symbolic limits that separate groups. By deciphering the symbolic structures with which a society distinguishes the unpolluted, the clean, and the immaculate from the contaminated, dirty, or stained, much can be learned about that society's social structures (Douglas 1984). The case of the untouchables in the Indian caste system comes immediately to mind. However, in other societies, including ours, there are also cultural markers that associate social groups with order and disorder, with cleanliness and dirtiness, and with purity and contamination.

In a study on relations between locals and outsiders in a small, working-class community in London, Norbert Elias analyzed the processes of stigmatization of the outsiders through which the members of the established group represented themselves as better human beings than the rest. The group fantasies of praise and condemnation, along with the complementary relationship between group dignity (of their own group) and group shame (of the others), create an emotional barrier that is fundamental to the reproduction of asymmetries in power relations (Elias 2006: 220–229).

Myths also play a role in the valuing and devaluing processes, as Maurice Godelier shows in his study on masculine domination among the Baruya. In this New Guinea community, a complex mythical narrative consecrates the supremacy of men, to whose semen a number of virtues are attributed (it produces conception, nourishes the fetus, feeds the wife, strengthens initiated youth, etc.), while the menstrual blood is considered a harmful and dangerous substance. This narrative is extended into differences in bodies (the man's body is considered beautiful; they may use bands, feathers, and other decorations) and in spaces (there are double paths, with the men's paths elevated, and an imaginary line divides masculine and feminine areas within the home). This complicated configuration contributes to the existence of gender-based discrimination in economic and political spheres (Godelier 1986).

Gender studies have contributed to understanding the cultural dimensions of inequality by showing that the asymmetries between men and women have been associated with symbolic constructions regarding what it means to be a man or to be a woman, along with the relationships of power between people of different sexes (Butler 1996; Comas D'Argemir 1995; Lamas 1996; Ortner 1979; Rubin 1975). Many cultures' worldviews are filled with oppositions of masculine and feminine, frequently over-valuing the positive qualities of men and under-valuing those of women, a fact that contributes to the production and reproduction of relationships of gender domination.

Working in the opposite direction, one can find the strategy of re-valuing the subordinate. This strategy produces a symbolic inversion of which are the positive

The symbolic construction of inequalities **149**

TABLE 8.2 Processes of valuation, devaluation, and re-valuation

Symbolic strategies in the construction of inequalities	Symbolic strategies in the deconstruction of inequalities
Overvaluing and undervaluing	**Re-valuing the subordinate**
Attribution of positive and negative characteristics to categories	Symbolic inversion of positive and negative characteristics
Overvaluation of one's own group, undervaluation of others' groups	Overvaluation of the popular, undervaluation of the elites
Qualifications of purity and impurity	Idealization of bandits and heroes of the poor
Stigmatization	Critique of pureness
Hierarchization	Resilience against stigmatization
Distinction	Questioning of hierarchies
Generalizations of superiority/inferiority	Counter-distinction, alternative scales of values
Rituals of exclusivity, mystiques of excellence	Claims of equality
	Defense of popular culture, derision of the powerful

Source: The author's own elaboration.

and negative characteristics, re-valuates the popular, and criticizes the discourses of pureness and excellence. It also includes resilience against stigmatization and questioning of hierarchies. Re-valuing the subordinate implies a counter-distinction narrative, supported by alternative scales of value, opposite of that of hegemonic groups. The evaluation of groups and individuals is not a unidirectional power device, with only one regime of truth (Foucault 1977: 23), or only one legitimate symbolic capital (Bourdieu 1988), but a contested arena where various groups dispute different regimes of value (Appadurai 1991).

Over the past decades, a period in which many other inequalities have got worse, there have been significant advancements in gender equity, although there is still a lot of ground to cover. These achievements cannot be understood without taking into account the symbolic processes that have deconstructed the roots of unequal relationships between women and men. Gender studies have made a fundamental contribution to understanding resistance to inequity. A few of the many contributions have been the re-valuing of women, the questioning of patriarchal oppression, the de-naturalization of gender, and the deconstruction of hegemonic categories according to which men and women have been classified for centuries.

3 Relations between difference and inequality

The third symbolic process points to the relation between difference and inequality. The hegemonic strategy is the conversion of differences in inequalities. The creation of a cultural and affective distance is fundamental to making distances and differences of another nature possible. The degree of inequality that a society tolerates

150 Luis Reygadas

has to do with how different the excluded and exploited are considered to be. In this sense, the strategy of turning those who are different into non-equals is fundamental. Here operates what Gerd Baumann (2004) calls the grammars of identity and alterity, that is, the rules of selfing or othering, the classificatory structures to define who belongs to the "us" and who is from the "others." The cultural construction of gender, race, and ethnicity is a very good example of these grammars. The homogenization and assimilation discourses exclude those who are different— or include them but as second-class citizens; they also establish levels of inclusion/ exclusion related to sameness and otherness.

In many aspects social inequality is an intercultural phenomenon because: (a) it is generated in asymmetrical interactions between people of different cultures, or (b) disparities among people of the same culture create boundaries and distinctions that with time give way to intercultural relationships. This is expressed in two mechanisms: those who are different become non-equals, and the non-equals become different.

Those who are different become non-equals. Frequently, *inequality* is generated and justified by way of *difference*: social distinctions are used to produce and legitimize asymmetrical accesses to advantages and disadvantages. Identity and alterity, the differences between "us" and "them," are essential components of the inclusion, exclusion, exploitation, and opportunity hoarding processes. Furthermore, it is common to find overlapping of the socioeconomic asymmetries with cultural markers such as gender, ethnicity, religion, or nationality, as it has been shown by the intersectionality theories (Crenshaw 1991; Collins 2000).

Intercultural relationships are imbued by difference: of language, physical features, ways of speaking and dressing, customs, values, and worldview. This presence of alterity does not become inequality automatically, however it does enable it. When coupled with a disparity of resources (economic, military, legal, social, educational, symbolic, etc.) it will most likely give way to an asymmetrical interaction that can become persistent inequality that is justified through difference: the "others," the "different" ones cannot have the same rights, benefits, or treatment as "us," the "equals."

Many examples can be found of inequalities produced from intercultural intersections: enslavement of war prisoners, subjugation of colonized peoples, etc. In the contemporary era this phenomenon is recreated in many ways, for example, ethnic segmentation of the transnational labor market (Lins Ribeiro 2003: 109–110); restriction of human, labor, and social migrant rights (Miller 2007: 38–40); and special privileges for expatriates of multinational corporations (Ong 2006: 16).

The non-equals become different. The bulk of inequities are generated in social relationships among people of the same culture. Nevertheless, when these inequalities aggravate and become structural, they can acquire similar characteristics to those forged in intercultural contexts. If the social disparities are abysmal and lasting in a society it is possible that they prompt opposed status groups, lifestyles, values, and worldviews that lead to forming dissimilar cultures and subcultures, so that what was a social asymmetry inside a culture becomes an intercultural relationship: the

The symbolic construction of inequalities   **151**

TABLE 8.3 Relations between difference and inequality

Symbolic strategies in the construction of inequalities	*Symbolic strategies in the deconstruction of inequalities*
Conversion of differences in inequalities	**Recognition and transformation of difference**
Grammars of identity and alterity	Assertion of the right to difference
Selfing and othering	Alternative selfing and othering
Cultural construction of gender, race, and ethnicity	Deconstruction of gender, race, and ethnicity
Racism, sexism, discrimination	Anti-discriminatory discourse
Discourses of homogenization and assimilation	Pluralistic discourses
Hierarchization of differences	Equality in the difference, intercultural equality
Grammars of exclusion	Grammars of inclusion
Levels of inclusion/exclusion related to sameness and otherness	Disentanglement of inclusion and sameness

Source: The author's own elaboration.

non-equals have become different. In Latin America, the region that has had the most income inequity in the world for decades, how many cultural affinities are there among the elites and most unprivileged social groups? Their worlds, daily experiences, opportunities, and standards of living are so contrasting that the relationships among them are closer to an intercultural experience than to an interaction among people who share similar values and worldviews.

The opposite strategy faces toward recognition and respect of the right to difference. The recognition strategy seeks that those who are different can participate in the community in equitable conditions. In order to do that it deconstructs gender, race, and ethnicity. It also includes alternative ways of constructing identity and alterity, whether it is affirming subaltern identities or promoting more open and flexible identities. This strategy includes the discourses in favor of pluralism and against discrimination, as well as all of those that follow an inclusive grammar, that break the link between alterity and exclusion. In this matter the distinction that Nancy Fraser makes among the discourses that affirm the difference and those who transform it (Fraser 1995) is very important. The former seek to promote equality using the existing categories and classifying regimes. In contrast, transformative discourses question and deconstruct the categories and the hegemonic classifying systems, which is why their potential for promoting equality is higher.

4 Production, acquisition, and distribution of symbolic capital

A fourth key process is the production, acquisition, and distribution of symbolic capital. In the inequality pole of this process are the cultural devices that generate asymmetries in the educational, symbolic, and cultural capitals distribution. The inequality of capacities is a social product; however, it has the appearance of being the result of the personal characteristics of the individuals. It is fundamental for distantiation, an inequality-producing mechanism that Göran Therborn considers: "The main road to increasing inequality today. It is the most subtle of mechanisms, the one most difficult to pin down morally and politically" (Therborn 2009: 5).

In a text on elites in Sierra Leone, Abner Cohen studied rituals of exclusivity that permitted one ethnic group to preserve their social, political, and cultural privileges. He speaks of the "mystique of excellence" and "elite cults" (Cohen 1981: 2) that allow a group to validate and sustain their privileged status by affirming that they possess uncommon and exclusive qualities that are essential for the society. The ideology of the elite is reified, developed, and sustained by an elaborate body of symbols and dramatic performances, which include manners, etiquette, ways of dressing, spoken accent, recreational patterns, customs, and rules about matrimony. That lifestyle is only acquired over long periods of socialization and training, in particular in informal social spaces, such as the family, peer groups, clubs, and extra-curricular school activities.

Pierre Bourdieu's notion of *habitus* (1988) expresses in a precise way how the symbolic structure produces individuals with deeply unequal willingness and capacities. *Habitus* are lasting schemes of thought and feeling that govern the behaviors and tastes of different social groups. Those schemes result in systems of classification that position individuals in determined social statuses, not only because of their money, but also because of their symbolic capital. A subject's position in the social division of labor is even inscribed in apparently insignificant details, like a way of speaking or of moving the body (Bourdieu 1988: 477, 490). Inequalities in *habitus* and capabilities are very difficult to remove because they are created through people's lives and frequently transmitted from one generation to another.

In some cases, the symbolic processes can produce inequality in a direct way. One of them is the one of the asymmetries in the access to symbolic goods (for example, education and culture), because in that case the symbolic devices directly generate an unequal distribution of such goods. Another case is what Göran Therborn calls existential inequality: "the unequal recognition of human individuals as persons. This creates an *existential inequality*, which allocates freedom and unfreedom in the pursuit of personal life projects, rights, and prohibition to act, and distributes affirmations and denials of recognition and respect" (Therborn 2006: 7, italics in the original). Here, the symbolic act (acknowledgment or lack of it) is also in a direct way an inequality-producing mechanism.

The opposite strategy is the equalization of capacities. This strategy includes all the narratives about the ontological equality of all human beings. More important than narratives are the symbolic mechanisms that produce equalization in the cultural, symbolic, and educational capitals. Achieving more equality in capacities is an inescapable requisite for fairness in contemporary societies. Asymmetries in *habitus* is one of the more stubborn features of inequalities, but there are also forces

The symbolic construction of inequalities **153**

TABLE 8.4 Production, acquisition, and distribution of symbolic capital

Symbolic strategies in the construction of inequalities	Symbolic strategies in the deconstruction of inequalities
Construction of unequal individuals	**Equalization of capacities**
Narratives of essential differences	Discourses of ontological equality of all human beings
Creation of unequal *habitus*	Creation of equivalent *habitus*, re-valuation and recognition of subaltern *habitus*
Asymmetries in cultural, symbolic, and educational capitals	Equalization in cultural, symbolic, and educational capitals
Symbolic distantiation	Symbolic rapprochement

Source: The author's own elaboration.

that push forward to reduce those asymmetries, especially the efforts of millions of individuals to catch up and get rapprochement.

The equalization of capacities implies the production of equivalent *habitus* among the members of the society. This can be understood in two ways. On the one hand, it means that most people have equal opportunities of access to those goods and services that are fundamental for acquiring the capacities that are valued in that society (for example, education, health services, cultural goods, job training, Internet access, access to scientific knowledge, etc.). On the other hand, in a deeper sense it also implies re-valuing capacities and *habitus* that have been historically seen as inferior, secondary, or less important (for example, nonscientific knowledge, the capacities normally considered as feminine, non-Western cultures, popular and subaltern cultures, manual labor, collaborative abilities, etc.). In this way, capacities that have been undervalued would be given equal value. It would mean *making those who are different the same*, but without homogenizing them, in a context of respect toward diversity and difference. This would generate a symbolic as well as economic and social rapprochement.

Symbolic struggles around the legitimacy of inequalities

Finally, there are the symbolic struggles around the legitimacy of inequality. Some of the strategies analyzed above (classing, overvaluing/devaluing, converting differences in inequalities, and constructing unequal individuals) contribute to the justification of inequalities, but a fifth strategy, aimed specifically at legitimization, could also be considered. It involves symbolic tools that present the particular interests of one group as if they were universal, that is, as if their satisfaction benefited the entire society. Discourses that naturalize inequality, or that consider it inevitable or normal, also fall into this category. For them to work, it is fundamental for the privileged to convince the rest of the society that the portions of wealth appropriated are legitimate rewards for contributions made in common enterprises (Kelley and Evans 1993). The narratives that legitimize inequality are very powerful; however, their strength must not be exaggerated. Most people disapprove of inequalities

154 Luis Reygadas

that are very large or that are not the product of effort. There are discourses that criticize inequalities and present them as the product of an abuse or result of an illegitimate process. Sometimes this criticism is not presented in a direct way, but as hidden transcripts and allegorical protests. Everything that contributes to legitimize equality and the actions that seek a more fair resource distribution must also be considered: the moral economy of the poor, the ritual redistribution, and the legitimization of everyday resistance against injustices.

There are symbolic tools that sustain, justify, and legitimate everyday resistance to inequality and the expropriations from below that exploited and excluded sectors carry out. In his famous essay on the subsistence riots of English peasants and workers in the eighteenth century, historian Edward P. Thompson (1971) provided important analytical keys for studying the cultural fabric that sustains lower-class egalitarian practices. During the riots, which in general appeared in periods of scarcity and high prices, the workers confiscated grain, flour, or bread and forced the farmers, bakers, and sellers to sell them at an accessible price, or they simply sold them themselves and returned the money from the sale to the owners. In these actions, we can observe notions of legitimacy. The men and women who carried them out believed that they were defending their rights or traditional customs. The riots were guided by a "moral economy of the poor," linked to ancient ideas of reciprocity and "a popular consensus as to what were legitimate and what were illegitimate practices in marketing, milling, baking, etc." (Thompson 1971: 79). In a similar way, Eric Hobsbawm analyzes the case of social bandits, supported and admired by peasants, who considered them "as heroes, as champions, avengers, fighters for justice, perhaps even leaders of liberation, and in any case as men to be admired, helped, and supported" (Hobsbawm 2001: 20 [1969]). Those social bandits expropriated, although on a minor scale, a portion of the wealth accumulated by the powerful. For the peasants, it was a just and valid taking-back. In the day-to-day activity of workers, similar disruptions, miniscule acts of social banditry, can be observed.

For his part, James Scott (1990) proposes the concept of "hidden transcripts" to explain the cultural substrata that nourish varied and numerous underground resistance actions carried out by peasants, slaves, and other poor sectors. He argues that when they are in the presence of the powerful, they can follow a public script of respect and deference, but in the spaces hidden from the vigilant eye of the dominant class, subaltern sectors tend toward other types of discourse and develop day-to-day resistance behaviors that, in spite of their small scale, gain relevancy through the number of times they are repeated. These hidden transcripts have arguments that legitimate actions of resistance and therefore play an important role in limiting and assuaging inequality (Scott 1990).

There is a dispute regarding the legitimacy of the wealth appropriated by each social agent. What is for some a fair or legitimate appropriation is for others an expropriation or an illegitimate extraction. Wealth (at least the great proportion of it) is produced socially, but it is susceptible to private appropriation, which is why there are constant tensions and negotiations regarding what portion of wealth each agent deserves, which is one source of conflicting interests over distribution.

The symbolic construction of inequalities **155**

But this opposition of interests about the distribution of wealth is also linked to social heterogeneity, cultural diversity, and differences in the criteria for legitimate appropriations, which in turn result in very different interpretations about what the most adequate distribution of wealth should be.

It is not possible to find objective criteria to discern where simple appropriation ends and where expropriation begins. I want to underscore the essentially disputed nature of any distribution of resources and the resulting inequalities. What for some is a suitable and fair appropriation, for others is seen as an unjustified expropriation. Obviously, objective factors are taken into account in measuring or evaluating the contribution of each agent in a common enterprise (scarcity, the number of hours worked, and amount of investment, among others), but power relations and sub-jective and cultural factors are also decisive in measuring each one's contribution (for example, in determining the quality of work, the value of ideas, the degree of dedication, or the level of risk) and in thus determining what is appropriate.

In some sense, any appropriation is an expropriation. I do not say this as a moral judgment, but rather as a way to describe that the portion of wealth that each person appropriates can always be questioned by others, and is often the result of negotiations, struggles, agreements, or exchanges that bring to light power rela-tions and different interpretations of reality. A certain degree of consensus can be arrived at, with regard to a given distribution, but it will always be provisional and will change along with modifications in the actors' conditions, the power relations between them, and even their perceptions on the matter.

Fifty years ago, the majority of the population considered the traditional sexual division of labor in the household to be legitimate, with all that it represented in terms of the inequality between men and women, whereas today that distri-bution is the subject of polemical dispute. Behind many contemporary battles over intellectual property, copyrights, free-trade agreements, and black-market economies, arguments can be found regarding the legitimacy of different agents' rights to appropriate, which their adversaries consider robbery or expropriation.

TABLE 8.5 Struggles around the legitimacy of inequalities

Symbolic strategies in the construction of inequalities	*Symbolic strategies in the deconstruction of inequalities*
Legitimization of inequalities	**Resistance to and de-legitimization of inequalities**
Naturalization of inequalities	Subversion
Justification of unequal results	Moral economy of the poor
Internalization of inequality's values, rules, and structures	Legitimization of everyday resistance
	Hidden transcripts
	Allegorical protests
	Ritual redistribution

Source: The author's own elaboration.

156 Luis Reygadas

The thresholds for tolerance of inequality vary from one society to another and from one historical period to another (Kelley and Evans 1993). If there is not widespread consensus regarding certain levels or types of inequality, it is to be expected that distrust, hostility, different kinds of discord, protests, and even violence will be produced among disagreeing sectors.

Symbol, power, social tie, and value: the long chain of inequalities

Putting together the five symbolic processes involved in the construction and deconstruction of inequality, what stands out is that there is no single factor that explains the influence of culture on inequality. There is a vast array of symbolic devices used by many different players, which can contribute to both increase and reduce inequality.

Inequality is not a fixed and invariable state, but rather a configuration that results from the tension between contradictory tendencies, continuously reproduced but always challenged. These tensions and contradictions deeply mark the symbolic processes analyzed in this chapter. It is useful here to recall Victor Turner's analysis of the connection between structure, counter-structure, and anti-structure, and their modification in the ritual field (Turner 1987). Bourdieu's description of the dynamic between classing, de-classing, and re-classing in contemporary societies is also pertinent (Bourdieu 1988). Both of them highlight the negotiated and disputed nature of boundaries and limits between groups of status and class, which must be constantly redefined. Norbert Elias also points out that the relations between established people and outsiders are subject to struggles for power equilibriums, in which the outsider groups tacitly or openly push for the reduction of power differentials, while the established groups push to preserve or increase those differentials (Elias 2006: 239).

Many rituals serve to elevate individuals' ranks, to allow them to acquire a superior status, and, in that sense, to give way to a variety of inequalities and hierarchies. Rituals can, however, equalize and balance as well. This same duality runs through all symbolic constructions. They exclude and include, elevate and denigrate, dissolve classifications as much as reinforcing them, erect and demolish boundaries, legitimate the powerful and question domination. There is no sense in attributing to cultural processes and devices an *a priori* function of producing equity or generating distinctions, since both possibilities exist and the effects of equality or inequality depend greatly on context, on the symbolic dynamic, and on agents' interests and actions. Therefore, the dynamics of interaction must be analyzed in each concrete case.

In most cases culture is just one of the many components of the causal chain that produces inequalities. In general, the influence of culture is indirect and acts along with other factors. A good example of this is the analysis that Charles Tilly made about the relation between paired categories and persistent inequalities:

> Categories do not in themselves produce deep, durable inequality. That depends on their combination with a second configuration: hierarchy.

Categorical inequality depends on the conjunction of a well-defined boundary separating two sites with a set of asymmetrical social ties connecting actors in the two sites. […] Categorical inequality survives, finally, to the extents that sites attach unequally to flows of resources that sustain their interaction.

(Tilly 1998: 99–100)

As can be seen, the symbolic processes (creation of paired categories and border definition among categories) are entwined with a political process (establishment of a hierarchy), with a socio-institutional process (development of asymmetric social ties), and with economic processes (resource flow). The conjunction of these four dimensions—symbol, power, social tie, and value—is the one that best explains the whole chain of production of inequalities. Accordingly, research on inequality will benefit tremendously if the symbolic dimensions are included in the analysis. It will gain even more if it finds the way to entwine cultural aspects with power relations, social interactions, and economic dynamics.

Note

1   Translation from Spanish by Daniel Russell and Adriana Reygadas.

References

Appadurai, A. (1991): *La vida social de las cosas. Perspectiva cultural de las mercancías*, México: Grijalbo-CONACULTA.

Balandier, G. (1994): *El poder en escenas. De la representación del poder al poder de la representación*, Barcelona: Paidós.

Baumann, G. (2004): "Grammars of Identity/Alterity: A Structural Approach," in: Baumann, G. and Gingrich, A. (eds.), *Grammars of Identity/Alterity: A Structural Approach*, New York, NY: Berghan Books, pp. 18–50.

Bourdieu, P. (1988): *La distinción. Criterio y bases sociales del gusto*, Madrid: Taurus.

Butler, J. (1996): "Variaciones sobre sexo y género: Beauvoir, Wittig y Foucault," in: Lamas, M. (ed.), *El género. La construcción cultural de la diferencia sexual*, México: PUEG-Miguel Ángel Porrúa, pp. 303–326.

Cohen, A. (1981): *The Politics of Elite Culture: Explorations in the Dramaturgy of Power in a Modern African Society*, Berkeley, CA: University of California Press.

Collins, P. (2000): *Black Feminist Thought: Knowledge, Consciousness, and the Politics of Empowerment*, New York, NY: Routledge.

Comaroff, J. (1985): *Body of Power, Spirit of Resistance: The Culture and History of a South African People*, Chicago, IL: University of Chicago Press.

Comas D'Argemir, D. (1995): *Trabajo, género y cultura. La construcción de desigualdades entre hombres y mujeres*, Barcelona: Icaria Antropología.

Crenshaw, K. (1991): "Mapping the Margins: Intersectionality, Identity Politics, and Violence against Women of Color," *Stanford Law Review*, 43, 6, 1241–1299

Douglas, M. (1984): *Purity and Danger: An Analysis of the Concepts of Pollution and Taboo*, London: Ark Paperbacks.

Durkheim, E. and Mauss, M. (1996 [1903]): *Clasificaciones primitivas (y otros ensayos de antropología positiva)*, Barcelona: Ariel Antropología, 23–103.

158 Luis Reygadas

Elias, N. (2006): "Ensayo acerca de las relaciones entre establecidos y forasteros," *Revista Española de Investigaciones Sociológicas*, 104, 3, 219–251.

Foucault, M. (1977): *Discipline and Punish: The Birth of the Prison*, New York, NY: Vintage Books.

Fraser, N. (1995): "From Redistribution to Recognition? Dilemmas of Justice in a 'Post-Socialist' Age," *New Left Review*, I, 212, 68–93.

Gledhill, J. (2000): *El poder y sus disfraces. Perspectivas antropológicas de la política*, Barcelona: Bellaterra.

Godelier, M. (1986): *La producción de grandes hombres. Poder y dominación masculina entre los Baruya de Nueva Guinea*, Madrid: Akal.

Hobsbawm, E. (2001 [1969]): *Bandits*, London: Abacus.

Keesing, R. (1992): *Custom and Transformation: The Kwaio Struggle for Cultural Autonomy*, Chicago, IL: The University of Chicago Press.

Kelley, J. and Evans, M. (1993): "The Legitimation of Inequality: Occupational Earnings in Nine Nations," *The American Journal of Sociology*, 99, 1, 75–125.

Kertzer, D. (1988): *Ritual, Politics and Power*, New Haven, CT: Yale University Press.

Lamas, M. (1996): *El género. La construcción cultural de la diferencia sexual*, México: PUEG-Miguel Ángel Porrúa.

Lamont, M. and Fournier, M. (1992): *Cultivating Differences: Symbolic Boundaries and the Making of Inequality*, Chicago, IL: The University of Chicago Press.

Lins Ribeiro, G. (2003): *Postimperialismo. Cultura y política en el mundo contemporáneo*, Barcelona: Gedisa.

Miller, T. (2007): *Cultural Citizenship*, Philadelphia, PA: Temple University Press.

Ong, A. (2006): *Neoliberalism as Exception. Mutations in Citizenship and Sovereignty*, Durham, NC, and London: Duke University Press.

Ortner, S. (1979): "¿Es la mujer con respecto al hombre lo que la naturaleza con respecto a la cultura?" in: Harris, O. and Young, K. (eds.), *Antropología y feminismo*, Barcelona: Anagrama, pp. 128–145.

Piketty, T. (2014): *Capital in the Twenty-First Century*, Cambridge, MA: Harvard University Press.

Rubin, G. (1975): "The Traffic in Women: Notes on the 'Political Economy' of Sex," in: Reiter, R. (ed.), *Toward an Anthropology of Women*, New York, NY, and London: Monthly Review Press, pp. 157–209.

Sahlins, M. (1988): *Cultura y razón práctica. Contra el utilitarismo en la teoría antropológica*, Barcelona: Gedisa.

Scott, J. (1990): *Domination and the Arts of Resistance: Hidden Transcripts*, New Haven, CT: Yale University Press.

Taussig, M. (1980): *The Devil and the Commodity Fetishism in Latin America*, Chapel Hill, NC: University of North Carolina Press.

Therborn, G. (2006): "Meaning, Mechanisms, Patterns and Forces: An Introduction," in: Therborn, G. (ed.), *Inequalities of the World*, London: Verso, pp. 1–58.

Therborn, G. (2009): "The Killing Fields of Inequality," *Soundings* 42: 1–10.

Thompson, E. P. (1971): "The Moral Economy of the English Crowd in the Eighteenth Century," *Past and Present*, 50, 1, 76–136.

Tilly, C. (1998): *Durable Inequality*, Berkeley, CA: University of California Press.

Turner, V. (1987): *Dramas, Fields and Metaphors: Symbolic Action in Human Society*, Ithaca, NY: Cornell University Press.

Weber, M. (1996 [1922]): *Economía y sociedad. Ensayo de sociología comprensiva*, Mexico City: Fondo de Cultura Económica.

PART III

Dynamics of production and transformation of inequalities

9

MULTIPLE LAYERS OF INEQUALITIES AND INTERSECTIONALITY[1]

Jairo Baquero-Melo

Introduction

Colombia has one of the highest levels of inequality worldwide, which is also reflected in high levels of land concentration. The Colombian case is an example of the relation between high levels of inequality, violence, and the role of violence as a mechanism that produces and reproduces inequalities. This is the case of the Lower Atrato region in Chocó Department. This region, belonging to the greater Darien region, was historically introduced to the world economy through colonial flows affecting territories in what currently is part of Panama and Colombia. During the twentieth century, there have existed the interaction of multiple racial groups, as well as land conflicts and competing economic interests. This chapter aims at studying the configuration of inequalities in this region through the overlapping of economic, political, and social processes, both historical and contemporary.

Previous research on the Lower Atrato region has neglected the processes that have produced the overlapping inequalities endemic there. This analysis adopted a methodology of a case study, studying several processes that have occurred in Lower Atrato historically (colonialism, looting, and governmental neglect); and how new processes have affected this region since the 1990s: the expansion of multicultural collective land rights granted to Afro-descendants, violence and dispossession linked to agribusiness.

This chapter notes that the populations historically affected by inequalities (Afro-descendants and mestizo peasants) have benefited from collective land titles since the 1990s. However, the violence and dispossession linked to global agribusiness have prevented those populations from enjoying or exercising those rights. In the region, the forces promoting equality (land rights, social resistance, and land restitution policies) counter the forces of inequality (dispossession and land re-concentration). Despite the collapse of the oil palm economy (which had existed

162 Jairo Baquero-Melo

until 2008), agro-entrepreneurs maintain control in the area, supported by the army and paramilitaries. In addition, the local communities have faced challenges regarding the implementation of Law 70, related to the definition of the beneficiaries of collective land rights.

The main question guiding the chapter is: how have historical and contemporary processes produced layers of inequalities, creating the overlapping and interplay of multiple forms of inequality related to racism, land conflicts, and labor disputes, evidencing the intersection of social categories of class, race, and ethnicity?

This chapter is structured as follows. The first section explains the layered inequalities concept. The second part analyzes the historical configuration of inequalities, including colonialism and processes up to the beginning of the twentieth century. The third part discusses the processes affecting this region and its populations since the mid-twentieth century. Finally, the chapter presents the interplay of two main processes since the 1990s: the expansion of the oil palm agribusiness and the adoption of multicultural policies that aimed at determining the structure of collective property rights and land uses.

1 Layered inequalities: explaining the concept

Inequalities overlap forming several layers. The literature on layers of inequalities has taken layers in various forms: historical layers of inequalities (Therborn, 2006; Wallerstein, 1974), layers of inequalities linked to intersectionality (Guhathakurta, 2012; Roth, 2013; Sandhu, Stephenson, and Harrison, 2013), and layers of inequalities related to mechanisms in the production and reproduction of inequalities (Talmud, 2001; Tilly, 1995). However, it is necessary to explain in a clearer way the relationship between the approaches to layers as historical configuration of inequalities, and the views on intersectionality.

Historically, the formation of a capitalist world-economy has been structured upon an international division of labor, but also through the reproduction of racism and class inequalities (Wallerstein, 1974). This world-economy has entailed the production of new layers of inequality with origin in slavery, social hierarchization, capitalist labor relations, and land concentration. Restrepo (2013) claims the existence of a sort of "sedimentation" of forms of understanding the blackness. Those cross from the colonial period, to the formation of nation-states, to contemporary multiculturalism. Authorities have classified in different ways the populations. However, these approaches note a sort of replacement of race by ethnicity without considering intersectionality.

Other works have related the layers to a sort of intersectionality (Hill-Collins and Bilge, 2016; Roth, 2013) in a transversal-cut perspective. It relates to the addition of new types of inequalities in determined social groups (Guhathakurta, 2012; Sandhu, Stephenson, and Harrison, 2013). A determined social group, accumulating various personal characteristics by race, ethnicity, gender, class, nationality, etc., can accumulate new layers of inequalities for having those characteristics, and by the impacts of some public policies. Social inequalities are shaped by many axes working together and influencing each other (Hill-Collins and Bilge, 2016) that determine unequal access to resources, opportunities, and personal traits. However, this approach lacks a deeper examination of the historical processes producing those multiple axes.

Other works note that inequalities are created and maintained in time due to the existence of social categories (Tilly, 1995), frequently adopted and legalized by the state, influenced by everyday social relations. Inequalities become durable due to several mechanisms: distanciation, resources and opportunity hoarding, and emulation (Tilly, 1995; Therborn, 2006). Although this perspective combines historical processes and social categories, it does not explain intersectionality.

This literature revision notes that in the works on layers of inequalities there is a dearth of analyses of the intersectional dimension of inequalities. At the same time, the intersectional approaches often ignore the historical accumulation of inequalities. This work defines layers of inequalities as the combination of historical processes that overlap, forming new forms of inequalities, and of processes of intersection of social categories that give form to social inequalities. This approach allows us at the same time to historicize the intersectionality and to intersectionalize the previous approaches to layered inequalities. This perspective notes that inequalities have been structured through the intersection of social categories constructed in history. The twentieth century was characterized by the proliferation of class conflicts in rural and urban areas. The historical social layers of racism overlap and mingle with layers of class inequalities. Thus, layers are not static, but dynamic processes (Costa, 2011). Inequalities are structured on diverse social axes, both in structural processes and in everyday interactions in which class, race, ethnicity, and gender intersect each other.

2 Colonial layers: the Darién, difference, and global inequalities

The Darién, including the Lower Atrato region and the neighboring territories of Urabá, has been affected by several historical and contemporary global processes. Different modalities of inequalities and alterities have been formed by the interaction of local, national, and global processes affecting this region.

The production and reproduction of layers of inequalities in the region have been linked with three elements: the effects of global processes such as colonialism and capitalist expansion, emphasizing the inequalities between centers and peripheries in the world system (Wallerstein, 1974); the establishment of economic projects (e.g., infrastructure, agribusiness); and, finally, the "otherness" constructed in the mentality of local white-Antioquian elites, who have regarded Urabá either as an "empty" space, to justify the appropriation of its resources (Uribe, 1992), or as a marginal area inhabited by populations whose differences—not only racial but also cultural—have legitimized the social, political, and economic exclusion of Urabá's inhabitants (Roldán, 1998, 5).

The Darién and Lower Atrato regions had several functions for the Spanish colonial powers. In the sixteenth century, the area provided them with the opportunity

164 Jairo Baquero-Melo

to embark on the initial explorations of the continent, as the entry point for the incursion into the interior. The conquerors called the Darién region "Tierra Firme" ("Mainland") (Vignolo and Becerra, 2011, 15). The Atrato river was the site from which the conquerors carried out their first explorations into the continent, with the first to sail the river being Vasco Nuñez de Balboa, in 1511, although he also faced the hostility of the indigenous populations along the river.

The Darién and Lower Atrato regions had also a commercial importance. Villages such as Santa Maria La Antigua del Darién lost their initial importance when the conquerors moved in 1549 to Panama due to the discovery of gold mines there. The foundation of Cartagena in 1533 and the closure of the Atrato river reduced the importance of the Urabá Gulf. The crown policy of preventing navigation along the Atrato river aimed to prevent other colonial powers from taking control of the wealth. One of the checkpoints of the crown was established at Curbaradó. Information about the strategic location of the Darién attracted colonial competitors, as well as pirates and buccaneers. The Darién was strategic for being the contact point between Cartagena and Panama (then called Portobelo) as well as the place for connecting the Atlantic and the Pacific, to control the Peruvian riches.

However, despite the influx of conquerors and colonial powers between the sixteenth and beginning of the nineteenth centuries, the region remained almost unchanged, and the territory stayed "outside" the colonial processes that affected other regions of New Granada, due to indigenous resistance and disputes between colonizers over this strategic area. Few towns and villages were established. Spanish establishments in the area were mainly of a military character. Various incursions into this area resulted in "slaughter and graves" for the Spanish (Uribe, 1992, 14; Valencia, 1983, 18).

Indigenous populations and African slaves

The Lower Atrato region belongs to the greater eco-region of the Chocó Biogeográfico, which contains the Darién region. These territories have been historically inhabited by different indigenous communities, whose survival has been threatened since the Spanish conquest. While some indigenous groups have disappeared, other groups have been obliged to move within the territory to other areas. The indigenous groups have had various locations, and the conquest chronicles describe two sets of social groups in the area of the Urabá Gulf. Main indigenous groups in this region include the Cuevas who disappeared in the eighteenth century; the Urabáes; and the Emberas or Chocós who occupy territories in which they have resisted the occupation to exploit territorial resources.

The numbers of the indigenous populations were reduced by the epidemic diseases brought by the Spanish and by violence. From the almost 60,000 Emberas and Waunamás who lived in 1600, there were only some 36,000 by 1768, and 15,000 by 1793 (West, 2000, 146). Communities who survived probably re-grouped with other indigenous communities with similar language and cultures, and they have been suffering the pressures of new settlers who have put at risk their lives, culture, and territorial rights (Uribe, 1992, 83). The main survivors have been the Emberas and the Cunas.

African slaves were brought by the Spanish, mainly for the exploitation of gold mines in regions such as Chocó. The black populations adopted the living customs of the local indigenous groups, including housing construction and agricultural methods (West, 2000). Most of the slaves arrived in New Granada between the end of the sixteenth century and the finalization of the colonial period (West, 2000, 152).

In the Pacific region, African slaves were forced to work in mines located mainly in the upper reaches of the Atrato and San Juan rivers, the Barbacoas district, and the upper and lower tributaries of rivers located between Buenaventura and Guapi (West, 2000, 155). Starting from those points, the black people settled in the rest of the region. The Nóvita province was the main center for the black population as it was surrounded by several mining camps. Another important point was the Citará province, currently the location of Quibdó, the capital of Chocó. In the last quarter of the eighteenth century, the number of slaves reached almost six hundred people (West, 2000, 157).

The achievement of freedom began during the colonial period in mining areas. By 1778, 38% of the black population was free in Chocó. This number included those slaves who bought their freedom, the cimarrones who escaped, and mulattos who were liberated by their masters. In 1821 the gradual emancipation of slaves was proclaimed, although bureaucratic problems and disobedience were obstacles to its implementation. In 1851 slavery was officially abolished in Colombia (West, 2000, 161). After abolition, a significant number of Afro-descendants emigrated toward areas with agricultural potential. Some blacks mixed with indigenous people, giving rise to the Zambos. Influenced by white revolutionaries of the independence movement at the beginning of the nineteenth century, groups of black people supported the revolutionary forces (West, 2000, 163).

Mining and slavery sowed the seeds of the future impoverishment of Afro-descendant communities in Colombia. After independence from Spain in 1810, mine owners lived in cities such as Popayan, Cartagena, and Medellin, cities that had received wealth from the looted minerals. Businessmen refused to settle along the Pacific, arguing that the high rainfall in Chocó made it difficult for them to settle and stay. However, Afro-descendants have been living there, consolidating cimarronaje processes—the struggles against slavery and the achievement of freedom.

Colonial social categories

At the end of the seventeenth century, in the New Kingdom of Granada, a society of castes was consolidated (Losonczy, 2008). Different legal and occupational statuses were given to differentiate socio-racial groups. Populations had "particular rights and consciousness of the body linked to their ancestry, mixed or not, and visible by phenotype" (Losonczy, 2008, 264). The main castes identified were whites, Indians, slaves, and *libres de color* (free people). This last category grouped several mixed social groups with regional variations, such as "*mestizos* (white and

166 Jairo Baquero-Melo

Indian), *zambo* (black and Indian), *mulato* (black and white), *pardo* (mulatto and black)" (2008, 264). Several diverse social groups shared a legal status based on color.

At the end of the eighteenth century, the *libres de color* co-existed with other social categories that included mainly the whites (descendants of European colonizers) at the top of the social strata; the *colonos* or settlers of metropolitan and diverse regional origin, located below the whites; and the white fugitives who, with the *cimarrones* and Indians, constituted populations outside of colonial control, creating refuge areas such as the *palenques* inhabited by *cimarrones* (2008, 265). The Indians were classified as *ladinos* (Christianized and Spanish-speaking), in resistance against evangelization and social incorporation. The arrival of new slaves filled spaces where the indigenous refused to work or perished from heavy work or disease. The Africans represented the category of "*negro bozal*," versus the categories of "*negro criollo*, those Afrodescendants who were born in the country and Spanish-speakers, and in some degree evangelized," and "cimarron or fugitive slaves, imagined as animals or savages by the colonizers" (Losonczy, 2008, 265). Several new identities, "*mestizajes*, escapees and purchasers of freedom, evangelization and manumission," enhanced the range of the *libres de color* category (Losonczy, 2008, 265).

At the end of the eighteenth century, disputes arose regarding the criteria for acquiring the status of white and *criollo*. The main legal instrument was the so-called *certificado de pureza de sangre* (certification of blood pureness) issued by the Real Audiencia, reclassifying and establishing the terms of the definition of whiteness (Losonczy, 2008, 265). Several *libres de color* of all the subcategories aimed for the acquisition of this certification to facilitate labor access and social mobility as well as establishing marriage rights. The *criollo* category became the goal or desire of several sectors for gaining access to rights.

3 Regional layers: race, difference, and regional elites in Urabá

Processes of independence in Latin America occurred in general at the beginning of the nineteenth century. There existed conflicts between the *criollos* and the Spanish populations at the time of the creation of the New Kingdom of Granada. The dominant power exerted by the *criollo* elites was and had been linked to the predominance of racism before and after the independence processes (Restrepo, 2010, 71). The *criollos* demanded their right to and need for self-governance independent from Spain, and they also sustained racist attitudes in social and cultural practices, as well as in their political and intellectual views.

In the nineteenth century, the indios and blacks represented the "Other" of the national people, although they were neither excluded nor made invisible, but were included in the discourses of the nation in a subaltern position (Arias, 2007, 50). The center of the nation was "built upon an inverse interpretation of its margins" (2007, 50). They were taken as subordinated, but also as problematic for the exercise of modern government. The scientists and intellectuals associated the indigenous and blacks with particular geographical territories and with specific climates, in "zones of the internal frontier" (2007, 51). In the nineteenth century, "black" was taken as the opposite to white, and race was related to physical strength for labor. The state did not produce laws for incorporating black people, as it did for the indigenous (2007, 57). The blacks, imagined as "savages" or "barbaric," were located in "the rainforests of Chocó, inter-mountain range valleys, the basins of rivers at the Caribbean Coast, far away from the economic, political and cultural national control" (2007, 57).

The separation of Panama affected this region. It occurred at the same time as the emergence of extractive economies and plantations. Between 1870 and 1930, the world experienced increasing global flows of goods and populations, due to the effects of the industrial revolution and to an accumulation crisis in Europe. The European powers sought to control the production of raw materials for emergent industrial capitalism (Araghi, 2003). The Darién was the site of one of the disputes between the European powers and the emerging powers such as the United States. The combination of internal political conflicts within Colombia (disputes between the liberals and the conservatives) and international geopolitical disputes was decisive in leading to the separation of Panama in 1903. The colonial and imperial powers aimed at integrating new territories into the world-economy (Baquero-Melo, 2015c).

The geopolitical transformation of the Darién was accompanied by the expansion of new economies such as rubber, tagua, timber, and the *raicilla ipecacuana* (Leal, 2008; Villa, 2011, 9; Uribe, 1992, 33, 38). The exploitation of forests produced land conflicts, with the involvement of national and transnational companies. At the start of the twentieth century, certain agro-industries were also established in the Lower Atrato, mainly for sugar cane and banana production, alongside the works of the Panama Canal (Palmer, 1932, 265). During the first half of the twentieth century, national and international actors proposed to build the so-called Panamerican Road that would cross the Darien region. However, the road to the sea failed to open the "Darien gap," and most of the colonizers from Antioquia migrated to the Sinú and San Jorge river basins (Uribe, 1992, 39).

Historically, Chocó was integrated across the Atrato river with the economic center of Cartagena and the international market (Villa, 2011, 6). Some business elites from abroad (Cartagena) settled in Quibdó, giving the city the character of a regional urban center (Aprile-Gniset, 1993). Small towns emerged as families from the interior settled along tributaries of the lower and middle Atrato river. The agro-industrial banana plantation in Acandí and the sugar mill in Sautatá attracted workers and colonization (Villa, 2011, 6). These ventures established particular types of social, economic, and labor relations.

The establishment of plantations produced the enclave model. It produced the expansion of the agricultural frontier, forming settlements of people from different cultures and regions. There, the various indigenous peoples, Afro-descendants, and Sinuanos established their own forms of territorial appropriation. Also some settlers from Antioquia arrived later to the region, expanding the livestock economy (Villa, 2011).

In terms of the structuration of racial inequalities in the Urabá region, between the end of the nineteenth and the beginning of the twentieth century, the regional elites from Antioquia reproduced what Roldán (1998) called "a discourse of cultural differences." It was rooted in the colony, which stemmed "from the climatic, economic and ethnic differences of different geo-graphic spaces within the region" (1998, 5). The elites had a regional imagined map, producing a differentiation between central areas of settlement and "peripheral areas" (e.g., Urabá) (Roldán, 1998, 5). The elites were self-imagined as embodying whiteness and values from Catholicism and capitalism (and civilization), and the people at the "margins" as embodying the inversion of those values (1998, 5). But the markers of difference were rooted not only in racial markers, but more in cultural differences. It helped to produce a regional identity and "helped to legitimize the political, social and economic exclusion" (Roldán, 1998, 5).

Areas such as the Lower Atrato were imagined as "insanitary, inhabited by people of African descent, indigenous or foreigners (non Antioquians), taken as [...] sickly, indolent, passionate, (and) prone to fetishism and anarchy" (Uribe, 1886, cited in Roldán, 1998, 6). The mainly white Antioquian elites, linked to political parties and trade, produced a "regional hegemonic project" (Roldán, 1998, 6). The territories at the periphery were identified as "objects of desire," due to "the strategic position, natural resources and potential" (...) "to enhance the political and economic power of Antioquia" (1998, 8).

4 Territorial regimes, settlements, and multi-ethnic character of the region

In the 1960s a banana economy enclave was introduced in the Urabá region, nearby Chocó, giving form to the so-called Eje Bananero. This process had regional impacts such as spurring the migration of populations to other areas, including the Lower Atrato, as well as prompting the emergence of further layers of inequalities, linked to land dispossession, labor conflicts, and the expansion of different modalities of violence.

During the first half of the twentieth century, "the colonization processes ruled from the elites and the government of the Department failed in their goal of populating the [Urabá], and the economic projects [such as rubber and banana] were ephemeral" (Uribe, 1992, 31). During this period, the bi-party violence between members of the liberal and conservative parties affected the Urabá as well as the rest of the country. Urabá's population was divided into the same party adscriptions. For this reason, "Urabá always has been a disputed territory and a war frontier with open violence, and its expressions have included insurgency, delinquency, resistance and offensive actions" (Uribe, 1992, 32). The outcomes of those processes have produced a state focused on a strong military presence in the area, rather than on being a supplier of social and other services. In addition, they have produced a resistance mentality among the local people, who organize their social relations outside the structures of the state (Uribe, 1992).

Various regimes of land ownership and environmental structuring have co-existed, interacted, and evolved in the region, in accordance with different governmental (and entrepreneurial) reasoning and goals.

Multiple layers of inequalities **169**

First, some areas in the Lower Atrato were included in indigenous reservations or *resguardos*. The main regulations included the creation of a reservation in 1927 at Kiparadó; a reservation created in Panama in San Blas (Law 59 of 1930); Resolution No. 85 of August 1920 that created a Reservation of the Cunas; Decree 1667 of July 1936 to create a reservation for the Cunas of Arquía; Resolution 059 of 1975 of INCORA; and Resolution 0026 of 1976 that created the Indigenous Reserve of Arquía (Valencia, 1983, 29).

Second, Law 2 of 1959 or the Law of Forest Reservations has been identified as the "first conservationist order in the Colombian Pacific" (Pardo, 1996; Meza, 2006). Law 2 aimed at regulating the forest economy and the conservation of resources (Acción Social, 2009, 11). Decree 0111 defined seven forest reservations in the country. The indigenous *resguardos* were extracted from the forest reservations through the ratification of the ILO Agreement of 1957 (Meza, 2006, 401). Besides producing environmental legislation, the government also gave concessions for timber extraction (Leal and Restrepo, 2003), which attracted peasants to the region.

Third, the National Natural Park Los Katíos is located within the Lower Atrato in Cacarica. This park was declared a World Natural Heritage Site by UNESCO in 1994. It occupies 72,000 hectares. In the nineties, this area was in good conservation condition (Molano and Ramírez, 1996, 70). This area and the indigenous reservation of Salaquí have remained as conservation areas with rich mega-biodiversity (1996, 71). The designation of this park aimed to prevent the expansion of settling. In some periods, colonization has been counteracted by expelling and/or re-allocating communities. The area has been affected also by the introduction of coca crops.

The peopling of the region involved several processes (Baquero-Melo, 2014). The majority of villages in Cacarica, Curbaradó, Jiguamiandó, and Bajirá were founded between the 1940s and the 1970s, by people coming from the Caribbean (Sinú and Cartagena) and the rest of Chocó (e.g., Baudó).

The Lower Atrato region gained a multi-ethnic basis. Anthropological (Ruiz-Serna, 2006a; Ruiz-Serna, 2006b; Ruiz-Serna, 2008; Restrepo, 2011; Villa, 2011) and historical works (Uribe, 1992) documented that the main human groups inhabiting the region have been: (i) Afro-descendants with origins in other areas of Chocó (Baudó and San Juan); (ii) mestizo peasants, known as *chilapos*—the term "mestizo" or "*chilapo*" refers mainly to a "mestizo ethnic belonging," identified by "a color of skin, different from that of the Afro-descendants from Chocó and the white 'paisa'; an origin in Sinú and other villages from Córdoba; and their peasant culture" (Ruiz-Serna, 2006a, 8, translated by the author); (iii) a few *paisas*, or white people from the country interior (Restrepo, 2011); and, (iv) indigenous communities (Embera, Wounaan, Tule, and Katío), known also as *cholos* (Ruiz-Serna, 2008, 355).

In number, the predominant groups are the Afro-descendants and mestizos. Those populations have lived in settlements that have a prevalence of Afro-descendants, but in some cases, both the mestizos and Afro-descendants have had family and social ties (Restrepo, 2011, 56). The difference between them is that the Afro-descendants are "water people" and the mestizos are "land people" (Ruiz-Serna, 2006a, 8–9). The Afro-descendants base their material and symbolic existence on

170 Jairo Baquero-Melo

their relation with the rivers and waterscapes; the mestizos have been linked to the land, engaging in agriculture and small-scale livestock farming (2006a, 8–9). The differences between the groups have become less evident with time, including several cultural and practices interchange and learning (2006a, 8–9).

5 Law 70 of 1993: collective territories of black communities

At the end of the 1980s, different political and social conflicts prompted the Colombian elites to rewrite the Constitution. In 1990, the government called for the election of a National Constituent Assembly (ANC). However, for various reasons, black organizations failed in the election of a representative, and they supported the Embera indigenous Francisco Rojas Birry, from Chocó, as their candidate for the ANC. In 1991, the new Constitution proclaimed Colombia as a multicultural and pluri-ethnic nation. After that, social pressure led to the introduction of Transitory Article 55 (AT-55), and paved the way for Law 70 of 1993, which defined the creation of collective territories of black communities, producing opportunities for communal titling (Agudelo, 2005). AT-55 focused on rural populations living in territories that were culturally differentiated, such as in Chocó. However, it excluded legal elements to support the black population in urban spaces (Rosero, 2005).

The indigenous and Afro-descendants gained visibility at the national and transnational level as collective subjects with rights, based on the re-invention and re-signification of their ancestral origins. However, while these groups have gained political instruments to fight for their rights, in Colombia several other sectors such as the mestizo peasants have been also historically affected by violence and inequalities. They have had restricted access to land, exacerbated by violence and forced displacement. The visibility of some ethnic groups has contrasted with the relative invisibility of the mestizo peasants (Lozonczy, 2008, 276). Despite these limitations, the Constitution of 1991 and AT-55 multiplied processes of social organization in the rural Pacific region and created legal opportunities for national social movements to support their claims (Agudelo, 2005, 133).

Decree 1745 of 1995 defined community councils as the local authorities in charge of the management of the collective territories. After that, up to March 2006, almost 60,418 families benefited, "with the expedition of 149 collective titles, reaching a coverage of 5,128,830 hectares" (García and Jaramillo, 2008). This shift in state policies was situated between two hypotheses (Wade, 2006): the interest of the state and capital in controlling lands and resources (Escobar, 1997; Oslender, 2002), and the outcome of the actions of social movements (Arocha, 1998).

Law 70 of 1993 had a progressive character that expanded recognition and clarified property rights for several Afro-descendant communities. However, it also created new challenges for the local populations. This had impacts on the modalities of land tenure and uses, due to the collective character promoted by the law. New actors (e.g., communities, academic advisers, NGOs, local leaders, social movements, public servants, the church), in a relational way, produced and interpreted this reorganization of identities. Since the 1990s, the local communities have complained about the contradictions in the co-existence of Law 70 with the spread of extractive projects (CAVIDA, 2002, 230).

Law 70 introduced the key concepts of black communities, collective occupation, and traditional practices of production. The communities had to be assimilated into the new institutions created by the law (Villa, 2011). The community councils are composed of a General Assembly and a Junta. In legal and formal terms, the legalization of the election of community councils depended upon approbation by the mayors of municipalities.

Impacts of Law 70 of 1993 in the Lower Atrato

Besides the positive impacts of Law 70, it also produced issues and transformations at the local level. These changes are entangled with the effects of violence in the region. This violence has made invisible the social transformations produced by multicultural policies (Restrepo, 2011; Bocarejo and Restrepo, 2011). A main effect of Law 70 was a renegotiation of identities (Baquero-Melo, 2014; Corredor, 2013), both for the Afro-descendants and the mestizos in order to gain and keep their land rights.

Law 70 produced the idea of eco-identities, indicating the Afro-descendants as "wardens of nature" (Wade, 2006; Asher, 2009; Cárdenas, 2012), imagined as "ecological natives" (Ulloa, 2004). This emphasis on environmental preservation is aimed at establishing some control and regulations for the uses of natural resources. However, the law also essentialized the identity to one social group (Afro-descendants) and to particular environmental practices. Afro-descendants are understood as linked to the *territorio*. Following former cooperation programs such as the Darién Project (Gobierno de Colombia, IGAC and OEA, 1978), Law 70 sought to stop processes of land appropriation in settlements. Thus, there emerged risks of exclusion of other population groups.

Law 70 also implied challenges for the re-identification of the mestizos or *chilapos*. Law 70 had to be interpreted in several forms (Ruiz-Serna, 2006a and 2006b). When the law began to be enforced, "the government told the mestizos that they would be removed from the region" (CAVIDA, 2002, 230). However, the mestizos and the black people negotiated to avoid conflicts, recognizing the historical rights of the mestizos. Since the 1990s the historical social ties have co-existed with the new social relations emerging from the application of Law 70 of 1993. This occurred amid the effects of violence and displacement (Ruiz-Serna, 2006b). The communities have avoided the production of new inequality layers through solidarity practices. Even so, Villa (2011) emphasizes the role of conflicts linked to Law 70 as a new mechanism of social relations.

6 The creation of new municipalities and the expansion of agribusiness

Since 1996 the Lower Atrato region has been affected by violence carried out mainly by paramilitaries and the army, whose chief goal was to attack the guerrilla presence in the region, but who simultaneously sought to exert territorial control for expanding oil palm cultivation. Thus, new layers of inequalities emerged in the Lower Atrato, as the agricultural frontier expanded toward Chocó, unleashing processes of territorial disputes, or struggles over territorial configurations. The territorial rights gained by the communities through Law 70 were contested by the paramilitaries and other actors with violence. In this way, the paramilitaries and agro-entrepreneurs aimed to gain and consolidate territorial (military) control, which also enabled the expansion of agribusiness.

New municipalities

There has been an effort to separate parts of the Chocó territory to include it in Antioquia, to develop infrastructure and productive projects. Formerly, only Riosucio existed (founded in 1880), but in 2000 it was sub-divided into three municipalities: Riosucio, Carmen del Darién (or Curbaradó), and Belén de Bajirá. Riosucio municipality currently covers an area of 10,373 square kilometers. The municipality of Carmen del Darién was established through Ordinance No. 018 of 22 September, 2000 (supported in Article 300, No. 6 of the National Constitution of 1991; Article 8 of Law 136; and Article 1 of Law 177 of 1994). The Belén de Bajirá municipality was created through Ordinance No. 011 of 2000.

Riosucio was a vast territory. However, the creation of Bajirá aimed to integrate these lands into Antioquia and to segregate it from Chocó. The control exerted by paramilitaries sought to serve those ends (Villa, 2011, 32). The new municipalities were established amid the violence; and they are related to regionalism, racism, and the continuation of the "regional hegemonic project" at Urabá (Roldán, 1998). The Antioquia authorities have included Chocó in their official reports as part of the development plans of Urabá. The document "Vision Antioquia XXI Century" mentions the Antioquia's goals to turn the Urabá region into "The Best Corner of America" by 2020. It would include megaprojects such as the Transversal de Las Américas road and possibly an interoceanic canal (Baquero–Melo, 2015c). These megaprojects would cross through territories of black communities and indigenous people. The disputes over Bajirá remain today, including legal ordinances.

Banana economy

The Urabá and Lower Atrato regions have been transformed by the introduction of agribusiness ventures, mainly of banana and oil palm. Those economies have been linked to violence and socio-political conflicts. However, they have also been entangled with global land and labor conflicts amid the neoliberal globalization. The regional elites have seen the Urabá region as an area suitable for the global insertion of Antioquia and Colombia. They produced inequalities by regarding Urabá as "empty territory," or as inhabited by culturally differentiated inhabitants (Uribe, 1992; Roldán, 1998), which was also used to justify the exclusions of those populations. New layers of inequalities emerged, linked to the development of the banana enclave since the 1960s, and the adoption of neoliberal reforms since the 1990s (Hough, 2012). Urabá has been considered by the elites as the "cutting edge of neoliberalism" (Chomsky, 2008). Colombian elites have sought to create a good "climate" for foreign investment, to attract capital in new economic sectors. The securitization of areas of production or "guarded" enclaves (Uribe, 1992) connected with global markets attempts to render the region attractive for foreign direct investment (FDI), at the cost of unsafe working conditions, violence against union workers, and the dispossession of peasants.

The banana economy was expanded in the 1960s, turning the region into the main production area in the country. The land and labor conflicts were "politicized" through their interaction with guerrillas and political parties in the 1960s and 1970s, and the emergence of paramilitaries at the end of the 1980s. The banana economy has been globalized with the strong participation of Colombia in the world market (Baquero-Melo, 2014). However, production has entailed land conflicts, and disputes over access to markets, amid intense global competition and local violent repression (Hough, 2012).

Oil palm

From the 1990s, the cultivation of oil palm spread in Lower Atrato in Chocó. This occurred after the violent displacement by paramilitary groups of peasants who were granted land titles through Law 70. The military Genesis Operation in 1997, and the related paramilitary Black September operation, sought to combat the guerrillas; but they removed the population to take their lands. The violence and forced displacement are an example of the relationship between the global economy and layers of inequalities characterized by the intersection of class, race, and ethnicity. The production of new raw materials (oil palm) in enclaves generated inequalities linked to pressures for new lands, harming communities historically affected by racism that recently gained territorial rights as ethnic groups.

Class inequalities are related to the role of actors from the banana enclave who aimed to expand the oil palm agribusiness, seeking to control new lands. The "regional hegemonic project" of Urabá (Roldán, 1998), initially controlled by urban elites from Medellín, evolved and became linked with the emergence of (mainly rural) paramilitaries at the end of the 1980s. Paramilitaries are part of the new "elites" who exert control in the enclave (García and Aramburo, 2011).

In Urabá the elites sought to enlarge the enclave by incorporating lands from Chocó. Thus, the labor conflicts lost prominence and land conflicts became more important. Armed actors suppressed factions, inhibited the behavior of trade unions, and thwarted their goals. The land conflict was transformed into a ethnic territorial conflict, involving a dispute over the population (Uribe, 1992; García and Aramburo, 2011). The Patriotic Union (UP) left-political party was exterminated. Trade unions and local governments changed their political composition. The paramilitarism was socially embedded, and actors controlling the enclave economy became politically hegemonic.

The layers of inequalities have been restructured since the 1990s by the expansion of paramilitary groups. There are agro-entrepreneurs, livestock breeders, regional members of the army, and local political powers. There emerged new elites or "*Los Señores de la Palma*" who controlled the oil palm economy in Lower Atrato. They were consolidated in the 2000s under the government of Uribe; they regarded the Lower Atrato region as an "annex" to the banana enclave. The region was integrated in a territorial project for producing oil palm, plantain, cassava, and livestock. The expansion of agribusiness involved complex processes, mixing legal and illegal actions. Oil palm changed the use of lands: mainly from forests, wetlands, and areas of food production to monocultures for agro-fuels. Oil palm cultivation spread during the Uribe government (2002–2010) through support from FINAGRO, reaching 23,000 hectares in Lower Atrato. The oil palm project lasted until 2008, and failed due mainly to social resistance, the impact of butt rot disease, and the intervention of several public institutions. A re-composition of agribusiness sectors is taking place in the region, with increased importance for cassava, plantain, and livestock (Baquero-Melo, 2014). Since 2010 the Santos government has adopted a policy for land restitution, aimed at reversing this counter-agrarian reform. However, these policies are contradictory, attempting to foster development through neo-extractivist policies (including agribusiness), while at the same time aiming to restitute lands (Baquero-Melo, 2015b).

Conclusion

This chapter has sought to analyze the relation between the approaches to layers of inequalities and the analyses on intersectionality. By analyzing the Lower Atrato region, this chapter sought to historicize intersectionality and intersectionalize previous debates on layered inequalities. Different layers of inequalities exist and affect populations such as those inhabiting the Lower Atrato region. The historical colonialism laid the foundations of social hierarchization, racism, and discrimination. Global capitalism introduced institutions such as agribusiness enclaves integrating this region into the global economy, producing class inequalities that intersected former racial inequalities. Contemporary processes such as the armed conflict and forced eviction of local populations have reproduced inequalities in which the intersection of class, race, and ethnicity is evident. Gender issues also play a relevant role in this process. However, due to the adopted research design, this dimension is not directly addressed in this chapter.

The displaced populations were granted land rights under multiculturalism. Those rights produced a population re-identification as the ethno-adscription "Afro-descendant." The interplay between agribusiness expansion and communal land rights produced complex processes that have affected intersectionality and the existing layers of inequality. New class inequalities (rooted in violent forced eviction and agribusiness expansion) are entangled with former racial inequalities related to the regional hegemony project (Roldán, 1998) in Urabá, and with labor and land disputes affecting the banana enclave.

However, the new land rights have also produced complex outcomes. On the one hand, the populations deploy those rights to raise their demands for inclusion; those rights have made visible new forms of racism (Wade, 2011); on the other hand, those rights also produce challenges for the communities to adapt to the new social categories and emerging power relations created by the law. The analysis of the intersection of class, race, and ethnicity is crucial to analyze if current policies are useful to overcome inequalities structured in historical layers.

Note

1 Some ideas presented in this chapter were firstly developed in Baquero-Melo (2014). The author is grateful to Sérgio Costa and Renata Mota for their comments. Also, he thanks the desiguALdades.net network (Berlin) for its support of this research.

Bibliography

Acción Social (2009): "Caracterización de las reservas forestales de Ley 2 de 1959," Bogota: Proyecto Protección de Tierras y Patrimonio de la Población Desplazada.

Agudelo, C. E. (2005): *Multiculturalismo en Colombia: política, inclusión y exclusión de poblaciones negras*, Colombia: La Carreta.

Aprile-Gniset. J. (1993): *Poblamiento, hábitats y pueblos del Pacífico*, Cali: Universidad del Valle.

Araghi, F. (2003): "Food regimes and the production of value: some methodological issues," *The Journal of Peasant Studies*, 30(2), 41–70.

Arias, J. (2007): *Nación y diferencia en el siglo XIX colombiano Orden nacional, racialismo y taxonomías poblacionales*, Bogota: Universidad de los Andes.

Arocha, J. (1998): "Inclusion of Afro-Colombians: an unreachable goal," *Latin American Perspectives*, 25(3): 70–89.

Asher, K. (2009): *Black and Green: Afro-Colombians, Development, and Nature in the Pacific Lowlands*, Durham, NC: Duke University Press.

Baquero-Melo, J. (2014): *Layered Inequalities. Land Grabbing, Collective Land Rights, and Afro-descendant Resistance in Colombia*, Berlin: LIT Verlag.

Baquero-Melo, J. (2015a): "The intersection of race, class, and ethnicity in agrarian inequalities, and the social resistance of peasants in Colombia," *Current Sociology*, 63(7): 1017–1036.

Baquero-Melo, J. (2015b): "Regional challenges to land restitution and peace in Colombia: The case of the Lower Atrato," *Journal of Peacebuilding and Development*, 10(2): 36–51.

Baquero-Melo, J. (2015c): "'Entanglements, nature and inequalities in the Darien: analyzing interoceanity in Panama and Colombia," *Forum for Interamerican Research*, 8(3): 45–67.

Cárdenas, R. (2012): "Green multiculturalism: articulations of ethnic and environmental politics in a Colombian 'black community,'" *The Journal of Peasant Studies*, 39(2): 309–333.

CAVIDA (2002): *Somos Tierra De Esta Tierra. Memorias de una Resistencia Civil*, Cacarica: CAVIDA.

Chomsky, A. (2008): *Linked Labor Histories: New England, Colombia, and the Making of a Global Working Class*, Durham, NC: Duke University Press.

Corredor, J. (2013): "Negociaciones identitarias y movilizaciones territoriales: el caso de los chilapos en el bajo Atrato," *Revista de Estudios del Pacífico Colombiano*, 2: 115–136.

Costa, S. (2011): *Researching Entangled Inequalities in Latin America. The Role of Historical, Social, and Transregional Interdependencies*, Berlin: desiguALdades.net Working Paper 9.

176 Jairo Baquero-Melo

Escobar, A. (1997): "Cultural politics and biological diversity: state, capital and social movements in the Pacific coast of Colombia," in Fox, R. and Starn, O. (eds.), *Between Resistance and Revolution: Cultural Politics and Social Protest*, New Brunswick, NJ: Rutgers University Press.

García, C. and Aramburo, C. (eds.) (2011): *Geografías de la guerra, el poder y la resistencia. Oriente y Urabá antioqueños 1990–2008*, Bogota: Cinep and Medellín: INER.

García, P. and Jaramillo, E. (2008): "Colombia: El caso del Naya," *Informe IWG 2*.

Gobierno de Colombia, IGAC and OEA. (1978): *Proyecto Darién. Estudio para la orientación del desarrollo integral de la región del Darién Colombiano*, Bogota: Gobierno de Colombia.

Guhathakurta, M. (2012): *Addressing Inequalities in a Post MDG Agenda: The Location of Minority Women*, Dhaka: Research Initiatives, Bangladesh, Addressing Inequalities.

Hill-Collins, P. and Bilge, S. (2016): *Intersectionality*, New Jersey: John Wiley & Sons.

Hough, P. (2012): "A race to the bottom? Globalization, labor repression, and development by dispossession in Latin America's banana industry," *Global Labour Journal*, 2(3): 237–264.

Leal, C. and Restrepo, E. (2003): *Unos bosques sembrados de aserríos*, Medellín: Universidad Nacional, Sede Medellín.

Leal, C. (2008): "Disputas por tagua y minas: recursos naturales y propiedad territorial en el Pacífico colombiano, 1870–1930," *Revista Colombiana de Antropología*, 44(2): 409–438.

Losonczy, A. -M. (2008) "El criollo y el mestizo. Del sustantivo al adjetivo: categorías de apariencia y de pertenencia en la Colombia de ayer y de hoy," in: Cadena, M. de la, (ed.), *Formaciones de indianidad. Articulaciones raciales, mestizaje y nación en América Latina*, Popayán: Envion, pp. 261–277.

Meza, C. (2006): "Territorios de frontera: embate y resistencia en la cuenca del río Cacarica," *Universitas Humanística*, 62: 385–429.

Molano, A. and Ramírez, M. C. (1996): *El tapón del Darién: Diario de una travesía*, Bogota: El Sello Editorial.

Oslender, U. (2002): "The logic of the river: a spatial approach to ethnic-territorial mobilization in the Colombian Pacific region," *Journal of Latin American Anthropology*, 7(2): 86–117.

Palmer, J. (1932): "The banana in Caribbean trade," *Economic Geography*, 8(3): 262–273.

Pardo, M. (1996): "Movimientos sociales y relaciones inter-étnicas," in Escobar, A. and Pedroza, A. (eds.), *Pacífico: ¿Desarrollo o diversidad? Estado, capital y movimientos sociales en el Pacífico colombiano*, Bogotá: Cerec-Ecofondo.

Restrepo, E. (2013): *Etnización de la negridad: La invención de las 'comunidades negras' como grupo étnico en Colombia*, Popayán: Universidad del Cauca.

Restrepo, E. (2010) "¿Quién imagina la Independencia? A propósito de la celebración del Bicentenario en Colombia," *Nómadas*, 33: 69–77.

Restrepo, E. (2011): "Etnización y multiculturalismo en el bajo Atrato," *Revista Colombiana de Antropología*, 47(2): 37–68.

Roldán, M. (1998): "Violencia colonizacion y la geografia de la difrencia cultural en Colombia," *Revista Analisis Politico*, 35: 3–22.

Rosero, C. (2005): *Intervention at the Foro Regional IIAP. El Chocó Biogeográfico. 12 años después de la Ley 70 de 1993, 1–3 June 2005*, Quibdó. IIAP.

Roth, J. (2013): *Entangled Inequalities as Intersectionalities: Towards an Epistemic Sensibilization*, Berlin: desiguALdades.net, Working Paper 43.

Ruiz Serna, D. (2006a): *Nuevas formas de ser negro. Consideraciones sobre las identidades entre la gente chilapa y negra del bajo Atrato chocoano*, Caracas: Universidad Central de Venezuela.

Ruiz Serna, D. (2006b): "Nuevas formas de ser negro. Consideraciones sobre las identidades entre la gente chilapa y negra del bajo Atrato chocoano," in: Bolívar, I. (ed.), *Identidades culturales y formación del Estado en Colombia*, Bogota: Universidad de los Andes, pp. 211–248.

Ruiz Serna, D. (2008): "Gente de agua: Comunidades negras en el Bajo Atrato," *Maguaré*, 22: 339–359.

Sandhu, K., Stephenson, M. A., and Harrison, J. (2013): *Layers of Inequality. A Human Rights and Equality Impact Assessment of the Public Spending Cuts on Black Asian and Minority Ethnic Women in Coventry*, Warwick: Centre for Human Rights in Practice, University of Warwick.

Talmud, I. (2001): "The multi layer structure of inequality," *HAGAR International Social Science Review*, 2(1): 25–32.

Therborn, G. (2006): "Meanings, patterns, and forces: an introduction," in: Therborn, G. (ed.), *Inequalities of the World*, London: Verso, pp. 1–60.

Tilly, C. (1995): *Durable Inequality*, New School for Social Research. Online version at: http://www.ciaonet.org/wps/tic02/ (Accessed: 30 June, 2013).

Ulloa, A. (2004): *La construcción del nativo ecológico*, Bogota: ICANH-COLCIENCIAS.

Uribe de Hincapié, M. T. (1992): *Urabá: ¿Región o Territorio?*, Medelli: Corpourabá and INER-Universidad de Antioquia.

Valencia, E. (1983): *Colonización en el Urabá Chocoano*, Bogota: Universidad Nacional de Colombia.

Vignolo, P. and Becerra, C. (2011): "Introduction," in: Vignolo, P. and V. Becerra (eds.), *Tierra firme: El Darién en el imaginario de Los Conquistadores*, Bogota: Universidad Nacional de Colombia, ICANH: pp. 15–29.

Villa, W. (2011): *Colonización y conflicto territorial en el Bajo Atrato. El poblamiento de las cuencas de la margen oriental*, Oxford: FUCLA-OXFAM.

Wade, P. (2006): "Etnicidad, multiculturalismo y políticas sociales en Latinoamérica: Poblaciones afrolatinas (e indígenas)," *Tabula Rasa*, 4: 59–81.

Wade, P. (2011): "Multiculturalismo y racismo," *Revista Colombiana de Antropología*, 47(2): 15–35.

Wallerstein, I. (1974): "The rise and future demise of the world capitalist system: concepts for comparative analysis," *Comparative Studies in Society and History*, 16(4): 387–415.

West, R. (2000): *Las tierras bajas del Pacífico colombiano*, Bogota: Instituto colombiano de Antropología e Historia.

10

MILLIONAIRES, THE ESTABLISHED, THE OUTSIDERS, AND THE POOR

Social structure and political crisis in Brazil[1]

Sérgio Costa

Introduction

On 1 January 2003, Luiz Inácio Lula da Silva, a migrant from the Brazilian northeast and former metalworker in São Bernardo do Campo (in the industrial area of São Paulo), was sworn in as the president of Brazil. His first term gave rise to a power system that André Singer (2012) labeled *Lulism*, implying a double strategy that maintained an orthodox economic policy with high interest rates, floating exchange rate, and balanced public budget while strongly expanding social disbursements and raising the minimum wage in real terms proportional to the country's economic growth (Fritz and Lavinas 2015). This strategy ensured gains both for the rich, who were exempt from tax increases or confiscation of goods or assets, and for the poor, who could benefit from cash transfer programs as well as from the economic growth that yielded new economic opportunities. From the political-institutional point of view, this power system was supported by the coalition between Lula's party, that is, the Workers' Party (PT) created during social struggles against the military dictatorship (1964–1985), and several conservative parties.

This power system proved extremely successful, ensuring Lula's re-election in 2006; the election of his chosen successor, then-unknown Dilma Rousseff, in 2010; and her re-election in 2014—even though the signs of Lulism's exhaustion were evident from 2013 onward. Between 2003 and 2013, Brazil's gross domestic product (GDP) grew 64% and the percentage of the population living in poverty was halved, according to measurements based on monthly income. In addition, social spending grew significantly, the minimum wage increased by 75% in real terms, and millions of new formal jobs were created every year (Bielschowsky 2014; Pochman 2014).

Since 2014, however, Brazil has faced a dramatic crisis, which has transformed the country into a "dreamland for social scientists [and] the nightmare for everyone else," as properly described by a University of London economist Saad-Filho (2016).

On the one hand, a political and an economic crisis fed themselves reciprocally, generating economic recession, lower formal employment, and higher household debt. While investigations into corruption paralyzed the political system, the GDP annual growth rate fell from 7.6% in 2010 to 0.1% in 2014 and contracted 3.8% in 2015. At the end of 2015, the Brazilian congress started an impeachment process against President Rousseff, who has allegedly violated Brazilian budgetary laws. The president was first suspended in April 2016 and finally removed from office in August 2016. Up to December 2016, when I concluded this chapter, the Vice-President Temer, who assumed the presidency in April 2016, had not been able to re-establish political and economic stability.

On the other hand, the crisis fueled the curiosity of social scientists. They wanted to uncover the political polarization of a country that, notwithstanding its violent past, experienced all major transitions—including independence, abolition of slavery, and proclamation of the republic in the 19th century, as well as democratic transitions in the 20th century—not through revolution, but through agreements between elites. This essay is an attempt to explain this paradoxical situation by combining socio-structural and political power analysis.

I argue that the contemporary political crisis in Brazil represents a distributive conflict involving four classes or strata, defined using not only socio-economic indicators but a multiplicity of vectors of social inequality. Initially, I recover some of the central arguments supporting the timeliness of the concept of classes and strata under late capitalism. I subsequently seek to understand recent changes in the Brazilian social structure, considering the following classes or strata: millionaires, the established, the outsiders, and the poor, classified according to five vectors of social inequality: material wealth, positions in hierarchical organizations and socially valuable spaces, socially valuable knowledge, exclusive associations, and existential rights. Finally, I interpret the contemporary Brazilian political crisis as an expression of distributive conflicts between these four classes or strata within three corporate hubs: wage labor, capital, and state.

Analytical framework: reconciling Marx and Weber

Classes and strata matter

Starting in the 1940s, the study of social stratification from a functionalist perspective became hegemonic in the field of sociological studies on social inequality, at least in the Anglo-Saxon world. According to this perspective, inequality is functional and necessary for societies, to the extent that those who engage in socially relevant activities and/or have a higher level of "training or talent" should be rewarded with more resources (Davis and Moore 1944: 243). Although they share a staunch opposition to this functionalist reading, inequality research following the Weberian tradition and the Marxist tradition evolved independently from each other in the post-war period. Only recently, efforts to bring those two traditions together have become more visible.

180 Sérgio Costa

In their many variants, Marxist approaches share at least two common premises, namely: (i) they consider that the capital/work relation shapes social structures to the extent that those with the means of production are the owning or dominant class and those who sell their labor power form the working or dominated class; (ii) they establish a necessary logical link between structural class belonging and cultural and political choices. This means that if the working class does not display the cultural and political behavior corresponding with its structural condition, this is due to ideological deviations (Wright 1985).

Approaches based on Weber share the Marxist claim that social classes are a shaping principle of the social structure of modern societies. However, they disagree with Marxists when questioning the necessary link between class—understood as class situation, that is, as the material insertion in the social structure—and forms of action and behavior, both at the cultural and political level. Thus, the Weberian tradition rejects any political determinism stemming from class situation or position. In the words of Weber himself, people belonging to the same class may, under certain circumstances, act politically in favor of their common interests as a community of interests, "but it does not have to be so; in any way, a class is not a community [Gemeinschaft] and to treat classes as a conceptual synonym for communities leads to distortions" (Weber 1956: 533 [1922]). On the other hand, in the sense that a class is defined by a group of people sharing a "specific determinant of their vital chances" (Weber 1956: 531 [1922])—namely, the place occupied in the hierarchies of wealth distribution, rather than whether or not they own the means of production—the possible positions in the social structure reproduce themselves beyond the owning and the working class conceived in Marxism.

In addition, as shown by Parkin (1974), there is, according to Weber's view, another reason for the multitude of structural positions, which is the variety of strategies of social closure in class formation:

> By social closure, Weber means the process by which social collectivities seek to maximize rewards by restricting access to rewards and opportunities to a limited circle of eligible individuals. This entails the singling out of certain identifiable social or physical attributes as the justificatory basis of exclusion.
> *(Parkin 1974: 3)*

To the extent that strategies of social closure go beyond the struggle to own the means of production, the existing class positions are also broadened.

Following this reasoning, the distinction between strata and classes is no longer relevant. That is, provided class or stratum are used as categories that define comprehensive positions in the social structure—with their respective strategies of social closure, and not just income groups, as functionalist stratification studies do—it makes no analytical difference whether we refer to classes or strata.

The links between power asymmetries and social inequalities, as outlined by Weber, are also present in the work of N. Elias. The model of established-outsider figuration, developed by Elias and Scotson (1994 [1965]), deserves particular attention here. It was based on research of discrimination and stigmatization processes of new residents in a small English suburban town named in the study as Winston Parva. As shown by the two authors, in this figuration, that is, in this web of interdependencies, established residents use all possible means—from defamation to the construction of access barriers—to jettison newcomers from social spaces as well as public and symbolic goods available in the community. According to the authors, the exclusionary practices within this figuration were not cultural or physical marks that differentiated the established group from the outsider group, but rather the power asymmetries that allowed the established group to give meaning to external traits, such that self-ascribed markers were decoded as symbols of superiority and instruments that legitimized advantages and privileges. In opposition, inferiority markers were assigned to outsiders to legitimize barring their access to socially valued goods and spaces.

Among contemporary contributions that sought to reconcile the Marxist and Weberian traditions to understand the role of classes and strata in constituting the inequalities that shape contemporary societies, the works of R. Kreckel (1992, see also Kreckel 2004) and G. Therborn (2013) are particularly relevant.[2]

Kreckel adapts and expands to late capitalism the sources or vectors of social inequality identified by Marx and Weber, establishing a matrix with four vectors that produce vertical inequalities in contemporary societies: material wealth, positions in hierarchical organizations, access to exclusive associations, and knowledge. For examining how the different positions in the social structure articulated through these distinct vectors correlate with political actors interested in maintaining or transforming a "specific system of social inequality" (Kreckel 1992: 150), Kreckel develops a *force field model*, according to which effective inequality is the result of distributional disputes among three corporate actors, state, capital, and wage labor, through the institutions and organizations that represent them, including parties, trade unions, and interest groups. Around this core, social movements and protest actors are also relevant for representing marginalized and diffuse interests. Finally, "on the outskirts of the force field is the *social-structurally organized population* that reflects the social conditions of inequality for everyday life, from values and potentials for action defined according to their stratum, environment or specific condition" (Kreckel 1992: 161).

Unlike Kreckel, Therborn (2013) is not concerned with developing a systematic theory of class or inequality. His aim is understanding existing inequality structures as an entangled product of national and global processes and flows. Accordingly, he first distinguishes three dimensions of inequality, namely, vital inequality, existential inequality, and resource inequality, analyzing how these different forms of inequality have recently changed at the global level. By observing these developments, he draws attention to the fact that the nation-state has become one of the institutions buttressing the reproduction of inequalities. According to him, nation-states still exercise in certain circumstances their historically assigned role of controlling the influence of capitalism on

182 Sérgio Costa

generating social inequalities and imploding social solidarity ties. However, since the 1990s:

> National cohesion and equality have been dumped for national attractiveness of foreign capital, in China and Vietnam as well as in Argentina, Eastern Europe and elsewhere. In this way, nations have become territories of cheap bodies, pimped by their elites to foreign capital, and as such almost unprecedented generators of inequality. [...] Nations and national boundaries [...] provide the national pimp governments with their exorbitant rents, and they constitute major barriers of exclusion to poor migrants.
>
> *(Therborn 2013: 175)*

In connection with this reconfiguration of nation-states, Therborn researches a central development in the global dynamics of class struggles during the first years of the 21st century, that is, the decline—at least on a discursive level—of the importance of the working class as a collective subject and the generalization of discourses on the middle class. This obviously has nothing to do with the hypothesis of structural leveling of global inequalities, which are actually increasing. In truth, these are ideological discourses that—according to Therborn—go in two different directions: the suffering and "larmoyant" tone of the upper middle class, which has supposedly been "left behind the soaring oligarchy of current financial capitalism" (Therborn 2013: 178); and the discourse of the middle classes in the Global South that, inflated by international agencies and business consultancies, goes against the former, being "jubilant, telling about the arrival or the imminent coming of the Messiah, in the shape of consuming middle class" (p. 178).

Approaching Brazilian social structure

Drawing on classical and contemporary attempts to reconcile Marxist and Weberian analysis of social structures as summarized in the previous section, we can identify at least five vectors that are crucial for structuring social hierarchies in contemporary Brazil:

1   Material wealth, including property, means of production, income, and other assets that can be converted into money (Kreckel 1992);
2   Positions in hierarchical organizations and socially valuable spaces. This vector includes both ranks occupied by individuals in organizations in the labor spheres as well as positions in social life that are, following the "meritocratic ideology" (Kreckel 1992), linked to different levels of prestige, power, and compensation. Particularly relevant in the Brazilian case are leisure spaces (recreational clubs, concert halls, etc.) or even contexts of consumption of goods and services (shopping malls, airports) in which discretionary criteria for access (economic or informal) are applicable.[3] Attending these spaces represents an important dimension of the class experience in Brazil. As a

consequence, preventing new aspirants to such spaces to accede is a particular form of social closure.

3   Socially valued knowledge. This category refers to skills required in contemporary capitalism that are usually expressed in degrees and titles as well as, for statistical purposes, in years of schooling. In the case of Brazil, degrees and years of schooling do not represent general equivalents with automatic consequences for social mobility: the extremely heterogeneous quality of education received during schooling by the rich and the poor functions as an instrument of social closure inasmuch as the socially more valued education received by the wealthiest assure them better positions in the social hierarchies (Quadros 2008).

4   Access to exclusive associations. This vector is translated into access to formally or informally established associations that guarantee benefits and privileges to their members (Weber 1956 [1922]; Kreckel 1992).

5   Existential rights. This vector expresses hierarchies in ensuring existential guarantees, corresponding to the "unequal allocation of personhood, i.e., of autonomy, dignity, degrees of freedom, and of rights to respect and self-development" (Therborn 2013: 49). The significant percentage of the economically active population working in the informal sector without any labor guarantees, the systematic violation of civil rights by state and private actors, and unequal access to justice justify addressing the existential hierarchies as a separate dimension of the existing inequalities in Brazil.[4]

The positions occupied in the hierarchy of possession of or access to each of these five features determine the classes and strata found in the Brazilian social structure, at least in general terms. They also define fairly clear groups, based on ethno-racial categories (Guimarães 2002; Costa 2015).[5] As will be seen below, this statement does not imply an entire overlap of strata arising from the five vectors. Nevertheless, the trend toward their convergence is undeniable: they define a vertical system of social structuring that is reasonably consistent and coherent with regard to the different dimensions of inequality. Thus, the stratum with the least material resources occupies the lowest positions in hierarchically organized organizations and spaces. These individuals are also those who hold less socially valuable knowledge, who have less access to powerful exclusive associations, and whose existential rights are less protected.

The concrete mechanisms and dynamics leading to both the perpetuation and the displacements or transformations in this system of vertical inequalities in contemporary Brazil are certainly quite different from those identified by Kreckel (1992) in his study of Germany, marked by a comprehensive and protective social welfare state. Nevertheless, the abstract description of the distributional disputes in German society, as offered by Kreckel, also applies to the Brazilian case. This means that in Brazil, too, these disputes take place in a force field comprising three corporate hubs: state, capital, and labor. Institutionally, political parties are the main actors behind distributional negotiations. Legally established interest groups, such as business associations or trade unions, also participate in these disputes. Also relevant are informal networks among representatives of the three corporate hubs, especially among those linked to capital and state. These informal channels are essential in the reproduction of existing inequalities and also constitute a central mechanism for the strategies of social closure adopted by the wealthiest.

Besides the political parties, a multiplicity of concrete actors (such as social movements, non-governmental organizations, pressure groups, mass media, etc.) as well as the formation of public opinion and political will at the level of the public sphere, are key to the legitimization of inequalities as well as to the struggle for their mitigation. This means that public debates do not merely influence the choices and preferences of individual voters, these debates also flow into the decision-making bodies in the corporate field, guiding and legitimizing decisions, including those with distributive impact (Habermas 1992; Avritzer and Costa 2004).

It is also crucial to adequately take into account the role of the international context in distributional disputes between the three hubs: capital, work, and state. The topic is certainly vast and involves discussing the inclusion of a country in the world economy, since, for example, there is evidence of a positive correlation between the production and export of primary goods and inequality levels (Korzeniewicz and Moran 2009; see also Boatcă 2015: 117ff.). It also involves analyzing various external linkages and flows, from the international transfer of profits and immigrants' remittances to cooperation agreements and international treaties concerning social or cultural rights. The latter may impact the social structure at the national level by inhibiting race or gender discrimination, for instance. At the same time, states alter domestic distributive parameters by "pimping" countries for foreign investors in Therborn's terms as described above. This has frequently occurred in Brazil: in the search for creating an institutional environment that is supposedly more conducive to attracting investment, Brazil adopted, especially during the 1990s, measures such as tax breaks, suppression of labor rights, or grants and special rights to investors, fostering the internal concentration of wealth and entitlements. These kinds of measures build also the core of the program adopted by the new Brazilian government after Rousseff's impeachment (Franco 2016).

Social structure in Brazil: recent changes

For analyzing the current crisis in Brazil, it is necessary to first assess changes observed in the Brazilian social structure, since the Workers' Party took power in 2003. The five vectors of inequality highlighted above will guide this exercise whose aim is not a detailed study of the Brazilian social structure through a precise quantification of the mobility of different groups. The central goal is to identify structural shifts that, according to my hypothesis, led to the current crisis. Therefore, there is no concern here in naming classes or social strata that cover the entire Brazilian population, but only those whose upward or downward mobility help explain the crisis. According to this logic, it is particularly interesting to follow the movements of four strata: the poor, the outsiders, the established (middle class), and the millionaires.

Poor

Fraser (2010: 370) suggests adopting the expression "transnational precariat" in place of "the global poor" to refer to the segment of the global population subjected to different forms of exclusion that "arise from the convergence of multiscaled processes, as when global economic structures intersect with local status hierarchies and national political structures." Although I recognize the "multiscaled processes" highlighted by Fraser, I adopt here the expression "the poor" to refer to the part of the population that occupies the most inferior positions in Brazilian social hierarchies in order to adequately differentiate the poor and outsiders as described below, who also used to live in precarious conditions. In reference to the debate on scales of inequality and of justice, it is warned that these positions, even when they are understood in their national dimension, reflect the entanglements between the local, national, and global as well as interpenetrations between different hierarchies, especially those of class, gender, and race/ethnicity.

The Brazilian poor, in the sense adopted here, corresponds to the segment of the population that lives below the poverty line and that either lives from social aid and other social transfers and/or occupies the positions least valued on the labor market, which includes strong participation in domestic labor. When we consider incomes, we observe that the poor were significantly reduced in number in the past decade. According to the data from the CEPAL (2016: 18), 37.5% of the population were poor or indigent in 2001, falling to 16.5% in 2013.

As far as the knowledge vector is concerned, if one considers the variable *years of schooling*, there has been a substantial increase in the situation of those considered poor and very poor in the official statistics: between 2003 and 2013, the period of schooling for the poorest 40% of the population increased an average of 1.5 years, reaching 5.9 in 2014, while the richest 20% added close to one year more of schooling in the same period, averaging 10.8 years (IBGE 2014).

With regard to exclusive associations, there is no reason to believe that the poor as such created new forms of special access to goods or socially coveted spaces in the period under consideration. Nevertheless, if we view the data on poverty, we can see that its reduction was slightly higher among the black population and women (IPEA 2015), which might indicate a fall in the impact of the exclusive associations of whites and men on inequality.

Regarding existential rights, the expansion of social and housing programs, besides the increase in the level of formalization of labor relations, even in less qualified jobs on the labor market, represents a considerable broadening of the existential rights of the poorest during the PT administrations.

Outsiders (newcomers)

The denomination "outsiders" is of course not a self-ascription. It fits in the context of the established-outsider figuration described above and expresses the dynamic activated when former poor groups experience upward social mobility

186 Sérgio Costa

and increment their level of income and consumption, going on to dispute social spaces and goods previously reserved for the established middle class.

In relation to the vector wealth, the increase in income and consumption capacity in the last decade is impressive for those who passed from the condition of poverty to become "the new middle class."[6] According to measurements carried out by Neri (2012: 27), no fewer than 39.6 million Brazilians made this journey between 2003 and 2011. The consumer power of this contingent, vastly based on the expansion of credit facilities, explains, to a great extent, the enormous expansion of durable consumer goods observed in the last decade, broadly sustained in the expansion of credit facilities (Lavinas 2016).

With regard to knowledge measured by schooling, there is evidence that the outsiders benefited substantially from the vertiginous expansion of higher education since 2003, when enrollment in institutions of higher education in Brazil jumped from 3.9 million to 7.3 million (MEC 2014: 26). The expansion in university attendance of outsiders is due to, inter alia, the quota system introduced at public universities and programs such as PROUNI and FIES, which offer grants or loans so that pupils with less purchasing power are now able to study at private institutions (MEC 2014). This does not imply that schooling guarantees higher positions in the labor market. Because of the structure of the labor market and due to the low "social value" of their certificates, even outsiders with academic degrees continue occupying less qualified jobs (Scalon and Salata 2012: 397; Quadros et al. 2013).

Nevertheless, if we consider the positions in hierarchical social spaces as exclusive areas of leisure, consumption, and the provision of services, it is evident that the increase in the outsiders' consumer power shifts their position within these spheres formerly dominated by the established.

With respect to exclusive associations, there is no evidence, as in the case of the poor, that the outsiders managed to create organizations capable of guaranteeing them any privilege in the period analyzed. Yet the reduction of gender and racial disparities in this segment highlights a reduction of power in the associations linked to gender and ethno-racial discrimination.

Established

The reference to the established middle class operates as a counterpart of the outsiders in the context of an interdependent web as defined by Elias (2004). It is not the case here of defining a precise income interval for the group of the established, as this is not the principal criterion used for its definition as a class or stratum in this text. Nonetheless, in the sense of evaluating the dislocations in the social structure based on the five vectors of inequality selected, and resorting to the model of five income classes, A to E, we can affirm that this group corresponds to those who already found themselves in class C in 2003, in addition to the members of class B. From the point of view of wealth, if one takes into account only the income variables, one sees that this group saw significant absolute gains in the period between 2003 and 2011 (Neri

2012; Pochmann 2014). From 2011 up to 2014, there was a rise in the number of Brazilians belonging to classes B and C, with their share in the total income also increasing. Regarding property and other assets, there was a clear rise in the wealth of the middle- and high-income groups in recent years (Castro 2014).

With regard to schooling, the average number of years in school for the richest 40% grew by nearly a year between 2003 and 2013, reaching 9.4 years in 2014, a little behind the years of schooling added among the poorest. Particularly relevant is the growing participation of the poorest among the university population and the resulting decline in participation among the richest in this group. In 2004, the richest 20% of the population corresponded to 54.5% of the enrollments in public institutions and 68.4% in private ones; in 2014, 36.4% and 40.9%, respectively (IBGE 2014).

There is no evidence that the established descended to inferior positions in the labor market, at least not in the period 2002 to 2009 analyzed by Scalon and Salata (2012). Nevertheless, the loss of positions of the established is evident in at least two contexts. The first regards socially segmented spaces such as shopping malls, airports, leisure spaces, etc. in which the growing presence of outsiders has provoked reactions of repulsion and rejection on the part of the established.[7]

The second loss of position for the established concerns a specific labor relation, that of domestic workers hired by close to 7% of the employed population in Brazil (IPEA 2015). Since 2003, the increasing of the minimum wage and new labor rights have led to the gradual disappearance of the model of exclusive domestic worker who is permanently at the employer's disposal, without a clearly defined contract or working schedule. No longer able to count on the comprehensive provision of service at an extremely low cost, the established middle class loses its social position and must undergo important revisions of family arrangements based on the externalization of the costs of gender inequality.

Regarding exclusive associations, there has been, during the PT administrations, a reduction of the relative efficacy of those instruments that the established have at their disposal for their strategies of social closure. After all, even though rejected and ridiculed, outsiders had one major achievement in the access to social spaces such as universities, shopping malls, and airplanes that the established understood as being for their exclusive use. Finally, existential rights for the established were not expanded, but they were not explicitly reduced in the period analyzed either.

Millionaires

There is surely a certain sociological arbitrariness to treating the richest 1% of a given population as a specific class or stratum among four considered groups. However, the importance they are acquiring in international debates on inequality, and the extraordinary percentage of wealth appropriated by them in Brazil, beyond their stronger resistance to crises, justify treating them as a group apart in the Brazilian stratification. The proportion of income appropriated by the richest 1%—namely, those who earned more than 203,100.00 reais a year in 2012—has recently increased, reaching 25% of the total income of all Brazilians after decreasing between 1987 and 2005 (Medeiros et al. 2005; Milá 2015). The concentration of wealth, for its part, is even greater and also persistent: the Gini coefficient for property and other assets was at 0.860 in 2006 and 0.849 in 2012. Little more than 400,000 taxpayers, corresponding to 0.2% of the total population, concentrated in 2012 about 47% of all of the declared wealth in Brazil (Castro 2014: 103). Based not on income statements but on the PNAD household surveys (see IPEA 2015), we know that the proportion of blacks among the richest 1% rose, between 2003 and 2013, from 9.6% to 14.9%.

Based on the variations of schooling of the richest 20%, the group to which millionaires belong, one can assume that there was an increase in years of schooling in all of the period, although this has remained slightly lower than the average rise of schooling among the whole Brazilian population.

With regard to positions in hierarchical organizations, there are indications of shifts among the different sectors of the economy given the loss of industrial productivity, the gains of agribusiness in the past decade, and the increment of financial gains. Nonetheless, the richest 1% maintain their prestigious positions in the economy. Even the loss of positions that affects stability in hierarchical social spaces does not directly reach the millionaires, given the great social and even spatial distance that separates them from the outsiders. Nor do the variations in the domestic labor market affect them, since their average monthly income reaches almost 100 times the minimum wage.

In relation to exclusive associations, informal agreements and criminal networks among politicians, parties, and large entrepreneurs, especially those in the business of construction (Anderson 2016), have traditionally constituted an effective strategy of social closure for the millionaires, guaranteeing a restricted group privileged access to public funds.

Finally, regarding existential rights, there are no factors that indicate any reduction in full validity for millionaires during the entire period studied.

Table 10.1 summarizes the shifts in the Brazilian social structure in accordance with what has been described up to now.

Since 2014, the economic recession has led to economic losses of wealth, especially income, for all four strata, although with different intensities. Accordingly, the poor as well as the outsiders are particularly affected since dismissals among less skilled sectors have been massive. The established, especially highly qualified

TABLE 10.1 Recent changes in Brazilian social structure 2003–2014

	Wealth	Position	Knowledge	Exclusive association	Existential rights
The poor	↑	→	↑	→	↑
Outsiders	↑	↑	↑	→	↑
Established	↑	↓	↑	↓	→
Millionaires	↑	→	→	→	→

Source: The author's own elaboration.

Legend: ↑: upward mobility; ↓: downward mobility; →: stability.

workers, are less affected by the increasing unemployment (Barufi 2016), although they are more affected by reduction in income, since higher salaries have recently suffered a higher proportional reduction than lower salaries (IBGE 2016). Also, millionaires are losing income in absolute terms, given the current downturn in the economy and the reduction in profits. Millionaires are also facing losses in their privileged access to public funds due to current investigations into corruption.

Social structure and political crisis

The movements observed in the Brazilian social structure correspond to shifts in the *force field* among state, capital, and labor that, in turn, reflect relations of dependency and interdependency with the global context. These interdependencies concern, firstly, financial flows such as foreign investments, remissions of profit abroad, or other profits obtained by Brazilian companies abroad. These flows affect the amount to be apportioned, in turn affecting the social distribution among the hubs capital, labor, and state, as well as among the different social classes or strata. Another important component of these interdependencies is the Brazilian insertion in transnational production chains that were modified substantially in the period, given the retraction of industrial activity (Pochmann 2013). The growing specialization in commodity exports ensured that the persistent fall in the international price of raw materials since 2010 dragged the economy into a recession and altered the parameters of the internal distribution of income and wealth. Beside this, global shifts observed in some sectors of the economy, such as the extensive subcontracting in the banking sector, dramatically modify the margin of maneuver of distributive negotiations at the national level, as Sproll (2013) shows.

At the political level, on the one hand, the amicable rhetoric concerning both national and foreign capital adopted by the Brazilian government in all of the period implied restrictions to economic policy and to the adoption of more emphatic redistributive measures, so as to maintain the so-called "confidence of the markets." On the other hand, international law conventions ratified by the Brazilian government and the transnationalization of social movements observed in this period influenced the national distributive game in favor of less privileged groups, as in the cases of women and blacks (Costa 2015).

If we consider the distribution of resources among the hubs capital, labor, and state, there was an increase in state participation in the general distribution of income in the period considered: tributary revenue went from 31.4% of GNP in 2003 to 33.5% in 2014 (Ministério do Planejamento 2015). When we observe the composition of the tax burden, however, the asymmetries of power among the three corporate hubs are fairly evident. In contrast to countries with a better income distribution that tax capital gains up to 42%, Brazil exempts profits and dividends from income tax. Levies on income, representing 26.5% of the total, and on the consumption of goods and services, representing 49.7%, formed the bulk of tax collection (Castro 2014: 25, data from 2012). That is, if it is true that the PT governments augmented expenditures on social policies to combat poverty, there

190 Sérgio Costa

were no shifts as far as revenue was concerned: the model continued to be based on regressive indirect taxes, that is, taxes that promote the concentration of income. In the period studied here, there was no organized movement whatsoever nor any systematic discussion in the Brazilian public space regarding the distributive consequences of this tributary structure.

Lula was elected president in 2002 with a government program that emphasized the fight against inequality. His votes were well distributed throughout the national territory and among the different income groups, with impressive results in larger cities and among better educated groups, historical electoral bases of the PT. Starting with his reelection in 2006, a tendency was initiated that deepened with the election of Dilma Rousseff in 2010 and her reelection in 2014. From then on, Lula's main electoral base and later that of his successor Rousseff began shifting more and more toward poorer groups, moving from the southeast toward the northeast of the country and from larger cities to smaller ones (Braig et al. 2015; TSE 2014). The party's discourse was also modified. While the redistribution of wealth did not disappear completely from the electoral programs, the focus did shift toward expanding the possibilities of consumption, individual social mobility, and the middle class.

Next to the political dedication to a "new middle class," the commitment to fighting racial and gender discrimination became explicit in the discourse used by the PT presidents and in many of their government actions. At the political level, this set of discourses and actions is seen as a threat to the established group characterized above. The losses are not economic, since the established increased their income and wealth in the period 2003 to 2013. They faced losses of position in hierarchical contexts and a loss of efficacy of their exclusive associations to guarantee their strategies of social closure. Early on, some of the media began vocalizing the fear of the established, constructing the discourse of the "larmoyant" established middle class in opposition to the "jubilant" "new middle class" (the outsiders), as demonstrated below:

> Nowadays, the middle class is the real 'black' of Brazil: It pays abusive taxes, it does not use our terrible public services and is forced to assume its health, education and security costs alone [...]. Let me remind you: Nobody protects the middle class, neither the state nor NGOs, churches ... nothing.
>
> *(Azevedo 2007: 106)*

This kind of discourse, which combines defending the class position of the established with discrediting the fight against gender and racial discrimination, has been crystallizing with time into an anti-PT discourse. This is easily comprehensible: the party and many of its representatives, among them their most important leader, Lula, embody the "invasion" of the outsiders in social and political spaces formerly reserved for the established. Although the larmoyant discourse of the established has accompanied the entire period in which the PT occupied the government, their power to mobilize broad segments of society remained inexpressive as long as the Brazilian economy was growing at accelerated levels and the poor, the outsiders, and the millionaires saw their material and social condition improve.

However, these critical discourses gained public resonance in the second half of Dilma Rousseff's first mandate and, starting in June 2013, fed a series of public protests with marches and demonstrations in various Brazilian cities. Little by little, more right-wing movements of the political spectrum started to organize demonstrations that, despite adopting a generalized tone of critique of institutionalized politics, are becoming more and more distinctly a protest against the government and the Workers' Party in general.

In the parliamentary context, the PT never managed to hold even one-fifth of the seats in Congress, despite having the most numerous fraction. This forced the party to establish alliances with the remaining parties. After the failure of the strategy of direct purchase of the loyalty of parliamentarians in 2005, the PT began, as mentioned above, to give ministries and positions to politicians and allied parties, who in turn administered directly their criminal associations with private initiative. The PMDB became the most important allied party and was represented by Vice-President Temer when Rousseff won the elections in 2010 and 2014 (Nobre 2013). In its own way, the model functioned fairly well until 2015, when a sweeping action against corruption in Brazilian politics was initiated, combining the forces of the judicial branch and the federal police. Besides impeding or at least limiting the access of politicians and parties to the channels of the generation of illicit resources that were lining their pockets, the attack generated panic among the politicians and entrepreneurs involved, due to the fear of being discovered and arrested, as has indeed happened in several cases. The investigations dismantled the bases upon which Dilma Rousseff's parliamentary majority lay, leading to her impeachment in August 2016, as mentioned above.

In public space, important changes also occurred. From the end of 2015, in view of the worsening economic crisis, entrepreneurial entities led by the Federation of Industries of the State of São Paulo (Federação das Indústrias do Estado de São Paulo or FIESP) entered into a political dispute in favor of deposing the president. At the same time, as the possibility of impeachment became more and more imminent, social movements and intellectuals who, in previous years had distanced themselves from the PT, rearticulated themselves to organize a reaction to what they saw as a parliamentary coup d'état against a president who was legitimately elected by popular vote. In this way, public protests began to alternate between those who, starting in 2013, were organizing demonstrations against the PT, and those who went out on the street to support the president. The average levels of schooling and income of the demonstrators both in favor of and against the impeachment were much higher than the Brazilian average, indicating that the poor and a large part of the outsiders were absent from the demonstrations (Alonso 2016).

Conclusions

By shifting to studies that combine Marxist and Weberian traditions in the analysis of social structure, this chapter sought to present the contemporary Brazilian political crisis as a distributive conflict involving four classes or strata (the poor,

192 Sérgio Costa

outsiders, established, millionaires), defined using five determinant vectors of social inequality: wealth, position, knowledge, selective association, and existential rights. The definition of these classes or strata considered not the position occupied in the social structure at a particular moment, but the social trajectory traversed by each group since 2003.

Generally speaking, the four classes or strata considered saw their wealth and their knowledge grow in the period between 2003 and 2014. Their existential rights increased or at least remained stable in this period. In relation to position and exclusive associations, the movement observed between 2003 and 2014 is fairly discrete for the different classes: while the poor and outsiders ascended significantly in their social position, the established lost social position to the extent that their power to exclude outsiders from social spaces formerly reserved for their own usage diminished. The same logic applies to exclusive associations with regard to gender and race. Even though gender and ethnoracial equality are far from being achieved in Brazil, between 2003 and 2014 there was a decrease in the power of men and whites to discriminate against women and blacks. This loss of position in the hierarchies of class, gender, and race fed the resentment of the established against the PT government even in times when, in terms of wealth, they experienced an ascendant trajectory.

Starting in 2014, the picture changed. The exacerbation of the economic crisis caused all of the groups, especially the outsiders, to lose income. The reduction of vacancies in the formal market produced a loss of existential rights, particularly for the poor and outsiders. The established, though less threatened by the outsiders (the most affected by the crisis), also experienced social decline as the recession advanced. Finally, the millionaires, who had until then been gaining at all of the levels of inequality with the PT governments, lost at least part of their exclusive associations as the investigations into corruption advanced and their criminal networks with the state and politicians were dismantled. It is precisely when the millionaires began to lose that the representative associations, such as the FIESP, entered into the political dispute in the public space. It is also at this moment that the effective changes in favor of the removal of the president began to occur. The impression that remains is that the established, given the resonance of their positions and opinions in the mass media, constitute a decisive actor in the formation of public opinion. Nevertheless, the formation of political will, in the sense of the agglutination of decisions with a binding effect, still depends on the dispositions of the millionaires. When they understood that their capital interests were threatened and their privileged channels of access to the state were obstructed, they joined the political fight unfolding in the public sphere, deciding the game in their favor. This was at least the partial result of the dispute among capital, state, and labor at the end of 2016.

Notes

1 Iasmin Goes and Clay Johnson translated a previous version of this paper from Portuguese into English, including all quotations. I thank Elizabeth Jelin, Renata Motta, Lena Lavinas, Krista Lillemets, and Jan N. Pieterse for valuable comments on

and criticisms of different versions of this essay. I alone am responsible for any remaining deficiencies and imprecisions.

2   Kreckel emphasizes a crucial and widespread misunderstanding in the Anglo-Saxon reception of Weber (this is also the case for the Brazilian reception), when it comes to three terms appearing in *Economy and Society* (§ 6 and chapter IV): Klassen, Stände, Parteien (Classes, Estates of the Realm, Parties) are wrongly understood as the material (classes), symbolic (status groups), and power (parties) dimensions of existing inequalities. As convincingly shown by Kreckel (1992: 57–63, 69–70), class does indeed correspond to the structural-material dimension of inequalities. However, *Stände* in Weber's work do not concern the symbolic dimension, but rather the extent of interactions, relationships, and social networking between peers, something close to Pierre Bourdieu's (1979) notion of social capital. And parties, in turn, cannot correspond to the power dimension since power is not *one* single dimension of inequality in Weber's reading, but a transversal category that permeates all other dimensions.

3   These spaces reflect and reproduce social hierarchies in a multitude of ways: through an architecture that often hinders the access of the carless or ensures more comfort and agility in service to those willing to spend more; through overt surveillance of "intruders," defined by appearance, ethno-racial criteria, etc. (Caldeira 2014; Nascimento et al. 2015).

4   Strictly speaking, one would have to include a sixth vector of inequality—the socio-ecological inequalities (see Dietz in this book). In contemporary Brazil, the expanded production of commodities has created new environmental risks and damages to the rural population, while the dramatic increase in the number of cars and motorcycles circulating in the cities has deteriorated the quality of urban life, affecting different social classes and strata with diverse intensities. This chapter does not take this sixth dimension into account, given the difficulties in estimating its impact on the social structure.

5   Gender hierarchies are not equally applicable to the five vectors considered here: while income disparities, participation in exclusive associations, and advantages in hierarchical organizations for the man are widely spread, women have more years of schooling than men. In the case of existential rights, a quite differentiated picture is observed: while men—and especially those who are black and poor—are, for instance, preferential victims of police violence, women are more affected by domestic or sexual violence (for indicators from different social spheres, see IPEA 2015).

6   In line with a rhetoric adopted by international organizations (World Bank 2013) and by the PT, Neri (2012) uses the expression "new middle class" to celebrate income improvements of groups that counted among the poor strata at the beginning of PT administrations. In due course, different Brazilian social scientists criticized the rushed enthusiasm about the "new middle class," pointing to the conceptual limits of basing a definition of classes only on income criteria (e.g., Xavier Sobrinho 2011; Scalon and Salata 2012; Quadros et al. 2013; Pochmann 2014).

7   One case of blame gossip that became paradigmatic for the public repercussion it received in social and mass media occurred in 2014. A university professor posted on her Facebook profile a photo of a man (who, as it later turned out, was a public prosecutor) dressed in a tank-top and Bermuda shorts in the terminal of the Santos Dumont Airport in Rio de Janeiro with the caption: "Airport or bus station?" Among many other posts that shared the indignation of the professor appeared the following: "The glamour of flying is definitely gone." "This is only a sample of what I've seen in Brazil" (Toledo 2014: 2).

References

Alonso, A. (2016): "Protesto e repressão," *Le Monde Diplomatique Brasil*, available at: http://diplomatique.org.br/protesto-e-repressao/.

Anderson, P. (2016): "Crisis in Brazil," *London Review of Books*, 38(8): 15–22.

Avritzer, L. and Costa, S. (2004): "Teoria crítica, democracia e esfera pública: concepções e usos na América Latina," *Dados*, 47(4): 703–728.

194 Sérgio Costa

Azevedo, R. (2007): "O movimento dos sem-bolsa," *Veja*, 2020: 106–107.

Barufi, A. M. (2016): "Movimento recente de retorno para as Classes D e E parece ser conjuntural," *Destaque Depec. Bradesco*, Ano XII (133): 1–3.

Bielschowsky, R. (2014): "O modelo de desenvolvimento proposto por Lula e Dilma," *Brasil Debate*, available at (accessed on 15 June, 2016): http://brasildebate.com.br/o-modelo-de-desenvolvimento-proposto-por-lula-e-dilma/.

Boatcǎ, M. (2015): *Global Inequalities Beyond Occidentalism*, Farnham: Ashgate.

Bourdieu, P. (1979): *La Distinction. Critique Sociale du Jugement*, Paris: Les Éditions de Minuit.

Braig, M., Power, T. J., and Renno, L. (2015): "Brazil 2015 and Beyond: The Aftermath of the 2014 Elections and Implications for Dilma's Second Term," *Lasaforum*, XLVI (3): 15–17.

Caldeira, T. (2014): "Qual a novidade dos rolezinhos? Espaço público, desigualdade e mudança em São Paulo," *Novos Estudos*, 104: 13–20.

Castro, F. A. (2014): *Imposto de Renda da Pessoa Física: Comparações Internacionais. Medidas de Progressividade e Redistribuição*, Brasília: Universidade de Brasília, dissertação de mestrado.

CEPAL (2016): *Panorama Social de América Latina*, Santiago de Chile: CEPAL.

Cortes da Costa, L. (2013): "Classes medias e as desigualdades sociais no Brasil," in Bartelt, D. (ed.): *A 'Nova Classe Média' no Brasil como Conceito e Projeto Político*, Rio de Janeiro: Fundação Heinrich Böll, pp. 43–55.

Costa, S. (2015): "Protection without Redistribution? Conceptual Limitations of Policies Meant to Reduce Inequalities Concerning Race and Gender in Brazil," in: Fritz, B. and Lavinas, L. (eds.): *A Moment of Equality for Latin America? Challenges for Redistribution*, Farnham: Ashgate, pp. 235–252.

Davis, K. and Moore, W. E. (1944): "Some Principles of Stratification," *American Sociological Review*, 10(2): 242–249.

Elias, N. (2004): *Was ist Soziologie?*, Weinheim: Juventa.

Elias, N. and Scotson, J. L. (1994 [1965]): *The Established and the Outsiders*, Dublin: University College Dublin Press.

Franco, B. M. (2016): "Ponte para o future," *Folha de S. Paulo*, 02 August, 2016, p. 2.

Fraser, N. (2010): "Injustice at Intersecting Scales: On 'Social Exclusion' and the 'Global Poor,'" *European Journal of Social Theory*, 13(3): 363–371.

Fritz, B. and Lavinas, L. (eds.) (2015): *A Moment of Equality for Latin America? Challenges for Redistribution*, Farnham: Ashgate.

Guimarães, A. S. (2002): *Classes, Raças e Democracia*, São Paulo: Editora 34.

Habermas, J. (1992): *Faktizität und Geltung—Beiträge zur Diskurstheorie des Rechts und des demokratischen Rechtsstaats*, Frankfurt am Main: Suhrkamp Verlag.

IBGE (2015): *Pesquisa Nacional por Amostra de Domicílios 2014*, Rio de Janeiro: Instituto Brasileiro de Geografia e Estatística, available at (accessed on 15 June, 2016): http://www.ibge.gov.br/home/estatistica/populacao/trabalhoerendimento/pnad2014/.

IBGE (2016): *Pesquisa Nacional por Amostra de Domicílios 2015*. Rio de Janeiro: Instituto Brasileiro de Geografia e Estatística. Available at (accessed on 25 November, 2016): http://www.ibge.gov.br/home/estatistica/populacao/trabalhoerendimento/pnad2015/default.shtm.

IPEA (2015): *Retrato das Desigualdades de Raça e Gênero*. Brasília: Instituto de Pesquisas Econômicas Aplicadas. Updates available at (accessed on 15 June, 2016): http://www.ipea.gov.br/retrato/.

Korzeniewicz, R. P. and Moran, T. P. (2009): *Unveiling Inequality*, New York, NY: Russell Sage Foundation.

Kreckel, R. (1992): *Politische Soziologie der sozialen Ungleichheit*, Frankfurt am Main: Campus.

Kreckel, R. (2004): *Politische Soziologie der sozialen Ungleichheit*, Frankfurt am Main: Campus, 3rd ed.

Lavinas, L. (2016): *How Social Developmentalism Reframed Social Policy in Brazil*, Berlin: desiguALdades, Working Paper 94.

MEC (2014): *A Democratização e Expansão da Educação Superior no país 2003–2014*, Brasília: Ministério da Educação.

Medeiros, M., Souza, P. H., and Castro, F. A. (2015): "O topo da distribuição de renda no Brasil: Primeiras estimativas com dados tributários e comparação com pesquisas domiciliares, 2006–2012," *Dados*, 58(1): 7–36.

Milá, M. M. (2015): *Income Concentration in a Context of Late Development: An Investigation of Top Incomes in Brazil Using Tax Records, 1933–2013*, Paris: School of Economics, Master Thesis.

Ministério do Planejamento (2015): *Evolução Recente da Carga Tributária Federal*, Brasília: Assessoria Econômica do Ministério do Planejamento, Orçamento e Gestão.

Nascimento, M. C. R., Oliveira, J. S., Teixeira, J. C., and Carrieri, A. P. (2015): "Com que cor eu vou pro shopping que você me convidou?" *RAC, Revista de Administração Contemporânea*, 19(3): 245–268.

Neri, M. (2012): *A Nova Classe Média. O Lado Brilhante da Base da Pirâmide*, São Paulo: Saraiva.

Nobre, M. (2013): *Imobilismo em Movimento. Da Redemocratização ao Governo Dilma*, São Paulo: Cia das Letras.

Parkin, F. (1974): "Strategies of Social Closure in Class Formation," in: Parkin, F. (ed.): *The Social Analysis of Class Structure*. London: Tavistock, pp. 1–18.

Pochmann, M. (2013): "Mobilidade social no capitalismo e redivisão internacional da classe média," in: Bartelt, D. D. (ed.): *A 'Nova Classe Média' no Brasil como Conceito e Projeto Político*, Rio de Janeiro: Fundação Heinrich Böll, pp. 156–171.

Pochmann, M. (2014): *O Mito da Grande Classe Média: Capitalismo e Estrutura Social*. São Paulo: Boitempo Editorial.

Quadros, W. (2008): *A Evolução da Estrutura Social Brasileira*, Campinas: Textos para Discussão IE/ UNICAMP 48.

Saad-Filho, A. (2016): "Watch Out for Judicial Coup in Brazil," *MR Zine*, available at (accessed 22 August, 2016): http://mrzine.monthlyreview.org/2016/sf230316.html.

Scalon, M. C. and Salata, A. (2012): "Uma nova classe média no Brasil da última década? O debate a partir da perspectiva sociológica," *Sociedade e Estado*, 27(2): 387–407.

Singer, A. (2012): *Os Sentidos do Lulismo: Reforma Gradual e Pacto Conservador*, São Paulo: Cia. das Letras.

Sproll, M. (2013): *Precarization, Genderization and Neotaylorist Work: How Global Value Chain Restructuring Affects Banking Sector Workers in Brazil*, Berlin: desiguALdades.net, Working Paper 44.

Therborn, G. (2013): *The Killing Fields of Inequality*, Cambridge, U.K.: Polity Press.

Toledo, J. R. (2014): "Aeroporto ou rodoviária?" *Estado de S. Paulo*, 10 February, 2014, p. 5.

TSE (2014): *Estatísticas Eleitorais 2014*, Brasília: Tribunal Superior Eleitoral, available at (accessed 1 June, 2016): http://www.tse.jus.br/eleicoes/estatisticas/estatisticas-eleitorais-2014-resultado.

Weber, M. (1956 [1922]): *Wirtschaft und Gesellschaft. Grundriss der verstehenden Soziologie*, Tübingen: J.C.B. Mohr, 4th ed.

World Bank (2013): *Economic Mobility and the Rise of the Latin American Middle Class*. Washington, D.C.: World Bank.

Wright, E. O. (1985): *Classes*. London: Verso.

Xavier Sobrinho, G. (2011): "'Classe C' e sua alardeada ascensão: nova? Classe? Média?" *Indicadores Econômicos FEE*, 38(4): 67–80.

11

TRANSNATIONAL CARE CHAINS AND ENTANGLED INEQUALITIES

Anna Katharina Skornia

Introduction

In recent decades, the increase in global care migrations has drawn attention to new interdependencies and inequalities between individuals, households, and countries. For families in poorer countries of the globe, emigration has become a central strategy of care and social reproduction, involving a growing proportion of women who migrate autonomously, assuming the role of economic providers in response to social, economic, and political crises. This feminization of migration is also spurred by new care needs in Europe and other countries of the global North, caused by the aging population, along with a change in the social roles and aspirations of women, which have contributed to a collapse of common modes of care provision. In this context, women's entry into paid work has not involved a substantial change in the gendered division of labor, but an outsourcing of care labor to migrant workers in the domestic sphere. These new care relationships have important implications for the reproduction of social inequalities across national borders and beyond.

A central concept for studying these processes, including the link between care and social inequality, from a global perspective, is the concept of "global care chains" (Hochschild 2000), referring to interdependencies in the care arrangements of individuals and families located in different places and regions. Global care chains are constituted through a global network of persons: While employer women in rich countries outsource care and domestic tasks to migrant women from poorer countries, migrant women again delegate part of their care responsibilities to persons from even poorer households in the country of origin. These practices are observed to perpetuate the gendered division of labor, while also producing new "care drains," especially on the part of children who are left behind (ibid.). Hence, with the purchase of care services, provided by migrant workers in the global

North, it is argued, care has become an unfairly distributed resource, which is withdrawn from one country and household and imported to another, similar to "the nineteenth-century extraction of gold, ivory, and rubber from the Third World" (Hochschild 2003: 23, 26).

These arguments have inspired ongoing research and controversial debates (e.g., Escrivá 2005; Zimmerman et al. 2006; Orozco 2009; Yeates 2009). Many scholars acknowledge a certain degree of agency in migration processes and therefore reject the dichotomized distinction between "winners" and "losers" of this global division of labor (ibid.). Rather than focusing on global care chains as a one-way transfer from poorer to richer countries, it is argued, attention should be drawn to the overall *transformation* of care practices and meanings among both migrant and employing families involved (Zimmerman et al. 2006; Yeates 2009). Further critique relates to the limited focus on long-distance mothering, which disregards the diversity and transitional character of transnational care (Yeates 2009), and to the little attention paid to extra-domestic actors in shaping transnational caregiving, including in particular the state and its influence exerted through migration policies (Herrera 2008).

The aim of this chapter is to critically engage with the global care chains concept and discussion, based on an analysis of empirical data on social inequalities in care chains between Peru and Italy. More specifically, I adopt a perspective focused on "entangled inequalities" (Costa 2013) to explore the reproduction of inequalities in transnational care chains as relational units of analysis. This perspective was elaborated as a contribution to the Research Network on Interdependent Inequalities in Latin America desiguALdades.net. It is well suited for studying the intersection of different inequality axes, which are of central importance in the global care chains literature, while also allowing a comprehensive analysis of inequalities at different local, national, transnational, and global levels.

As I seek to show, transnational care chains involve a transformation of care practices, which is based on a dynamic reproduction of entangled inequalities. My central argument is that beyond global asymmetries between regions, countries, and households, the particularities of national social-institutional and policy configurations play an essential role in contributing to a reproduction of inequalities related to care. Hence, I deal with the following main questions: How are social inequalities reproduced in transnational care chains between Peru and Italy? And what is the role of states in shaping and contributing to these inequalities? The case of Italy is particularly interesting to examine this question, due to a series of migration, care, and labor market policies, which influence the migrants' employment relationships in the care sector.

The findings presented in this chapter are drawn from a multi-sited ethnographic case study on Peruvian migration to Italy, conducted between 2011 and 2012, which included fieldwork trips to Milan as well as Lima, Huancayo, and Cuzco/Urubamba in Peru, and examined the employment and transnational care relationships of Peruvian migrants hired as home-based caregivers for the elderly in Milan, Italy (Skornia 2014).[1]

Researching the link between care and social inequalities

Understanding the emergence of transnational care chains requires a closer look at the link between care and social inequalities. Care can be defined as the (paid and unpaid) work of looking after the physical, psychological, emotional, and developmental needs of one or more people (Kofman and Raghuram 2009). While care constitutes a key dimension of human development and welfare, which relates to needs shared by people across social groups and societies, the social organization of care work is shaped by persistent inequalities in the distribution of care responsibilities.

The unequal distribution of these practices is revealed first and foremost within families and households, where the major part of domestic and practical, 'hands-on' care work falls on women, as time surveys have shown (for Europe see: Lutz 2008; for Latin America: CEPAL 2012). This is true despite the fact that women's labor market participation has significantly increased over the past decades. At the same time, the distribution of care work is also based on class and ethnicity, as revealed by the hiring of internal migrant women to provide domestic work in urban, upper-class households. This practice has been common in the history of both Europe (Sarti 2008) and Latin America, where it has been strongly marked by inequalities of race and ethnicity, in addition to class and social status (Bunster and Chaney 1985).

In addition, an uneven distribution of care responsibilities can be observed between families and other, non-domestic agents in the context of welfare and care regimes or, in other words, the "infrastructure of care, namely how care is organized and delivered" (Raghuram 2012: 163). Considered in this context, the social organization of care work depends on multiple sectors, including not only families, but also state, market, and community sector (Razavi 2007). In this infrastructure, the state plays an important role, being not just a provider of care but also a significant decision maker and actor in shaping and influencing both the formal and informal modes of care provision.[2] Historically, states have largely contributed to constructing the family as the central agent of care provision. This applies in particular to "familistic" care regimes in Mediterranean and Latin American countries, which intensively resort to the family for care provision (Aguirre 2008).

Care work often goes along with limited or absent remuneration and social benefits, the non-existence or non-application of legal regulation as well as social devaluation (Orozco 2006). Thus, care work may contribute to the caregiver's financial hardship and poverty during their working lives as well as in old age. In short, the absence of a sense of social responsibility regarding care, coupled with the relegation of care to households (and subsequently to women), has produced a deep-rooted link between care, social inequality, and exclusion from citizenship (ibid.). With the emergence of transnational care chains, this link is taking on new global dimensions.

To study the link between care and entangled inequalities from a transnational perspective, this research followed an inductive approach, aimed at understanding the ways social inequalities are reproduced and reshaped through the dynamic social practices and interactions of Peruvian migrants with their employers and their own family members. This meant looking at *processes* rather than at static categories of difference and domination. Here, the analysis of care practices, as well as expectations, strategies, and negotiation processes in transnational care chains between Peru and Italy, will provide insight into global as well as national asymmetries, including the influence of state policies related to care, gender, migration, and labor regimes.

In looking at transnational care practices, existing research has tended to limit its focus to the experiences of the so-called caregivers, especially migrant mothers and their female employers. Based on the understanding of care as an interdependent social practice and relationship (Orozco 2006), which involves both caregivers and receivers, I suggest to broaden the focus by studying the perspectives of a variety of actors: Peruvian migrant women and men, with and without children, with experience as elderly carers in Milan, Italy, as well as their employers and transnational family members, including the perspectives of care receivers, such as children and the elderly.

The transnationalization of care regimes

Global care chains emerge as part of a transnationalization of care regimes. According to structural approaches, they are a product of a "reprivatization" of social reproduction occurring in the context of neo-liberal restructuring and large-scale social, cultural, and demographic transformations, which have contributed to multiple "care crises" (Zimmerman et al. 2006: 15). These developments, however, occur differently, depending on the social organization of care within the broader context of welfare regimes.[3] Following Esping-Andersen's (1990) typology of welfare regimes, the Mediterranean countries—Italy, Spain, and Greece—have been identified as a distinctive cluster of regimes in which the management of care is delegated almost entirely to the family (Bettio et al. 2006). In these countries, the development of wider social services by the state has been halted by the restructuring of familiarist care arrangements through the hiring of migrant care workers in private households. In the northern European countries, in contrast, migrant workers are introduced into care regimes characterized by a shift from state to marketized provision, both in home-based and institutional arrangements (Erel 2012). Independently from the different organization of care in each country, however, there seems to be a trend toward "commodification" of care—exemplified, for instance, through cash benefits, such as direct payments for elderly and disability care (e.g., Italy, UK, the Netherlands, and Austria) (ibid.). These developments have encouraged the outsourcing of care work to transnational migrants, to be further examined in the Italian case.

At the same time, the transnationalization of care regimes is spurred by structural changes in the countries of the "South," which have contributed to the increase in international migration. In Peru and other countries of the Andean region, neo-liberal structural reforms, along with political and economic crisis, have contributed to a deepening of inequalities, especially based on social class (Gonzales de Olarte 2005). These developments have serious repercussions for the care capacities of families, and above all women, as the central agents of care provision, who compensate for inadequate social and public services. In this context, emigration and the sending of remittances have become an important strategy of social reproduction. Since the late 1980s, Peruvian emigration has increased considerably, with the consequence that in 2007, 1,635,207 Peruvians—more than 10% of the national population—were residing permanently outside the country (OIM and INEI 2009).[4]

Italy, along with Spain, is the European country that concentrates the highest numbers of Peruvian migrants. At the beginning of 2012, 108,000 Peruvians were residing in Italy with a regular residence status (ISMU 2013). Almost half of this population lives in Lombardy (45,550), with a spatial concentration in the city of Milan (19,450). It is estimated that in addition there are around 13,000 Peruvians residing in Italy in irregular conditions (ISMU 2009). Peruvian migration to Italy is characterized by the steady increase of presences over the decades since the late 1980s, including migrants of different social classes and geographical origins; the predominance of women who constitute 60.1% of Peruvians in Italy (Caritas 2011); the concentration of these migrants in a number of well-defined occupational niches, especially domestic work, care of the elderly, and construction work; the strength of family networks in sustaining migration as well as an ongoing process of family reunification.

Peruvian migrants have come to fill the growing "care gap" (Gerhard 2010: 105) that has emerged in Italy due to a series of demographic and socio-cultural factors, including the aging of the population, the change in family models, women's increasing participation in the labor market, and a limited provision of social services by the state (Degiuli 2007). In this context, the outsourcing of elderly care to migrant workers has involved a far-reaching restructuring and transnationalization of a "familistic" care regime, which has also been described as a shift from a "family" model of care to a "migrant-in-the-family" model of care (Bettio et al. 2006: 274).

From the perspective of transnational migration studies, these processes are supported by the agency of migrants and their families in constructing new social spaces through practices, identities, and communities that extend across national borders (e.g., Glick Schiller et al. 1992; Pries 1999), including transnational families (e.g., Baldassar et al. 2007; Herrera 2008; Drotbohm 2013). New forms of "doing family," however, involve not only transnational but also employing families. In this sense even relationships between paid domestic workers and their employers can be described as quasi-familial (Lutz 2007), reflecting the changeability of care relationships and fluidity of private and public spheres in the construction of domesticity.

Here, it is interesting to consider non-market-related forces, including lifestyle and social status as further driving factors of both emigration and the hiring of migrant caretakers in private homes (Yeates 2009). In Peru, both internal and international migration is socially constructed as a way of achieving progress by climbing up the socio-economic ladder. At the same time, the employment of a migrant domestic worker may also be aspirational (Abbots 2012). In Italy, many employing women stay outside of the labor market but expect to enhance their social status and independence by hiring a paid caregiver for the elderly. Among the Italian employers I interviewed, there was a significant proportion of housewives, who decided to delegate the work of elderly care in order to save time for other types of unpaid care work, provided mainly in their roles as wives and mothers. This suggests that migrant caregivers to the elderly are not only hired to allow the permanence of Italian women in the labor market, as frequently noted (e.g., Sarti 2008), but also enable women employers to make decisions on which types of care work they prefer to do themselves (caring for husbands, children, and/or grandchildren) and which to delegate to others (caring for elderly parents). In addition, the cultural preference for home-based, as compared to institutional, care is another important reason for the employment of home-based carergivers for the elderly in Italian households.

Finally, states play an important role in shaping and contributing to care trans-nationalization. In the global care chains literature, the role of the state has been addressed mainly through a critique of its failure to guarantee social and economic rights of its population, especially of women and children (Herrera 2008). Sending and receiving states, however, have played a more active role in contributing to migration and care chains through discourses and political frameworks. In a trans-national context, this is reflected by the importance of migration regimes, and their intersections with care, gender, and employment regimes. Migration regimes include the political, legal, and normative frameworks related to immigration and citizenship as well as to the organization of labor markets and treatment of the migrant workforce (Lutz and Palenga-Möllenbeck 2010).

In the case studied here, such frameworks, norms, and discourses contribute to the formation of care chains and reproduction of inequalities between Peru and Italy. The Peruvian state sustains emigration mainly through an open discourse in favor of migration as well as recent policies and programs in the fields of remittances and co-development (Berg 2010). The Italian state plays a more powerful role, based on a series of social and migration policies, which have institutionalized the employ-ment of migrant domestic workers. On one hand, these include subsidies for the dependent elderly. The most important one, the *Indennità di Accompagnamento*, is an attendance allowance of around 480 Euro per month (in 2011) for dependent persons with severe disabilities, which is granted irrespective of the receivers' age and financial situation. This benefit is often used to employ migrant caregivers to the elderly (Gori 2011). On the other hand, the Italian state has promoted their employment through the cyclical declaration of immigration amnesties. Since 2002, however, immigration is mainly regulated by annual quotas for migrant domestic workers, which have increased markedly within a very short period of time from 19% in 2005 to 38% in 2007 and to even 70% in 2008 (Catanzaro and Colombo 2009: 28). This procedure has been used by many employers for the admission of immigrants who are already staying and working irregularly in the country. As most Italian employers wish to hire a female care worker, these measures have sustained the feminization of Peruvian migration to Italy. Overall, they have been central in promoting a transnationalized model of care based upon the indispensable role of migrant workers.

The renegotiation of gender inequalities: care as women's responsibility

In both countries examined here, care relationships have been strongly shaped by the normative ideal of women's domesticity, which is linked to their protagonist role as caregivers toward both the younger and older generations in the domestic sphere. This brings me to the central question examined in this study: How are gender inequalities reproduced and renegotiated through their intersection with other interdependent axes of stratification, such as ethnicity, citizenship, and migration status? In the following I will analyze this question by presenting some observations and examples from my empirical data.

First of all, the strategies of employer and migrant women, in the case of Peruvian migration to Italy, reveal multiple practices of "doing gender" (Lutz 2007). By hiring a migrant caregiver for the elderly, Italian employer women distance themselves from certain gender and intergenerational expectations and make choices unavailable to previous generations of women, which are experienced as a form of emancipation and privilege. Their emancipation, however, remains incomplete, as most of them remain in charge of the domestic chores and care of other family members. These tasks are often described as exhausting. Talking about her responsibility of supervising the work of several migrants who take care of her elderly mother, Alessia, an Italian woman, points out:

> It's also quite some work to supervise all of them. (...) And I have difficulties, a lot of difficulties to do so. (...) Because then I dedicate myself to children at the hospital, to my grandchildren, I have quite a demanding husband. (...) I dedicate myself to the cooking, the arts of cooking, I *have* my interests, I have a very intense life, but I dedicate it *very* much to the family, very much. And I *dislike* that because sometimes I also feel that it's a bit suffocating.
>
> *(Alessia, 62 years, employer)*

Shown by this statement, the distribution of care and domestic tasks within employer families remains highly unequal. As in this case, most female employers interviewed do not free themselves from their caregiving roles but prioritize one care practice over another.

The continuity of gender ideals is also reflected by the perspectives of elderly care receivers in Italian employer households. Elderly women seem to have particular difficulties to accept a live-in caregiver, as this means ceding the autonomy of household management that used to be among their main responsibilities. Hence, gender norms are reproduced and simultaneously challenged by the newly established care relationships.

Similar observations can be made with regard to the care arrangements in the transnational families of Peruvian migrants. Commonly these migrants rely on the support of another female family member, or paid woman of a lower ethnic and class status for the care of their own family dependents. Most frequently, the migrants' mothers or sisters act as co-caregivers of small children or aging parents (see also Anderson 2012). While delegating or assuming caregiving tasks, transnational women also continue to struggle with gender norms that sacralize women's domestic caregiving roles as daughters and/or mothers and are more involved than men in the various dimensions of practical, financial, and emotional care on a transnational level. Not only migrant mothers but also non-migrant mothers in Peru, whose children have emigrated to Italy, struggle to accept the distance to their children, while also developing new forms of motherhood at a distance that include continuous communication by phone and internet as well as remittances.

At the same time, migrant women, including childless women, also renegotiate their family roles as they become financial providers and may experience new forms of autonomy and independence from gender and intergenerational obligations, for instance, by protecting themselves against the pressure exerted by family members, as a migrant mother of four children from Lima noted:

> To be honest, in the past I communicated continuously, but actually my job also stresses me and I don't call anymore, because sometimes you call to your country and they always come with problems, I mean, they tell you about problems or ask you for money, you see what I mean? So it's better not to call so that you're left in peace (laughs).
>
> *(Ines, 44 years, from Lima, in Italy since 1999)*

All in all, the increase in women's individual and financial autonomy, on the part of both employer and migrant women, may also contribute to a process of "undoing gender" (Benería 2008: 10). This process, however, goes along with the continuity of the gendered division of labor, as revealed by the protagonist role of women in the reorganization of care work in both employing and transnational households (see also Herrera 2008).

For migrant women, the continuous involvement in transnational caregiving has serious implications for their working strategies and conditions. Migrant mothers and other women with intense care obligations tend to be most likely to submit themselves to live-in jobs and the conditions imposed by employers, mainly in order not to run the risk of losing their job and of compromising the continuity of income and remittances (see also Dota 2009; Catanzaro and Colombo 2009; Oso Casas 2010). These jobs are considered to entail the greatest limitations to independence, privacy, and self-care, and, ultimately, to the migrants' power to decide upon the use of their time beyond employment. In sum, compared with Italian employing women, most migrant women do not experience the same flexibility of deciding upon how to use their time and to distribute the care work within their own families. As a consequence, they experience higher levels of conflict in the attempt to reconcile multiple care obligations at the same time.

The participation of men in transnational care chains

Compared with women, to what extent do men participate in transnational care chains and in which ways do their strategies contribute to a renegotiation of gender inequalities? Research on transnational families and care chains has emphasized the absent or insufficient participation of men especially in unpaid domestic work (Sarti and Scrinzi 2010). My study revealed that men, at different ends of the chains, are not absent as paid and unpaid caregivers, but tend to assume care responsibilities only where no female family member is available to do so. In addition, they often assume different tasks as compared with women or tend to be more autonomous than women to make decisions regarding their involvement in paid or unpaid care. Migrant fathers, for instance, participate in the financial care of their children, but do not necessarily send money to other family members. Compared with migrant mothers, they tend to send lower amounts of remittances and do not maintain similar levels of transnational communication. Especially, single and childless men often privilege their personal independence and see their involvement in transnational caregiving as optional.

A further notable aspect is the gender-specific tasks and strategies of migrant caregivers to the elderly. In Italy, the hiring of male domestic workers is more frequent than in other receiving countries. In the mid-1990s a fourth or even a third of declared migrant domestic workers in Italy were male. Recently, the proportion of men among all declared (migrant and national) employees in the domestic and care sector has fluctuated at around 10–11% (Sarti and Scrinzi 2010). My interviews indicate that while the majority of caregivers for the elderly are women, male care workers may be preferred when the elder is also a man. This is based on the idea that men are physically stronger and thus better prepared to cope with the care needs of the elderly. Due to these ideas, the tasks of male caregivers tend to be more clearly defined and limited to caring for the elderly in a stricter sense, which means that other tasks, such as cooking and cleaning, are more often taken over by the elder's wife or by a female care worker. Female workers, in contrast, are commonly expected to assume the whole range of activities that are part of domestic work, in addition to caring for the elderly (see also Catanzaro and Colombo 2009).

At the same time, compared with men who are left behind, *migrant* men are to a greater extent required to subject themselves to new dependencies. As paid caregivers for the elderly, they assume tasks that involve not only physical but also emotional and practical dimensions of care work, and may also suffer from emotional strains, exploitation, and the frequent lack of recognition by employers. However, in dealing with such difficulties, they develop a series of strategies of 'professionalization' to enhance their status as workers or keep a certain emotional distance from employers. Migrant men, to a greater extent than women, express dissatisfaction about the lack of social recognition of their work as caregivers for the elderly and seek ways to enhance their status as workers, for instance, by asking for higher salaries or improved working conditions. In addition, they are more autonomous than women to move to a different employment sector over time. Gustavo, a Peruvian migrant who decided to quit his job as a caregiver for the elderly after some years, told me:

> For me it was emotional *waste*. Because when I started working with the elderly, I identified with him. And I saw them die and the only one who

cried was *me*. And that's what *frustrated* me. I better dedicated myself to other things.

(Gustavo, 37 years, from Lima, in Italy since 2004)

Such strategies are closely linked to their transnational family roles. Gustavo, the man cited above, is a single and childless migrant, who clearly differentiates his care obligations from those of Peruvian migrants who leave children behind. In addition, he stresses his personal projects linked to migration:

I don't have a wife who is waiting for me, I don't have children that I'd *miss*. I do have my *parents*, my brothers and sisters who are still there [in Peru]. I think about them and, when I can, I send money to them so that they are able to *support* each other. (…) I *do* think about my family, I think about them. But it would be a lie to say that I miss them, that I want to go back to Peru. (…) Rather, I'm still thinking about my project to make my career here.

(Gustavo, 37 years, from Lima, in Italy since 2004)

Similar to Gustavo, most migrant men continue to care for parents and siblings, and at times children, at a distance, but highlight their personal projects linked to migration. Clearly, their transnational involvement is considered optional and thus not comparable with that of most migrant women. As a consequence, they are more flexible to improve their working conditions, for instance, by taking a job as a live-out caregiver or in another employment sector, which, in comparison with live-in work, allows a higher degree of independence (see also Catanzaro and Colombo 2009). Several of the men interviewed for this study created their own business, corresponding to their professional knowledge in fields such as informatics, graphic design, or engineering, which allowed them to enjoy better working conditions and the continuity of their professional career. Yet, these steps may also entail income reductions resulting from the more reduced demand for workers outside the care sector, which has further declined as a consequence of the recent economic crisis.

Shown by these observations, migrant men are required to renegotiate their positions as they form part of new care relationships and adapt to the specific conditions of Italian migration and employment regimes. Still, their roles and strategies often contribute to a reassertion of gender roles.

Inequalities based on ethnicity, citizenship, and migration status

The renegotiation of gender and intergenerational obligations cannot be examined independently from their intersection with other axes of stratification. In this context, it is particularly interesting to look at inequalities of ethnicity, citizenship, and migration status.

In employer households, inequalities are often justified through the construction of ethnic and national differences. A closer look at the expectations of

Italian employers reveals that the decision of hiring a migrant caregiver for the elderly is also the product of ethnic categorization, as reflected by the important role of nationality-based ethnic constructions in the views of Italian employers.[5] Accordingly, migrants from Peru and other Latin American countries are often preferred as caregivers for the elderly, because they are held to be particularly "respectful," "kind," and "caring" regarding the elderly as well as "self-sacrificing" and "gifted" for this type of work, in opposition to Italians and to other migrant groups. This was noted by several employers interviewed:

> A characteristic that South Americans have to a higher extent (...) than people from Asia or Russia is this humanity. They have, I guess by tradition, a respect for elderly people. (...) They have this sweetness, they are strong, they are persons who aren't afraid of working, they keep working and don't back out.
>
> *(Alessia, 62 years, employer)*

> Peruvians are persons who adapt themselves very much to the person they will care for and with whom they have to work. (...) They are willing to work (...) they are able to sacrifice themselves.
>
> *(Stefania, 65 years, former employer)*

The employers cited here, similar to many others interviewed, portray an essentialized image of Peruvian migrants, in which the work of care is constructed as a dimension of character and, thereby, as natural and effortless.

At the same time, Italian migration and employment regimes contribute to new citizenship and migratory-based inequalities within the employing and transnational families of migrant workers. Subsidies for the elderly have encouraged the frequent practice of illegal employment, especially on the part of employers of middle to lower class background (see also Gori 2011). These often mentioned that subsidies and pensions were insufficient to cover the costs of a worker who was regularly employed. It is estimated that only one out of three elderly carers employed by families in Italy has a work contract, while 60–70% are employed on an irregular basis (Pasquinelli and Rusmini 2009).

However, Peruvian migrants in Italy, unless they have a long-term residence permit or Italian citizenship, depend on their legal employment as domestic workers, that is, the existence of a work contract to obtain access to a residence permit. As a consequence of the quota system, they are only granted "partial citizenship" (Parreñas 2010): Their residence is conditional on their membership in a family and, specifically, in a family for whom they provide domestic work. Because of this legal dependence on employers, many Peruvian migrants accept the difficult working conditions in this sector—including long working hours, exploitation, abuse, and drawbacks for their own health condition. The dependence on employers also affects their access to a series of rights, such as social security, health, and family reunification. Family reunification is linked to requirements of legal residence, income, and housing comfort and thus only granted to those migrants who have achieved a certain degree of legal and economic stability (Bonizzoni and Cibea 2009). In short, Italian policies contribute to inequalities between employers and migrant workers that are not primarily shaped by class, but by differences in terms of citizenship and migration status.

These conditions may have negative implications not only for workers but also for elderly care receivers. For both migrants and the elderly the 'familiarization' of employment relationships, based on the development of emotional bonds, may allow them to turn a hierarchical employment relationship into one of mutual support and intimacy, which contributes to the continuity of the care relationship and, in some cases, to an improvement in the migrants' working conditions. However, these practices and emotional bonds with migrant workers remain extremely vulnerable to the decisions of those who manage the employment relationship, including the precarious and exploitative working conditions that predominate in the sector of elderly care. These may result in emotional drawbacks for both migrants and the elderly, for instance, when workers are dismissed or quit their jobs because their rights are violated.

Adela, a Peruvian migrant woman, had developed a close relationship with the elderly for whom she cared. In her words: "It's no longer the employer and worker but you're already united by a relationship that is a bit more like a family." Yet, when Adela's employer decided to dismiss her overnight and to send the old woman to a health care institution, she was shocked, not as much about the violation of her rights as a worker as about the violent way in which the old woman was suddenly separated from her home and daily company, which caused pain and sadness for both of them, as she mentions:

> She (the old woman) did not want to go. (...) She cried and implored me not to leave her. (...) How can they grab that person and deposit her in another place, as if she wasn't a human being! That's the saddest thing that can happen, because a job I may find it again, but the person was already used to me.
> *(Adela, 51 years, from Trujillo, in Italy since 1998)*

As this statement reveals, the emotional closeness between migrant caregivers and the elderly remains unstable and fragile, due to the relationships of domination to which it is subjected. As in this case, the elderly, similar to the migrant workers, are often excluded from the processes of decision-making and may suffer drawbacks from this condition.

New dependency relations also emerge in the migrants' transnational families. Within their families, migrant workers find themselves in a position similar to that of their employers, as they earn the resources needed for care provision and hold the power to decide how to spend the money and organize the care of family dependents. In contrast, the margin of action of non-migrant family members, such as children, aging parents, and co-caregivers left behind, is restricted due to the conditions that predominate in most Peruvian households of origin, which are shaped by inadequate social policies and services. For them, the migration of family members may bring important benefits to those left behind, such as access to new economic resources, education, health care, and material comfort. However, they are highly dependent on the contingencies faced by migrants in the receiving country. All elements of transnational caregiving—including the continuity of remittances and gifts as well as regular communication and interaction and occasional visits—are shaped by structural conditions. Therefore, the migrants' illegal residence and difficult working conditions may contribute to a decline in transnational support and prolonged periods of separation between migrants and non-migrants and thereby reinforce existing or create new care deficits among children and parents who stay behind. Hence, migration may also produce reactions of abandonment, especially on the part of family dependents with intense care needs left in Peru, such as children and aging parents, as well as additional costs, increasing workloads, and limitations to self-care and independence on the part of those who support migrants as co-caregivers.

In addition, new inequalities can be observed in migrant households in Italy, for instance, when female relatives with a subordinate legal and socio-economic status support better-off migrant mothers, including family members, with unpaid childcare or domestic work and thereby allow for their permanence in the labor market.

One example is that of Carina, a Peruvian migrant mother, who was hosted in the household of her two female cousins after arriving in Italy. Her cousins offered her free housing, allowing her to save money while searching for a job in the new place. In return, however, Carina was expected to support her cousins with childcare and domestic work. As a newly arrived migrant in irregular conditions, she could not afford the high housing costs, did not have other contacts in the country, and hoped her cousins would guide her search for a job. She had indebted herself to pay the high costs of illegal migration to Italy and was pressured to pay back her debts, while also wishing to financially support her mother and children left in Peru. For these reasons, Carina decided to stay at their place, yet her cousins kept raising new expectations. After one year, she finally moved out of her cousins' place. As she notes: "I have already helped them a lot and they wanted to take advantage of me. I've seen that they don't respect me." This decision was supported by Carina's job as a live-out caregiver for the elderly, in which she earned the income necessary to afford her own room.

This example reveals the importance of new inequalities based on citizenship and migration status in shaping transnational care relationships. The differential outcomes of these processes are reflected in mainly two aspects. A first aspect relates to the unequal transnational division of care labor between women, which is linked to unequal possibilities to reconcile different types of care work, including self-care, with other (paid and unpaid) activities. While migrant women may achieve higher levels of autonomy within their families, they also reproduce the pattern of their employers by delegating care work to women of a lower status in terms of citizenship, legal status, or place of residence, who assume this work on an unpaid or a low-paid basis. These inequalities, however, are constantly renegotiated as caregivers may also break with conditions of subordination, when they become unsustainable and interfere with their own care needs.

Transnational care chains and inequalities **209**

A second observation is that transnational care chains may result in unequal possibilities to receive care. Researchers of global care chains have argued that employer households "clearly benefit" from the care provided by migrant workers (Orozco 2009: 6). In these accounts, however, the perspectives of the care receivers are seldom considered. As this study revealed, not only Peruvian migrant workers but also elderly care receivers in employer households find themselves in a condition of dependency and may both suffer drawbacks and care deficits. At the same time, I have observed ambiguous outcomes within the migrants' transnational families. Overall, this study identified a continuum of situations in the migrants' households of origin, ranging from cases of children or parents who thought of migration as an improvement for the family and their own wellbeing to those of others who perceived the migration of their parents or children in predominantly negative ways. Perceptions of abandonment and care deficits, however, are not the result of migration as such, but often emerge due to the structural conditions that shape migration and employment conditions in the care sector as well as the conditions of the households of origin, which reorganize the care of family dependents in the (continued) absence of public support. These results challenge Hochschild's conceptualization of care chains, introduced at the beginning of this chapter. As my findings suggest, there is no sign of an overall "care drain," but of new inequalities within employer and transnational families, which are supported by the regulative frameworks of states linked to care and migration.

Conclusion

The findings presented in this chapter have revealed the complex and dynamic reproduction of entangled inequalities in transnational care chains between Peru and Italy. My focus on entangled inequalities has drawn attention to the importance of extending the concept of the global care *chain*, which suggests a relatively stable and linear arrangement. Considered from this perspective, transnational care chains are dynamically reproduced by the practices of the individuals involved.

In this process, care work continues to be gendered, privatized, and socially devalued. However, while care work keeps being passed on to social groups of a subordinate social status, *transnational* care chains are clearly distinct from those that have existed within the boundaries of the nation-state. This is reflected by the growing importance of inequalities based on nationality, citizenship, and migration status in shaping transnational care relations, which are more important than class in influencing not only employment relationships in the domestic work sector (see also Lutz 2002) but also transnational family relations. Due to the continued gendering and privatization of care provision, female members of transnational families are particularly affected by the intersections of gender with nationality, citizenship, and place or status of residence.

As these findings suggest, global power and socio-economic asymmetries between states are reproduced in the new transnational division of care labor— not only in relationships between migrants and the national population of the

210 Anna Katharina Skornia

destination country, or between poorer and richer households, but also *within* the families involved. States play an active role in contributing to these inequalities through their influence on intersecting gender, care, and migration regimes. The care strategies outlined in this chapter do not eliminate the inequalities that emerge in the context of unequal policy regimes, but rather contribute to reproduce them through a re-stratification of transnational care and family relations.

From these observations, it can be concluded that particular national contexts are central in shaping the dynamic structuration of inequalities on a global level and contribute to the reproduction of such inequalities at the micro-level of households and inter-personal relations of care. At the same time, transnational care chains are shaped not only by global structural dynamics, but also by the agency of individuals. A perspective on entangled inequalities, as adopted in this chapter, revealed that inequalities in transnational care chains are a product of interdependencies between global dynamics, political frameworks, and individual action. Moving toward a more equal global framework for the social organization of care work will therefore require changes at different levels—individuals, households, states, and global standards for political action.

Acknowledgments

I am grateful to the International Research Network on Interdependent Inequalities in Latin America desiguALdades.net for funding this research and to Prof. Dr. Sérgio Costa and PD Dr. Heike Drotbohm for supervising my work. I would also like to express my gratitude to the editors of this volume, Sérgio Costa, Elizabeth Jelin, and Renata Campos Motta, for their valuable comments on earlier versions of this chapter.

Notes

1   The data was gathered through two fieldwork phases in Milan of a total duration of four and a half months and an intermediate phase of three and a half months in Peru, including research trips of approximately one month to each of the sending localities. The principal methods included participant observation and interviews with 55 Peruvian migrants with experience as home-based elderly carers; 42 Italians with employment experience in this sector; 74 family members left behind, who were related to the migrants interviewed mostly as parents, siblings, or children; and 23 experts and representatives of organizations in both countries. Interviews with employers were conducted in Italian and those with migrants and family members in Spanish. The quotes from interviews used in this chapter were translated into English.
2   Here, informal care refers to the unregulated, mostly unpaid, care for children, the elderly, or others, which is closely related to social discourses, relations of power, and inequality, as well as to cultural practices and norms or 'care cultures'—the dominant national and local cultural discourses on what constitutes appropriate care and who should provide care (Williams 2012). Formal provisions of care, in contrast, are those regulated by law or other contractual agreements, which depend on a variety of inputs, including provisions concerning working conditions, monetary benefits, and benefits or services provided in kind (Bettio and Plantenga 2004).

3   Here I refer to the term welfare "regime" introduced by Esping-Andersen (1990), which shows how social policies and their effects differ between European countries. Esping-Anderson's model applies to capitalist societies that have been transformed into welfare states and that differ according to several characteristics, including, among other aspects, the degree of "de-commodification" through state action, referring to the social right to receive an adequate income independently from the market value of the labor force, as a measure of protection against total dependence on market forces, and to the particular way in which state, market, and family interact in the provision of welfare.

4   This process is also linked to previous and ongoing internal migration as a common strategy employed by rural Andean families to maximize individual and family options as well as life conditions (Bourque and Warren 1981).

5   Here, I understand ethnic categorization as the "positing of an immutable communal difference" (Anthias and Yuval-Davis 1992: 112), which is reflected by the construction of nationality-based cultural differences between employers and various groups of migrant workers. This process needs to be differentiated from racial classifications, which are legitimized through ideological constructions of a "biological," "physiognomic," or "natural" difference (ibid.).

References

Abbots, E. -J. (2012): "In the absence of men? Gender, migration and domestic labour in the Southern Ecuadorean Andes," *Journal of Latin American Studies*, 44 (1), 71–96.

Aguirre, R. (2008): "Familias como proveedoras de servicios de cuidado," in Astelarra, J. (ed.): *Género y Cohesión Social*. Madrid: Fundación Carolina.

Anderson, J. (2012): *La Migración Femenina Peruana en las Cadenas Globales de Cuidados en Chile y España. Transferencia de Cuidados y Desigualdades de Género*. Santo Domingo: ONU Mujeres.

Anthias, F. and Yuval-Davis, N. (1992): *Racialized Boundaries. Race, Nation, Gender, Colour and Class and the Anti-racist Struggle*. London and New York, NY: Routledge.

Baldassar, L., Vellekoop Baldock, C. and Wilding, R. (2007): *Families Caring Across Borders. Migration, Ageing and Transnational Caregiving*. New York, NY: Palgrave Macmillan.

Benería, L. (2008): "The crisis of care, international migration and public policy," *Feminist Economics*, 14 (3), 1–21.

Berg, U. (2010): "El Quinto Suyo: contemporary nation building and the political economy of emigration in Peru," *Latin American Perspectives*, 37 (5), 121–137.

Bettio, F. and Plantenga, J. (2004): "Comparing care regimes in Europe," *Feminist Economics*, 10 (1), 85–113.

Bettio, F., Simonazzi, A., and Villa, P. (2006): "Change in care regimes and female migration: the 'care drain' in the Mediterranean," *Journal of European Social Policy*, 16 (3), 271–285.

Bonizzoni, P. and Cibea, A. (2009): "Family migration policies in Italy," January 2009, Node Research, International Centre for Migration Policy Development (ICMPD).

Bourque, S. C. and Warren, K. B. (1981): *Women of the Andes. Patriarchy and Social Change in Two Peruvian Towns*. Ann Arbor, MI: The University of Michigan Press.

Bunster, X. and Chaney, E. M. (1985): *Sellers and Servants. Working Women in Lima, Peru*. New York, NY: Praeger Pubishers.

Caritas (2011): *Immigrazione. Dossier Statistico 2011. 21° Rapporto*. Roma: IDOS.

Catanzaro, R. and Colombo, A. (eds.) (2009): *Badanti & Co. Il Lavoro Domestico Straniero in Italia*. Bologna: Il Mulino.

CEPAL (2012): *Panorama Social de América Latina 2012*. Santiago de Chile: CEPAL.

Costa, S. (2013): "Entangled inequalities in Latin America: addressing social categorisations and transregional interdependencies," in Célleri, D., Schwarz, T., and Wittger, B. (eds.):

212   Anna Katharina Skornia

Interdependencies of Social Categorisations. Madrid/Frankfurt am Main: Iberoamericana/ Vervuert, 41–61.

Degiuli, F. (2007): "A job with no boundaries: home eldercare work in Italy," *European Journal of Women's Studies*, 14 (3), 193–208.

Dota, F. (2009): "Peruviani e romeni nella capitale: esperienze migratorie a confront," in Caritas di Roma e Provincia e Camera di Commercio di Roma: *Osservatorio Romano sulle Migrazioni. Quinto Rapporto.* Roma: IDOS, 128–142.

Drotbohm, H. (2013): "The promises of shared motherhood and the perils of detachment: a comparison of local and transnational child fostering in Cape Verde," in Alber, E., Martin, J., and Notermans, C. (eds.): *Child Fostering in West Africa: New Perspectives on Theories and Practices.* Leiden: Brill, 177–199.

Erel, U. (2012): "Introduction: Transnational Care in Europe—Changing Formations of Citizenship, Family, and Generation," *Social Politics*, 19 (1), 1–14.

Escrivá, A. (2005): "Aged global care chains: a Southern-European contribution to the field," Paper presented at the International Conference on Migration and Domestic Work in Global Perspective, Wassenaar, 26–29 May, 2005.

Esping-Andersen, G. (1990) *The Three Worlds of Welfare Capitalism.* Cambridge, U.K.: Polity Press.

Gerhard, U. (2010): "Care und citizenship," in Apitzsch, U. and Schmidbaur, M. (eds.): *Care und Migration. Die Ent-Sorgung menschlicher Reproduktionsarbeit entlang von Geschlechter- und Armutsgrenzen.* Opladen and Farmington Hills, MI: Verlag Barbara Budrich, 97–111.

Glick Schiller, N., Basch, L., and Blanc-Szanton, C. (eds.) (1992): *Towards a Transnational Perspective on Migration. Race, Class, Ethnicity, and Nationalism Reconsidered.* New York, NY: The New York Academy of Sciences.

Gonzales de Olarte E., (2005): *Crecimiento, Desigualdad e Ingobernabilidad en el Perú de los 2000,* Buenos Aires: CLACSO Biblioteca Virtual, 49–69.

Gori, C. (2012): "Home care in Italy: a system on the move, in the opposite direction to what we expect," *Health and Social Care in the Community*, 20 (3), 255–264.

Herrera, G. (2008): "Políticas migratorias y familias transnacionales: migración ecuatoriana en España y Estados Unidos," in Herrera, G. and Ramírez, J. (eds): *América Latina Migrante: Estado, Familia, Identidades.* Quito: FLACSO, 71–86.

Hochschild, A. R. (2000): "Global care chains and emotional surplus value," in Hutton, W. and Giddens, A. (eds.): *On the Edge: Living with Global Capitalism.* London: Vintage.

Hochschild, A. R. (2003): "Love and gold," in Ehrenreich, B. and Hochschild, A. R. (eds.): *Global Women: Nannies, Maids, and Sex Workers in the New Economy.* New York, NY: Henry Holt and Company, LLC, 15–30.

ISMU (2009): *Quindicesimo Rapporto sulle Migrazioni 2009.* Milano: FrancoAngeli.

ISMU (2013): *Diciottesimo Rapporto sulle Migrazioni 2012.* Milano: FrancoAngeli.

Kofman, E. and Raghuram, P. (2009): "The implications of migration for gender and care regimes in the South," *Social Policy and Development*, Programme Paper Number 41, July 2009, United Nations Research Institute for Social Development.

Lutz, H. (2002): "At your service Madam! The globalization of domestic service," *Feminist Review*, 70 (1), 89–104.

Lutz, H. (2007): *Vom Weltmarkt in den Privathaushalt. Die neuen Dienstmädchen im Zeitalter der Globalisierung.* Opladen and Farmington Hills, MI: Verlag Barbara Budrich.

Lutz, H. (2008): "When home becomes a workplace: domestic work as an ordinary job in Germany?" in Lutz, H. (ed.): *Migration and Domestic Work: a European Perspective on a Global Theme.* Aldershot: Ashgate, 43–60.

Lutz, H. and Palenga-Möllenbeck, E. (2010): "Care-arbeit, gender und migration. Überlegungen zu einer theorie der transnationalen migration im haushaltsarbeits sektor in Europa," in Apitzsch, U. and Schmidbaur, M. (eds.): *Care und Migration. Die Ent-Sorgung menschlicher Reproduktionsarbeit entlang von Geschlechter- und Armutsgrenzen.* Opladen and Farmington Hills, MI: Verlag Barbara Budrich, 143–161.

OIM (Organización Internacional para las Migraciones) and INEI (Instituto Nacional de Estadísticas e Informática) (2009): *Migración Internacional en las Familias Peruanas y Perfil del Peruano Retornante.* Lima: OIM.

Orozco, A. (2006): *Perspectivas Feministas en torno a la Economía: el Caso de los Cuidados.* Madrid: Consejo Económico y Social.

Orozco, A. (2009): "Global care chains," *Gender, Migration and Development Series*, Working Paper 2, United Nations INSTRAW, 1–9.

Oso Casas, L. (2010): "Movilidad laboral de las mujeres latinoamericanas en España y empresariado étnico," in Grupo Interdisciplinario de Investigador@s Migrantes: *Familias, Jóvenes, Niños y Niñas Migrantes. Rompiendo Estereotipos.* Madrid: IEPALA. Sandra Gil Araujo, 33–46.

Parreñas, R. S. (2010): "'Partial citizenship' and the ideology of women's domesticity in state policies on foreign domestic workers," in Apitzsch, U. and Schmidbaur, M. (eds.): *Care und Migration. Die Ent-Sorgung menschlicher Reproduktionsarbeit entlang von Geschlechter- und Armutsgrenzen.* Opladen and Farmington Hills, MI: Verlag Barbara Budrich, 128–140.

Pasquinelli, S. and Rusmini, G. (2009): "I sostegni al lavoro privato di cura," in Network Non Autosufficienza (ed.): *L'assistenza agli Anziani Non Autosufficienti in Italia—Rapporto 2009.* Rimini: Maggioli, www.maggioli.it/rna (01.07.2012).

Pries, L. (1999): *Migration and Transnational Social Spaces.* Aldershot: Ashgate.

Raghuram, P. (2012): "Global care, local configurations. Challenges to conceptualizations of care," *Global Networks*, 12 (2), 155–174.

Razavi, S. (2007): "The political and social economy of care in a development context. Conceptual issues, research questions and policy options," *Gender and Development*, Programme Paper No. 3, June 2007, UNRISD, 1–38.

Sarti, R. (2008): "The globalisation of domestic service: an historical perspective," Lutz, H. (ed.): *Migration and Domestic Work: a European Perspective on a Global Theme.* Farnham: Ashgate, 77–97.

Sarti, R. and Scrinzi, F. (2010): "Introduction to the special issue: men in a woman's job, male domestic workers, international migration and the globalization of care," *Men and Masculinities*, 13 (4), 4–15.

Skornia, A. (2014): *Entangled Inequalities in Transnational Care Chains. Practices Across the Borders of Peru and Italy.* Bielefeld: transcript Verlag.

Williams, F. (2012): "Converging variations in migrant care work in Europe," *Journal of European Social Policy*, 22 (4), 363–376.

Yeates, N. (2009): *Globalizing Care Economies and Migrant Workers: Explorations in Global Care Chains.* Basingstroke: Palgrave Macmillan.

Zimmerman, M., Litt, J., and Bose, C. (2006): *Global Dimensions of Gender and Carework.* Stanford, CA: Stanford University Press.

12

SOCIO-ENVIRONMENTAL INEQUALITIES AND GM CROPS

Class, gender, and knowledge[1]

Renata Motta

Soybeans, maize, cotton, and canola, the main genetically modified (GM) crops[2] available on the market, serve as inputs for animal feed, industrial food processing, and agrofuels. These biotech crops are thus part of a complex chain between farming and the consumer's table. These connections have been comprehended through a world-systemic perspective with the help of the concept of global commodity chains. It was coined to study the links and mediations from raw material supplies to final consumption, including production, processing, trading, wholesale, and retail. Such connections shed light on how value is constructed, which might happen at different geographical locations, integrating them into asymmetrical positions in the global division of labor of the world economy (Hopkins and Wallerstein 1986).

While this perspective raises the distributive question within the productive chain, a broader consideration of the various dimensions of inequality at stake in the large-scale production of GM crops needs to inquire into the global division of its socio-environmental burdens. Scholars have been calling for an ecological turn in the analysis of the political economy of food and agriculture, by taking into consideration the environmental and health impacts of spatially and socially disembedded food relations between consumption and production (Campbell 2009).

For that, in addition to a macro-analysis of the processes by which agrarian capitalism establishes global connections for generating value, it is necessary to follow the concomitant processes by which it produces disconnections between the places, communities, and bodies involved along the chain. Just as the concept of global division of labor provides the clue for tracing economic asymmetries in the production of commodities, an analysis of the socio-environmental impacts of global agrarian chains could benefit from concepts that have been crucial to understanding social inequalities. Based on this premise, in this chapter, I will rely on the concept of reproduction as key to connect such critique of agrarian capitalism with a broader understanding of inequalities, inspired by a feminist critique (see Chapter 6 by Jelin in this volume) and the literature on gender and environment.

The Southern Cone of Latin America is the largest area of producers of GM crops in the world, with 75.8 million hectares, with the major producers being Brazil (44.2 mi ha), Argentina (24.5 mi ha), Paraguay (3.6 mi ha), Uruguay (1.4 mi ha), and Bolivia (1.1 mi ha). The region accounts for more than one-third of the global total area of GM crops (179.1 mi ha), a production only comparable to that of the USA (70.9 mi ha), the holder of most technological patents (James 2016). The governments of the region have relied on agrobiotechnology as part of a technological package that strongly capitalized the production of grains, in particular, soy, maize, and cotton, destined for export in the world market. The renewed attention to agrarian commodities in the region has not only reinforced historical patterns of inequalities such as those related to land, but also brought with it a number of conflicts over socio-environmental inequalities (see Dietz in this volume).

My argument is that the alliance between global agrarian capitalism and state commercial strategies betting on the market expansion of GM crops and its purported highest economic productivity went hand in hand with the erosion of state and corporate responsibilities for both social and environmental reproduction. Such convergence is not accidental or an unintended effect of risky technologies. Rather, as I further argue, the expansion of GM crops depends on neoliberal globalization as the institutional basis of agrarian capitalism, characterized by a lax state regulation of their health and environmental effects while at the same time pressuring for a strong state presence for enforcing intellectual property rights. Contesting the disjuncture between the productive and reproductive spheres on which the defenders of GM crops rely, social movements and affected citizens have, in their reactions to situations of dispossession, traced the relations between these spheres.

The chapter starts with a conceptual discussion, followed by a brief contextualization of Brazil's and Argentina's politics and export policies. Based on my research on the social mobilizations against the expansion of genetically modified organisms (GMOs) in Argentina and Brazil,[3] I then present two cases of struggles that establish the connections between the production of transgenic crops and the threats to reproduction, constituting socio-environmental inequalities. The first relates to the struggle against contamination by pesticides associated with GM soy in Argentina, when a group of neighbors succeeds in making visible the threats to social reproduction. The second concerns the reactions to the approval of GM corn in Brazil as it impacts in the loss of biodiversity and farmers' rights over seeds. The chapter then draws conclusions from these cases on the overall purpose of conceptualizing and researching inequalities generated by global commodity chains beyond the productive sphere.

Economic, social, and ecological (re)production

In her theoretical overview of the relationships between hierarchical inequalities in class relations and categorical differences, Jelin (this volume) argues that the analysis of the development of capitalism has often led to the centrality of class struggles and socio-economic inequality as the main axes of analysis. The feminist critique on Marxism has broadened the scope of analysis by developing the conceptual differentiation between processes of production integrated into the market sphere through labor and social reproduction that takes place at home or in the domestic sphere. While the former produces commodities for the market, the latter refers to the biological reproduction, the socialization, and the care of human beings, based on a gendered division of labor within the family, with the highest burden taken up by women.

In the nineties, there was a fruitful exchange of ideas between feminist scholars and environmentalists that culminated in a vast and diverse literature on gender and environment. Authors differ considerably on the relative importance of hierarchies of class, gender, and environmental exploitation and how they intersect. Ecofeminists posited a shared history of domination by patriarchal and Western institutions on women and nature. They identified the scientific revolution as establishing a separation between culture and nature and causing the domination of the latter by the former, as nature becomes known in scientific laws and subjected to technical transformation (Mies and Shiva 1993; Shiva 2010). Ecofeminist thought claims that women have a biologically or socially constructed closeness to nature that empowers them as conservationists. For instance, women's social experience of caretaking makes them attentive to life threats; often, women are the first to notice that miscarriages and family health problems are not "environmental accidents" (Diamond and Orenstein 1990, 55).

Ecofeminism raised the importance of gender in tackling issues of environmental protection and sustainable development. Problematic was its essentialism, assuming homogeneity amongst women and positing harmony "before" patriarchy and scientific revolution. A further critique is that some strands of ecofeminism postulate an essentialist connection between women and nature (Mellor 1992). Identified with green feminist socialism, Mellor proposes, instead, to look into motherhood and its constraints (as early feminists did), claiming that there is nothing natural about motherhood, but a complex social construction of motherhood, including birth. Against the problematic proposition of a "natural" affinity of women with the natural world, Mellor suggests the need to think the other way round: that motherhood needs a supportive environment, social and physical, and this raises the question of why men lack affinity for care work and environmental conservation.

The neglect of class inequalities in dealing with gender and environmental issues has been the point of departure for authors within political ecology that draw on historical materialism (Agarwal 1992; Di Chiro 2008; Mellor 1992; Salleh 2009). These authors "en-gendered" the political economy analysis of environmental issues using, among others, the concepts of production and reproduction. They claim that the social division of labor based on gender led women to establish particular relations with natural resources, to develop gendered knowledge on nature based on that experience, and, therefore, to, more often than men, defend the need for sustainability. These authors emphasize the importance of material practices, work practices, and cultural and class-specific gender roles that shape gender-environment relations. Salleh (2009) suggests to "triangulate political ecology" in order to connect: (a) political economy, which looks at relations between economic classes; (b) political ecology, in order to include ecosystems; (c) feminism and post-colonialism, to take into account gender and race. In her argument, the labor theory of value can offer a starting point for a conceptual discussion of the ecological debt, that is, the appropriation of people's livelihood resources, and of the embodied debt, which includes the reproductive work and intergenerational supply.

My aim in these cursory notes on some of the literature on gender and environment is to show how the concept of reproduction has undergone a further theoretical development as scholars inquiring into the ecological question have expanded its reach to understand relations of domination between society and nature. It became a central category that mediates between the (female) care work and the processes responsible for the continuous reproduction of the environmental commons, both of them taken for granted (or "externalized") by the market sphere, and therefore, not valued. More than that, social reproduction and the environment, as sharply pointed out by Di Chiro (2008), are increasingly threatened by the rise of neoliberalism and its associated reforms that further the processes of privatization, commodification, and deregulation of social welfare. Countering such disconnections between the productive sphere and social and environmental reproduction, civil society and social movements react to make visible their relationships and fight against the various dimensions of inequalities associated with them. In short, the conceptual triad of economic, social, and ecological (re)production provides a broad analytical framework to inquire into various disputes regarding social inequalities that have arisen surrounding the adoption of GM crops.

The market, the state, and civil society in relation to GMOs in Argentina and Brazil

Brazil and Argentina are, respectively, the second and the third largest producers of GM crops. These countries have specialized in the production of commodities for a global chain, in which oligopolies of transnational corporations control important nodes (inputs, commercialization, processing, and retailing). Dependency on agrarian commodities (in which biotechnology is applied) is not new in these countries; it grew in the twenty-first century, after a decade in which it had been relatively lower, as measured by participation in gross domestic product (GDP), exports, and state revenues. Argentina and Brazil are classified as having high commodity dependence, with commodity exports (in millions of US dollars) accounting for, respectively, 67 percent and 65 percent of merchandise exports in 2012 and 2013. Among all commodities, agrarian products destined for feed and food correspond to 81 percent (Argentina) and 52 percent (Brazil). During the period from 1990 to 2011, soy and corn—the main GM crops in these countries—and their processed products were responsible for almost 25 percent of Argentinean and 10 percent of Brazilian export values (UNCTAD 2015).

218 Renata Motta

The year 2003 marked the beginning of 'pink wave' politics in Argentina and Brazil with the elections of Néstor Kirchner and Luis Inácio Lula da Silva, respectively, whose governments, though lacking a radical agenda for social change, did promise a commitment to passing reforms in social policy. Both presidents were elected on the basis of a campaign discourse of differentiation from previous governments, who were identified as responsible for implementing damaging neoliberal structural adjustment reforms, as dictated by the Washington Consensus. Both countries did achieve significant levels of poverty reduction after bringing the issue to the center of the political agenda (data from ECLAC/CEPALSTAT, 2015). The extent to which these new governments would actually mark a rupture with past administrations in terms of neoliberal policies in the realm of agriculture was an open question for most of the social movements that had long been fighting for an alternative agrarian model and resisting the negative effects of the advancement of agribusiness. Indeed, the year 2003 coincided with the beginning of a phase in which commodity prices peaked, including the price of agrarian products such as soybeans and their derivatives. With Argentina and Brazil among the world's top three producers and exporters of soy, governments' continued emphasis on neoliberal and market-oriented agricultural policy seemed likely, as it turned out to be.

Despite their similar position in the global agrarian market, namely, as big producers of commodity for export, these countries experienced very different trajectories in this process. The ten-year lag between the conversion of the majority of soy fields to GM soy in Argentina (1999) and Brazil (2009) relates to differences in social mobilization. In 1996, Argentina was a pioneer in adopting GM crops, together with the USA, where the technology holder, Monsanto, is based. The agricultural authorities approved the new technology in a bureaucratically insulated way, without allowing the issue to be part of the public agenda. This resulted in a rapid conversion to a new model of agriculture anchored in transgenic soy, in which dissident voices and small protest actions were ignored. Expecting that Brazil would follow the relatively unchallenged script that guided the technology adoption in the pioneer countries, the proponents of GM crops were faced instead with sharp opposition from civil society organizations and social movements, and also from subnational governments. In the late 1990s, a long dispute over Brazilian policy for agrobiotechnology began, and a moratorium on GM soy was established as a result of social mobilization. However, the initial social movements' victories were to be reversed, with Brazil approving GM soy in 2005, GM corn in 2008 and, after that, topping Argentina in hectares of GM crops. Meanwhile, the transgenic agrarian model in Argentina became increasingly contested at the local level. The following sections will provide sketches of these two trajectories.

Fighting pesticide contamination in the GM soy chain: the mothers of Ituzaingó, Argentina

Perhaps the main node of contention against GM crops in Argentina has been the use of pesticides associated with the soy boom in the country. Neighborhoods living next to GM soy fields started to mobilize in networks self-called sprayed peoples (*pueblos fumigados*), referring to the way pesticides were applied on a large scale by airplanes or large machines. They mostly targeted the pesticide glyphosate, which is associated with the use of transgenic soy developed to be resistant to this active ingredient. Ituzaingó Anexo is a locality in the province of Córdoba, with 200 cases of cancer in a population of 5,000. The mobilization of this neighborhood became a symbol of the struggles against the agrarian model in Argentina. Here I will sketch episodes of their struggle, from its emergence to the judicial ruling, based on which I will advance my argument.

Making sense of contamination and mobilizing

In the year 2000, Sofia Gatica (Madres de Ituzaingó, interview, 2012), after having suffered the death of a new-born child, started to ask herself why many of her neighbors were ill. Sofia affirms that they "got used to ill people": She saw kids with chinstraps (due to the treatment of leukemia), and young women with headscarves (signs of the effects of the cancer treatment chemotherapy). She began talking to the people about it, and they started to exchange their perceptions that, when the airplanes sprayed pesticides over the soy fields that surround their houses, many suffered with immediate reactions of their skin and of their breathing and with headaches. In this way, they associated their health problems with the practice of spraying pesticides. Sofia denies having had a special enlightened idea to connect everything; rather, she affirms, it was the suffering of having lost a child, which one does not easily accept, that prompted her to actively interpret the situation. Also, to her, children are innocent, they cannot be held accountable for their diseases. When she heard of other cases from neighbor mothers, they shared their suffering, their emotions, and their moral indignation and started looking for the common reasons. This is why they became known as Madres de Ituzaingó, or "The Mothers of Ituzaingó." They defined their struggle as defending the lives of their children.

In order to yield credibility to their claims, the Madres de Ituzaingó decided to make their own epidemiological map. They mobilized their main resource: Their network in the neighborhood that gave them access to all families. From house to house, they collected data on the health situation of the neighborhood, counting the incidence of cancer and abortions. They compared the data found with the average estimations and concluded that the number of ill people in their neighborhood by far exceeded average rates. This resulted in an innovative strategy to fight GM crops: The construction of 'counter-hegemonic epidemiological data' (Arancibia 2013). However, the provincial Ministry of Health (Córdoba) disregarded their data, maintained the official position that the pesticides posed no danger to health, and, at the same time, invited experts to investigate the health situation of Ituzaingó. Experts conducted blood tests on the children, confirming the health situation of a contaminated community. Three municipal ordinances were issued in 2002: Declaring the neighborhood in a state of emergency,

220 Renata Motta

prohibiting air spraying of pesticides in the city of Córdoba, and prohibiting land fumigation in Ituzaingó.

Witnessing the continuing practice of pesticide spraying over their homes, the mothers kept up their protests, among which were road cut-offs in which the ill people from Ituzaingó took part. They received death threats and realized that the police, instead of enforcing the ordinances, were on the side of soy producers. Thus, they decided they had to mobilize more scientific knowledge, draw allies to their side, and bring their demands to the judicial system. They learned a lot from searching on the Internet (by conducting simple keyword searches on each pesticide that was used in their area). In 2005, they went to Buenos Aires to demand that national authorities provide a solution to their plight: They went to the Ministries of Human Rights, Health, and Environment; they also went to the National Congress where, with the support of three deputies, they presented a law project for prohibiting pesticide spraying near villages. While these demands did not prosper, their presence in the national capital awoke solidarity from other organizations. As their message spread, with the aid of media coverage, many (national and foreign) social movement organizations contacted them, offering support in varied ways, providing information, and disseminating their case.

They developed a clear diagnostic of the injustice of their situation as a contaminated community, relying for that on expertise with scientific proofs of contamination. They framed it in terms of discrimination and unequal distribution of environmental burden, "as the price that we have to pay for a supposedly progress that benefits a few" (Grupo de Madres de Córdoba 2005). They state that their fight is to make visible what the country has been trying to conceal: The victims of its record harvests and of the adoption of the transgenics agro-exporter model, which they characterize in an elaborated fashion as the cause of their suffering.

> The globalization process imposed a model of a GMOs-producer and forage-exporter state on Argentina in the 1990s. The consequences are now easy to notice: immense territories emptied from their rural populations, hundreds of villages in a state of extinction, four hundred thousand small producers bankrupt and many more ruined with the banks due to the incorporation of new technological packages with high dependence of inputs, GM seeds and herbicides from Monsanto. The concentration of ownership in the fields and the expulsion of populations sum up the neo-colonial model imposed by the globalization process. This agro-exporter model expressed the abdication of the state vis-à-vis the market policies, the absolute absence of a project for the country; or maybe even worse, the existence of a project of a laboratory-state for the corporations and producer of forage to export for meat production at the metropolis.
>
> *(Grupo de Madres de Córdoba 2005, 9)*

The Mothers of Ituzaingó did not stop short of attributing responsibilities for the health and environmental contamination of villages near soy fields: They consider it to be a crime marked by state omission for not enforcing environmental laws and thus showing connivance with transnationals. In sum, this group of neighbor mothers who started to act in defense of the health of their families have developed an elaborated action repertoire, including production of counter-hegemonic data, elaboration of law projects, and legal mobilization, as well as the establishment of an increasingly national and transnational solidarity network. As a result of their mobilization, the Public Prosecutors' Office entered with a judicial action against three men who violated the above mentioned ordinances. The case reached the courts in 2008.

Ituzaingó in the courts

The legal case of the Mothers of Ituzaingó was judged in 2012. This case presents an important departure from previous judicial rulings on pesticide use, in that this is characterized as a criminal act of environmental contamination and not an administrative failure. It penalized three individuals who sprayed pesticides over GM soy fields. Although these men carried the whole burden of responsibility, the Public Prosecutors discussed the underlying causes and made recommendations of legal and policy changes that are pertinent not only to the Argentinean regulations but also the global state-of-the-art on pesticides.

Challenging the often-invoked argument that the use of pesticides is a safe and legal activity guaranteed by the state bodies, the Prosecutors drew on the precautionary principle, foreseen in the *Environmental Bill*. They argued that the authorization of pesticides cannot be invoked when there is contamination and evidence of damage to human health and the environment. The argumentation contrasted a bureaucratic procedure of authorizing pesticides—based on laboratory data on animals—and the actual use of the product after approval. More than an issue of bad agricultural practices, the Public Prosecutors called attention to the dimensions of pesticide use in Argentina, stating that its increase was as high as the increase in harvests. They further argued that, although regulators classify pesticides like glyphosate in the lowest classes of toxicity, any pesticide may provoke damage depending on the degree of exposure. Using data from the chemical industry, the Public Prosecutors mentioned that in Argentina 300 million liters of pesticides were used in 2010 on 22 million hectares, affecting 12 million people living in those areas. As evidence of damage to human health, they referred to a health survey conducted in 2010 in Ituzaingó, emphasizing the statistic that 33 percent of causes of death were attributed to cancer, much higher than the national average, as well as the high number of spontaneous abortions.

In addition to penal sanctions and community services prescribed to the three accused men, the Public Prosecutors made recommendations to public authorities. The local Ministry of Health in Córdoba was ordered to prohibit air and terrestrial sprayings within 1,000 meters of villages and to initiate campaigns to enforce the law and to educate producers in pesticide applications. Also, they recommended that a *National Bill on Pesticides* should be passed, prohibiting aerial spraying and setting limits on terrestrial spraying. The regulatory body was to reclassify all toxicological products taking into account not only acute but also chronic intoxication, prohibit highly toxic products, anticipate the prohibition of endosulfan, and make sure that analytical toxicological studies are conducted by official state laboratories or federal universities to ensure an objective assessment of health risks.

This was the first time that a legitimate activity was considered to be a crime. For some, the judicial rulings involved a symbolic change in the conflict between, on the one side, the right to health and to a safe environment and, on the other, agribusiness as an economic activity. The cultural and historical legitimacy of the farmer in Argentina, espousing a social identity of hard worker and morally charged with a strong symbolism, has been an obstacle to the debate on the negative effects of the agricultural activity. Sofia Gatica (Madres de Itunzaingó, interview, 2012), although satisfied that justice was done in the particular case at hand, is well aware that the three accused people have only a very limited responsibility. For her, the ultimate responsibility lies with the government and the multinationals. Although the state is held accountable, Sofia does not believe that change will come from there: "If the state is absent, you have to do it"; actualizing the historical frame of women's participation in politics in Argentina in face of human rights violations (Bonner 2007).

Motherhood and beyond: making connections between health, environment, and agriculture

How did this group of mothers trace the connections between the productive activities related to GM soy and the threats to both social and environmental reproduction in their neighborhood? Gender is a key category to explain this case of mobilization, as well as class and space. In contrast to the Mothers of Plaza de Mayo, who became known by the name of the square where they protested, located at the center stage of Argentinean political affairs, the Mothers of Ituzaingó belong to a poor neighborhood in the semi-urban territories, unknown to most Argentineans. Motherhood is deployed as a political identity in both cases, but there are important differences in terms of class and position in the geopolitical space (Giarracca 2003).

These differences help to explain why they and not middle-class urban women became one of the strongest nodes of resistance to GM crops in Argentina. As environmental justice scholars and activists have long claimed, environmental contamination mostly, and not casually, occurs amongst poor communities, often intersecting with axes of hierarchical differences such as race and ethnicity. Indeed, the Mothers of Ituzaingó denounced the feeling of injustice in suffering the negative consequences of the agrarian model. In addition, in tune with ecofeminist scholarship, mobilization took place in a specific gendered context, where women have ascribed roles in the realm of reproduction and care. They rejected fatalist explanations for the health problems suffered in their families and community and collectively searched for causes, creating powerful collective action frames and protest repertoires.

From their social roles as mothers, women living close to GM soy fields created their own political culture of citizenship. They went much beyond the traditionally ascribed roles of caregivers and were able to politicize an issue that was otherwise taboo in Argentina, due to the hegemonic view of agrarian activities as representing the general interests of society. They were able to create frictions in this hegemonic understanding from their marginal position in the political realm. They did so by establishing connections between agrarian production, environmental contamination, health deterioration, including cancer, and abortions. They made visible the threats to the social and environmental reproduction that they were experiencing in their bodies, household, and neighborhood. More than that, they attributed responsibility to the state and agrarian actors, domestic and transnational, in their actions and omissions vis-à-vis the pesticide contamination. In Argentinean history, the dictatorship had politicized women as the state violated the rights of all; now, agrarian activities, when threatening life and violating rights, had also politicized women. Fighting the *modelo agrobiotecnológico*, women acted not as 'women *without* rights' that fight to obtain rights, but rather as 'women *for* and *in relation* to human rights,' namely, fighting for the universal right to have rights and to participate in the definition of what are human rights in a specific context and time (Jelin 1996, 194). Therefore, instead of relying only on concepts of motherhood and care to explain their mobilization, it is necessary to understand it also in terms of citizenship (MacGregor 2004; Schild 1994).

Fighting GM corn in Brazil: biodiversity and farmers' rights over seeds

After so many years of controversy over GM soy, the approval process for GM corn was seen as crucial to define on which side of the balance Brazil would tip: Was soy going to be an exception or would the country turn from an ambiguous to a clear pro-GMO policy? Therefore, as GM corn landed on the agenda of the regulatory commission, it was a disputed process. I will narrate two moments of reactions from peasant movements: The debates prior to the approval of GM corn and during the approval process.

Peasants concerned about the risks of GM corn

Maize raised specific concerns in comparison to soy. First, maize is the most disseminated cash crop for small farmers, and, second, there is a high probability of genetic contamination due to its biological characteristics. While there is always the danger of contamination of conventional crops by GM varieties, in the case of soy this only occurs through physical means within close proximity. By contrast, the maize plant cross-fertilizes, which can lead to genetic flux between the GM variety and the conventional one across large distances. This is when the discussion about farmers' rights assumed centrality in the debate over GM crops in Brazil: The right to decide what to plant and what to harvest, the right to select seeds to make their

224 Renata Motta

own genetic improvement, and the right to reserve part of the harvest, multiply it, exchange with other farmers, to serve as seeds for the next season (AS-PTA, interview, 2012). GM seeds thus posed a double threat: biological and legal.

The biological threat relates to farmers' control over their processes of seed selection. Because of the concreteness of this threat, it was easier for the leadership of peasant movements to make the debate about GM crops with their grassroots (MPA, interview, 2012), who promptly shared the diagnostic of a future contamination. Due to their accumulated experience with corn, they knew that maize crops cross-fertilize. The same characteristic that had empowered them as agents of genetic selection now was threatening them. They knew that if there was GM corn, contamination was a matter of time. The traditional practices of saving and exchanging corn seeds provided the concrete basis for the discursive articulation of varied issues such as agro-biodiversity, peasant culture, and farmers' rights over seeds. As small farmers and peasants were the ones who historically selected seeds, they promoted biodiversity of corn. These practices are culturally oriented by needs other than economic productivity: Some seeds are selected for yielding bigger grains, others for their taste in particular food dishes, yet others for resistance to locally specific weather and soil conditions or pests. Thus, these practices ensured the agro-biodiversity of corn in Brazil. These practices were embedded in family traditions, giving an emotional guise to their relation to corn.

Contamination directly affected their control over the seeds they had received from their families over generations. With genetic contamination, there is an external gene that is not a corn gene, and due to the uncertainties associated with the techniques of genetic modification, this new gene might or might not express desired properties such as insecticide function or pesticide resistance.

The legal threat concerns farmers' rights over seeds multiplication as intellectual property rights becomes an unavoidable problem. Saving part of the harvest as seeds for the next sowing season is part of the cultural identity of farmers; a tradition passed from generation to generation, "a historical practice of peasantry" (MPA, interview, 2012). Small farmers were alarmed by rumors of the prospect of planting a year, harvesting, and, when planting again, the seed would not germinate. GM corn is composed of a genetic modification inserted on a hybrid seed designed to be sown only once, and thus it forces farmers to the seed market every season. GM technology brought additional concerns, due to the fact that it is a proprietary technology legally protected by a patent. If hybrid seeds already forced farmers to buy new seeds every season, it at least allowed them to make their own genetic mix with other varieties. With a patented gene, this is no longer allowed nor desired by farmers (AS-PTA, interview, 2012).

Appealing the approval of GM corn

In September 2007, three varieties of GM corn were approved for commercial use. During the meeting of the regulatory commission, the Movimento de Mulheres Camponesas (Movement of Peasant Women, MMC)[4] staged a protest event with pregnant women holding posters with the slogan *Meu filho não é cobaia* (My son is not a guinea pig). This action brought to the fore the dimension of health risks arising from the consumption of transgenic foods. The activists warned about the risks for pregnant women, infants, and babies, citing studies that indicated reproductive alterations in animals; the possibility of absorption of the insecticide inserted in transgenic maize and its contamination of breast milk causing toxic reactions in the mother and the baby; and the possibility that foods made with transgenic maize will cause allergy in children if the bacteria inserted in the maize combine with those of the intestinal flora, leading to anaphylactic shocks or death (Pereira and Fernandes 2007). NGOs and social movements also organized a petition to the president and filed an injunction to suspend the decision, contesting the absence of environmental risk assessments.

The approval of GM corn drew allies from the executive power, with the disagreement of state agencies responsible for health and environmental protection, which appealed the decision, challenging its technical and scientific basis for not having fulfilled all formal requirements, as many studies were lacking. The council of ministers, which met in February 2008, decided that the regulatory body for biotechnology had the final word on issues related to the biosafety of GMOs. So, the three varieties of corn were approved without considering appeals from civil society or the appeals from the health and environmental agencies. The council of ministers issued two recommendations: First, that the regulatory commission consider scientific studies conducted by third parties in order not to rely on studies made by the proponent firms, justifying when this is not followed; and second, the creation of an interministerial working group to conduct studies of the medium- and long-term impacts of GMOs and their effects on health and environment. These were never followed.

In 2008, GM corn reached the fields. Meanwhile, the majority of corn farmers who planted hybrid seeds sold at the commercial market had fallen victim to the market strategies of the biotech industry. There was less and less supply of non-GM corn varieties. Based on data from the Ministry of Agriculture, AS-PTA estimates that, by 2010, more than three-quarters of new seed releases were genetically modified. Relying on industry data, it calculates that 20% of corn farmers use creole seeds and 80% rely on commercial seeds (AS-PTA, interview, 2012). Indeed, whereas GM soy took about ten years to cross the threshold of 70% of cropped area, GM corn did it in the space of three years.

Crossing biological, juridical, and generational borders

Peasant movements in Brazil established linkages between the commercial approval of GM corn and the threats to peasant production, to social and environmental reproduction. They integrated class, gender, and environmental issues into their actions against transgenic maize. This is the result of a process of renewal in the rural movements, which today represent one of the most globally active sectors in the struggle against inequalities related to global capitalism. The social identity of the "peasant," based on experience yet reinforced and conveyed in these spaces

226 Renata Motta

of mobilization, includes a mode of food production that relates to nature in a particular way, often under the label "agro-ecology."

The political decision about an agricultural technology that generates immediate economic benefits created a typical asymmetric situation of conflict about technological risks (Luhmann 2008). Peasant movements raised concerns about its impacts on at least three levels: The environment, peasant farms, and the body. They called attention to the risks of genetic contamination of GM maize in the environment, a threat to agro-biodiversity as it was until then practiced. Farmers selected corn seeds without having, in the genetic mix, the gene now inserted in a maize seed that came from bacteria with insecticide properties. The biological contamination led to legal and socioeconomic risks because that gene is protected under a patent and its use must be paid for. Peasants as a class and as a political subject, not wanting to engage in agribusiness on a small scale (*agronegocinho*) but rather struggling to maintain a different mode of production—one that is often based on non-monetized forms of exchange of farming inputs—felt threatened of being forcefully incorporated into the seed market. More than that, the biological risk of cross-fertilization meant that farmers' control over such decisions was undermined: producers of non-GM corn could have their crops contaminated and therefore be incriminated and have to pay fines and royalties to the patent owners, as would happen later.

Peasant women, in turn, incorporated the public health dimension. For that, they brought in another level to identify the impacts of transgenics: The level of bodies. Gender identity was mobilized to draw attention to the health risks that transgenic foods bring to consumers, a topic that goes beyond agricultural production and is not emphasized by other agrarian movements. On the one hand, in the protest against the approval of transgenic maize, the participation of pregnant women referring to their future children highlighted care and reproductive work of women. The discussion of the meaning of "being a peasant woman," of the role of women as family caregivers and producers of healthy foods, is central to the MMC. Activists were not reacting to problems suffered by their own families; they were raising public attention, of experts and authorities, to future risks for the entire population resulting from approving transgenic maize. The presence of their bodies in the condition of pregnant women demonstrates the performativity of the gender (Nightingale 2006), bringing to the debate the impacts on future generations of present political decisions.

Conclusions

The widespread adoption of GM crops has put renewed pressure on known damages stemming from industrial agriculture, such as pesticide contamination and the loss of biodiversity, while at the same time raising new risk issues, such as genetic contamination. Agrarian elites and political interests profit from global market demands and rely on the state and its national policies to promote the production of agrarian commodities. The environmental impacts of its cultivation are concentrated in the production nodes of global commodity chains. The gap between the countryside and the urban centers makes the grievances of the former even more abstract to the latter. Those living close to the production nodes of a global chain have denounced the threats to economic, ecological, and social (re)production caused by the expansion of GM crops. Although the global unit of analysis is necessary to understand the causes of socio-environmental inequalities associated with GM crops, it does not necessarily provide the best scale to make visible its consequences.

In this chapter, I drew on the cases of the Mothers of Ituzaingó and the sprayed peoples in Argentina, and peasant movements fighting GM crops in Brazil, to argue that social mobilization established connections between the productive and reproductive spheres, bringing to the fore the socio-environmental inequalities associated with GMOs. Pesticide contamination and genetic contamination, with the common denominator of being different instances of the same phenomenon "contamination," convey, in this very word, that the borders between the productive sphere and its effects on social and environmental reproduction are blurred, and that they are crossed by pesticides and by genes.

However, although the word *contamination* might denote an unintentional event, an accident that might occasionally occur, the cases narrated here hint at the rather inconvenient conclusion that these trespassing relations are part of the "technological package." Due to all "purifying efforts" on the part of the network of actors promoting GM crops, pesticide and genetic contamination are not unintended effects but appear to be so because of the institutional arrangements on which global agrarian capitalism relies.

Here lies the second part of the argument, that is, social movements face a hard time in "proving" the connections because the disjuncture between GM crop production and its effects is made possible by lax state regulation on health and environmental risks, and therefore, by the erosion of state and corporate responsibilities for both social and environmental reproduction. Yet this is not at odds with demands for strong state regulation of intellectual property rights.

Although one might want to interpret the cases of pesticide and genetic contamination as instances of weak states, it rather represents the state-of-the-art in the global regulation of GM crops. The absence of independent assessments of long-term environmental impacts of GM crops in regulatory decisions is a key characteristic in the geopolitics of knowledge that sustains the global diffusion of GM crops. Regulatory authorities rely on industry data based only on short-term studies on health and environmental effects of GM crops and pesticides. Moreover, the studies are conducted in very few exemplars and for only 90 days (Motta and Arancibia 2016). It should come as no surprise that regulatory agencies testify the safety of such products and have no instruments to identify, assess, and interpret situations like Ituzaingó, where people have been sprayed for over 15 years.[5] Similarly, experiments conducted by global seed industries assuring the safety of their products and the possibility of coexistence are taken into account in decision-making while experiential knowledge of local farmers about the risks of cross-fertilization and thus genetic contamination is neglected.

Therefore, in the disputes about the environmental and health effects of biotechnology, asymmetrically positioned types of knowledge compete. International agreements and national regulatory bodies, which have the power to define what counts as knowledge deemed relevant to decide on the use of agro-biotechnologies, have assigned scientific knowledge the monopoly to identify risks. In this way, the political economy and political ecology of biotech crops are sustained by a dominant arrangement in the geopolitics of knowledge.[6] The latter privileges knowledge situated in places such as laboratories at the headquarters of transnational seed and agrochemical industries that produce evidence of "safety" of their products, while disregarding knowledge of people experiencing locally the effects of the use of GM seeds.

Both in Argentina and Brazil, risk discourse resonated well among the poor rural constituencies where production takes place, more than in the urban dwellers, including upper classes, who consume industrial food containing GM ingredients. The social question does not come first in a linear model that would posit that risk concerns would be of a post-material nature (Beck 1986). Rather, the cases studied show that concerns about risk deeply intersect with social issues: The poor are those who most suffer the effects of GM crops in their bodies and environments. More than targets of campaigns to raise their awareness, they themselves are making sense of the very concrete damage experienced in their bodies and environments. Risk becomes material. Popular epistemology establishes correlations between the expansion of GM crops and their sufferings; they do not depend on scientists in distant laboratories to calculate probabilities based on a few rats.

Women have played a central role in establishing these relations between agrarian production, the environment, and bodies. In the two instances analyzed there are elements of ecofeminism, such as the use of common sense about the social role of women in reproductive work to expand it to care for the environment as a basis for their political mobilization. Feminists have criticized this type of argument because it strengthens patriarchal ideas about women and nature (Leach 2007; MacGregor 2004). However, in both cases, the performativity of gender was at play when women drew on this (traditional) role in a context of strong mobilization in the public arena of disputes over the negative effects of agrarian activities. In other words, their mobilization was not so much focused on the feminine but on the feminist potential of uncovering relations of domination, in the case of GM crops, between the productive sphere, on the one side, and social reproduction and nature, on the other.

Finally, the inequalities generated by the widespread adoption of GM crops are not only global but also entangled (see introduction to this volume), since the increase in profits of the headquarters of transnational seed and chemical companies goes hand in hand with the concentration of environmental contamination in the margins of the production nodes of the global commodity chains. Thus, the question of responsibilities acquires a central significance. Although the causes are global, the responsibilities are asymmetrically distributed, and, faced with interests of global and domestic agrarian capitalism, states have mostly proven "weak." Therefore, social analysis must incorporate the geopolitics of knowledge and the political ecology of GM crops alongside their political economy, as environmental burdens and the ability to define them are also asymmetrically distributed.

List of interviews quoted

Movimento dos Pequenos Agricultores (MPA), São Paulo, 24 January 2012.
Assessoria e Serviços a Projetos em Agricultura Alternativa (AS-PTA, Advisory and Services for Projects in Alternative Agriculture), Rio de Janeiro, 13 February 2012.
Madres de Ituzaingó Anexo, Córdoba, 7–8 August 2012.

Notes

1 I would like to thank Elizabeth Jelin and Sérgio Costa for their very constructive comments and suggestions on previous versions of this chapter.
2 Biotechnology applied to plant breeding, or agrobiotechnology, uses a genetic engineering technique to design a seed with specific properties, such as resistance to herbicide and the production of insecticides by the plant. They are referred to as genetically modified (GM) crops or organisms (GMOs). I use these terms interchangeably.
3 The empirical research upon which this chapter is based consists of different types of data relating to the period 1996–2013, including official databanks, documental sources, secondary literature, and primary data collected from newspaper articles, social movements' campaign documents on the internet, and semi-structured interviews with activists (Motta 2016).
4 Initially named Movimento das Mulheres Trabalhadoras Rurais (MMTR), which was launched in 1989 in Rio Grande do Sul, the movement started with women mobilizing for gender issues inside other agrarian movements, until they decided on autonomy. A growing national network culminated in the national movement MMC (Rosa 2010).
5 Only in 2013 did the European Food Safety Agency design protocols for chronic studies, following the controversy surrounding the publication of results by a critical research institute, showing the increased probability of cancer among rats exposed to glyphosate (Séralini et al. 2012).
6 The geopolitics of knowledge is, in turn, institutionalized by international legal regimes. The stronger advancement of international law in the protection of free trade vis-à-vis its slower progress in environmental protection reinforces global socio-environmental inequalities.

References

Agarwal, B. (1992): "The Gender and Environment Debate: Lessons from India," *Feminist Studies* 18(1): 119.
Arancibia, F. (2013): "Challenging the Bioeconomy: The Dynamics of Collective Action in Argentina," *Technology in Society*, 35(2): 79–92.
Beck, U. (1986): *Risikogesellschaft. Auf dem Weg in eine andere Moderne*, Frankfurt am Main: Suhrkamp Verlag.
Bonner, M. D. (2007): *Sustaining Human Rights: Women and Argentine Human Rights Organizations*, University Park, PA: The Pennsylvania State University Press.
Campbell, H. (2009): "Breaking New Ground in Food Regime Theory: Corporate Environmentalism, Ecological Feedbacks and the 'Food from Somewhere' Regime?" *Agriculture and Human Values*, 26(4): 309–19.
Di Chiro, G. (2008): "Living Environmentalisms: Coalition Politics, Social Reproduction, and Environmental Justice," *Environmental Politics*, 17(2): 276–98.

230 Renata Motta

Diamond, I. and Orenstein, G. (1990): *Reweaving the World: The Emergence of Ecofeminism*, San Francisco, CA: Sierra Club Books, 2nd ed.

Giarracca, N. (2003): "De Las Fincas y Las Casas a Las Rutas y Las Plazas: Las Protestas y Las Organizaciones Sociales en La Argentina de Los Mundos 'rururbanos' Una Mirada Desde América Latina," *Sociologias*, 10: 250–83.

Grupo de Madres de Córdova (2005): *Destrucción del Espacio Urbano: Genocidio Encubierto en Barrio Ituzaingó de Córdoba. Informe Alternativo Sobre La Salud en América Latina*, Quito: Observatorio Latinoamericano de la Salud CEAS.

Hopkins, T. K. and Wallerstein. I (1986): "Commodity Chains in the World-Economy Prior to 1800," *Review (Fernand Braudel Center)*, 10(1): 157–70.

James, C. (2016): "Global Status of Commercialized Biotech/GM Crops: 2015," *ISAAA Briefs*, 51, Ithaca, NY: ISAAA.

Jelin, E. (1996): "Women, Gender, and Human Rights," in Jelin, S. and Hersberg, E. (eds.): *Constructing Democracy: Human Rights, Citizenship, and Society in Latin America*, Boulder, CO: Westview Press, pp. 177–196.

Leach, M. (2007): "Earth Mother Myths and Other Ecofeminist Fables: How a Strategic Notion Rose and Fell," *Development and Change*, 38(1): 67–85.

Luhmann, N. (2008): *Risk: A Sociological Theory*, New Brunswick, NJ: Aldine Transaction.

MacGregor, S. (2004): "From Care to Citizenship: Calling Ecofeminism Back to Politics," *Ethics and the Environment*, 9(1): 56–84.

Mellor, M. (1992): *Breaking the Boundaries: Towards a Feminist Green Socialism*, London: Virago Press Ltd.

Mies, M. and Shiva, V. (1993): *Ecofeminism*. Halifax, Nova Scotia: Fernwood Publications.

Motta, R. (2016): *Social Mobilization, Global Capitalism and Struggles over Food: A Comparative Study of Social Movements*, London: Routledge.

Motta, R. and Arancibia, F. (2016): "Health Experts Challenging the Safety of Pesticides in Argentina and Brazil," in Chamberlain, M. (ed.): *Medicine, Discourse and Power*, London: Routledge, pp. 170–206

Nightingale, A. (2006): "The Nature of Gender: Work, Gender, and Environment," *Environment and Planning D: Society and Space*, 24(2): 165–85.

Pereira, P. and Fernandes, G. (2007): "Mulheres Protestam contra Milho Transgênico em Reunião da CTNBio," available at: http://www.cptne2.org.br/index.php/publicacoes/noticias/noticias-do-campo/1734-mulheres-protestam-contra-milho-transgenico-em-reuniao-da-ctnbio.html.

Rosa, M. (2010): "Para Além Do MST: O Impacto nos Movimentos Sociais Brasileiros," in Carter, M. (ed.): *Combatendo a Desigualdade Social: O MST E a Reforma Agrária no Brasil*, São Paulo: Unesp, pp. 461–78.

Salleh, A. (ed.) (2009): *Eco-Sufficiency and Global Justice: Women Write Political Ecology*, London; New York, NY; North Melbourne, Victoria: Pluto Press.

Schild, V. (1994): "Recasting 'Popular' Movements: Gender and Political Learning in Neighborhood Organizations in Chile," *Latin American Perspectives*, 21: 59–80.

Séralini, G. -E., Clair, E., Mesnage, R., Gress, S., Defarge, N., Malatesta, M., Hennequin, D., and Spiroux de Vendômois, J. (2012): "Long Term Toxicity of a Roundup Herbicide and a Roundup-Tolerant Genetically Modified Maize," *Food and Chemical Toxicology*, 50(11): 4221–31.

Shiva, V. (2010): *Staying Alive: Women, Ecology, and Development*, New York, NY: South End Press.

UNCTAD (2015): "The State of Commodity Dependence 2014," New York and Geneva: UNCTAD, available at http://unctad.org/en/PublicationsLibrary/suc2014d7_en.pdf.

FINAL REFLECTIONS

Sérgio Costa, Renata Motta, and Elizabeth Jelin

Any attempt to bring together such diverse research endeavors under the common goal of advancing conceptual debates always brings with it the complex task of drawing lessons from the existing scholarship and defining ways forward. The global entangled inequalities perspective is under construction and draws on insights from the different approaches discussed in this book (transnationalism, world systems, categorical inequalities, intersectional studies, among others). Therefore, we briefly join, in these final reflections, research findings from the various book chapters highlighting how these results, when combined, significantly expand the state of the art in research on social inequalities. Far from trying to write a concluding chapter, we reflect on how our analyses and concepts offer a timely and important contribution to understanding dynamics of global inequality and social inequalities in Latin America. This exercise follows the levels of analysis according to which the book is organized: structures, categories, and the dynamics of social inequalities.

Concerning structures of inequalities, a combined analysis of the findings presented in the chapters compiled in the book grasps, at first glance, the historical persistence of income inequalities between countries as well as the durability of patterns of inequality found in the different countries, in line with the world-historical approach adopted by Korzeniewicz (in this book). That is, even if domestic income inequalities in wealthiest societies have recently increased (Piketty 2014), the groups of countries with low and high levels of income inequalities, with only a few exceptions, have not substantially varied since the 19th century. The expansion of citizenship rights, responsible for producing more equality at the domestic level, is also co-responsible for keeping the income distance between citizens from different countries as these rights are reserved for nationals—the "transnationalization of social rights" (Fischer-Lescano/Möller 2016) remains an unfulfilled promise.

Based especially on the rise of China as a major economic player, world-historical analysts (Korzeniewicz in this book) expect a shift in global structures that sustain long-term between-country income inequalities. Current trends in Latin America (as described by Dietz, Segura, and Góngora-Mera in this book) allow a more comprehensive perspective.

This implies first raising the broader question regarding "inequalities of what?" in order to incorporate not only differences in income distribution but also inequalities in terms of power, welfare, and environmental assets. Accordingly, Dietz establishes a clear correlation between the recent cycle of economic growth in Latin America and increasing ecological harms that affect especially the poor and more vulnerable populations such as indigenous and Afro-descendent communities. The ecological lens also sheds light on the interdependencies between income increases in China and the increase in ecological inequalities in Latin American and African countries that supply raw materials to China's growth.

Segura, in turn, shows that recent economic growth in Latin America goes hand-in-hand with a deterioration of welfare in terms of quality of life in Latin American cities due to a lack of public investments in infrastructure and urban services. This affects especially the poor and those who do not have power to influence local and national decisions. Based on these findings, one could state that even if the prediction of the reduction of between-country *income disparities* due to the rise of newcomers in the world economy as in the case of China, this will not necessarily lead to a transformation of the global structuration of inequalities. This is a consequence of the fact that in less affluent societies, increases in income are linked to the deterioration of other unequality dimensions. Thus, social distances measured in terms of power, welfare, and ecological assets between nationals from the contemporary wealthy societies and from the less affluent countries will persist.

From another perspective, Góngora-Mera also makes the case for the durability and the interdependent production of inequalities beyond national borders. Thus, the study of jurisprudence on race at the *longue durée* reveals the importance not only of national citizenship rights to shape between-country inequalities but also international law for shaping and maintaining global inequalities. International law functions as a transregional entanglement that, in modern history, has connected productive and social structures in different world regions by regulating, for instance, trade or capital flows. At the same time, international law has separated subjects of rights according to national, gender, ethnic, and racial criteria, as Góngora-Mera shows.

The entangled inequalities perspective also innovates the analysis of categorizations as discussed in the second section of the book. It claims that de-centering inequality research should have first priority in order to incorporate research findings produced in different world regions. The academic celebration of the intersectionality approach in the Anglophone academia since the 1980s loses its originality when considering the long-term scholarship that, at least in Latin America, has researched since the 1940s entanglements between class and race, class and gender, and class and ethnicity (Jelin in this book). The entangled inequalities approach also calls for, at different levels, a revision of the categorical inequalities paradigm as

Final reflections **233**

inaugurated by Charles Tilly. The categorical inequalities approach as well as many contributions in the field of intersectionality studies (see Roth 2013) conceive of social categorizations as dichotomist differences that are historically durable components of social structure.

We do agree with Tilly that being classified as black, female, or indigenous has been historically associated with consistently lower positions in socio-economic and/or power hierarchies (Perez Sáinz in this book). In modern history, these classifications have also been institutionalized in policy bodies and legal frameworks where they have been transformed in hard facts of social structures. However, the studies collected in this volume argue, in the first place, that just as in the case of continuities, discontinuities also characterize the "biography" of social categorizations. They have changed not only through history but also vary according to specific social contexts. Social categorizations are more contextual than structural variables (Canessa and Jelin in this book). Second, the studies argue that, for shaping social inequalities, social categorizations have to be interpreted and negotiated in everyday life and within institutions. Thus, the mere existence of categorizations as a cultural repertoire is prima facie neutral for social structure. These categorizations influence the positions assumed by individuals or groups in existing social hierarchies only once they have begun to influence social positions and strategies of social closure. In this sense, they are not pre-political but political categories that have to be actively constructed and reconstructed in social interactions in order to impact social inequalities (Reygadas in this book). Third, the different axes of categorizations (race, ethnicity, gender, etc.) are irremediably interdependent. That means that the references to black and white, women and men, or Muslim and non-Muslim, as described by the categorical inequalities approach and also some intersectional studies, are analytical tools that are not found independent of each other in social life or in the social structures. In fact, it is not possible to isolate the effect for social inequalities of being, for instance, black without also taking into account that one has a gender, is a citizen of a certain country, etc. (Jelin in this book).

Finally, in this book, the entangled inequalities approach has been further developed in the study of the dynamics of inequalities in Latin America. This enabled us to be precise about how historical entanglements shape present social inequalities. For this, the geological metaphor of "layered inequalities" (Baquero-Melo in this book) proved to be useful. It allows for articulating present dynamics of social structuration with social distances accumulated through centuries. In this context, even when compensatory policies or contemporary cycles of expansion of the labor market function as powerful driving forces for reducing inequalities concerning ethnicity, gender, or race, structural changes occur at a slow pace due to the fact that existing distances in terms of hoarding of opportunities or socially valued skills continue operating to keep or even enlarge social distances.

By using relational unities of analysis as in the case of care chains, the entangled inequalities approach has enabled a more elaborated reconstruction of certain linkages between local, national, and global social structures than studies based solely on the world systems perspective. Thus, even in cases in which migration processes lead to a reduction of income inequality between citizens of different countries, they leave a track of new forms of inequalities (racial, gender, international, intergenerational) along the chains that connect sending and receiving localities of migrants (Skornia in this book).

For stressing interdependencies between global and local structures of inequalities as well as between the different dimensions and the various axes through which social inequalities are produced and reproduced, the entangled inequalities approach applied and developed in this book also illuminates some dilemmas faced by Latin American countries for reducing inequalities in contemporary times. Accordingly, the cycle of economic growth during the first fifteen years of the 21st century that has contributed to reducing income inequalities and also to mitigate asymmetries between men and women and blacks and whites in the cities in most Latin America countries has led to more land concentration in the countryside and to new levels of environmental deterioration in both rural and urban areas (Motta in this book). It has also led to a "reprimarization" of Latin American economies and to increasing economic dependence on the rising power of China.

Furthermore, the cycle of economic growth has brought to the surface serious disjunctures between democratic legitimation and contemporary capitalist development. Grounding their legitimation on the promise (fulfilled to a certain degree) of promoting upward mobility to "new middle classes," "pink tide" governments, as in the case of Brazil (Costa in this book), have been politically kidnapped by liberal economists and their strategies for enlarging domestic markets and opening new spaces of accumulation for (foreign) capital. In this context, democratic stability becomes entirely dependent on economic growth, which is by definition cyclical, unpredictable, and dependent on external factors not controllable by national governments.

During the first decade of the 21st century, Latin America had shown significant results in poverty reduction and in the growth of labor markets, constituting an exception when compared to other world regions. Yet these results did not mitigate income inequality. More recently, the decrease in commodity prices and economic stagnation have strongly affected the national political economies of the region. In a context characterized by major changes in power in countries like Argentina, Brazil, and Paraguay, where leftist governments committed to both pro-market and pro-poor policies were replaced by ultraliberal presidents, the state is now contributing to increasing income and non-monetary social inequalities via new privatizations, cuts in social rights, tax facilities for investors, revisions in land rights for indigenous peoples, etc.

Therefore, it is to be expected that a future research agenda on global entangled inequalities, in analytical terms, will deal with this growing disjuncture between democratic politics, taking place mainly at the level of national units, and the capitalist economy, global in its reach and dynamics. However, this development is unpredictable as it depends on the actions of political and economic actors, which not only establish linkages across productive and financial activities globally but attempt, at the same time, to disconnect and disembed such processes from societal influence. It remains to be seen how emancipatory politics responds and counters such trends. Future research might inquire into how civil society engages in contestations on the streets and how social mobilization builds solidarity and coalitions across borders, as well as how grassroots economic and political practices continuously create value and meanings that challenge dominant views of democracy and of capitalist laws beyond human agency.

References

Lescano-Fischer, A. and Möller, K. (eds.) (2016): *Transnationalisation of Social Rights*, Cambridge, U.K.: Intersentia.

Piketty, T. (2014): *Capital in the Twenty-First Century*, Cambridge, MA: Harvard University Press.

Roth, J. (2013): *Entangled Inequalities as Intersectionalities: Towards an Epistemic Sensibilization*, Berlin: desiguALdades.net, Working Paper 43.

INDEX

References to graphs, tables and other illustrations are in **bold**

Agarwal, Bina 79
agrarian capitalism: consequences 214; and GM crops 215
Albrecht, Scott & Korzeniewicz, Roberto Patricio 33
alterity, and identity 150
American Constitution: 14th Amendment (1868) 50; and racial discrimination 50
anti-racism 54
anticapitalism, women as 120; *see also* capitalism
appropriation, expropriation, distinction 155
Argentina: commodity exports 217; economic growth 69; GM crops 15, 215; GM soy 215; income inequality 67, 69, 72n6; income share 99; Madres de Ituzaingó campaign 219–23; pesticide contamination 218–23; social mobility 33
Avatar (film): cartoon **129;** and indigeneity (*indigenismo*) 128, 139, 140
Aymara New Year, Bolivia 133, 139

Balandier, Georges 146
banana economy, Urabá region (Colombia) 168, 172–3
Baquero–Melo, Jairo 13–14
Bauman, Zygmunt, historical memory concept 123–4
Baumann, Gerd 150
Berlin Conference, General Act (1885) 52

blanqueamiento policies 52; *see also* Jim Crow laws; white status
Bobbio, Norberto 96
Bolivia: Aymara New Year 133, 139; Chapare region 135, 138; coca growers 135–6; coca production 130–1, 135; extractionist policies 130; GM crops 215; highlanders, vs lowlanders 134, 135, 138, 140; indigeneity (*indigenismo*) 129, 130; indigenous citizenship 134; indigenous colonists 136–8; indigenous discourses 12; MAS party 128, 135; mining 135, 136; pluriculturalism 135; poverty reduction 218; social mobility 33; Tiwanaku site 132, 133; 'vivir bien' policy 133; Wila Kjarka people 139; *see also* TIPNIS
Borsdorf, Axel 64
boundaries 145
Bourdieu, Pierre 144, 156; *habitus* concept 152
Brazil: commodity exports 217; corruption 179, 191; domestic work 187; family values 120–1; GDP 178, 179; GM corn 218; GM corn, opposition to 223–6; GM crops 15, 215; GM soy 218; NP 189; middle class 186–7, 190; middle-class schooling 186; millionaires 87–9; "Negro" 114; outsiders 185–6; the poor 185; slavery, abolition (1888) 114, 120, 179; social classes, vectors 14, 182–3;

238 Index

social inequality 28; social inequality, vectors 179, 181, 184, 186, 192; social spending 178; social structures 182–4; social structures, changes 184–9, **188**, 192; social structures and political crisis 189–91, 192; taxation 189–90; urbanization 120; Workers Party 14, 178, 184; *see also* São Paulo
Brubaker, Rogers 110
Buenos Aires: inequality and poverty 62; Permanent Household Survey 72n6; population growth 69
Buenos Aires (Metropolitan Region): gated communities 67; housing 69, 70; income distribution 66–7; jurisdictions 72n5; nomenclature 72n5; population growth 69; poverty **68**; social inequality **68**; unemployment **68**
Burgos, Laws of (1512) 47

Cadiz, Constitution of (1812, Spain) 51
Caldeira, Teresa 65
Cameron, John, *Avatar* 128
Canessa, Andrew 11–12
capabilities 97
capacities: equalization of 152, 153, **153**; and *habitus* 153
capitalism: family in 121; Latin America 114, 123; and race 114–16; Schumpeter on 28–9; *see also* agrarian capitalism; anticapitalism
capitalist development, women in 120
care deficits 14
care relationships, and inequalities 14–15
care work: and character 206; commodification of 199; definition 198; ethnic categorization 206, 211n5; as family responsibility 199; gender inequalities 202–3; gender–specific tasks 204; informal 210n2; infrastructure 198; outsourcing of 196, 199; and social inequalities 198–9, 233–4; as women's responsibility 198, 200, 202–3; *see also* global care chains; transnational care chains
care workers: citizenship status 206–7; motivation for employing 200–1
Casanova, Pablo González 124
caste systems 45, 47–9; purchase of white status 48
Castel, Robert 101, 102–3
Castree, Noel 82–3
categorical inequalities 35, 37, 145, 232–3

categorical pairs 106n16; processing of differences 103
Cattaneo Pineda, Rodrigo 64
CEPAL *see* ECLAC/CEPAL
Chapare region, Bolivia 135, 138
Chile: income share 99; Law of Selective Immigration (1845) 53
China, economic growth 26, 231, 232, 234
Chinese Exclusion Laws (1882–1943, US) 52
Ciccolella, Pablo & Baer, Luis 67, 68
city: as privileged space 63, 71; and social inequalities 60, 71; *see also* Latin American city; urban space
Civil Rights Act (1964, US) 50
class memory 115, 123
classes *see* social classes
classification, social inequalities 145
climate change 83, 84, 132
CO_2 emissions 83
coca growers: Bolivia 135–6; indigeneity 135–6
coca production, Bolivia 130–1, 135
Code Noir (France, 1685) 48
Cohen, Abner 152
Colombia: Afro-descendants 165, 169–70; colonialism 163–4; community councils 170
colonialism: Guatemala 117; internal 118; Mexico 117; persistence of 117–18; *see also* internal colonialism
colonisation, and indigeneity
color, and race 45
Committee on the Elimination of Racial Discrimination 42
conflict, and power 10
Constitution (1991) 170; gold mining 77, 87; income share 99; independence (1810) 165; indigenous populations 164–5, 169; inequalities 161; land rights 161–2, 174–5; Law 70: 162, 170–1; new municipalities 172; Patriotic Union party 173; slavery, abolition 165; social categories 165–6; social inequalities 161; white status 166; *see also* Darién region; Lower Arato region; Urabá region
Cook-Martín, D. & and FitzGerald, D. 53
Costa, Sérgio 14
creative destruction concept 29, 31
Cruces, Guillermo 67
culture, and social inequalities 156–7

Darién Region 163–4; economic growth 167
data scarcity and inequalities 6

Declaration of the Conference of the Americas against Racism 42

DesiguALdades.net 6, 197

deskilling 29; *see also* skill

Dicken, Peter 88

Dietz, Kristina 9–10, 232

difference: and categorical pairs 103; and inferiorization 104; right to 151; and social equality 119; and social inequality 11, 124, 146, 149, 149–51, 150, **151**; transformation of 151

dispositives 44

diversity, and neoliberalism 109–10

domestic sphere, and public sphere 121, 200

domestic work, and social reproduction 121–2, 123

Domingues, José Mauricio 124

Douglas, Mary 148

dualization, urban structures

Duhau, E. & Giglia, A. 64

Dulitzky, Ariel 42

Ebert, Anne 133

ECLAC/CEPAL 113, 185

ecofeminism: essentialism of 216; GM crops issues 228

ecological inequalities 2

economic growth: China 26, 231, 232, 234; Darién Region 167; Lower Atrato region 167

Elias, Norbert 148, 156

Elias, Norbert & Scotson, J.L. 181

elites, Sierra Leone 152

emigration, Peru 201

encomenderos 47

encomienda system 47, 48

entangled inequalities: applications 233; definition 6; in transnational care chains 209

environment: and gender 15, 215, 216, 217

environmental inequalities 2, 9

environmental justice 80–1

epistemic hybridization 78

equality *see* social equality; social inequality; social inequalities

equalization, of capacities 152, 153, **153**

Escobar, Arturo 80

Esping-Andersen, G. 199

ethnic categorization, care work 206, 211n5

ethnicity: and gender 124; and social inequality 205–6

exclusion *see* selective exclusion

exploitation 100–1

expropriation, appropriation, distinction 155

Fabricant, Nicole 134

family: in capitalism 121; public and private spheres 121–2

feminism 119; *see also* ecofeminism

Fernandes, Florestan: on capitalism and race 114–16; on the "Negro" 123

Fitzsimmons, Margaret 78

force field model, and social inequality 181

Fordist economic model 65

Foreign Direct Investment (FDI), Urabá region (Colombia) 173

Foucault, Michel 80

Frankfurt School 82

Fraser, Nancy 151, 185

Fraser, Nancy & Scott, Joan 119

Freyre, Gilberto 113; *Casa-Grande & Senzala* 54

Gasparini, Leonardo & Cruces, Guillermo 67

gated communities: Buenos Aires (Metropolitan Region) 67; Latin American cities 64, 67

Gatopardism 51

gender: and environment 15, 215, 216, 217; and ethnicity 124; performativity 226, 228; pervasiveness 119; *see also* feminism

gender asymmetries, social inequality 148

gender equity, and symbolic processes 149

gender identity 226

gender inequalities 112: care work 202–3

gender relations: "Negro" 115

Germani, Gino 124

Gini coefficient 71n2

global care chains 196, 197

global care migrations 196

global commodity chains 214, 215, 226, 228

global inequality, transformation 34–9

Global Production Networks 87

Global South 79

global spaces 61

globalization: and Latin American cities 62; and social inequality 39, 61, 62; and urban fragmentation 72n3; and urban structures 62

GM (Genetically Modified) corn, Brazil, opposition to 223–6

GM (Genetically Modified) crops: and agrarian capitalism 215; Argentina 15, 215, 218; Bolivia 215; Brazil 15, 215;

240 Index

contamination 227; ecofeminism 228; intellectual property issues 15, 215, 224, 227; Paraguay 215; political ecology of 228; regulation of 227; risks 226–7; and social inequality 228; United States 215; Uruguay 215

GM (Genetically Modified) soy, Argentina 215; opposition to 219–23; pesticide contamination 218–23

Godelier, Maurice 148

gold mining: Colombia 77, 87; spatiality of 88

Góngora–Mera, Manuel 8, 232

Groisman, Fernando 69

Guatemala: colonialism 117; Decree 126 (1874) 53; indigenous peoples, extermination of 54; social mobility 33; Vagrancy Law (1934) 53

Gunder Frank, André 114

habitus: and capacities 153; definition 152

Haddad, Fernando 16n2

Haiti: abolition of slavery 50; Constitution (1805) 50; slave rebellion 50

Harvey, David 60, 79, 81

"hidden transcripts" concept 154, 155

historical memory concept 123; *see also* habitus

hoarding *see* opportunity hoarding

Holocaust 54

home, work, differentiation 121

housewife, as worker 122

Hurricane Katrina 83

identity, and alterity 150; *see also* national identity; racial identities

Inca slogan 132

income disparities, reduction 232

income distribution: Buenos Aires (Metropolitan Region) 66–7; national **24**; United States 23; and urbanization, case study 66–70

income inequality: Argentina 67, 69, 72n6; Latin America, decline 59, 96–7, 99

income share: Argentina 99; Chile 99; Colombia 99; Uruguay 99

indigeneity (*indigenismo*): and *Avatar* (film) 128, 139, 140; Bolivia 129, 130; coca growers 135–6; discourses 12, 134, 140; as global commodity 132; and the hyperreal indian 131, 139–40, 140; and integration 118; Mexico 118; as political discourse 139; privileging of 12; varieties of 12

indigenous citizenship, Bolivia 134

indigeneous consciousness 134

indigenous, meanings 12, 138

indigenous colonists, Bolivia 136–8

indigenous populations, Colombia 164–5, 169

indigenous reservations, Lower Atrato region (Colombia) 169

inequalities *see* social inequalities

inequality *see* social inequality

inequality and poverty *see* social inequality and poverty

inequality regimes 8, 41; compensatory regimes 46, 47, 109, 233; definition 46; racial 46, 47–55; transregional articulations 46

inferiorization 103; and difference 104

integration, and indigeneity (*indigenismo*) 118

intellectual property issues, GM crops 15, 215, 224, 227

Inter-American Development Bank 98

International Mother Earth Day 132

intersectionality 5, 9, 11, 232; and layered inequalities 162, 163, 174; and social categorizations 112, 232; and social inequalities 77

Italy: attendance allowance provision 201; care gap 200; Peruvian migrants 15, 197; role in migration 201

Janoschka, Michael 64, 65

Jelin, Elizabeth 11

Jim Crow laws, United States 42, 52

Kessler, Gabriel 69

Kirchner, Néstor, President 218

knowledge: geopoltics of 228; and risk 227–8; socially valued 183, 185

Korzeniewicz, Roberto Patricio 3, 8, 114

Korzeniewicz, Roberto Patricio & Albrecht, Scott 25, 26, 33

Korzeniewicz, Roberto Patricio & Moran, Timothy Patrick 22, 34; global stratification, country deciles 23, **24**, 25; *Unveiling Inequality* 37

Kreckel, Reinhard 183; force field model 181

Kuznesof, Elisabeth Anne 45

labor market: and social inequalities 113

labor theory of value 217

Laing, Anna, Evotar cartoon **130**

land rights, Colombia 161–2, 174–5

Larguía, Isabel & Dumoulin, John 121

Latin America: abolition of slavery 51; assimilation projects 54, 55; capitalism

114, 123; change 123; income inequality, decline 59, 96–7, 99; independence movement 49; law and race 48–9; as liminal space 125; mining 84; modernization 112; multiculturalism 11, 47; post–Second World War developments 112–14; racial discrimination 42; racial inequality regimes 47–55; urbanization 112; and Western modernity 125; women in labor market 122–3

Latin American cities: fragmentation 63–4; gate communities 64, 67; and globalization 6; inequality and poverty **62**; model 60–1; transformations 61

Latin Americans, rich 98–9

law and race 44–6, 56; approaches 55–6; Latin America 48–9; layered inequalities 233; and racial discrimination 42, 46; and racial discrimination, examples 42

layered inequalities 233; and intersectionality 162, 163, 174

Leal, C. & Van Ausdal, S. 86

Lima, inequality and poverty 62

Lópex–Calva, Luis Felipe & Lustig, Nora 71, 96, 97

Louis XIV, King of France 48

Lower Atrato region (Colombia) 13, 14, 161; Afro–descendants 169–7; economic growth 167; indigenous reservations 169; Law 70, impact 171; multi–ethnicity 169; National Natural Park Los Katíos 169; oil palm cultivation 85–6, 173–4; violence 171–2

Lukes, Steven 100

Lula da Silva, Luiz Inácio, President 178, 190, 218

Lulism 178

lusotropicalism policy 54

machismo 10

Madres de Ituzaingó, Argentina, campaign 219–23

Mariategui, José Carlos 113

Marini, Mauro 114

Marshall, T.H. 103

Marxism, feminist critique of 216

MAS (Moviemento al Socialismo) party Bolivia 128, 135

materiality: concept 86–7; of oil palm fruit 87

de Mattos, Carlos 63

Mellor, Mary 216

men: migrant 204–5; in transnational care chains 203; *see also* women

mestizaje (miscegenation) 43, 45, 54

mestizo nationalism 52–5

mestizos 5

Mexico: abolition of slavery 51; colonialism 117; Constitution (1917) 53; economic growth 31; indigeneity (*indigenismo*) 118; inequality and poverty 61; Migration Law (1930) 53; social mobility 33

Mexico City, social inequality and poverty 62, **62**

middle class, Brazil 82, 190; schooling 186

migration: feminization of 196; and income differentials 33; and inequalities 14; international 31, **32**, 33; role of Italy 201; role of Peru 201; as social mobility 31, **32**, 33, 34; and social reproduction 196, 200; and stratification 33; transnational 3

Milan, Peruvian migrants 200

millionaires, Brazil 187–9

mining, Latin America 84

mobility *see* social mobility

Montevideo, inequality and poverty 62

Morales, Evo, President: *Avatar* image 128; Evotar cartoon 129, 130, **130**; *Global Defender of Mother Earth* award 132, 136; indigeneity, privileging of 12, 133; indigenous credentials 128–9, 131–2; indigenous rhetoric 132; 'vivir bien' philosophy 133

Moran, T.P. & Korzeniewicz, R.P. 3

Motta, Renata 15

Movimento de Mulheres Camponesas (MMC) 224–5, 229n4

Multiculturalism, Latin America 11, 47

Mumbai, average hourly wage 25

myths, role 148

nation, and race 49–50

nation-state: and social inequalities 181–2; as unit of analysis 21, 22–3, 76

national identity 36, 49, 54, 134

nature: and social inequalities 9, 81–4, 88–9; social production of 82; society, dualism 9, 77, 78; transformation of 81, 82

"Negro": in Brazil 114; Fernandes on 123; gender relations 115; in São Paulo 115; use of term 125n3

neoliberalism: and diversity 109–10; and social reproduction 217

New Imperialism 52

New Kingdom of Granada 165, 166

New Laws (1542) 47

New York average hourly wage 25, 26

Nuñez de Balboa, Vasco 164

242 Index

oil palm cultivation, Lower Atrato region (Colombia) 85–6, 173–4
oil palm fruit, materiality 87
opportunity hoarding 101, 101–2

Pachamama 132, 139
Panama 167; Constitution (1941) 53
Paraguay, GM crops 215
paramilitary groups, Urabá region (Colombia) 173–4
Parkin, Frank 180
patriarchy 121, 216
Patriotic Union party, Colombia 173
Pelligrini, Alessandra 135
Peltier, Leonard 132
Pérez Sáinz, Juan Pablo 10–11
Peru, role in migration 201
Peruvians and Italy: 15, 197, 200; conditional citizenship 206–7; emotional issues 207; essentialised images of 206; and family dependents 207–8; Milan 200
pesticide use: Argentina 218–23; and social reproduction 215
Piketty, Thomas 99, 144
pluriculturalism, Bolivia 135
PNUD see UNDP
Polanyi, Karl 100, 109
political ecology: concept 78; connections 217; feminist 79; of GM crops 228; neo–Marxist approach 78–9; post–structuralist 79
poor people, Brazil 185
poverty: Buenos Aires (Metropolitan Region) **68**; and inequality see social inequality and poverty; reduction, Brazil 218
power: asymmetries, and social inequalities 180–1; and conflict 100; inequalities 2; Weberian concept 101
Prebisch, Raúl 113
Prévot–Schapira, M.F. & Pineda, Cattaneo 64
production modes 121
protagonism 98, 104
PT see Workers Party
public sphere 184, 192; and domestic sphere 121, 200
Purchasing Power Parity (PPP) 40n6

Quispe, Felipe 139

race: and blood purity 45; and capitalism 114–16; and color 45; legal lineage 8, 42, 44–6; and nation 49–50; and

social stratification 52, 81; Spain 45; as transregional inequality 44–6; see also law and race
racial discrimination: American Constitution 50; Latin America 42; and law 42, 46
racial identities 45, 48, 81
racial inequality regimes, Latin America 47–55
racist nationalism 49–55
Ramos, Alcida 131
Rawls, John, theory of justice 40n11
re-valuing, the subordinate 149, **149**
Real Cédula (Spain, 1789) 48
regime analysis 46
Research Network on Interdependent Inequalities (LA) see *desiguALdades.net*
Restrepo, E. 162
Reygadas, Luis 12–13
Rio de Janeiro, inequality and poverty 62
risk, and knowledge 227–8
rituals, role 156
Roberts, Bryan 62–3
Rousseff, Dilma 178, 190; impeachment 179, 191

Saad-Filho, Alfredo 178
Sack, Robert David 85
Saffioti, Heleieth 123; *A mulher na sociedade de classes. Mito e realidade* 120
Sahlins, Marshall 144
Salleh, A. 217
Santiago: social inequality and poverty 62
São Paulo: black women in 115; inequality and poverty 62; "Negro" in 115; spatial segregation patterns 65
Schumpeter, Joseph: on capitalism 28–9; creative destruction concept 29, 31
Scott, James 154
Scott, Joan W. 119
segregation, modalites 104
Segura, Ramiro 9, 232
selective exclusion 34–5, 35
Sen, Amartya 1, 97
Shakow, Miriam 135
Sierra Leone, elites 152
Singer, André 178
skill 28; see also deskilling
Skornia, Anna 14–15
Slave Trade Act (1807, GB) 50–1
slavery, abolition: Brazil 114, 120, 179; Colombia 165; Haiti 50; Latin America 51; Mexico 51; Venezuela 51
slavery, codes of treatment 47–8

Index **243**

slavery, transatlantic 44
slavery, United States 50
Smith, Adam: on opportunity hoarding 22, *The Wealth of Nations* 21, on town and country differentials 22, 30, 34, 36, 37
social categorizations 10, 111–12; and intersectionality 112, 232
social citizenship, and social inequalities 103
social classes 102; and social inequalities 111; and social stratification 81; and strata 180
social closure 148, 180, 183, 187
social equality: and difference 119; meanings 109
social imaginary 95–6; limitations 96–8, 104
social inequalities: and care relationships 14–15; and care work 198–9, 233–4; categories 113; classification 145; Colombia 161; and culture 156–7; and data scarcity 6; deconstruction, symbolic processes **149**; dimensions 181–2; durable 145; and intersectionality 77; and the labor market 113; layered 13; meaning 83; and migration 14; multiple 111–12; and the nation-state 181–2; and nature 9, 81–4, 88–9; plurality of 7; and power asymmetries 180–1; research 1, 2–5; social actors 3; and social citizenship 103; and social classes 111; socio–ecological perspectives 77–8, 88, 89; structuring of 7–8, 231; and symbolic processes 12, 144–5, 146, 156–7; and symbolic strategies **147**, **149**, **153;** and symbolic struggles (de-legitimization) 153–5, **155**, 156; and symbolic struggles (legitimization) 153–5, **155**, 156; transformations 13; and transnational care chains 197, 208, 209; and urban space 9, 59, 60, 65–6, 66, 70, 71; *see also* ecological inequalities; environmental inequalities; layered inequalities
social inequality: analysis of 3, 4, 11, 76, 112; basic questions 96; Brazil 28, 179, 181, 184, 186, 192; Buenos Aires (Metropolitan Region) **68**; categorical 145; and difference 11, 124, 146, 149, 149–51, 150, **151**; dimensions of 4; and ethnicity 205–6; and force field model 181; gender asymmetries 148; and globalization 39, 61, 62; and GM crops 228; horizontal 4; as intercultural phenomenon 150; justification for 153; national perspective 23; nature of 156; patterns 3; and poverty, world–historical

perspective 38–9; and spatial segregation 71; transnational approach 3, 14; and urban fragmentation 63–6; and violence 14; *see also* global inequality; income inequality; inequality regime; stratification
social inequality and poverty: Buenos Aires 62; Latin American cities (table) 62; Lima, patterns 62; Mexico City **62**, **62**; Montevideo **62**; Rio de Janeiro **62**; Santiago **62**; São Paulo **62**
social mobility 15; Argentina 33; between-country 30–1; Bolivia 33; global patterns 27–34; Guatemala 33; jumping categorical inequality 31, 33–4; Mexico 33; migration as 31, **32**, 33, 34; obstacles 28; and stratification 25; within–country 27–30; *see also* migration
social question 96, 228; depoliticizing of 11, 95; repoliticization 95, 97, 105
social reproduction 13, 228; and domestic work 121–2, 123; and migration 196, 200; and neoliberalism 217; and pesticide use 215; place of 216; reprivatization of 199
social stratification: contradictions 146; functionalist perspective 179; global 30, 37, 38; Marxist approach 180; and migration 33; and race 52, 81; and skin color 49–50; and social classes 81; and social mobility 1, 23, 25, 27, 28; Weberian approach 180; *see also* caste systems; social inequalities; social inequality
social structures: Brazil 182–4, 184–9, **188**, 189–91, 192; symbolic structures 148
society: nature, dualism 9, 77, 78; and space 68
socio–ecological perspectives, social inequalities 77–8, 88, 89
soya beans *see* GM (Genetically Modified) soy
space: empty, and appropriation 163; leisure 182; liminal 125; privileged, city as 63, 71; public 191, 192; segregated 64, 65, 125; socially produced 71, 85, 116, 152, 181, 200; socially segmented 187; and society 68; transnational 3, 6; *see also* global spaces; territorialization; urban space
Spain, race 45
spatial fix 84
spatial segregation 8, 65; and social inequality 71
spatiality, of gold mining 88
status groups, symbolic structures 148

244 Index

Stavenhagen, Rodolfo: on agrarian capitalism and ethnicity 116–19; *Las clases sociales en las sociedades agrarias* 116
Stewart, Frances 4–5
stigmatization processes 148
strata, and social classes 180
subordinate, re–valuing of 149, **149**
Sundberg, J. 81
surplus, production of 100
Swyngedouw, Erik 82
symbolic capital 144, 149, 151–2, **153**
symbolic processes: and gender equity 149; social inequalities 144–5, 146; and social inequalities 12, 144–5, 146, 156–7; social inequalities, deconstruction **149**
symbolic strategies, and social inequalities **147, 149, 153**
symbolic structures, social structures 148
symbolic struggles and social inequalities 153–6; de-legitimization 153–5, **155**, 156; legitimization 153–5, **155**, 156

Temer, Michel, Vice–President 179, 191
territoriality, definition 85
territorialisation, definition 85
Therborn, Göran 152, 181–2
Thompson, E.P. 116, 154
Thorp, Rosemary 112
Tilly, Charles 4, 100, 233; *Durable Inequality* 96, 145, 156–7
TIPNIS: road project 130, 138–9; territory 12
Tiwanaku site, Bolivia 132, 133
town and country, differentials 22, 30, 34, 36, 37
transnational care chains 7; care deficits 209; entangled inequalities in 209; individual agency 210; influences on 199–201; male involvement 203–5; and social inequalities 197, 208, 209; state role 201
transnational, transregional, distinction 56n4
Turner, Victor 147, 148, 156

Ulloa, Astrid 80
UNDP (United Nations Development Program) 59, 689, 70
Union Bank of Switzerland (UBS), prices and salaries data 25, 26
United States: Chinese Exclusion Laws (1882–1943) 52; citizenship criteria 50; Fourteenth Amendment (1868) 50; GM crops 215; income distribution 23; Jim

Crow laws 42, 52; Naturalization Act (1790) 50; slavery 50; *see also* American Constitution; New York
Urabá region (Colombia): banana economy 168, 172–3; Foreign Direct Investment (FDI) 173; land conflicts 173; paramilitary groups 173–4
urban fragmentation: and globalization 72n3; and social inequality 63–6
urban space: configuration of 70; as microcosm 6; and social inequalities 9, 59, 60, 65–6, 66, 70, 71; and urban structures 71
urban structures: and globalization 62; and urban space 71
urbanization: Brazil 120; and income distribution, case study 66–70; Latin America 112; private 64, 67
Uribe, Alvaro 85
Uruguay: GM crops 215; Immigration Law (1890) 53; income share 99

valuation, processes **149**; *see also* re–valuing
Vandergeest, Peter & Peluso, Nancy 85
Venezuela: abolition of slavery 51; Constitution (1811) 51
violence, and social inequality 14
de Vitoria, Francisco, *De Indis Noviter Inventis* (1532) 55
'vivir bien' philosophy, Bolivia 133

Wall Street Crash (1929) 53
Washington Consensus 218
Weber, Max 101, 148
welfare regimes, typology 199, 211n3
white status: Colombia 166; purchase of 48; *see also blanqueamiento* policies
Wila Kjarka people, Bolivia 139
women: as anticapitalism 120; black, in São Paolo 115; in capitalist development 120; care work, responsibility for 198, 200, 202–3; in labor market 122–3; social invisibility of 122; subordination of 113; traditionalism of 119; *see also* men
work, home, differentiation 121; *see also* domestic work
Workers Party, Brazil (PT) 14, 178, 184, 185, 189–90, 191
working class 182
World Bank 63
world population, distribution by income levels **38**, 39